No Peace Without Spain

No Peace Without Spain

In Memory of J.A.C.H.

British Library Cataloguing in Publication Data
Hugill, J. A. C. (J. Antony C.) *1916—1987*
    'No peace without Spain'.
    1. War of Spanish Succession
    I. Title
    940.2526

    ISBN 0–946041–58–X

Published by The Kensal Press
Riverview, Headington Hill, Oxford

**Printed and Bound in Great Britain by
Hartnolls Limited, Bodmin, Cornwall.**

Contents

List of Illustrations

List of Battle Plans

The Spanish Succession

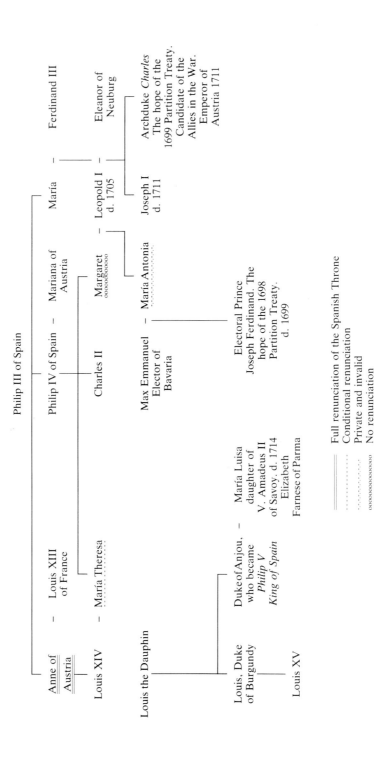

Philip III of Spain

Anne of Austria — Louis XIII of France

María — Philip IV of Spain — Mariana of Austria

María — Ferdinand III

Eleanor of Neuburg

Louis XIV — María Theresa

Charles II

Margaret — Leopold I d. 1705

Joseph I d. 1711

Archduke *Charles* The hope of the 1699 Partition Treaty. Candidate of the Allies in the War. Emperor of Austria 1711

Max Emmanuel Elector of Bavaria — María Antonia

Louis the Dauphin

Electoral Prince Joseph Ferdinand. The hope of the 1698 Partition Treaty. d. 1699

Duke of Anjou, who became *Philip V King of Spain* — María Luisa daughter of V. Amadeus II of Savoy. d. 1714 Elizabeth Farnese of Parma

Louis, Duke of Burgundy

Louis XV

———— Full renunciation of the Spanish Throne

··········· Conditional renunciation

·-·-·-·-·- Private and invalid

ooooooooooooo No renunciation

Acknowledgements

A<small>N</small> example of supreme courage, 'a heroic feat of arms', wrote Winston Churchill in *Marlborough, His Life and Times*. He is describing an incident which took place on March 3rd, 1709, towards the end of the Siege of Alicante. Early that morning, the Governor, Major-General John Richards, with some of his officers and a guard, took their stand on the parade ground of the Castle, immediately above a mine laid by the French besiegers of the town. At six a.m. the explosion took place, and Richards and those with him vanished for ever as the parade ground split open.

This almost laconic description of a long-forgotten incident of war, was to lodge in my late husband's memory and to give him the idea, first of all for a novel and, later, for the account which follows of the War of the Spanish Succession. Little military history had been published about this war since 1888, when much of the material now available was not accessible to nineteenth century historians. They tended to treat the campaigns in Spain as something of a sideshow, turning back to decisive events in Northern Europe. The intrigues among the Royal courts and the personalities of the Commanders on both sides of the conflict, were to provide the background for a new study.

Persuaded at school to become a scientist, when my husband's inclination had been towards an academic career as a historian, it was to be years before he had time to steep himself in the period, to travel and relive the land and sea battles and the appalling sieges of this long and costly war, the continuance of which had been assured by the Parliamentary parrot cry: 'NO PEACE WITHOUT SPAIN.'

The heady excitement of reading bundles of contemporary papers, many with the sand still trickling from the pages, provided him with solid work for many years. Sadly, he died before the sand was even sprinkled on the pages of his book.

He would have wished me to thank the numerous historians whose encouragement never failed, and particularly Dr. Fernández-Armesto for his sympathetic editing of an over-long manuscript. My own thanks go to Iris

Dalton and Hilda Pengelly who coped with reams of typing, to John Carter who drew the battle plans, and to my brother-in-law, Michael Hugill, for his invaluable help.

This is a fascinating story, and its publication is a fitting memorial to a brave man of intense humanity, who had himself experienced the carnage of a war in Europe, and whose memory is fresh in the minds of all who knew him.

FH – ASHTON KEYNES, February, 1989.

Dates

Europe was just changing from the Old Style or Julian to the New Style or Gregorian Calendar, adding eleven days to the date. England did not do so until 1751 and then to the accompaniment of riots because the public thought they were being robbed of time. English correspondents writing abroad often but not invariably gave both dates. In this account all dates given are New Style.

Foreword

Much of the history of Spain remains unwritten. Nor is this surprising, in view of the problems: those of combining sources scattered all over the world; those faced by Spain, on a more general level, in the course of her eventful recent history; and those caused by the existence of a number of different foci of interest in the subject in Spain, where the past looks different from Madrid, Barcelona and other centres of intellectual and political life. The War of the Spanish Succession, which is the subject of the present book, is itself a case in point, because Madrid fought for Philip V and Catalonia for his rival.

This is a most interesting book about a key moment in our history. After a period of Spanish political preponderance in Europe, and repeated interference by us in the internal affairs of other leading nations, we in turn became the butt of other powers' policies. Relying chiefly on British, French and Spanish sources, the book shows exactly how England's policy cleverly exploited internal divisions over the inheritance of the last Spanish

La Historia de España está bastante por hacer, lo que se comprende por las dificultades de reunir unos datos dispersos por el mundo entero; por las dificultades generales que el país atravesó en su movida historia contemporánea; y tambien por el carácter policéntrico del interés histórico, con visiones distintas desde Madrid, Barcelona y otras cabeceras intelectuales y políticas. La propia Guerra de Sucesión a la que se refiere el presente libro es un ejemplo de ello, porque Madrid apoyaba a Felipe V y Cataluña al Archiduque.

El presente e interesantísimo libro trata de un momento clave de nuestra historia, aquél en el cual, tras el periodo de hegemonía política de España, y de nuestras reiteradas intervenciones en la política interna de los principales países de Europa, nos convertimos, a nuestra vez, en un objetivo de la política de otras potencias europeas. Escrito fundamentalmente desde fuentes británicas, francesas y españolas muestra con precisión el inteligente aprovechamiento de nuestras divisiones ante la sucesión del último Austria, por la política de

Londres, que Habsburg; as a result, England managed at one and the same time to weaken Spain and France, perfect her own naval ascendancy, gain control of Gibraltar and other important pieces in the game, and set the seal on her emergence as a power, in the Mediterranean and overseas.

The author's declared intention is to provide an essentially military narrative and he relates, accurately and in detail, previously little-known events, like the attack on the Vigo galleons. Other episodes of major importance, like the siege of Barcelona, receive a fuller account than in existing books in English, such as those of David Francis and Henry Kamen. With the help of various friends (and, in particular, of Professor Fernández-Armesto, a member of the Oxford history school of whom much can be expected), the writer's widow has therefore done well to rescue this important study, which now at last appears in print.

Although this is basically a military account, it casts a more general light on a great turning-point of European history; and the reader will find a great deal of valuable information about Spain's own experience of change, political and cultural alike. The sustained lack of mutual comprehension between the Spaniards and the French, even though they were fighting on the same side, is clearly shown; so is the progressive hispanisation of the Bourbon pretender,

logra debilitar a la vez a España y a Francia, completar su supremacía naval, ontener Gibraltar y otras importantes bazas, instalándose definitivamente como una potencia mediterránea y colonial.

El autor define su objetivo como el de una historia esencialmente militar, y narra con gran precisión hechos hasta ahora mal conocidos, como el ataque a los galeones de Vigo y otros de gran interés, como el sitio de Barcelona, con un detalle no expresado antes, en otros importantes libros ingleses, como los de Henry Kamen y David Francis. Ha sido, por ello, un acierto de la viuda del autor y varios de sus amigos (entre los que destaca esa firme promesa de la escuela histórica de Oxford, el Prof. Fernández-Armesto) el rescatar este importante manuscrito, que ahora sale a la luz.

El lector de esta historia, esencialmente militar, pero ilustradora de una de las grandes crisis europeas, encontrará muchos datos interesantes para nuestra propia transformación histórica, política e incluso cultural. Podrá ver el sistemático mal entendimiento entre españoles y franceses, a pesar de combatir del mismo lado; la creciente españolización del Borbón Felipe V y de su esposa saboyana; como tambien del Duque de Berwick, nacido inglés, más tarde gran militar francés, y finalmente Duque de Liria (sus descendientes enlazan con la Casa de Alba). Tendrá

Philip V and of his Savoyard wife, as well as that of the Duke of Berwick, who was born an Englishman, became a great French soldier and ended as Duke of Liria (his descendants married into the House of the Dukes of Alba). Here extraordinary insights will be found into a war which displayed basic features of modern warfare alongside survivals from the age of medieval chivalry, in instances of personal combat and individual valour. Thus while the Battle of Almansa – the most unexpected and most decisive of victories – was to be hailed by Frederick the Great as 'the most scientific battle of the century', at Almenara the English General Stanhope actually killed the Spanish cavalry leader Sarno (a descendant of the Medicis) with his own hand; he thus obtained, for the last time in European history, the distinction known to the Romans as 'spolia opima'. The reader will see Philip V found a new dynasty, while the Habsburg pretender amuses himself with Italian opera; and will learn how the Battle of Brihuega, which was also decisive, could have been even more impressive had the Spanish cavalry not scattered to take sackfuls of rich booty from the Archduke's partisans in Madrid.

The author died without drawing his final conclusions but he did leave an interesting last thought. In the Peninsula, the War of Succession produced no plagues and no wholesale destruction. It was a war of

noticias increíbles sobre una guerra que, ya moderna en sus planteamientos, aún participaba de elementos de combate y coraje personal, como en la caballería medieval. Así como la batalla de Almansa, la más inesperada y decisiva de las victorias, habría de ser llamada por Federico el grande 'la más científicas de las batallas del siglo', en la de Almenara todavía el general inglés Stanhope mató con su propia espada al jefe de la caballería española, Sarno (un Médicis), obteniendo por última vez, en Europa, lo que los romanos llamaran los 'spolia opima'. Podrá ver a 'Felipe el Animoso' fundar una nueva dinastía, mientras el pretendiente austríaco se dedicaba a la ópera italiana en Barcelona; y saber que la tambien decisiva victoria de Brihuega hubiera podido serlo aún más si nuestra caballería no se hubiera desbandado para meter en sacos el rico botín de los partidarios madrileños del Archiduque.

El autor no pudo rematar las conclusiones de su análisis, pero sí un mensaje interesante final. La Guerra de sucesión, en la península, ni produjo epidemias ni miseria; típica guerra limitada de gabinete, respetó las grandes ciudades (menos Barcelona), y abrió paso a un inevitable proceso de unificación y modernización, que a su vez iba a llevar a excesos centralizadores, que como todos los excesos habrían de pagarse más tarde. Es pues un trabajo

policy, typically limited; apart from Barcelona, the great cities were respected; and the way was opened for an irreversible process of unification and modernisation, which would lead in turn to excesses of centralisation. Like other excesses, these would exact their own price later on. This book not only makes interesting reading but is also therefore, highly relevant today.

Manual FRAGA IRIBARNE

Member of the Royal Academy of Moral and Political Sciences; formerly Ambassador at the Court of St James's.

de interesantes lectura y notoria oportunidad.

Manuel FRAGA IRIBARNE

De la Real Academia de Ciencias Morales y Políticas; ex-Embajador en la Corte de Santiago

Preface

Q UEEN Anne was unable to attend in person, owing to an attack of
gout, but she awarded Mr Handel a pension of £200. The occasion
was the performance of a *Te Deum* in St Paul's Cathedral to give
thanks for the Treaty of Utrecht and the end – more or less – of the
War of the Spanish Succession. The Queen's encouragement of the
young composer was, perhaps, the happiest outcome of eleven years of conflict,
from which most of the participants gained little enough. The military history of
the Peninsular theatre has remained largely neglected and widely forgotten.

To Anglo-Saxon readers the War – if indeed it means anything – conjures
up a recollection of Blenheim. Some may recall that, within a few days of
Marlborough's 'famous victory', British squadrons took possession of the Rock
of Gibraltar. Others may remember the duke's three other great victories, but
few, I think, that there was a whole series of campaigns in the Spanish Peninsula
itself. Yet the war was intended to decide which of two candidates should
occupy the throne of Spain: the Archduke Charles, second son of Emperor
Leopold of Austria, who was backed by the Grand Alliance of the Empire,
Britain and the Netherlands (later joined by Portugal, Savoy, and the Principality of Catalonia); or his eventually successful rival, Philip, Duke of Anjou,
second grandson of Louis XIV of France. The confrontation of these two made
Spain the chief cause and cockpit of the war.

The notes (with references, for want of space, normally in general form),
and some further references important enough to be included in the text, should
show the range of available secondary work and primary sources and will
suggest, I hope, the usefulness of the archives which I have quarried – especially
those of the Dépôt de Guerre, Vincennes, and the Archivo Histórico Nacional,
Madrid, which have hitherto been relatively neglected by historians of this
subject. Four recent books demand a prominent mention. The first is Henry
Kamen's *The War of Succession in Spain* (1969). Although this concentrates
principally on economics and politics, the author consulted many documents of
military interest, and I am grateful to him for much assistance in finding the

originals. David Francis *The First Peninsular War* (1974) covers much of the same ground as I do, and he quarried deeply the relevant British documents, the Dutch and the Austrian, and some of the Catalan but not the French and Castilian. All scholars are indebted to him for depositing copies of so many of the documents he used in the Bodleian Library. Antoni Portà i Bergadá in *La Vitòria Catalana de 1705* (1984), which deals with the early part of the war up to the capture and siege of Barcelona in 1705, has also drawn on many hitherto unpublished Dutch and Catalan documents, as well as English ones. Prior to these, the latest studies were those of Mahon (1832) and Parnell (1888).

This book is not intended to compete with these authors but to complement them. The last chapter deals at some length with the final siege of Barcelona in the summer of 1714 (over a year after the Treaty of Utrecht). This is a subject virtually never treated in English history books, though a number of Spanish writers have covered it – Bruguera, La Llave y Garcia, Sanpère y Miquel and Voltes Bou. The tragic story of the last fight of the Catalans still deserves more than a chapter.

This is strictly a military history and essentially a narrative. The justification for providing it in detail is simply that it has not been done before. The consequences of events in the Peninsular theatre were modest, except for the Catalans, who reaped the whirlwind. There were no innovations in tactics or in land strategy, though for the Royal Navy the war brought the first development of a consistent Mediterranean strategy. There were few exceptional feats of generalship. But it is instructive to have a study of a series of representaive episodes of the warfare of the period and exemplary, perhaps, to see the heroism and suffering it caused. The reader who looks for general lessons may find them in the picture which emerges of the oscillations of the fortunes of war, the *bouleversements* caused by accidents and the effects on the course of the fighting, of events outside the arena.

CHAPTER ONE

'Over the Hills and Far Away'

Here's forty shillings on the drum
For those that volunteers do come,
With shirts and clothes and present pay,
Then over the hills and far away.
Over the seas and over the Main
To Flanders, Portugal and Spain.
Queen Anne commands, and we'll obey,
So over the hills and far away.

– Contemporary English Marching song.

S IR John Munden, Rear-Admiral of the Red, must be considered an unlucky man. War was declared simultaneously in London, the Hague and Vienna on 15th May 1702, and the first action of the war was one proposed by the outgoing Lord High Admiral, the Earl of Pembroke, and adopted on 23rd May.

Munden was dispatched under sealed orders with nine modest ships-of-the-line and two frigates to intercept a French squadron believed to be on its way to Corunna. Four days out, off the coast of Galicia, he showed his orders to his captains and sent the frigates, *Salisbury* and *Dolphin*, close inshore to observe and report. They captured a small Spanish boat and a French barque whose crews confirmed that thirteen French warships were due at Corunna from La Rochelle; so Munden took his squadron to lie between Cape Prior and Cape Ortegal. When the French appeared they out-sailed him, and though he gave chase they reached the harbour of Corunna, well fortified with a narrow entrance. Intelligence sources, such as they were, now reported seventeen French vessels.

The admiral had an excellent record as a captain for dealing with piracy in the Mediterranean but was now faced with a different kind of problem. Not only was the French force apparently larger than his own and well protected, but his ships were beginning to run short of provisions. He therefore held a council of war and with the agreement of his captains returned to Soundings in the Channel to protect in-coming British merchantmen – the secondary part of his instructions. By 16th July he was out of food and returned to Portsmouth.

Here he found himself accused of misconduct. It was said that nine of the French ships in Corunna were merely transports and that there were only eight warships in the harbour. It was alleged that he had recalled the *Salisbury* while she was fighting successfully and that he had released his French prisoners too soon. He faced a court-martial on board H.M.S. *Queen* before Rear-Admiral Sir Cloudesley Shovell, and fifteen captains on 24th July. In his defence Munden justifiably said that the sea is 'a wide place' and that he had only missed his enemy by an hour and a half.

The court-martial acquitted Munden of misconduct for the curious reason that 'he lacked sense', but public clamour arose at this. The strictness and impartiality of the new administration 'might better appear', by making an example, however unfairly. Munden was 'ordered by the Queen to be broke'. As *London Gazette* 3835 reports, he was therefore 'laid aside' – driven into retirement. He died sixteen years later, unused during the rest of the war. One contemporary, Bishop Burnet, wrote later of Munden's stupidity and cowardice and blamed Admiral Rooke (whom Burnet could not stand) for appointing him. Another, Oldmixon, in his *History of England*, said on the contrary that Munden suffered because he was out of favour with Rooke. There appears to be some deep natural law whereby at the outset of a major war, Britain always makes a hash of things and those who hold high command are blamed. The unlucky Munden was an early example.[1]

Sir George Rooke was undeservedly luckier, and his good fortune held for a further two years, though he too would in time be 'laid aside'. His name is still associated with the taking of Gibraltar in 1704 but first in 1702, after a shaky start at Cadiz, he would reap rather fictitious fame by an attack on the Spanish silver fleet at Vigo. Before these episodes are described it is perhaps as well to examine briefly the place occupied in the Spanish war effort by this legendary argosy.

★　　★　　★

In his study of the economics of the interlocking war efforts of Spain and France, Henry Kamen points out the immense importance attached by the maritime powers and by France alike to the wealth of the Indies. Its importance to Spain was not only traditional but actual, for the confusion of her financial and fiscal affairs made the supporting and supplying of her armed forces problematic. Yet the true value of that wealth seems to have been much exaggerated, and its importance illusory.[2]

France is basically a rich country and despite the difficulties of Louis XIV's early years he had inherited a sound financial system, which for the next halfcentury he proceeded to dissipate. Powerful, unquestioned, wilful, he spent money prodigally, on grandeur, on building, and on wars. By 1672 France was running a budget deficit which grew year by year. Her agriculture lapsed into disorder, to the extent that in bad years such as that of 1709 thousands died of famine. Her interest in obtaining windfalls from the Indies, directly or indirectly, was therefore strong.

In England the funding of the war was for long in the capable hands of Godolphin, the Lord Treasurer, friend and close colleague of Marlborough, and money was voted virtually without demur each year by Parliament for the maintenance of the Army and Navy, the subsidies to the Empire, Portugal and the Dutch, and for the support of 'Charles III'. Yet there was a strong desire for the spoils of war, particularly in the shape of Spain's overseas wealth.

In Spain itself, so chaotic was the financial situation that it had to be taken in hand by a number of able Frenchmen. For the most part the Spanish grandees who should have taken responsibility were without cash or credit and unwilling to make much effort apart from finding paid posts for themselves and their friends and relations. Relatively few were effective, one such being the Conde de Mariana who was *tesorero mayor* (treasurer general) for six years. Later replaced by Campoflorido and then by de Arco, he returned to the post after the war. His task was to raise contributions from the various kingdoms and provinces, cities and towns as best he could and, under instruction from the Minister for War, to make over what he collected to the *caudales de guerra* or War Chest, most of it going to the Army. Contributions were of various kinds. First there was the *alcabalà*, a percentage tax on goods, somewhat like VAT. Initially the items taxed were salt, wine, oil, vinegar and meat, but *alcabalàes* were later levied on cocoa, chocolate, spirits, tobacco and even fishing rights and all foodstuffs. And as the cost of the war inexorably rose, still further impositions were required. Money from the *asiento de negros* or licence to trade with the western hemisphere, particularly in slaves, was brought into play. Confiscations of up to one third of the value of estates were levied. The Church, which was exempt from most taxes, was persuaded to make loans but did so only grudgingly, demanding swift repayment and high interest; and even when the bishops agreed to contribute the lower clergy frequently dragged their feet. Monies were raised by farming out this collection to *arrendadores*, to whose fingers considerable sums inevitably stuck. The troops were paid through salaried officials, *comisaris ordenadores*.

The *tesorero mayor* himself could not raise enough and it was for this reason that the French took a hand. The system was a dual one. Political representation was through a series of ambassadors of varying ability and effectiveness. Harcourt's successor Blécourt, was replaced by the Cardinal d'Estrées, and he in turn by his nephew, the *abbé* of the same name, who was succeeded by Gramont. The most successful and longest lasting was Amelot who owed his long survival chiefly to his ability to get on with Philip V, his Queen and their favourite, Madame des Ursins and to his unremitting work. He also collaborated fairly well with another French civil servant, Orry, who for a number of years was responsible for financial matters. Orry managed the finances of the Royal Household, and busied himself as well in obtaining loans and generally scraping together the additional funds needed for war. Early in the war much was mulcted from English and Dutch merchants, chiefly in Spanish ports, but soon afterwards trading with the enemy was stopped and French merchants and artisans established themselves in Spain instead. For some years these claimed special legal privileges and exemption from taxes, and Spain lost thereby.

Orry and his successors such as the Fleming, Bergeyck, used finance houses and banks in raising loans. A particularly important Madrid banker was one Arthur, an Englishman, who contrived at different times not only to serve Spain but also to provide loans to his compatriots such as Stanhope. He seems to have got away with such benevolent neutrality. Amelot described Orry in a letter as doing his best, though 'he would have been wiser to stick to finance and not meddle in everything often without reference to anyone'. Hard-faced and haughty, Orry frequently broke his word and as frequently antagonised many Spaniards, though he contrived to remain on excellent terms with the King and Queen. He was for long unpaid and although regarded as honest his own personal finances were always in disorder. Since even these two men quarrelled from time to time it is not surprising that their less compatible predecessors and successors were often at loggerheads, or that the correspondence between Madrid and Paris is a long series of complaints. The presence and pretensions of Louis XIV's soldiers and civilian subjects in Spain was a continual source of irritation, while at the same time there was frequent friction between different ministers and their departments in Paris itself.

And all the while the cost of the war increased. Partly, perhaps, because Philip V took money from the Spaniards and used it in part to pay the French, there was generally thought to be a famine of gold and silver in Spain. But this contributed to making Spanish silver coins more valuable than their French equivalent, and therefore grossly inflating the war expenses of the French treasury. With all these problems it is only to be expected that the attention of the Spanish court and its councils should focus on the fabled cargoes of specie and other commodities from the west and that to England, the Netherlands, and France alike the War of the Spanish Succession was seen as a continuance of the long struggle for mastery of the wealth of the Indies. For, as Kamen points out, however much the profits of New World trade were alienated to foreign creditors or usurped by foreign interlopers, foreign appetites were only whetted and Spanish anxieties increased.

In the earliest years of the trade, Seville had become the principal port for the Indies *flotas* but corruption and smuggling had grown with time, and Seville was something like 100 miles from the coast, upstream along the Guadalquivir. So, while ships and cargoes were still registered there, the city had dwindled in importance and Cadiz had thriven in influence – and in corruption. And the Spanish Atlantic trade had dwindled too. Each year two Armadas had for decades sailed westwards. One, the *Armada del Barlovento*, the Windward Squadron, set sail for *Nueva España*, New Spain, in the Caribbean, in the spring, carrying cargoes chiefly for Mexico. The other, the *Armada del Mar del Sur*, made for Nombre de Dios, in August with cargo to be unloaded and taken south overland to Peru. Returning, the *flotas* would assemble in convoy at Havana in January and sail eastwards for Spain in March. But as time went on practice became lax and by the end of the seventeenth century, just before the war, everything was highly disorganised. And of course, smuggling and peculation had spread from Seville to Cadiz.

The *Casa de Contratación*, or House of Trading, in Seville continued to keep records of names of ships, tonnages and cargoes carried, but the figures though meticulously recorded, are largely putative, because of the growth of peculation, piracy, smuggling and bureaucratic inefficiency. These records and those of the *Consejo de Indias* or Council of the Indies are kept in the *Archivo de Indias* and housed in the *Lonja* or Exchange Building, erected in the late sixteenth century in Seville. It lies just across the way from Seville's gorgeous cathedral and the jangle of bells from the Giralda tower still falls on the ears of those studying such documents, as it did on those of the men who wrote some of them nearly three centuries ago. The account of Cadiz and Vigo in the following pages is based in part on these voluminous papers, carefully collected and relatively easy of access.

In the 200 years since they began the *flotas* had become irregular in their sailings and the convoy system had fallen into disuse. The *flota* from *Tierra Firma*, the South American mainland, did not sail for a decade after 1695. That from

Nueva España still sailed more regularly. Both were the responsibility of the *Consejo de Indias* and this body at least seems to have been less indolent than many other Spanish authorities. It consisted normally of about twelve grandees. Its president was the Duque de Medinaceli and its deputy-president the Marqués del Carpio. A quorum seems to have been five and the council met once a week and sometimes more often. Its minutes were kept in an exquisite clerkly hand and initialled by all those present. On the outside page of each set is a one-paragraph summary 'placing in the hands of Your Majesty' such and such a letter or 'advising Your Majesty' of some event.

In 1699 the council appointed Don Manuel de Velasco as admiral, and Don José Chacón de Medina y Salazar as *capitán* or convoy commodore. The former had sailed to the Indies in 1696 to 1698, and the latter's experience dated from 1689. Both were to be involved in battle in 1702. But though the council proposed, the condition of the ships disposed otherwise. Even in 1696, Chacón had been requesting permission to cut timber on the mountains of Gibraltar to repair the flagship of the convoy, and before the 1699 *flota* could sail both this vessel and the *almiranta* or vice-flagship of the escort had to be careened at Cadiz in April. They were not ready till June, when guns for them were sent from Seville. The weather was fearfully hot, and this meant that loading was slow, so it was not until 8th July that the convoy sailed. News of its arrival at Havana was received eventually by the council in October. Apart from mercury and cloth and other commodities, this *flota* carried ecclesiastics in large numbers, and many officials. (There were governors, captains-general, and other bearers of imposing titles in Lima, San Juan de Puerto Rico, Havana, Cartagena, Vera Cruz, Florida and elsewhere, who needed staff.) And in addition to these over 200 married merchants are listed as sailing. Many of these would settle in the New World with their families for ever. Another *flota*, dispatched in 1700, returned to Cadiz on 1st January 1701, one day before Philip V crossed into his new kingom. In addition to indigo, leather, sugar, cocoa and tobacco, its eight ships carried a million and a half *escudos* for the king and over a million for the merchants of Seville. Philip V received only about a third of his due, the remainder being used for the purchase of military supplies in Andalucia.

In principle, a *flota* was led by the *capitana* while the *almiranta* brought up the rear with the escort, and took the windward station. Both these vessels carried bullion in addition to providing protection. But escorts were not always available and merchantmen had often to make their transit unprotected. Under pressure of dire need the war was to cause a revival of regular sailings. But since Spain's navy was in desuetude, most of the *flotas* were escorted by French warships. Latterly this often resulted in ships from the convoys arriving in

French ports while at the time French privateers were active on their own behalf. All this was bitterly resented in Spain. As early as December 1702, Pontchartrain, Louis XIV's Chancellor, in a letter to the French ambassador in Madrid, Blécourt, refers to Spanish objections to French ships 'trading in America.' All he can suggest is that they and their cargoes should be confiscated if caught. Louis XIV 'cannot impose any other penalty, since he is unable to stop English and Dutch ships from trading there'. As the war continued, more and more trading of this kind went on, exacerbating Franco-Spanish relations; more and more goods including bullion arrived at French ports, and at the same time the French continued to insist that French ships in Spanish ports should not be inspected by Spanish authorities. Even twelve years later, when the war was over, a French ship, commanded by one Lieutenant de la Jonquière, loaded under licence with tobacco at Havana, would be impounded and her sails burned to prevent her leaving Los Pasajes which she had entered without a permit. The correspondence on this would last for months.

So zealous were all concerned about these *flotas* that it has long been thought that their cargoes were vital for Spain's participation in the war. But as Kamen has established, even the average cargo of a *flota* in terms of bullion reaching Spain did not bring in more than about fifteen million *reales*, whereas the cost of the war was about 100 million a year early on and rose to three or four times that figure and more later. And as far as Spain was concerned, much of what came in had to be used for paying Louis XIV for arms and other supplies.

Many of the ships involved were quite small, varying in tonnage from 66 to some 500 tons burthen and they were only permitted to carry up to two thirds of this figure as cargo – Velasco had trouble when he exceeded the figure on one occasion. But their names, recorded in Seville, are often resplendent. At Havana, in January of most years after 1702 there would assemble from Trinidad, Cumaná, Puerto Rico, Buenos Aires, Vera Cruz, Florida and Santo Domingo ships with such names as *Santo Cristo de San Agustín*, or *Nuestra Señora del Rosario*. During the war French ships, the *Apollon*, *Triton*, *Saint François* or *Glorieux*, for example, would join them. Setting forth for Spain, these *flotas* were awaited with anxiety by Spain and France and with hopeful anticipation by England and Holland.

On 11th June 1702, one month after the declaration of war, one such, consisting at the start of fifty-eight vessels all told, left the Indies under overall command once more of Velasco and with Chacón as commodore. The escort, largely provided by France, was commanded by the Comte de Chateaurenault. This officer, whose name was spelt 'Chaternaut' or even 'Chaterno' by the Spaniards, and 'Shatterno' by the English, was fully aware of the dangers. While at Havana the local Spanish authorities suggested that he should sail his *flota* to Los Pasajes, but he refused, saying that that port was unsuitable for discharging cargo and in generally bad order. He wished to go to some other Spanish port or to a French one, and Velasco mentioned Vigo.

Velasco a year earlier had reported that the English commander-in-chief in the West Indies, John Benbow was calling in on Havana and other Spanish ports announcing that England and Holland recognized the Archduke Charles as king, and wished to help Spain rid herself of French tyranny. Benbow had shortly thereafter received 'secret orders' from England. This report reached the Council of the Indies on 5th October 1701 and represents accurately what Benbow had been up to. He had also been endeavouring, as recorded in an Admiralty minute of 24th June 1699, to persuade the Spanish commandant at Santo Domingo to restore some English ships which had been confiscated for illegal trading. The secret orders to which Velasco refers were to recall Benbow to serve in the Downs. He put in a few months thereafter as Vice-Admiral of the Blue in Rooke's Grand Fleet before being sent again to the Caribbean in November 1701. Here he awaited the arrival of a French fleet at the outbreak of war, and, joined by Rear-Admiral Whetstone on 8th May 1702, began to seek out the French. On 19th August, just as Rooke was approaching the coast of Spain, Benbow sighted a French squadron of four ships of the line, a transport and four frigates. His own squadron of seven ships was very scattered and when he attacked only his flagship the *Breda*, and the *Ruby* (Captain Walton) and *Falmouth* (Captain Vincent) kept company. These three took on the French squadron for three days. On the 24th, Benbow's leg was shattered by a grapeshot, and he continued the battle from a cradle rigged over the quarter-deck. Some of his officers, particularly Kirkby of the *Defiance* and Wade of the *Greenwich* refused to join in the chase. For this these two were court-martialled in Jamaica and later shot in Plymouth Sound on 16th April 1703. The others were suspended during the queen's pleasure. Benbow died of his wounds at Port Royal on 4th November and his tomb is still there in the Parish Church of St Andrew in Kingston.

He had himself been somewhat leisurely and the *flota* was not apparently affected by his presence in the Caribbean. Of the vessels originally in the convoy, twenty-two were Spanish galleons and merchant ships and the remainder either French merchant ships or warships most of which would break off for French ports once in European waters. No doubt from information gleaned by Benbow the English Government knew that the convoy was coming and indeed delayed sailing its fleet in the hope of grabbing the *flota* on its way, it was believed, to Cadiz. By July it was sailing across the Atlantic, but, as Munden said, 'the sea is a wide place', and there were no aids to interception. Even navigation was then a primitive and imprecise craft. So in the end Rooke sailed for Cadiz.

The *flota* was in fact not making for that port; for the Spanish authorities were fully alert to the dangers. On 18th August, the Comte d'Estrées, still nominally Vice-Admiral of the Spanish fleet, advised the Council of the Indies that he had intelligence that an English fleet would shortly sail, possibly to the Azores, to intercept the *flota*. He did not give the report great credence, for it had been obtained from an English merchant ship carrying wine, and might therefore be a plant. But he recommended sending out sloops to meet the *flota* and take reports of the latest situation. By 7th September the Council confirmed that it had just received a report that fifty warships under Admiral Rooke would shortly leave Spithead for Lisbon and then Cadiz in order to 'insult' the *flota* and capture its contents.

It is not surprising that a good deal was known in Madrid of Allied intentions, for discussions had been going on in London, The Hague, Lisbon and Vienna before even William III died, Anne acceded or war was declared. Secrets were certainly kept but the systems must have leaked like sieves. Francis, in *The First Peninsular War* gives a most lucid account of the diplomatic to-ing and fro-ing which involved in addition to the English Cabinet, among others Prince George of Hesse-Darmstadt; the Imperial ambassador in London, Wratislaw; the English ambassador in Vienna, Stepney; the Imperial and Dutch Ministers in Lisbon, Waldstein and Schonenberg; and the newly-appointed English ambassador to Lisbon, John Methuen, who, with his son Paul was to have a considerable influence on affairs over the next period. Methuen, as an ambassador out-ranked his two colleagues and he was, although a commoner and of middle-class origin, entitled – having held the title of Lord Chancellor of Ireland – to call himself Lord Ambassador.

Moreover, thanks to his having spent six years as Minister to Lisbon from 1691–97 and left his son there to keep up contacts, he was on more intimate terms with King Pedro than were his two Allied colleagues. All three were engaged in trying to persuade the Portuguese king to break alliances he had formed with France and Spain, and Methuen had attempted to get him to join the Anglo-Dutch-Imperial Alliance. None of them was successful and it became a matter of waiting to see whether a French squadron or an Allied fleet appeared at Lisbon.

Meantime there was disagreement between the Emperor, who wished to grab the Spanish possession of Naples, and the maritime powers who wished for a Spanish port – Port Mahon in Minorca, for example, or Cadiz. At all events, after a period of fluctuating fortunes as first London and then Vienna favoured his ideas, Prince George was appointed to go as representative of the Emperor with an Allied fleet to attack one or other of a number of Spanish ports and to act as liaison with the Spaniards, inspiring and directing any pro-Habsburg insurrection which the Allies were hoping would break out in Spain when they landed. As usual this was all muddled as between Mr. Secretary of State Hedges (a Tory), his opposite number the Earl of Nottingham and Stepney in Vienna, and by the time they had sorted things out the prince was embarking at Portsmouth for Lisbon – to whose court he had no credentials. John Methuen had meantime returned to England for his own purposes, leaving his son to carry on negotiations with King Pedro, but was ordered to turn back at once to Lisbon to help smooth Prince George's way. The prince, however, had already sailed in H.M.S. *Adventure* with a large retinue and Methuen had to wait weeks for another ship.

It was the worst kind of mess. The prince arrived in style but ran into protocol difficulties. Waldstein, who like Schonenberg, mistrusted Methuen's activities, heard that Spain was in a ferment to greet pro-Habsburg forces, the Portuguese were said to be keen on an invasion of Spain and the Catalans hoping for the prince's return. He issued fiery statements and inspected military parades. There was no sign of an Allied fleet, the French and Spanish ambassadors complained and at least part of King Pedro's court, led by the Duque de Cadaval, took the same line.

So King Pedro proposed – though very politely – that the prince should leave. The Methuens refrained from arguing and the Portuguese allowed H.M.S. *Adventure* to drop down to the mouth of the Tagus, and at last the prince, frustrated and angry, sailed southwards. Methuen meantime renewed his efforts to persuade King Pedro to extract himself from his commitments to France and Spain. But while Waldstein and Schonenberg wanted the Allied fleet, when it arrived, to sail up the Tagus in a show of force, Methuen demurred, for the French had sent eight ships of the line and four galleys and a battle might not have been the best way of bringing Portugal over. As it was, Prince George's activities had if anything shifted the Portuguese back into neutrality, given cause for dissension between the English, Dutch and Imperial embassies, and provided ample opportunities for Allied plans to be openly discussed and reported to Paris and Madrid. Moreover, the prince's presence in the expeditionary force had initially been unwelcome to Ormonde, the Allied commander-in-chief, though by the time he met up with the force off Cape St Vincent, Ormonde had overcome his dislike of the idea.

With all this going on there had been a great deal of loose talk bandied around in Allied circles and the intelligence available to Madrid and Paris was considerable. There were two strike forces being sent from England. The first was an amphibious one of thirty English and twenty Dutch ships-of-the-line, together with auxiliaries and a landing force of some 14,000. This was under joint command of Admiral Sir George Rooke for the navy, and of the Duke of Ormonde for the army, the latter being in overall but loosely defined command. Part of the orders for this force concerned the capture of the *flota*. The second strike force, under Admiral Sir Cloudesley Shovell, was intended principally for interception on the high seas. It was to sail later, when it was hoped that news of the *flota* would be more certain.

$$\star \qquad \star \qquad \star$$

On 12th June 1702 Prince George of Denmark dined on board Rooke's flagship, the *Royal Sovereign*, and reviewed the first strike force. This consisted of thirty English and twenty Dutch ships-of-the-line, and together with auxiliaries and the transports carrying the troops, numbered 160 sail. A week later, on the 19th, the armada weighed from Spithead and anchored at St Helen's, whence a squadron of twenty warships under Admirals Fairborne and Graydon was detached to look in at Corunna and blockade any French ships there. If there were none the squadron was to proceed to a position ten or twelve leagues off Finisterre and await Rooke there. They were to have quite a wait, for there were delays for which Rooke blamed the Dutch, and he did not sail till 23rd July just after Munden had returned from his fruitless expedition and his report had been read. Shovell's interception squadron, the second strike force, sailed a month later.

The orders given to the first force were over-optimistic and diffuse: first to prevent an anticipated [but unlikely] junction of the French Brest and Toulon fleets; secondly to intercept the silver fleet if it should arrive in Spanish waters; and thirdly 'to reduce and take the town and island of Cadiz, but if the attempt appear impractical, Vigo, Pontevedra, Corunna or any other place belonging to France or Spain as shall be judged proper'.[3]

Amphibious warfare requires close co-operation between the services and it is generally more likely to succeed if there is an effective commander-in-chief. Neither of these conditions applied in 1702. The senior officers were inevitably those who had been appointed before war broke out. Of the admirals, George Rooke was the son of Sir William Rooke, Bt., and was now fifty-two years old.

He had entered the Royal Navy against his father's wishes and had served with varying distinction in Irish waters during William III's campaign in 1689, taking occasional advantage of the mismanagement of the French fleet. He had flown his flag as rear-admiral in H.M.S. *Coronation* (Captain John Munden) at the Battle of Beachy Head in 1690 and as vice admiral in H.M.S. *Royal Oak* at Harfleur in 1692. In 1696 he had failed through lack of strength to attack Cadiz but had made up for this by taking possession of a fleet of Swedish vessels bound for France.

William III had thought well of him, considering him loyal and honest (at least in money) and he was now in favour with Queen Anne. A staunch high Tory and MP for Portsmouth, he disagreed in principle with Marlborough's (and William's) strategy and policy, believing that the Grand Fleet should in time of war be stationed in the Channel and that no detached squadrons should stay as far off as Spain after September.

Bishop Burnet, the whiggish comtemporary historian, lost no opportunity of speaking ill of Rooke but is an untrustworthy witness. Trevelyan, while considering him competent to manage a fleet or command an operation, describes him nevertheless as cautious, sulky, unimaginative, unwilling, recalcitrant and limited. His despatches after a battle show him to be a man who enjoyed a fight, but when it was a question of coming to action there was never more than an even chance that he would seize the opportunity. Plethoric and a martyr to gout, his temper was uneasy. He had been married three times and his latest wife had been ill. The news of her death reached him the very day he sailed.

The land force was commanded by James Butler, Second Duke of Ormonde. Popular with those who served under him and for long with the public as a whole, he was the official commander-in-chief of the expedition. Born in 1665 and educated partly in France, he had fought at the Boyne and at Landen. A high churchman loyal to William III, he was wealthy and gentlemanly, brave, able, and something of a leader of men because of his charm, but too pliant, too kind perhaps to take a strong line. Later, he would accept command of the English armies in Flanders after Marlborough's dismissal, and, carrying out 'restraining orders' from London, would be considered treacherous. In 1715, moreover, he would be involved in the abortive Jacobite rising, and, snubbed by George I, would have to live abroad for years. He was certainly not one to stand up to Rooke. Nor was he capable of dealing firmly with his staff of generals, some of whom were rogues or worse.

Prince George of Hesse-Darmstadt was a long-service officer. Highly critical of the general lack of discipline in the scratch force which had been thrown together for the expedition, he wrote scathingly to Wratislaw the Imperial ambassador in London after the affair had failed. Major-General Sir Charles O'Hara he described as 'a lackey and one-time highwayman'. O'Hara's origins were somewhat obscure but he may well have been a riding-master to Ormonde: he claimed to have been his tutor. Later he became Lord Tyrawley, fought well on occasion and appears to have been a jovial Irishman without too much brain. He was however one of those accused after Cadiz of looting but was cleared by his fellow officers. His senior Lieutenant-General Sir Henry Bellasis was, said Prince George, known since William III's Irish campaign for looting and was incompetent. He would later be broken by Queen Anne's express instructions and dismissed the service. The other Major-General, Lord Portmore, was conscientious and well-meaning but according to Prince George, too cautious. The prince spoke well of the two Dutch generals, Pallandt and Sparre, but though they knew their business they were inclined to be argumentative and Sparre was accused of looting.

Cadiz, towards which this expeditionary force was making, had earlier in the year been reported by secret intelligence, received in London, to be virtually undefended – as was Gibraltar. It was known that French engineers were now preparing plans to repair the fortifications in both places but it was confidently – and rightly – assumed that the inertia of Spanish officialdom would ensure that nothing would be done about this in a hurry. Cadiz Bay runs south-east to north-west and the city is virtually an island, the town and fortress being built on rock at the outer end of a promontory. At the inner end there is a narrow causeway called then the Bridge of Zuazo. Approached from the sea the city – though its walls were dilapidated – looked formidable, and the harbour, as well as being sheltered to the east by the strip of land, is protected on the west by two promontories. On one of these was sited Fort San Lorenzo and on the other Fort Matagorda (now a university site). These approach each other closely enough to have permitted a cable to be stretched between them and close the harbour, which is of good size.

The coast has numbers of fine beaches – of which much use is now made by tourists – but most of the land behind is swampy and brackish. West of the city is the Bay of Bulls. At the western end of this is Rota where there was then a fort, and at the eastern end is Puerto Santa María, protected by Fort Santa Catalina.

Cadiz, ancient and narrow-streeted, is hot and smelly in summer and wealthier citizens in the 1700's not unnaturally sought coolness and quiet in Puerto Santa María, an enchanting little place still full of lovely houses and plazas, cosseted and elegant, and only two or three miles away by boat or ten by land. Jeréz de la Frontera is fifteen miles or so away and wine has been grown in the region for millennia – a fact which would have some bearing during the English landing in August 1702.

As the expedition approached, King Philip V was in Italy. It was of course in the interests of the Bourbons to maintain the adherence of the Italian states to the Spanish crown, since strategically the western Mediterranean was a single unit. But the king's visit was untimely and ambassadorial letters from Madrid to Paris were highly critical, for Philip was away from his capital for months at the very beginning of a major war. He fought a few indecisive though fairly successful minor battles against the Imperial forces under Prince Eugene of Savoy, but their importance was peripheral and the campaign made many demands on Spain's scarce resources.

In his absence a Council of Regency, presided over by his now fourteen-year old queen, was left in charge and to the surprise of many, Her Majesty with her *camarera mayor*, Madame des Ursins, at her side, proved more than equal to the situation. The Spanish administration was generally unimpressive, for it was nominally in the hands of Cardinal Portocarrero, and His Eminence, jealous of Madame des Ursins, was sulking. Orry, reporting this to Torcy in Paris, said that the cardinal was holding up any decisions because of a disagreement with the President of the Council of Castile.

When, however, news was received from the Viceroy and Captain-General of Andalucia, the Marqués de Villadarías, of the parlous state of the defences, the young queen-regent used it to electrifying effect. Swiftly she called the council and coaxed and charmed it, persuading the grandees, even Portocarrero, to contribute financially and to raise troops at their own expense. She was nevertheless unsuccessful in a request to the immensely rich and influential hereditary Admiral of Castile, Don Juan Enrique de Cabreras, to take command in Andalucia. He refused, because he was fearful of his reputation, saying that he could not carry out the task without the means. So the Andalucian command remained with Villadarías. A few years later Villadarías would with justice be blamed for the severe defeat suffered by the Spanish army at Saragossa and would become hated in Andalucia; accused of injustice and avarice, because he was tough on the local inhabitants and retained the excise duties on tobacco in order to pay for defences, he was in the summer of 1702 however, the right man in the right place.

In April the garrison of Cadiz had been about 100 strong and there had been no military stores. Now under pressure from the queen-regent, ten regiments of infantry each of 500 men were raised. Supplies were rushed to Cadiz and Villadarías stocked the city and put in the best troops available. He persuaded

Cordova and Seville and other Andalucian cities to make gifts and the local grandees to take up arms. The clergy preached against the heretics and the peasants enlisted as infantrymen. In a matter of weeks he had at his disposal 900 cavalrymen and several thousand foot volunteers, ill armed, untrained but enthusiastic. Colonel Stanhope described them later in a letter as 'rascally foot militia', but they proved effective when the time came.

Strung out along the coast the militia were instructed to light fires at night so as to give the impression of a large army, a ruse which succeeded. A strong boom was laid between the *Puntales* and across the harbour entrance and two merchant ship hulks were sunk behind it. By August, the garrison consisted of nine regiments of foot, plus cavalry, and seventy cannon well sited in the various forts, while seven French men-of-war and eight (probably unseaworthy) galleys were drawn up behind the boom. Cadiz, under the immediate command of its governor, the Milanese Duce di Brancaccio, awaited with outward calm the arrival of the Allied force.

Fairborne's and Graydon's squadrons, dispatched in late June, had taken prizes in off-shore waters but had found nothing in Corunna. They therefore rejoined Rooke on 19th August and the whole force of fifty ships-of-the-line anchored off the mouth of the Tagus but did not sail up to Lisbon. Methuen had hoped that the sight of the fleet would help King Pedro to make up his mind to defect from his treaties with France and Spain but did not feel the fleet should make too active a show of force as it might offend the king's susceptibilities. Waldstein and Schonenberg, the Imperial and Dutch envoys to Lisbon, felt that Methuen should have been more insistent, and wished the fleet to sail up the river. But his tactics seem to have been right for a few days later, although two more French ships arrived, Pedro said he would now consider his new treaties void though he did not yet commit himself to join the Grand Alliance. Methuen, with his previous experience was on more intimate terms with the king than his two colleagues, though they knew Spain better than he. Indeed, immediately on his arrival in April he had been able to have audience of Pedro though the latter was taking his annual cure, while Schonenberg and Waldstein were less able to approach the monarch. They had not been best pleased when Methuen had left for England in June, only returning in August a few days before the fleet arrived.

Frustrated in his attempts to enlist Portuguese support and smarting under his summary though polite eviction from Lisbon, Prince George joined the fleet in H.M.S. *Adventure* off Cape St Vincent. Rooke received him civilly enough but was not in the best of tempers, what with his gout and the number of well intentioned but infuriating messages of advice he was receiving from different quarters. Among such was one from Methuen: 'Show you come not as enemies but only to force the Spaniards from France and enable them to establish themselves under the House of Austria.' This was sound enough in principle but may have been based on over-optimistic reports from some Spanish sources and from Darmstadt's news from his contacts in Spain. He appears to have thought that the Spaniards had a natural affection for the Austrians but this was by no means general. In any case his advice was not to be taken, as we shall see, despite attempts by Ormonde and Rooke to do so and despite the presence of Hesse-Darmstadt with the expedition.

There had been two councils of war on the way over from St Helen's but no firm course of action had been decided, and though Rooke knew Cadiz – having looked in there in 1696 – the topographical information available was not up to date and of course little or nothing could be known of the frantic Spanish efforts of the past two or three months.

On the fleet's arrival at anchor on 23rd August six miles from Cadiz, in the Bay of Bulls, indecision still reigned. Rooke in any case had been at heart unhappy about the whole affair. He had just heard the news that his wife had died and according to his vice-admiral, Hopsonn, in a letter to Captain John Jennings of H.M.S. *Kent* he had the gout in his right hand 'so that he cannot write his name'.

The situation needed a Drake, it had instead the likeable but not very forceful Ormonde and his immediate subordinates, some of them unreliable, and the sick and sulky Rooke.

Admiral Fairborne wished to force his way into the harbour but Rooke refused, considering it unreasonable 'to hazard the least frigate' on such an attempt. Ormonde sent his Chief Engineer, Carles, his Quartermaster, Smith, and a Lieutenant Cowe of H.M.S. *Ranelagh* to reconnoitre for landing places. They reported that there were three bays there 'very proper to make a descent in'.

Another council of war was held on 24th August, whose proceedings were vividly described by the direct and impetuous Stanhope. 'We are not only divided sea against land but land against land and sea against sea. Now if it be true that a house divided cannot stand I am afraid it is still more true that an army and fleet divided each against itself and each against the other can make no conquests.'

Ormonde first suggested landing on the strip of land called the Bridge of Zuazo between the island on which Cadiz stands and the mainland, but it was objected that there was insufficient space and no water. He then suggested a blockade and a bombardment but this, it was held would alienate the inhabitants. Ormonde then vehemently advocated a landing in one of the reconnoitred bays before the defence had time to do anything, but Bellasis and other generals demurred and Rooke disagreed, saying that the garrison was too numerous and that the fleet could do no more than cover a landing and bombard the town. If, moreover, it came on to blow, he would have to weigh anchor so as not to be forced on to a lee shore and the army would be unsupported. The opposition of the naval officers prevailed.

There are always excuses for error. Ormonde, though only thirty-seven years old had gout. Rooke was elderly and also gouty and like everybody else had been away some time at sea in discomfort. The stinks and insects were probably little worse than at home, but the weather was very warm. Although informal meetings were held in informal clothing, a council would require formal dress, far too thick and liable to encourage rashes and prickly heat. Vast perukes, *de rigueur* as a sign of rank, must have itched and weighed heavy. Drink was a part of life, antiseptic, analgesic and anaesthetic, but also in biblical terms a mocker and a rager.

So one can imagine that the twenty or so admirals and generals, Dutch and English, incompatible and opinionated, assembled in Rooke's great cabin with its low deckhead, arguing until out of sheer exhaustion they inevitably agreed on the wrong course of action.

The fleet should anchor closer in in the Bay of Bulls. The troops should land in that bay and attack first Santa Catalina Fort and Puerto Santa María. Fresh intelligence about the situation within Cadiz of which they knew little or nothing should be sought, so as to enable the command to reflect at leisure on the next step. Meantime, in the light of ambassador Methuen's advice, a propaganda war should begin.

Ormonde wrote to Governor Brancaccio with whom he had once served, suggesting a parley. Brancaccio refused, saying curtly that 'he would acquit himself in the service of his king'. Darmstadt wrote a series of letters to various authorities in Cadiz. Villadarías, who had often served against the French in the past, received one from Ormonde, who thought he might be disaffected. Captured Spanish fishermen were used to carry ashore copies of a proclamation to the local populace. As the latter were largely illiterate and in any case suspicious of heretic foreigners, the *envolées* had little effect.

Had a landing begun at once they might have achieved their object, but it was a further two days before the first troops went ashore at daybreak on 26th August from transports anchored some three miles offshore. It was a difficult operation, for although the weather was calm, the 'steep Atlantick stream' can build up a heavy surf on the western coast of the Peninsula, and the rise and fall of tide is up to nine feet. Twenty boats were sunk but although a few men were drowned in their heavy rig and those who got ashore were wet up to their necks, only a handful were lost, thanks to the efforts of the Navy. Stanhope wrote, 'To do them justice, I never saw fellows bolder than they were to rescue our men in distress.' There was only a scattered resistance and it was subdued by covering fire from H.M.S. *Lenox* (Captain William Jumper) and some smaller craft.

Among the first ashore was Prince George of Hesse-Darmstadt, who exclaimed, 'I swore to reach Madrid through Catalonia. Now I shall reach Catalonia through Madrid.' But he was still some way even from Cadiz. His position in the force was anomalous. He was not officially recognised and Stanhope acted as his liaison with Rooke and Ormonde, but Rooke called on him from time to time and occasionally listened to his views, though he insisted that he had had no orders to accept Darmstadt as Imperial commisary and as yet the Archduke Charles had not been proclaimed King of Spain.

While the first wave was establishing itself, its weapons wet and its gun-powder sodden, a cavalry counter-attack was mounted by Villadarías. The English numbered some 1,200 grenadiers commanded by Lord Donegal, and the Dutch Brigadier-General Pallandt. Grenadiers were men selected from all regiments because of their good physique (and, some said unkindly, their thick heads) to be the spearhead of an attack. Each carried a pouch containing three bombs, called grenades because they were the shape of pomegranates, together with a port-fire or slow-match, in addition to their normal equipment. Their objective was to blow up obstacles and effect multiple killing in confined spaces.

In the van of the landing was Lieutenant-Colonel Thomas Pearce, who was to spend much time in the Peninsula, with eighty men of the 1st Guards. To meet the Spanish cavalry attack he coolly ordered his men to take dry powder from their grenades and use it in their muskets. Standing firm they drove off the Spanish horse, killing the commanding officer, Don Félix Vallero. This officer, clearly loyal to the new dynasty, had nevertheless been one of the recipients of letters from Prince George, whom he had once known in Catalonia. Villadarías, to whom he had shown the letter and who must have teased him before about possible collusion, now said; 'Here comes your friend, Darmstadt'. It was enough to make Vallero put spurs to his horse and gallop to his death.

After this the remainder of the first Allied wave were unmolested except by Spanish fire from Fort Catalina to which Jumper in the *Lenox* replied. Some twenty English soldiers were drowned while disembarking but only five killed by gunfire. Stanhope, once in action, was in his element, writing soon after-wards, 'You may easily imagine that men landed in such a condition, with their arms and ammunition all wet, could not be very fit to encounter the enemy

... yet some of them had an opportunity to show what Englishmen are capable of.'

The land force was marched westwards towards Rota on the other side of the Bay of Bulls. Jumper's guns had silenced the fort. According to some accounts the governor, whose name does not appear to have been recorded, surrendered, having been a secret partisan of the Allies. According to others the place was deserted and it was only later that the *alcalde* and some others returned to greet the arrivals. At all events these had now a small jetty, at which the dragoons, their horses and part of the train were landed – albeit some fifteen miles from Cadiz itself overland and six by sea.

Darmstadt, hoisting the Imperial flag on behalf of Charles III, is reported to have conferred the title of marquis on the un-named governor, the only man of consequence in Spain to come over to the Allies, and together with Ormonde issued a series of proclamations in the name of their sovereign stating that their objective was not to capture towns but to assert the rights of the Empire. The disembarkation at Rota took two days, after which Ormonde, leaving a garrison of 380 men under Lieutenant-Colonel John Newton of the 1st Guards, marched eastwards through the savannah and swamp towards Puerto Santa María whose capture was intended as the first step in setting up a blockade of Cadiz.

Stanhope, whose Spanish was good, sent a letter on behalf of his com-mander-in-chief to the governor, clergy and gentry of the port, advising them of the Allies' intentions and inviting them either to declare for Charles III or to remain quietly in their houses. Using what had happened at Rota as an example, he promised them good treatment if they did so. When an English drummer arrived to deliver this message Villadarías was there. Threatening at first to hang the drummer, he later used him instead to carry back a proud message: '*Nos Españoles no mudamos de religíon ni de Rey. (We Spaniards change neither our faith nor our king)*'.

When, next day, on 1st September, Ormonde's troops reached Puerto Santa María, they found the houses shut and the place empty except for a party of 200 Spanish troops, on their way to Jeréz, who had mistaken their orders. These took refuge in a house but surrendered at discretion when Stanhope invested it.

Darmstadt's hope had been that many Spaniards would declare for the House of Austria and he helped Ormonde in distributing manifestos while the latter strictly ordered against plundering and directed that any Spaniards who came over to the Allies were to be well treated. The prince had no troops but had brought some Imperial banners and if any civil government were set up it was to be his responsibility. He had even tried to bring Spanish priests from

Lisbon but had been prevented from doing so by the papal nuncio. So in effect his influence was slight and very few Spaniards defected to the Allies.

Ormonde hanged a soldier for looting and condemned six more allowing them to dice for the lives of four. The local inhabitants although wary, asked mercy for the remaining two. The Spanish authorities had in fact ordered strict measures against desertion to the Allies or acceptance of Allied manifestos. So Prince George, marching with the leading dragoons was disappointed in his hopes. He was moreover unable to intervene to prevent a disgraceful outbreak among the Allied troops.

After Puerto Santa María was taken the troops were at first encamped outside the place but O'Hara, possibly with a view to protecting Allied property, brought them back into the town. They had marched a long way, water was a problem, and they were warned that they should fill their flasks – a loosely-worded order that was bound to lead to trouble in a town full of warehouses and cellars.

And now the demon drink took over. The absence of the inhabitants and the fact that they had fled leaving most of their possessions was too much of a temptation for the English troops. Since wine is grown almost up to the door-step it is not surprising that the cellars were full and Thomas Atkins proceeded to get thoroughly out of hand here and in the nearby villages. What he could not appropriate he destroyed, including the contents of churches, which even in impoverished villages contained plate of value. Women who had been unwary enough to stay behind were raped. Any seamen who were able to get ashore joined in the pillage – their assistance was needed in getting the loot on board.

Ormonde and some of his officers were appalled at this but were able to do little to stop it since some of the senior officers, notably Bellasis, participated in the plunder, and others were reported to have removed loot from private soldiers for their own use. The main victims were not in fact Spaniards but English and Dutch merchants living there. these later complained bitterly of their losses, saying that the soldiers 'left behind them such a filthy stench among the Spaniards that a whole age will not blot it out'.

Darmstadt, himself a Catholic, complained in writing to Vienna, with the result that London soon heard about Bellasis and O'Hara. Stanhope, when the expedition finally departed from Cadiz said cryptically that it did so 'with a deal of plunder and infamy'. The effect on Spanish attitudes was as predicted by Methuen. The priests had described the English and Dutch as heretics, and such they had turned out to be. Influential Spaniards would have nothing to do with the Allies. And these feelings were to spread throughout Spain from now on.

On 2nd September the governor of Fort Santa Catalina had an exchange of gentlemanly incivilities with Ormonde. The latter ordered him to surrender or be hanged. The governor replied that 'if he must be hanged it was all one to him whether he was hanged by the Duke of Ormonde or the Governor of Cadiz'. In the end he was hanged by neither when the Fort surrendered. Its capture did not do much to help the attack on Cadiz.

Two days later at a joint council of war, Rooke at last agreed to try and break into the harbour, but insisted that Ormonde first silence Fort Matagorda on the eastern *Puntale*. Accordingly on 8th September Baron Sparre and Colonel Carles with 2,400 troops, mostly Dutch, and a small train, advanced on Matagorda. They were under fire from the fort itself, from the batteries across the harbour, and from French and Spanish galleys under the command of the Conde de Fernán Nuñez behind the boom which, together with two sunken merchant ships, closed the entrance. Some sixty-five men were killed, but many more died as a result of the intense heat to which they were not accustomed. And the fort held out.

Rooke now wrote to Ormonde telling him to by-pass the fort and take up a position so as to cut off the escape of the citizens of Cadiz while the navy bombarded the city, but Ormonde refused to lift the siege. With four guns and four mortars he exchanged fire with Fort Matagorda for three days, until the English train, which was on marshy soil, began to sink; and although approaches had been dug to within 140 feet these filled with mud and water to a depth of two feet. Losses, chiefly from heat, continued heavy and on the 17th Ormonde finally ordered Sparre to retire with his troops westwards to headquarters at Santa Vitoria.

Ormonde and Rooke were now in full discord, the former complaining of Rooke's delays and the latter of the behaviour of Ormonde's troops. Furthermore, Rooke's decision to bombard Cadiz, taken because no Spaniards of any consequence had come over, was a further subject of disagreement. Ormonde disapproved, but Bellasis and O'Hara argued openly against him. Darmstadt, who had not been consulted, wrote a memorandum addressed 'to all who complain that none of the principal officers of the kingdom of Spain are yet come to join the army'. In it he said that the Spaniards could not be blamed 'seeing that the measures which have hitherto been taken seem not directed to do anything but find out some pretence, after unanswerable delays, to go with the first fair wind to England'. He added that the proposed bombardment of Cadiz would alienate the Spaniards from the Austrian cause. Rooke reacted angrily to this and complained to Ormonde, who now, under pressure from Bellasis agreed with the joint council's resolutions. The council of generals added that Rooke should, before bombarding, ask for a ransom of 100,000 *pistoles*. Next day the admirals met and changed their minds. 'The swell of the sea continues so as to render the bombardment of Cadiz ineffectual', they decided, and the troops should now be re-embarked.

Villadarías continued to harass Ormonde's force and the latter broke camp at Santa Vitoria on the 23rd and after blowing up Santa Catalina fort, marched towards Rota to re-embark. Accounts of what happened next differ. Mahon describes how 'by a sudden attack [Villadarías] retook Rota where the English had left a garrison of 300 men commanded by the former Spanish governor who was now condemned to death and executed as a traitor.' Mahon appears here to be following San Felipe, who is often too emotional to be reliable and who adds that the Allies lost 600 men, dead during the re-embarkation. Needless to say 'the governor surrendered vilely'. But neither he nor Mahon gives a date, and it is odd that he does not mention the governor's name. He is never backward in naming those of whom he disapproves, only occasionally refraining 'out of respect for the church' or 'because they are still alive'. And this man, if indeed he existed, had been hanged. Parnell, basing himself on English dispatches, says that Colonel Newton was in command of the garrison and the English were still there on 28th September, when they began to embark, 'accompanied at his own request by the *alcalde* of Rota'. Colonel Fox of the Marines commanded a rearguard of grenadiers from Pearce's Guards who fought off an attempt by the Spaniards to enter Rota and then withdrew. They had been the first to land and were the last to leave.

The campaign had so far achieved nothing, at a cost of about 100 men killed in fighting and some hundreds by illness and the torrid heat of August and September. Marlborough's comments, when he heard, were blistering:

'My people tell me that the Duke of Ormonde is governed by people that will incline him to accuse Sir George Rooke. By what I am told here [at The Hague] I should think it would be more for his grace's service and all the rest of the officers that the conduct at Cadiz should not be inquired into; for what can be said for staying 26 days at Port St Mary; for, if Cadiz was to be attacked they should not have stayed there; and if the taking Cadiz was not thought feasible, then they should not have lost time but have re-embarked to have attempted what [also] was in their instructions.'

A Committee of the House of Lords was appointed to enquire into the whole affair. In fact nobody can escape blame. The home authorities deserve censure for having selected Rooke and Ormonde (though admittedly they had little alternative); for having failed to provide good intelligence and even sufficient supplies; for having issued a complicated and vague directive; and above all, for selecting a target which had had the effect of making the Spaniards send their *flota* elsewhere.

Those in command on the spot were guilty of irresolution, and lack of strategic sense and tactical drive. There were some cases of disloyalty, at least one of personal dishonesty, and many of inability to control the troops. The senior officers were lucky to redeem – in some cases – their reputations, for though they did not know it, they were to be given another chance.

They also did not know that their arrival off Cadiz had been reported by sloops to Velasco on 31st August. He and Chateaurenault had considered sailing the *flota* into the roadstead of San Lucar de Barrameda; at the mouth of the Guadalquivir, but this was only some 12 miles up the coast from Rota, more vulnerable to attack than Seville, and facilities for unloading were not available; so Velasco and Chateaurenault were sent hurriedly drafted orders to proceed northwards to station between Capes Finisterre and Ortegal at the north-west tip of Spain. Chateaurenault refused, giving his reasons in a long letter written in a clerkly hand but bearing his authoritative signature. These were: navigational difficulties and the expectation of enemy vessels which could intercept him in the area designated. He held a council of war and instructed each of his captains instead to go to Vigo because it was more secure. He repeated these reasons in a letter in his own spiky, vigorous hand to the queen-regent on 27th September.

There was joy in Madrid at the divine mercy, which had caused the *flota* to go to Galicia rather than Cadiz. Orders were sent to the Viceroy of Galicia and the *corregidores* of four ports near Vigo to lend all possible help. Corunna and other towns were ordered to send wood for making cases. General the Prince Barbanzon took on the task of transporting the bullion as quickly as possible away inland from Vigo, and the Council of the Indies ordered one of their number, Don Juan de Larrea, Knight of the Order of Calabrana, to keep accounts of the bullion as it arrived and was discharged. (He will provide us with a first-hand account in due course of the battle in the harbour.) Only one local Governor, the Marqués de Cassadevante, at San Lucar where one vessel had arrived, showed a lack of urgency in speeding his parting guests and at Chateaurenault's request he received a rebuke.

There was no doubt that the passage to Vigo was fraught with danger. Barbanzon, writing on 21st, spoke of the dangers of being sighted by the enemy off the Andalucian coast – indeed they had seen ten warships off Portugal, but he was able to confirm in that letter that the *flota* had reached the Bayona islands just outside Vigo, many of them leaking and all short of victuals. 'This happy arrival', he said, 'is thanks to the Comte de Chateaurenault and Admiral Velasco.' Five vessels, three of them French, missed Vigo and went to Santander instead.

On the 27th Velasco wrote to Their Majesties announcing the *flota's* arrival and saying that fifteen vessels were already in the inner Vigo harbour at Redondela. 'They are as far away as possible from the mouth of the bay' and he intended to place a boom across the opening to the inner harbour and mount batteries at either end to protect this. Unloading was held up until in Barbanzon's and Chateaurenault's view sufficient land transport was available. Chateaurenault was supplying French army units under Colonel de Combes and in addition some naval personnel including a gunnery officer and ten gunners. Larrea also reports all this, asking for 30 *doblones* to cover pay for these men, and the Council of the Indies confirmed the arrangements on 3rd October. By the 6th Barbanzon reported that unloading was proceeding apace. Nevertheless Medinaceli wrote on 9th October from the Council of the Indies warning that the Anglo-Dutch fleet might come to Vigo and on the 12th advising that the Allies had left Cadiz. On this same date Velasco reported that the weather outside Vigo was very rough. On 16th Chateaurenault wrote to the Council that all but two of the ships were now in Vigo and that he himself was going to Corunna to arrange for the repatriation of French sailors 'needed urgently by King Louis.' He followed this with a letter dated 18th October in his own hand to the queen-regent reporting that the enemy had been sighted off Lagos in Portugal on 3rd October, that two English warships had been seen in the Tagus, and that he believed that 'twenty-three English line of battle ships and two frigates had been detached for America, while the rest were sailing home on 6th October.' He assured Her Majesty that he had taken such precautions that the *flota* was safe in the inner harbour at Redondela and that she could count on disposing of its cargoes. He added that he would like the English to attempt Vigo but was convinced that they could not do so. By then he was on his way from Corunna to Santiago de Compostela, seeking an overland route for repatriation of sailors. Before his letter reached its royal recipient he would have been shown to be wrong about the intentions and capabilities of the Allied fleet.

★   ★   ★

Slinking ignominiously away from Cadiz on 30th September the Allied command had to decide what if anything they could do to recoup the situation. They had received no indication of the presence of the *flota* further north. They had lost face and wasted men and munitions. Their physical situation, late in the year, was an uneasy one, they were short of supplies and no doubt they expected criticism on their return home.

Some ten days before, even while Ormonde was extricating himself from the siege of Fort Matagorda, a deputation of Austrian sympathisers from Madrid, led by Don Francisco de Santa Cruz and Don Luis de Pavedo, had arrived via Faro in the Portuguese Algarve by frigate and had urged on Prince George the need for the Allied expedition to winter in Spain, suggesting as sites San Lúcar, Vigo, Pontevedra or even Lugar Nuevo in the Mediterranean, near Alicante. Prince Greorge wrote to Ormonde, strongly pressing this and in turn Ormonde wrote to Rooke suggesting that Corunna or some other Spanish port should be captured 'for it is of the last [greatest] consequence to the queen and her Allies that we should stay in some port of Spain'. He later added: 'I desire nothing more than that you would set us ashore either in the Isle of Cadiz, Ayamonte, Vigo or Pontevedra, or wherever it shall be thought reasonable, with such a number of ships as shall be judged sufficient.'

Rooke would have none of it and seemed unable to think at this time of anything other than sailing home. A second attempt on Cadiz, he replied, would expose the fleet to bad weather. At Ayamonte the larger ships could not approach and the smaller would be in danger, so a landing was out of the question. Vigo or Pontevedra were possibilities but he set a final date of 23rd October for these because of lack of provisions and the onset of winter. Corunna was too far away.[4]

At a joint council on board H.M.S. *Ranelagh* Rooke and the Admirals refused to approve any further attack on Spain. They were backed by Bellasis and O'Hara (for reasons which can be supposed) but Ormonde, the Dutch generals and Prince George refused to sign the resolutions of the council, the last named returning in disgust to Lisbon as the expedition weighed anchor apparently for home.

News was now received from Methuen in Lisbon that King Pedro of Portugal would be 'extremely pleased to assist the expedition in anything you shall desire here or in any part of his dominions'. Ormonde interpreted this as an invitation and pressed Rooke at the very least to call in at Lagos in the Algarve on the way home, but again the Admiral would not hear of it. On 5th October in accordance with previous instructions he detached a small squadron under Commodore Hovenden Walker in H.M.S. *Burford* to take four regiments, Erle's, Hamilton's, Donegal's and Charlemont's to the West Indies. It was this detachment to which Chateaurenault referred in his letter to the queen-regent. His intelligence was up to date though a little exaggerated, but he was certainly right about Rooke's intentions to sail home.

Yet just at this time something happened to make Rooke change his mind and make Chateaurenault's information misleading. On 5th October some English ships put in at Lagos in the Algarve for water, and the chaplain of one of these, the 60-gun *Pembroke* (Captain Thomas Hardy), was a Jersey man, a Mr Beauvoir. While ashore he 'met a gentleman in the street whom by several circumstances he judged not to be Portuguese; he accosted him in French, which the other, who proved to be the French consul, returning in a very obliging manner, invited him to his house. Mr Beauvoir, extremely willing to embrace this offer, continued there two nights; during which the consul, in their several conversations, could not forbear to boast of his master's strength at sea and at last gave some hints of the arrival of the galleons [from the Indies] at the coast.' On this, Beauvoir, 'understanding that a gentleman was arrived in that town bound for the fleet with letters to the Prince of Hesse and Mr Methuen (who were gone from the fleet to Lisbon some time before) he invited him to go aboard the *Pembroke* without taking the least note of their departure. The gentleman gladly accepted this invitation and told him just as they were leaving the shore that M. de Chateaurenault was arrived at Vigo with 30 men of war and 22 galleons and that he was sent by the Imperial minister to the Grand Fleet. They went together on board the *Pembroke*.'

Mr Beauvoir was an early example of naval intelligence. On board ship Captain Hardy was found to be asleep but the chaplain had him roused and after a discussion with the senior captain, James Wishart, as the *Pembroke* was the fastest sailer, she left at once. But although he caught up with Rooke on the 14th 'the wind blew so hard he could not speak with the Admiral till the 17th'. At the inevitable council of war the Allied admirals, for once unanimous, decided that it was their duty to attack Vigo, though it could be done only just within the time limit set by Rooke. Ormonde does not seem to have been consulted.

Victorious admirals and captains grew rich on prizes and for the lower deck a sovereign or two of prize money made up for months of discomfort. Duty and greed were thus compatible, for this after all was legitimate plunder and there appeared to be a great deal of it. It was only a few days' sailing away, on the way home, and it could redeem the fiasco at Cadiz. So, on to Vigo!

Here the Spaniards had shown considerable diligence in discharging bullion and strengthening the defences. Larrea, on behalf of the Council of the Indies had issued passes from Redondela to those employed in taking the valuables to various towns, including Segovia and Santiago de Compostela, and although Cadiz owned in principle the monopoly on the receipt of 'indults' or tolls on bullion landed, and registered a complaint about Vigo being used, the council insisted on discharging first and arguing about tolls later. The less valuable cargoes, pepper, snuff, cochineal, cocoa, indigo, etc., were left on board. These were in any case the property of English and Dutch merchants and of relatively slight concern to the Spanish government.

To help the defences of the boom, Fort Randa at the southern end was now being furnished with guns (8 bronze and 12 cast-iron) from French ships and Chateaurenault had, as we have seen, supplied French personnel. He was by now at Santiago still trying to obtain money to pay and repatriate seamen and had had to use, as he put it, 'some violence' in keeping a Spanish banker under restraint until he produced the cash. There was also present in Vigo a force of cavalry. By the 13th October the Council of the Indies were being advised by Larrea, 'Redondela is well defended. 3,753 cases of bullion are on their way to Lugo and elsewhere under guards provided by Barbanzon and there have been no delays.' The batteries were now ready and the guns from the ships were to be mounted next day, while Chateaurenault wrote proposing that launches from the *flota* should row guard.

So pleased was everybody with Chateaurenault that the council shortly discussed presenting him with his portrait set in diamonds to the value of 1,000 *doblones*. This was eventually altered to a gift of 25,000 *piastres* from the king and queen. To them he wrote an elaborately gracious letter saying that his service to Louis XIV did not allow him to receive 'monetary gratification' so he would pass it on to the crown's receiver in Galicia. Meantime Larrea was concerned at the shortage of food and clothing being suffered by the Spanish seamen and soldiers and was demanding succour, though expectedly without any result. This letter is dated 19th October. There were now only two days to go before the attack, though he did not know it.

The Franco-Spanish side of what now happened is described in a very long minute later presented by the Council of the Indies to the queen-regent, but this in turn is based on three first-hand accounts by Larrea, by Velasco, and by Chacón. The first of these, sent off post-haste on the 23rd was also the first to reach Madrid. The English and Dutch armadas were off the Bayona islands [just outside Vigo] on 21st October. On the following day, Sunday 22nd, they entered the channel to Vigo but were 'surprised' by the strong boom. However, they were well out of range of the guns of the French fleet and had a favourable wind and tide which continued throughout the day. Most of the ships were two-deckers but there were some three-deckers as well. Next day (23rd) they were held up by the forts guarding the boom, so that they put ashore 2,000 men. Although Fort Randa was well defended by French and Spanish soldiers it fell to superior force. The Anglo-Dutch fleet was then able to approach the boom which it broke without difficulty. 'There was much firing,' wrote Larrea, 'such as I have not seen or heard before, and it is impossible at present to establish the losses on either side, but many ships in the Redondela were damaged. The terrified populace of Vigo fled to a monastery 8 leagues away, taking with them any valuables they could carry. Undoubtedly some silver was captured by the English.' He added that he had been unable to get in touch with Chateaurenault as he did not know where he was. A few days later he wrote again, from Porrin, saying that luckily most of the plate had long since been taken to Lugo, Villafranca and elsewhere and he was following it to check, but that someone 'practical and intelligent' should be sent to Vigo to see what further could be recovered. It was while his first message was on its way that on the 24th the Council of the Indies was debating the matter of the diamond-framed presentation portrait for Chateaurenault.

Velasco's report was written a week later from Pontevedra and contained much the same information. He added that once the English had, after the fall of Fort Randa and the breach in the boom, placed themselves between the Fort and the French ships he had personally given the order to set fire to the *capitana* and *almiranta*, he himself intending to go with as many men as he could find to help man the batteries. When, however, he landed from his barge he could not find many men, though he did meet up with Larrea.

The confusion reigning can be further imagined from an even more vivid account written by Don José Chacón. Describing the entry of the enemy armada into the port he says that Velasco ordered *all* ships to be set on fire and this was done. Only where the charges failed to go off or there was insufficient powder did they not catch fire. He says the enemy fleet consisted of 120 vessels including auxiliaries such as bomb ketches. His brother, Fernandez Chacón, who had been sent to help hold Fort Randa, had been wounded in the head and was very ill and a prisoner. 'Everything', he says, 'happened so fast that I was able to save nothing and am without even a shirt or any other clothes,' adding with some pathos a plea that 'His Majesty (whom God preserve)' should intervene on his behalf with the Ministry of Finance to re-imburse him after his sacrifices. He notes that some silver and other articles had 'probably' been taken by the English.

The English account is somewhat fuller. On 20th October, Rooke was off the Bayona isles which are as it were the foothills of the wild bare hills of Galicia, and while still out of sight from Vigo sent in a couple of frigates to reconnoitre. Vigo Bay is a deep, narrow inlet half-a-mile wide, a little like a fjord, sheltered by the Bayona hills. It widens at the innermost end to form the Redondela harbour, where the *flota* lay, a fact established by the frigates whose landing party captured and interrogated a friar. The town of Vigo, then of small importance, is about halfway along the fjord on the south side, and then contained about 3,000 people within its dilapidated walls. Two old towers, the Randa and the Corbeiro defended the entrance to Redondela and the English assumed – rightly as we know – that these, though part-ruined, were manned and gunned.

Early on the 21st a frigate sent ahead by Sir Cloudesley Shovell brought Rooke news that Shovell's squadron was off Cape Finisterre and sailing to join him. When on the afternoon of the 22nd in hazy weather Rooke came to anchor he found the boom, which he described as very thick, and saw a captured English warship, the *Hope*, at one end of it.

At the council of war which followed there was much debate. Ormonde was now unimpeded by Bellasis and O'Hara who were under arrest (by orders from London) and were to be court-martialled on their return. Vigo was a harder nut than Cadiz and the decision to attack it was not unanimous, being carried only by the votes of the Dutch generals.

The plan was for the army to land at Feis on the south shore and attack Fort Randa. The fleet was to be split into three divisions and attack in line ahead because of the narrowness of the channel. In order to encourage all ranks the flag-officers were to go in with the first wave and only Lieutenant-Admiral van Allmonde was to remain off Vigo with the rear. Rooke shifted his flag from the *Royal Sovereign* to the *Orford*, 70 guns, Captain John Norris, and is described as going from ship to ship during most of the night giving orders. Next day, when the attack took place he appears to have succumbed once more to gout and the active command fell to Vice-Admiral Hopsonn, 'Queen Anne's handsome captain'.

Early in the morning of the 23rd Ormonde landed unopposed at Feis in a sandy bay. (Although some peasants had been formed into a militia they could do little against an Armada which, as Prince George had remarked, carried more troops that were then to be found in the whole of Spain.)

The 2,500 English and Dutch troops were in four brigades, led by Lord Shannon, Gustavus Hamilton, Lord Portmore and Baron Sparre. Shannon had served with distinction at Landen and Namur in the 1690s – he was to become a field marshal in 1739 – and he led the vanguard swiftly into an attack on the Fort Randa battery, his grenadiers storming the outer part of the fort and silencing the battery.

Commanded by a French naval captain, de Sorel, the garrison retreated into the fort's keep which could only be entered up sixteen steps. Shannon's grenadiers 'plied them briskly with their hand grenades as soon as they appeared on the wall' and de Sorel opened the gates intending to cut his way out and make for some nearby boats. But the grenadiers charged into the fort and de Sorel with his 300 French marines and seamen, and fifty Spaniards (including poor Fernández Chacón) surrendered at discretion. Shannon had lost six officers and eighty men but he had opened the way for the boom to be tackled.

Hopsonn's squadron now sailed towards it. As the first-rates drew too much water the van consisted of second-rates. The squadron was composed of H.M.S. *Torbay* (50 guns), *Mary*, *Grafton*, *Kent* and *Monmouth* (all 70 guns). In company was Vice-Admiral Van der Goes in the *Zeven Provincien* (92 guns) with three Dutch two-deckers. Next came the Dutch Lieutenant-Admirals Callenburg, Pietersen and Graydon with eleven two-deckers. The *Association*, a first-rate (96 guns) (Captain William Bokenham), was ordered to try and silence the Corbeiro battery at the north end of the boom. Frigates and five ships accompanied the larger units. Hopsonn led in the *Torbay*.

As the squadron approached the boom the wind fell away and the ships had to anchor. A message from Ormonde arrived announcing that Fort Randa was out of action and just then there was another breath of wind. The *Torbay* cut her cable and, crowding on all sail, bore up on the boom, crashing through it under heavy fire to carry away the wreckage. Hopsonn ordered the ship to anchor between the *Bourbon* and *Espérance* and engage both. Meantime the wind died away again as the rest of the van squadron approached in line abreast, and without it the ships were unable to complete the smashing of the boom, described in the official English account as 'masts and cables frapped together to the thickness of nine feet buoyed up in its length by empty casks, moored with anchors at its extremities and flanked by two large ships'. Hopsonn and the *Torbay* were thus left on their own for an anxious few minutes. Rooke in his journal records something that may well then have been in his subordinate's mind. 'Hopsonn at first deemed that any ship attempting the boom must be lost. But I upon looking at the boom thought that it had little strength; so I ordered Mr. Hopsonn and the rest of the officers to execute their orders.' He had, however, earlier described it as 'very strong'.

Fortunately the breeze now blew again and Van der Goes found the gap made by the *Torbay*, passed through and laid the *Zeven Provincien* alongside the *Bourbon* forcing her to strike her colours. But now the *Torbay* was grappled by a fireship and her bows were soon on fire, her foreyard 'burned to a coal', most of her sails destroyed and 'her larboard shrouds burned to the dead-eyes'. Sixty of her crew who jumped overboard were drowned. A petition dated February 1st 1703 from one Benjamin Bryer, a gunner, claiming recognition for his activities, describes how flag-captain Leake was 'thrown overboard' at this time. Certainly the captain did not deny it, certifying that Bryer had been 'very active and useful on my return'.

Hopsonn had to shift his flag to the *Monmouth* (Captain John Baker) while his crew endeavoured to get the fire under control. He was helped by the fact that the fireship, probably a lighter hurriedly brought into service, was loaded with snuff. When she blew up her cargo enveloped the *Torbay* and partly extinguished the fire. Leake and his crew, sneezing violently, were able to save the ship. She had lost 215 men and was so battered and burned as to be virtually helpless for the rest of the battle. But she had done very well, and Hopsonn and Leake were both knighted by Queen Anne for their work.

Bokenham in the *Association* now managed to bombard and silence the Corbeiro fort at the northern end of the boom and the Allied squadron began to stream into the Redondela harbour. The battle was now at its noisiest but it lasted only half-an-hour. Rooke describes his enemy as putting up only a 'mean resistance'. He seems to have been under the impression that Chateaurenault was there. If he had been the outcome might have been different, but he was on his way to Santiago de Compostela. It was therefore Velasco, as we have seen, who gave the orders to blow up the French and Spanish ships in the harbour. The French flagship *Forte* of 70 guns was the first to go.

As darkness fell, although not all the ships were destroyed, the air was filled with the crash of magazines exploding, the roar of cannon and the rattle of muskets, while masts and merchandise and occasionally the bodies of men were sent flying through the sky. Working feverishly the English and Dutch managed to save fourteen ships and galleons. Eleven, too badly damaged to save, were run ashore and burned. The ships taken included the *Bourbon* (68), *Prompte* (75), *Ferme* (75), *Modéré* (54), *Assuré* (66) and *Triton* (42). These figures tally reasonably with those reported by Velasco (on 18th November) and Larrea (20th) to the Council of the Indies, whose minutes record five ships of the *flota* burned out; five burned by the English after removing their cargo, five or six seized and sailed away with their cargo and six set on fire by the French.

Casualties were not heavy. The *Torbay* suffered the most; but of the others involved, the *Association* lost only two killed, the *Kent* one, the *Barfleur* two killed and two wounded, and the *Mary* none, the total being about 250 all told. Among the French and Spanish the numbers killed are not known but some 400 prisoners were taken, including Chacón's brother, the French Commodores d'Alègre and de la Gabissonière and the captains of the *Assuré* and *Volontaire*.

Many French seamen and soldiers escaped 'because the English, having no horse could not pursue them', says Tindal, using a contemporary report. 'Spaniards appeared at some distance in a great body but they did not offer to enter into any action against the Duke of Ormonde.' He attributes this to 'the resentment felt by that proud nation, which now was governed by French counsels [which was] so high that they would not put themselves in any danger or to any trouble even to save their own fleet when it was in such hands.' One must allow here for a little of the francophobia which was rife in England during the whole eighteenth century but certainly only a little later we shall find many examples of ill feeling at all levels between French and Spaniards.

The loss of warships at the beginning of hostilities was of considerable annoyance to the French king, whose finances were severely stretched. Most of the Spanish ships, including the galleons, were chartered and of little immediate concern to the Spanish Crown, except in so far as ships would be needed for future silver fleets. As far as the bullion was concerned, Philip V had a windfall. For one thing Vigo was far from Seville and its smugglers, and as we have seen, Larrea and Barbanzon had acted with speed to secure the plate. So to that extent Chateaurenault had been right when he assured the queen that she would be able to dispose of what the *flota* had brought. Moreover, Philip used the Anglo-Dutch attack as an excuse to confiscate any silver intended for English and Dutch traders.

The accounts took several months to bring together but examination shows that the total amount of bullion was of the order of 12.5 million silver pesos, of which some 7 million went directly into Philip's Treasury. Blécourt, writing from Madrid to Torcy gives a figure of 12 million *écus* and almost immediately there was pressure from France to pay off debts for arms and other supplies. This took about one third and there were further payments to Milan, and to the Prince of Bavaria. Much bullion therefore left Spain but the royal treasury benefitted handsomely from what was represented by the Allies as a disaster for Spain.

The English treated it as a triumph and for long after Vigo was regarded as a stunning success. Parnell gives a figure of a million pounds as being captured but this is a clear exaggeration. Almost all the English ships' logs still exist and there are records of the amounts paid for French ships taken in prize; four third-rates and a fourth-rate averaging £1,200 each. Again, H.M.S. *Ranelagh* (Captain Fitzpatrick), for example, took 987 lbs 8oz. of silver and 6 oz. 8 dwt of gold. The mathematician, Isaac Newton, then Master of the Mint, reported in 1705 that the total haul was 4,504 lb. of silver and 7 lb. of gold, worth altogether £14,000, not a very great sum. The losers all round were the English and Dutch merchants whose bullion went to Philip and whose merchandise to England. It is not surprising that the news of Vigo was unwelcome in some circles in Amsterdam and London!

Clearing up after the action took some days. During the night of the 23rd October Ormonde had captured Redondela town and he forthwith tried to persuade Rooke to leave ships and supplies to enable the army, if it captured Vigo town, to remain there for the winter. Rooke, still poorly and as anxious as ever to go home before the autumn gales, said he could spare only six weeks' provisions and five or six frigates – and that these would only be safe while cruising, not in harbour.

On 27th October Shovell came in with his squadron and Rooke ordered him to destroy French and Spanish ships which had run ashore and demolish batteries and to bring away the captured vessels while he and Ormonde sailed home, preceded by Lord Shannon and Captain Hardy with dispatches for Queen Anne. (She made each of the messengers a handsome present and knighted Hardy.)

Shovell deserves particular mention here, for he was one of England's finest admirals until his untimely – and avoidable – death after a shipwreck. Born of humble parents in Suffolk, he was the same age as Rooke, but a tall, lithe and active man, with a round face marked by a strong nose and chin. He had begun as a shoemaker but joined the Royal Navy as a cabin-boy in 1664, during Pepys's time as Secretary to the Navy Board. This helped him, for Pepys approved of those who came in 'through the hawse hole', i.e. without favour. For a time Shovell served as a marine. He owed his promotion to Admiral Sir John Narborough who made him his flag-lieutenant, and with whom he saw action in the Mediterranean in 1674. After Narborough's death he married the widow, Elizabeth, and they had two daughters. He served off Ireland in 1689 and 1690, and at La Hogue in 1692. He had been knighted and made Rear-Admiral, and appears to have been willing, efficient, and selfless and popular with those serving under him. We shall meet him again.

He now set about exchanging prisoners, refitting ships and collecting the captured cannon. One of his subordinates, Captain Stephen Martin, passed on to his son an account of those days. The captain was in command of a shore party keeping at bay the local peasantry. These would watch from a distance often shouting words of abuse at the 'English dogs, rogues, heretics and cuckolds' and firing an occasional shot. In reply similar abuse and a volley of ball or 'partridge-shot' were discharged.

On 6th November Shovell sailed for England, one of his squadron, the *Barfleur*, taking in prize an English ship, *Dartmouth* (50 guns) which the French had captured in 1695. He re-christened her *Vigo Prize*. As soon as the Anglo-Dutch fleet had sailed, the Council of the Indies sent one Pedro Colón to help verify where all the cases of bullion had got to – Larrea was now writing to Santander, Segovia, Seville, Burgos and all over Spain. They also arranged for a diving expert, Don Fernando Ventura, with a team to report on what in the way of plate remained in the sunken hulks. His voluminous report, dated 29th December and accompanied by individual statements from his team, makes it plain that there was little or nothing there. In the centuries since then there have been occasional proposals to dive in search of wealth in these sunken vessels. Such endeavours would not, it seems, have been very rewarding.

Back in England Ormonde continued to complain of Rooke's inertia and obstructiveness. He was rewarded with the Lord-Lieutenancy of Ireland and acclaimed everywhere by cheering mobs and he received a charming letter from Methuen in Lisbon:—

'I shall be glad to hear that Your Grace and the fleet are safe arrived in England . . . renewing the fleet and army for better success next year. No one imputes either want of success of anything else which is not liked to Your Grace's conduct. Even the French and Spanish themselves [say] that Your Grace's whole carriage in every particular answers the character Your Grace would wish always to have.'

Ormonde's subordinates fared only fairly well. Shannon had his gift and Stanhope was mentioned in despatches. Bellasis and O'Hara came to court martial. The former was dismissed the service at Queen Anne's request, but the latter was cleared and returned later to serve after he had inherited the title of Lord Tyrawley. Bellasis, having been cashiered, was later, surprisingly, re-instated in his regiment. When the court martial took place Ormonde did not press the charges too hard – the two officers being accused solely of going ashore without leave. Stanhope, who had been present as a volunteer since his regiment was still in England, had been Bellasis' guest and did not testify against him. There was clearly some closing of the ranks and the fact that some of the prince's suite were suspected of selling loot in Lisbon made protests from Vienna look a little less than virtuous.

Rooke's gout kept him from public appearances but he was made a Privy Councillor. Nevertheless his instructions and journals were closely examined by a committee appointed by the House of Lords which produced an adverse report. His Tory support ensured that his behaviour was formally approved, though only by one vote, and during 1703 and 1704 he remained Admiral of the Fleet. His fellow admirals were: Shovell, George Churchill, Fairborne, Graydon, Leake, Hopsonn, Byng, Dilkes and Beaumont, not a few of whom we shall meet again.

At a service of thanksgiving held by Queen Anne in the as yet incomplete St Paul's Cathedral, Vigo was coupled with some minor successes of Marlborough's in Flanders. However gallantly carried out, it had been at best an unremunerative victory, worth far more to the Bourbon interest.

It seems unlikely that Don José Chacón's plea to the king to assist him in refurbishing his wardrobe was successful. In the *Archivo de Indias* the copy of his letter forwarded to the monarch by the Council of the Indies carefully omits that *cri de coeur!*

★　　★　　★

There was very little military activity in the Peninsula in 1703 but it was a year of intense diplomatic activity. Within Spain there were changes. Philip, although alarmed by the news of the Vigo action, returned in a somewhat leisurely fashion to his kingdom. On reaching Saragossa he was urged to ratify the decisions taken in his absence by the *despacho* and his queen. At first he refused to do so, considering that to accept them would usurp his position.[5]

On September 19th 1703, Charles III, aged eighteen, left Vienna to confront his rival claimant in the Peninsula. Meanwhile, in the Mediterranean, Admiral Sir Cloudesley Shovell had arrived off Toulon on 12th July with a mixed Anglo-Dutch fleet. His directive from the Admiralty was a typical Whitehall production. He was to aid the Cevennois who were rebelling against King Louis. He was to obtain the return of Naples and Sicily to Habsburg rule. He was to attempt to get the rulers and people of Algiers and Tunis to side against France. He was to provide a safe convoy for the English Levant trade. And all this was to be done before winter. He had no landing force and the Emperor had sent no troops to meet him.

Such a mixture of tasks was manifestly impossible to complete and to make matters worse Shovell's fleet had been equipped and victualled at a level which was poor even by the lamentable standards of the day. He lost many men through sickness. For example, when the *Prince George* returned to the Downs on 28th November one in ten of her crew had died of sickness and few of the remainder were fit to sail her. Moreover, just after his return, on the night of 7th December the greatest storm in English history fell on the south of England. Blowing from the west-south-west and accompanied by thunderstorms it swept across the country, flooding a huge area round Bristol, tearing up trees by the thousands and stripping the roof off Ely cathedral. London looked like a city after a bombardment and the damage there alone was estimated at a million pounds.

It was, however, the Royal Navy and the merchant fleet which suffered most. The queen's ships and thousands of merchantmen put to sea to avoid being blown ashore and lay hove-to in the North Sea and the Channel for a week. It was reported in Versailles that England had lost her fleet, but most of it was in fact saved, even in Shovell's sickness-ridden squadron, by seamanship of high order. Admiral Fairborne in H.M.S. *Vanguard* was blown as far as Gothenburg in Sweden. The losses were none the less serious; an admiral (Beaumont), at least 2,000 men and around the coasts twelve major units, including four 70-gun, a 60-gun and two 50-gun ships, one being the *Vigo Prize*, and many smaller vessels. The Commons on 12th December voted to make good all the losses and even to compensate the families of drowned seamen.

Before his return to home waters, Shovell had had a minor success in the Gulf of Lions, where he had captured prizes and succeeded in bottling up the French Mediterranean fleet in Toulon. This example of the effect of sea power had helped to bring in a further ally, the shifty unpredictable Victor Amadeus II, Duke of Savoy. This prince seems to have felt it his duty to keep the balance of power in Europe even to the extent of detaching himself from whichever side was on top at any time and joining the other. This was not, however, out of dispassionate interest in the general good, but was occasioned by an appetite for cash and land. He had deserted the Empire in 1696 for France, and as a consequence had been able to marry one of his daughters to the Duke of Burgundy, Louis's eldest grandson, and the other to Philip of Anjou, now Philip V of Spain. But in 1703 he received an offer from the Emperor of Montferrat, Alessandria and other territories and from the English of a large subsidy, and on 24th October he accepted this bargain even though it might mean the dethronement of his own daughter. A contemporary French lampoon puts it:

> 'Notre cousin le Savoyard
> A quitté sa mandrille
> Pour prendre celle du César
> Contre ses propres filles.'

Voltaire remarked that the Austrian Emperor was happy to share out what did not belong to him in order to get what he could in Spain. The deal was not entirely satisfactory to the Allies. Louis XIV was with difficulty persuaded of Savoy's treachery, but when he realised what was going on he sent Marshal Vendôme to disarm and imprison the 3,000 Piedmontese troops who would otherwise have been available to the Austrian Empire. The letter which

Vendôme carried from Louis to Victor Amadeus must be one of the sternest ever written by the urbane Sun King:

> 'Since religion, honour, interest, our alliance, and your own signature are to be nothing between us, I am sending my cousin the Duke of Vendôme, at the head of my troops, to explain my intentions to you. He will give you only forty-eight hours to make up your mind.'

At the end then of 1703 the maritime powers and the Empire had acquired two new allies, Portugal and Savoy, and a Mediterranean policy, adopted in spite of Rooke. England had negotiated one short-term military and one long-term commercial treaty with Portugal, the Methuen Treaties. The government and people of England had shown themselves ready to support the Royal Navy in dire adversity. Grudgingly the Emperor had permitted his second son, the Archduke Charles to visit England on his way to confront Philip V in Spain. Here and in France the Bourbons were preparing for a deeper war in the Peninsula, though Spain's financial straits were so appalling that she could not pay for arms and supplies. Yet she had to fight, for the Allies were now committed to a policy which would lengthen hostilities to a degree not realized at the time: 'No Peace without Spain'.

CHAPTER TWO

War in Earnest

¡ Ay! de tí, Reyno sin Rey
Y ¡ ay! infelis Rey sin Reyno.
                    – Spanish squib of the time of Charles II

THE year 1704 looks in retrospect like the end of the phoney war in 1940. For some eighteen months both sides had been engaged in minor and inconclusive skirmishes, manoeuvres and sieges, and in diplomacy. Vigo had had something of the appearance of a major act of piracy. Marlborough in Flanders had been trammelled by his Dutch colleagues, frittering away his time and energy, and only late in 1703 planning his masterstroke which was to culminate far away from Flanders, 'high up in Germany', at Blenheim in 1704. It seems to have been the 'defection' by Portugal to the Allies which lit the slow-burning fuse which resulted in a royal decree by Philip, while he was at Plasencia on 13th April 1704, that he was placing himself at the head of his armies 'to do battle to defend the honour of his subjects' in war, 'the ultimate court of appeal for the sovereigns of this world'.

Louis XIV was the recipient of much advice, not all of it helpful. An elderly gentleman, Monsieur Chamblay, produced each year for him a long memorandum on possible courses of action. Meticulously argued in cartesian fashion, the memoranda seem to be based on false premises and therefore, though lengthy, valueless. Being a sensible man, King Louis probably disregarded them. A more realistic but still over-optimistic 'state of the nation' memorandum, addressed to Philip V at the end of 1703, makes the following proposals. Since the enemy fleets are so strong, the King of Spain cannot maintain one capable of holding them off. But in order to keep the King of Portugal 'under the reins', Spain must have a squadron in Andalusian waters and another in the Mediterranean to protect the Levant trade and support the Kingdoms of Naples and Sicily. Philip should cut all other expenditure and use his revenues solely for paying and supplying his armed forces and make all the 'great men' raise troops in his support. With Portugal thus 'under the reins', with the English and Dutch respecting Philip and his subjects fearing him, he could then send troops to the Indies and to Italy. But, 'The King of Spain has no money, though he should have considerable resources.'

At the turn of the year, indeed, he had announced his wish to raise 17,00 infantry, 6,000 cavalry, and 2,000 dragoons (mounted infantry). But there was no way in which these could be paid or supplied with bread, clothing or munitions. Even barley for the cavalry could not be bought. And a commander was needed. Orry, one time exciseman and former steward to the Duchess of Portsmouth (fired for theft), was full of plans for raising cash, but his letters show how hard a task it was. Quite apart from the internal rows taking place at Court which would later explode, Spaniards hated the French 'because of the brigandage and harassment taking place' under the shelter of ambassador Cardinal d'Estrées. Although a fusspot and a tiresome colleague, Orry had commonsense.

In the end there was no alternative, if Philip V was to be maintained on the throne of Spain, to a generous injection of generalship, organisation, troops, supplies and money from his grandfather. For example, on 2nd July 1703 it was reported that Cadiz, attacked the year before, had only 3,521 defenders and although some supplies reached them these were nothing like sufficient. Lists of the artillery required by Spain, giving the calibres, and of the clothing and arms needed 'in case Portugal enters the war', had been pouring into Paris for months.

At length Louis XIV reached his decision. He would send twenty battalions of foot, six regiments of cavalry and two of dragoons to Spain. And to command them and whatever Spain could raise, he appointed on 29th November 1703, James FitzJames, Duke of Berwick, aged thirty-three years and the oldest of four illegitimate children of King James II of England and Arabella Churchill, sister of the soldier who was to become the first Duke of Marlborough. Berwick was to have the title of Captain-General of the Armies in Spain, and before leaving he wrote a fifteen-page memorandum to Chamillart asking for clear instructions on a large number of points. For example, are French generals senior to Spanish? If the King of Spain is with the army, will Berwick command both French and Spanish troops? Should French and Spanish troops be mixed or kept separate? And so forth down to minute detail. The memorandum is still extant, with the answers – sometimes ambiguous – noted in the margin.

Berwick has been the subject of several studies and still remains a personality of the highest interest.[1] His mother took little notice of him and at the age of seven he was sent to a Jesuit college in France, where he was reported to be serious, religiously inclined, and very methodical. At sixteen he was sent to take part in a campaign against the Turks under the Duke of Lorraine and a year later in another under Marshal Villars. In the first he is reported by an eye-witness, Jacob Richards, the Irish engineer, to have behaved with remarkable gallantry at the siege of Budapest. At the second, he learned much about the movement of large armies in battle. The two marshals under whom he served had a major influence on his development. Another potent influence was King Louis XIV for whose exquisite manners and strong personality Berwick offered to worship, and who in turn thought highly of his young cousin. For his father, James II, Berwick seems to have preserved his filial loyalty, for he has left no written criticism of this foolish, obstinate, unfortunate man, and he successfully carried out some delicate errands for him. Family loyalty, indeed, is a virtue he inculcated in his own children, and extended to include his uncle, Marlborough. Even when the two of them were on the eve of battle on opposite sides, they kept up a perilously frank correspondence, which neither ever betrayed. Family ties were in a way more important than nationality to someone like Berwick, whose parentage, upbringing and training were so mixed, and whose ties with his father's country had been severed by the revolution of 1688.

He seems to have shared his uncle Marlborough's cool military professionalism, and his early experiences in Eastern Europe, Ireland and elsewhere were put to good use when he achieved high command. He has a reputation for cold ruthlessness. Indeed in his *Memoirs* he describes himself as having neither friends nor enemies but for the good of the service. He was capable of hanging pilferers without mercy, and in the Cevennes of ordering two *camisards* to be burned alive and others to be broken on the wheel; and he conducted operations such as the final siege of Barcelona with an almost mechanical lack of feeling. This was of a piece with his attention to detail, a characteristic shared with his uncle, who for the care with which he fed and clothed his troops was known by them as Corporal John. Most of Berwick's correspondence is written by secretaries, but letters to Louis XIV and others exist in his own hand, a clear, no-nonsense, determined script. Perhaps as a soldier's soldier he was happiest on campaign. Certainly when the news of his being killed by a cannon-shot at Philipsburg in 1734 reached his former commander, Villars, the old marshal, himself dying, said, 'I was always right in saying that Berwick was more fortunate than I.'

Yet there was another side to him, He married twice, first the widowed Countess of Lucan, who died after presenting him with a short-lived son; and second, Anne Bulkeley, daughter of James II's master of horse. A large, good-looking, but – according to her stepson – ill-tempered lady, lacking in wit, she had thirteen children by Berwick, of whom only a few survived. It was a love-match, for he had only 20,000 *livres* a year and should have married for money. According to Anthony Hamilton, a poet at James II's court, she was known as Nanette and Berwick as Brochet, and they did not relish the frequent absences imposed on him by the service. It is easy to think of Berwick as an insensitive military machine, but the face in his portraits is surprisingly gentle. The mouth is curved, not thin-lipped, and there is a smile in, not just round the eyes. There is nothing here of the harsh bitterness to be seen in his father's face.

Ahead of him, accompanying the troops as Lieutenant-General, was Jean François de Castenet, Marquis de Puységur. A fine soldier, well known to Louis, for he had been Lieutenant-Colonel of the *Maison de Roi* (Household Brigade) and Quartermaster-General to Villeroy and Luxembourg, he was opinionated and quite capable of jealousy. At the battle of Oudenarde in July 1708 he would be so insistent that the French left-wing under Marshal Biron was protected from attack by an impassable marsh that its movement was paralysed, and Marlborough won the day. He was to be at cross-purposes with Orry soon after his arrival in Spain. He was responsible for victualling and paying the troops, providing forage, and building hospitals for the sick. Everything had to be brought into Spain via Bayonne. He was also responsible for intelligence and discipline, and clearly all this was more than one man could undertake. Louis therefore ordered Chamillart to appoint a number of commissaries to assist. The senior was Le Marié, with Dudoyer as assistant, and they were later assisted by Méliaud, Jourdain, Daubenton and du Barbier, and by sub-intendants at various points along the frontier, de la Gibaudière and Dupont. From their letters, sent regularly to the Ministry for War, much can be gleaned of the conditions in which the armies of France and Spain fought. These men's duties were divided, sometimes regionally, sometimes – in Madrid – functionally, as in the case of Daubenton whose job it was to supervise naval supplies and trade between Spain and France.

Although Le Marié initially reported optimistically that all should be well and that the troops should have nothing to complain of as regarded their subsistence, it would not be long before logistics became extremely difficult. Roads were appalling, there was a chronic lack of mules – these cost 15 *louis d'or* each – and oxen, and those available were slow. Food and forage were scarce, and money even scarcer. By 1st March 1704 Le Marié reckoned the French troops had cost over two million *livres*. The only way to obtain money was to draw bills of exchange on Paris, and as we have seen, the money had to be available in Spanish currency as French money was not accepted. Billeting of French troops was difficult, and yet billets must be found, not just to save the men having to carry tents but also because the ground was so hard in much of Spain that tents could not be erected and men were reduced to sleeping in the open. This in turn resulted in sickness and the need for hospitals. Mails, nominally once a week, were unreliable. And so it went on.

As a back-up, and since the French had a low opinion of the Spanish military organisation, the need was foreseen of someone to command the new troops to be raised by the King of Spain. A letter from Chamillart to Ambassador d'Estrées announced that King Louis had selected an Irishman, Colonel Daniel O'Mahony. This officer, a member of Dillon's Regiment (one of the units of Wild Geese, who had left Ireland after the treaty of Limerick), had served with distinction in Italy. St Simon describes him as witty as well as brave and Louis himself said of him that he had never seen anyone give so good an account of himself, so clear-thinking, so exact, and so agreeable. We shall see much of him, and of the other Irish who served Louis XIV and Philip in Spain. O'Mahony later married when he was widowed the sister of Berwick's second wife and there was thus a family tie with the Captain-General. His time in Spain was to be quite as difficult as that of any of them.

★   ★   ★

Prince George of Hesse–Darmstadt had reached London late in the autumn of 1702 and had spent time arranging with the English Government and through them with the Dutch for 4,000 English and 2,000 Dutch troops to be available for the Peninsula. He was still there at the end of the year when his young royal master was expected. The young man's father, Emperor Leopold, had delayed his decision to let him go, and, possibly out of dislike of the project but no doubt also because of money shortages, he failed in his ramshackle way to make adequate financial arrangements for the cost of Charles' entourage and the young man had to pawn some of his jewels on the way. The emperor had, however, renounced his claim to the Spanish throne in September. The entourage gathered in strength on the way and would soon number over 400. His chief adviser and equivalent to prime minister was his former tutor, Prince Lichtenstein, whose academic and tutorial talents may have been sound but who as a person was arrogant, timid, irresolute, obstinate and liable to take wrong decisions almost invariably. Charles clung to him for old times' sake for a long while but eventually began to disregard his advice. Other senior people were the Counts of Mansfeld and Caserta, the Marquis of Vasto, Counts Baur and Zinzerling, Major-General Count Uhlfeldt and Colonel Count Zinzendorf. They would soon constitute, as 'the German crew', a major irritant for the Allied body politic in the Peninsula, for they were for the most part greedy, idle, obstinate, full of self-importance and insistent on stiff etiquette. The Royal Navy was hard put to it to find cabin space for them and deck space for their impedimenta which included *inter alia* forty-odd post waggons and coaches. Half the guns had to be taken out of the flagship and staterooms with crimson hangings arranged under the low deck-heads. Charles and his Court were an expensive and cumbersome burden, but they represented for the first few years of the war the emperor's sole contribution to the Peninsular sector. Even Prince George, appointed as Charles' commander-in-chief and military adviser, was a general without an army, whose influence was largely dependent on force of personality.

Charles' journey across Europe was leisurely, partly because of the demands of protocol, partly from incompetence, and partly from shortage of cash.[2] He had stopped at Prague and Essen. At the latter he met Marlborough, fresh from a fairly successful campaign, and had given him his own gold and diamond-studded sword. He had to wait three weeks at Düsseldorf before the Dutch were ready to receive him. He should have left Holland in November but the weather was building up to the great storm which blew at the end of the month.

Admiral Rooke had sailed to Helvetsloes to await him with a squadron compatible with his dignity but this had been dispersed by the gales, and Admiral Callenburg's ships had been blown up to northern Norway and would not reappear for weeks. However, Charles at length embarked on 4th January at Brill and reached Spithead on 6th January. He was met by Queen Anne's Consort, Prince George of Denmark, and on 7th January landed at Portsmouth. From thence he was taken along the wintry roads to Windsor, where the queen feasted him. The Imperial ambassador to London, Wratislaw, had taken a good deal of trouble about protocol and Charles saw Marlborough, Godolphin and other important personages. Word of his visit reached Spain only a fortnight later. An English packet boat had reached Lisbon in six days and spread the news. During the visit alternative strategies for the Peninsula were discussed and the whole affair was a great social success. Queen Anne gave him £100,000.

The public in England liked a king. Charles, now eighteen, was tall and good-looking. A contemporary Catalan popular song describes him as 'Bell Senyor bonie virtuós i bo' (fine Lord, bonny, virtuous and good). When occasion offered he could be somewhat livelier than Philip, more attractive and capable of boyish enthusiasm. But despite this it was noted, 'He seemed pleased with everything without so much as once smiling all the while he was at Court which was only three days.' This may have been due to shyness and to the oppressive etiquette of his retinue, and it is true that though he spoke some languages, English was not yet one of them. But it may also have been due to an exaggerated sense of his own dignity. As he grew older he cultivated a certain reserve. He appears to have been musical and to have had some artistic taste and we shall see him showing almost excessive religious observance and also enthusiasm for gunnery at Barcelona. Rooke noted that he had a good appetite, eating enough 'to keep a Lazarus for eight months', though he drank little except for the purpose of toasts, even though Canary wine and Hermitage were available in quantity; and his personal tastes were modest.

He sailed for Lisbon in H.M.S. *Royal Catherine* on 17th January (N.S.) although Callenburg's Dutch squadron had still not come in and there were rumours that the French were hoping to capture him. He was accompanied by a fleet of 188 vessels including transports. He appears to have been determined to face up to storms at sea and to show interest in all the fleet's activities and the entertainments devised for him. In the transports were the 4,000 English and some of the 2,000 Dutch troops under the command of the Duke of Schomberg, an Anglo-Dutch survivor of King William's day and the undistinguished son of a far more worthy father. The Dutch contingent was under General Fagel. With the English contingent was also Colonel Stanhope, on his way back to the Peninsula after a stint under Marlborough in Flanders. Some at least of the Dutch contingent were delayed waiting for Callenburg.

Now, however, the weather took a hand. Gales blew up, and after an unpleasant two and a half weeks most of the fleet was driven back in disorder to Spithead, unable to sail again until 24th February, though Darmstadt, characteristically, had held his course for Lisbon in the frigate *Panther*, arriving with three transports of very seasick soldiers on 31st January. Chamillart, in Versailles, wrote to Tzerclaes in Spain, reporting intelligence that the archduke had been driven back by 'furious tempests'. News of the Allies soon reached Berwick who wrote to King Louis on 23rd February; 'It seems visible that God protects the justice of your arms.' Yet on 12th March Charles reached Lisbon, and the French ambassador, Chateauneuf, left the city but not the country on the same day; by the 16th all the English transports had arrived and the bulk of the soldiers began to disembark. The Almirante of Castile kissed hands and some Biscayan prisoners offered homage, though one little boy of ten among them refused. Charles was said to be looking pale, disturbed, and uncertain in speech after his rough trip. By 23rd April Le Marié, now at Alcántara, reported hearing from eight Irish deserters from the Allied force that fifteen days earlier there had arrived at Lisbon eight regiments of English infantry, one of cavalry, and one of dragoons (three squadrons). He was even able to name the regiments. There were also, he learned, five or six Dutch regiments of infantry, one of cavalry and one of dragoons.

On Charles' arrival King Pedro welcomed him warmly. He had intended to marry his daughter, the Infanta Teresa, to Charles but she had unfortunately just died. So important was the archduke's arrival politically that Pedro even went so far as to postpone official mourning for three days and organize fireworks and *feux de joie* to greet him. He boarded the *Royal Catherine* in person, deferred to Charles in rank and led him ashore under triumphal arches to the royal palace at Belém.

John Methuen was prevented by gout from attending the celebrations but was relieved that matters were taking the course he had pressed for. Rooke was given a diamond-hilted sword. It may be imagined that conversation between the two kings was not without its difficulties. Charles had some Spanish but no Portuguese and King Pedro had an impediment of speech.

The Portuguese had spent lavishly (excessively, da Cunha in London thought) on Charles' reception. Pedro had received £150,000 to maintain his auxiliaries for six months and another £75,000 to equip them, but much of the money had gone, not on arms and stores but on embroidered royal tents, and he had to borrow another £250,000 privately to buy muskets and horses. Most of the cash provided was English for the Empire had none and the Dutch provided their subsidies by making book entries in the accounts of the Dutch West Indies Company to which Portugal was in debt. Gunpowder and artillery were to be supplied by the Allies but were often late arriving. Altogether war preparations on the Allied side paralleled in effectiveness those on the other.

At Belém was held a grand council which both monarchs attended and plans for the campaign were discussed. In general the strategy was to be an offensive by the navy against Spanish coastal fortresses and ports, while the armies remained on the defensive. This was perhaps inevitable. The French and Spanish armies were believed to be stronger. The English and Dutch contingents were not large, and the Portuguese army after a long period of peace was in a lamentable state. Its 20,000 men were often unpaid, always ill-clad, and sometimes disaffected. There was much speculation among the officers and idleness was endemic. Fortresses were dilapidated, magazines were empty and horses hard to find. Indeed, although in the nature of things, the priestly attendants of St Anthony of Padua are unlikely to have permitted any lowering of the saint's pecking order, even they may have had to scrape the barrel a bit. This military shambles was compounded by the system of command. The nominal commander was, of all people, the Duque de Cadaval, thought to be leader of the pro-French faction at court, a civilian who did not trouble to consult any of his generals, even the most professional, António Luis da Souza, the Marqués das Minas. Each province conducted its own defences under a captain-general, and there was no co-ordination. The troops were mostly slumming in billets. The situation required a stout professional input from the new arrivals. It did not receive it. As Stanhope put it, 'The Duke of Cadaval has the chief direction and command ... He caressed our Duke [Schomberg] extremely at his arrival and governed him in everything.' So Schomberg and Fagel conformed to the local system, dispersing their troops widely as garrisons in half-fortified towns, the Dutch north of the Tagus and the English south. Sickness began to spread and the only *masse de manoeuvre* was a few regiments of cavalry. It was a recipe for disaster, only counter-balanced as we shall see by the soldierly though erratic zeal of the elderly das Minas, and by the problems, military and above all political, on the other side of the frontier.

First of all, the military problems in Spain. As early as 22nd January, Puységur, whom St Simon once called 'the soul of the army in Flanders', sent a thirty-page report to Chamillart on the needs of the Spanish troops, describing how he intended to organize matters. Berwick, by the time it arrived, was just leaving Versailles. By 3rd February he had reached Bordeaux and by the 6th he was at Bayonne where he had found the French artillery in such a bad way that he wrote to Versailles asking for de la Motte, 'the most capable artilleryman in France', to be sent to help. He also asked for General de Thouy, and was expecting General de Geoffreville, which would enable Colonel d'Asfeld to move. All these officers will appear and reappear in these pages during the years to come. Meantime there were indications of disagreement between Puységur and Orry. The former wanted everything to be ready but Berwick thought 'this cannot be' and intended to go to Madrid to see what was going on.

Puységur meantime had gone from Castile to Extremadura. 'Compared with Extremadura, Castile is a paradise', he reported. Here, so hard was the ground that 'the soldier cannot set up camp but has to sleep in his *justaucorps*'. In another report to Chamillart of thirty-two folios, written on both sides, he gloomily listed the growing difficulties. Puységur's letters spurred Chamillart into writing a rebuke to Orry for not doing as he promised, and he also found time to warn Berwick to make the most of the Spanish troops available, particularly the cavalry. 'Do not flatter youself that you can only work with King Louis' troops.'

Spanish correspondence was equally despondent. Tzerclaes writing from Badajoz said that Alcántara had only a third of the men needed and was short of guns. And a further forty or so letters, together with a long report on the state of Spanish infantry, are a litany of lacks: guns, powder, supplies, and above all money. Tzerclaes and Ronquillo named over a hundred supernumary officers. How were they to be paid? There was a backlog of pay due to the Regiment of Asturias and no equipment. Ronquillo described the shortage of bayonets in

April in Ciudad Rodrigo, and said firmly, 'I am not in a position to provide miracles.' He was heartened only to know that twenty-seven pairs of shoes he had left in Salamanca were safe.

Reading the letters – which continue for months and months – one is conscious of every sort of difficulty big and small that can and does fall on the shoulders of commanders. An officer (Lieutenant Richard) takes off from Spain to France for family reasons and says he has been granted leave; he has not, says Berwick grimly. Officers are asking to be reimbursed for forage but, as Chamillart says, 'This has never been the practice.' Berwick asks plaintively what is to be done about valets who leave their officers; they are hard to replace. Put them in gaol if you catch them, says Chamillart. Movement control suffers from its perennial breakdowns and the Regiment of Sillery is lost for seven days. Another regiment, the 2nd Berwick, is continually reported as causing disorder and upsetting the population wherever it goes. One wonders why, until one finds a report in French of a court martial of three private soldiers of the 2nd Berwick for desertion. They are found not guilty, for 'they had got lost but had kept their uniforms and muskets and had difficulty in rejoining, not speaking French.' This makes one look again. In the French army but speaking no French? Then the names of those involved explain it all. The president of the court is a Major Dwyer and the other officers all have names like Fitzpatrick and Kavanagh. The three defendants, 'Ezekyas Foot, Jean Best and Abraham Halsworth', are all from Ireland. Probably Foot, Best and Halsworth had had a jar or two and were sleeping it off when the 2nd Berwick Regiment marched off leaving them behind. And who will blame them, poor chaps? They had left everything in Ireland for ever and had so little to live for. *Plus ça change*. After this there is no further light on those three musketeers. For nearly three centuries they have been in some corner of a foreign field.

Berwick entered Madrid on 15th February in state, followed by more than 300 coaches filled with grandees. Here he found a political turmoil from which, while observing and reporting on it, he did his best to distance himself. As it had considerable bearing on the military events of 1704 it must later be described in another chapter. For the present, the duke had an audience of King Philip who formally appointed him Captain-General. 'I went through the ceremony of putting on my hat in his presence, being introduced to the audience by the Duke of Arcos as my sponsor, according to the Spanish custom.' He could not but be conscious of the tensions in the palace of Buen Retiro and between that Court and the French embassy, for each of the individuals approached him. 'But I said I would have nothing to do with what was going on. I had business of too much consequence.' His first action was to disentangle the argument between Puységur and Orry. This turned out to be a simple matter of the tense of a verb.

Orry had told Puységur in the presence of King Philip that the magazines 'would be supplied' with the necessary stores. Puységur heard it as 'were supplied', and finding this not to be so, complained. Orry pointed out that until Puységur arrived he had nothing to do with military affairs and did not even know where the magazines were, so he could not have replenished them. Nor would he be such a fool as to tell a lie which would rapidly be discovered. The king confirmed this, and the queen asked Berwick not to take against Orry, 'the only man with any resource'. Since Puységur was staying with the Abbé d'Estrées, who was caballing against Orry, the incident was magnified out of all proportion. Berwick assured her that he was there only to wage war against the enemy, and indeed, in his letters he is always fair to Orry. In his *Memoirs* he moreover says of him, 'I owe this justice to him that he neglected nothing which he thought might be necessary or helpful, for though he had no public standing he had a hand in everything and did all he could.'

Taking care to inform himself fully, as Louis had ordered, of the political and personal squabbles that were going on but to avoid participation, he reported on the situation to King Louis and left Madrid shortly afterwards, no doubt with relief, accompanied by Puységur, to prepare the Spanish army and its French companions in arms for the campaign he intended to wage against Portugal. Based on Alcántara he set about re-arming the Spaniards, calling up fresh troops, mounting cavalry and rapidly building up a Spanish replica of the French army. In this he was greatly helped by Orry who somehow contrived to raise most of the money initially required. In the space of a few weeks a force of 30,000 infantry and 10,000 cavalry, including the 12,000 French and Spanish veterans sent from Flanders, was standing on the Portuguese frontier.

★   ★   ★

Military events during 1704 neatly illustrate and set a pattern for the rest of the war in the Peninsula.[3] France and Spain possessed internal communications and could therefore in theory move by land wherever they wished, but their battle fleets were largely Mediterranean-based. The maritime powers enjoyed relative freedom of movement by sea and this enabled them, again in theory, to attack wherever they liked along the coasts of Spain, though availability of transport vessels limited the strength of the land forces they could put ashore at any given time. While, therefore, the osmotic effect of sea power could and did draw Bourbon forces away from northern Europe in accordance with Marlborough's strategies, and while Allied strength in the Mediterranean inexorably built up, the maritime powers could not attain sufficient preponderance on land to overwhelm their opponents. They would at times seem to produce situations which could result in Philip V's being driven from the throne, but again and again complete victory escaped them, sometimes because of less than effective generalship, sometimes by reason of disagreement and lack of co-ordination and sometimes because of lack of strength. The sharp thrust of an amphibious descent was often blunted by lack of powerful follow-up. And imperceptibly the navy changed its rôle from that of a fleet in being to that of a transport system and mobile artillery train. This began to manifest itself during a year in which each side, waging a campaign with some confidence, would in turn find itself surprised by the actions of the other. On the whole, sea power made surprise easier for the Allies to inflict than for the Bourbons, but initially it was internal communications which looked like prevailing.

Berwick's plan, which he outlined in long letters to Louis XIV dated 22nd and 29th February, was sound. Alcántara, high up on the Tagus, was to be the chief magazine for supplies and the 'centre of the war'. Although he was disturbed by the divisions and cabals in Madrid, Berwick found King Philip's attitude encouraging. 'I have never seen a prince who liked war more or showed better signs of doing well ... And most Spaniards, great and small, are well disposed to their king.' He went into great detail on logistics, including for example such matters as the cost of Spanish horses. These, at twenty-five *louis d'or* each, were excellent, whereas French horses died too quickly. And he set out where all the troops were stationed and their future movements. Such reports to the monarch were duplicated to the Minister for War, and it is clear that Louis found their relentless detail something of a bore, for it was not long before Chamillart was writing to Berwick asking him merely to give the main points when writing to the king. It took a little while for this injunction to be effective, for weeks later he wrote another long letter asking Louis *inter alia* that French soldiers in Spain should receive 4 *sous* a day without deduction for bread and other rations, since these arrive irregularly, and 'the soldier will console himself with wine or other things'. Louis later agreed. War in Spain, Berwick added, was very different from elsewhere. 'Anywhere else you give orders and they are carried out. Here you cannot find anything or anyone to deal with it. Lack of preparation means that the forthcoming campaign in Portugal cannot be finished in two or three weeks.' His strategy was to invade Portugal with five separate columns, of which three would converge on Lisbon. He himself with

17,000 men would advance down the right (northern) bank of the Tagus to Villa Velha, capturing on the way Salvatierra, Monsanto and Castelho Branco. Here he would be joined by Tzerclaes who was to advance along the left bank with 5,000 men and build a bridge of boats so as to maintain communications, having captured Portalegre on the way. To protect the right flank, Don Francisco de Ronquillo was to invade the Portuguese province of Beira with 9,000 men. Other columns were to operate further north still, under the Duke of Hijar, and in the extreme south under the Marquis of Villadarías.

It should have worked. But most of the troops were raw, the Spanish generals were unused to – and resentful of – serving under French command, and Tzerclaes was timid and incompetent. Moreover, as Berwick points out in a letter to Louis, 'nobody knows anything about the enemy's dispositions.' He had therefore arranged for an Irish officer named Lawler, serving under Colonel O'Mahony with Spanish troops, to go into Portugal and find out what he could. Since Lawler was officially going as a messenger between Torcy and Chateauneuf, the French ambassador still at that time in Portugal though not at Lisbon, he could not be at any risk for he had diplomatic immunity.

Berwick was full of confidence, though irked by the delays. Four weeks later he wrote again from Alcántara. The Spanish artillery was in poor condition, and he would have liked to wait till the French guns arrive in April. He could not build pontoons for lack of money. French guns and engineers were essential. 'Places in Flanders which are looked on as poor are like impregnable fortresses in comparison with what one finds here.' Some of these he wished to fortify and make 'beyond insult', and this would need French skills. He intended to keep Segura, Segrada, Monsanto and Castelho Branco so as to safeguard his communications. Philip V would come shortly to join him but would be based at Plasencia in safety until the campaign begins.

Lieutenant Lawler's report, when he returned at the end of March, was vivid and accurate. If the Spaniards were unprepared for war, the Portuguese were even more so. Portuguese forces were few and scattered. The Allies were awaiting wheat from England but would have difficulty transporting it to their store at Elvas. The only significant Portuguese magazine was at Montemor, an open town with an unguarded castle, and there were no troops between Lisbon and Estremós, this area being left for Allied troops who were still to disembark. The Portuguese hoped to have 8,000 infantry and 3,250 cavalry in the field but most of these were still at home, and from what Lawler had seen, were of poor quality. As to fortresses, Castelho Branco had a garrison of only 250 militia and like São Miguel and Monforte would be easy to take. From Castelho Branco to Lisbon the terrain was fertile and there was nowhere where Berwick's invading troops could be stopped. 'The King of Portugal is, of course, more interested in defence than in attack.'

This was an extremely valuable piece of intelligence work, confirming Berwick in the view that his plan of campaign should be successful. But there still remained the delays imposed by lack of artillery, mules and oxen, and doubts about supplies. Delay at this time was moreover of critical importance. In northern Europe war was generally a summer occupation, and by late October troops usually went into winter quarters until March. Here in the Peninsula they also had to go into summer quarters for the extreme summer heat made fighting or even marching virtually impossible. Extremadura means 'extreme and hard', and although that region is more extreme than most, the Spanish landscape in general is merciless in the summer. Much of the countryside was and is of quite excruciating dullness, miles and miles of scrub with an occasional small village or town, then usually walled, with its castle above on a hilltop, sometimes an olive or orange grove or pine wood, and often a cork forest in the south. Water is scarce and food scarcer. The inhabitants did not then welcome strangers, particularly armed men. In the rocky sierras the light glints sharply off the harsh stones, and everywhere insects plague by day and night. So it was not only prudent but essential to seek a few weeks of shelter from June to late August, for man and beast, and this limited the scope of campaign.

It was intended that King Philip should be with the army, chiefly in order to demonstrate that he was worthy to be monarch. He was keen to do so and Berwick encouraged him, although having the king present, with his huge staff – 'a great number of nobles of highest rank' says San Felipe – cannot but have added to the burden of command. There was another – political – reason why the king was encouraged to go with the army. Just at this time the pressure on King Louis to defuse the tense political atmosphere in Madrid was at its highest. Berwick had reported on the situation there, but was only indirectly involved in the crisis, though he would in time be regarded as in part responsible by Queen María Luisa, and this would occasion his recall from Spain in six months' time. Now, however, he impatiently awaited Philip's arrival.

Facing Berwick the situation was as Lawler described and as we have seen, with the Allies in defensive state and disastrously spread out. The 20,000-strong Portuguese army was still largely in garrison, the command split between the ancient Galveas in the Alemtéjo, south of the Tagus, and the spry sixty-year old das Minas in Beira, to the north, and only some 12,000 were potentially mobile. It was widely recognised that cavalry and dragoons were the best part of the Spanish army. King Pedro had served in battle and knew this and he tried to buy good mounts (at £11.50 each) for his dragoons as well as his cavalry. He was unable to find 5,000 horses for his own and 2,000 for the Allies as the French ambassador had secretly bought all he could find and got them away. Pedro even left his own cavalry short in an effort to supply his Allies but they considered (wrongly) that Portuguese mounts were not strong enough to carry heavy English and Dutch troopers. English horses could not however live on Peninsular forage and although during the course of the war importations were made by the Allies from Morocco, Ireland and elsewhere, the Spanish cavalry remained generally superior as they used local animals. Marshal Berwick was also to discover that local beasts were adapted to local forage.

At the lower levels of command were some good men, the Irish Major-General O'Farrell, General Montandré and Colonel Lundy. In particular there was, too, Colonel John Richards, also an Irishman. The Richards were a military family. The father, Jacob I, had served at the Boyne and had produced three sons, Jacob II (1660), John (1669) and Michael (1673) all of whom became soldiers, and a daughter who married one James Craggs. Jacob II, a Protestant, had served in Tangier, in Hungary, and with the duc de Vendôme, as well as with William III in Flanders. It was he who praised Berwick's gallantry at Budapest. He had died in 1701. The second son, John, was a Roman Catholic and as such could not hold a commission in the English Army. He had served with the Venetians against the Turks and in the Polish Army, which he had just left to come to the Peninsular. He was well known to Marlborough who had a high regard for him as a well-educated and scientifically trained soldier. His Portuguese commission in 1703 should have entitled him to English rates of pay but some local regulation prevented him from receiving more than 20 shillings a day. His correspondence during the war with his brother, with Stanhope, and many others, has survived his end at Alicante in 1709. Michael, a Protestant, was at present in Flanders but he was to come to the Peninsula after Ramillies (where he was one of Marlborough's A.D.C.s). We shall meet him again too, and we shall meet the Richards' brother-in-law, Craggs, who was to serve as secretary to Colonel Stanhope. The higher command on the Allied side was riddled with incompetence. Reinhardt Schomberg, second Duke of Leinster, now aged 49, was a disastrous appointment as English commander. Admittedly he spoke Portuguese, but he was idle, bad-tempered and self-indulgent, and cared little for the men he commanded. The higher command was weakened, moreover, by an argument between Schomberg and the Dutch commander, Fagel, resulting in the latter taking all his fit men (only about 1,900 foot and 100 horse) to serve in Beira with das Minas, while Schomberg with now only about 3,000 English went to Elvas to join Galveas. Horses were in very short supply and the English cavalry a mere detachment.

Thus, when the campaign opened, the Bourbon forces facing Portugal were larger in numbers than their opponents, although some of the Spanish had been placed as garrisons. But Berwick's leadership and military science were of a high order and his men, despite all difficulties, were in good spirits, while Schomberg, Galveas and Fagel between them were frittering away their strength. It would be das Minas who saved the day, and ensured that the Allies were not more severely mauled than they deserved.

★   ★   ★

All through March and April Berwick waited in what he described to Louis XIV as a 'defensive/offensive position' which gave him a choice. He was always short of sure intelligence and worried about money – the Spanish bankers were being 'inflexible' about the rate of exchange on a bill for 100,000 *écus* drawn on Paris. He was forever uncomfortably aware of the kitchen-cabinet quarrels at court and was irresistibly drawn into them. He was also on his dignity a little, complaining to Chamillart for putting Puységur and himself on the same level in his letter, as this might make Puységur difficult to manage.

At length, however, the armies were ready and on 2nd May Philip moved with his staff from Plasencia to Alcántara.[4] Perennially short of cash he brought only 100,000 *écus* to pay his troops, when 500,000 were needed. Berwick in a letter to Versailles said, 'It is really sad to be obliged to make war without money or munitions.' It was, he added, essential that money should enter Philip's coffers the whole time. Everything was dying for want of money and he was 'mortified' because things were not as he had hoped.

Reports had been received that all the English corps were in the Alemtéjo and that the archduke would open the campaign with a siege of Badajoz. Until these were discounted, Berwick had advised Philip 'not to go into enemy country perhaps to be driven out again after fifteen days for lack of supplies'. But now all was clear, and after a few days of parades and inspections, Berwick set in motion his five columns.

The main one, of twenty-three battalions and forty squadrons which he led in person, had its first action, as he intended, at Salvatierra which was held by about 6,000 Portuguese under Dom Diego de Fonseca. Heavy and accurate gunfire at first held off Berwick's forces for forty-eight hours and he began to fear that the place might take ten days or more to reduce. He summoned Fonseca to surrender to 'his catholic majesty', and to his surprise – as recorded in his letters and *Memoirs* – Fonseca, upon learning that King Philip was actually present, did so, even apologizing to the king for lack of respect in having fired on him. Fonseca's behaviour is still a mystery. It could have been due to respect for one's king – stronger in Iberia than elsewhere. It can hardly have been cowardice unless Fonseca was having an off day, for he was reputed to be brave and experienced. It could have been due, though one would have expected Berwick to know and he says nothing, to some influence on Fonseca from the pro-French party in Lisbon. Indeed, Stanhope wrote to his father from Lisbon a couple of weeks later, 'I fear withal there is something more than ignorance (in high places) and that the King of France has his friends here as in other courts.'

At all events, de Thouy's capture of Salvatierra enabled Berwick to keep up his momentum. The fortresses of Segura, Rosmarinha, Idanha-á-Nova, Galveros and Peña Garcia surrendered. Monsanto, naturally a strong place, resisted for three days only. Then the Spaniards burst in, killing the garrison and looting the civilians' goods. Idanha-á-Velha was similarly stormed before Fagel could reach it. Paradoxically, while the castles and strong places often opened their gates or fell easily to an attack, Berwick records that he was astonished at the resistance offered by mere villages. This would seem to be because the inhabitants had not yet been touched by the politics, often corrupt, which affected the cities and, being little travelled, were inclined to resist any incursion into their territory, from whatever source it came. But with only a few weeks to achieve his goal by marching on Lisbon and, 'causing confusion and fear there among the people to persuade King Pedro that his only course was to petition for peace', Berwick could not waste time. So he gave his troops full rein and villages and little towns were mercilessly sacked while their younger menfolk took to the hills.

The summer heats were on the army as it surged towards the next major objective, Castelho Branco, the siege party of 4,000 being again under the command of General de Thouy. Lawler had reported it as manned only by militia. But, once upon a time a Roman camp and now still possessed of a Moorish citadel, its fortifications had been repaired in the last few weeks, rendering it once more one of the strongest places in Portugal; and a hundred Dutch infantry had been added to its garrison. Berwick's Spanish artillery, moreover, was poor in quality and lacked ammunition, and he had had to leave without the French. Nevertheless, de Thouy's force attacked with vigour. They were short of food and their entrenchments were waterlogged by sudden heavy rain. But the presence of King Philip who, in San Felipe's rather sycophantic words, 'visited them often and sometimes, disdaining pomp and circumstance, ate on foot using a drumhead as a table, more pompous than the most splendidly adorned, thus setting a good example to princes and military leaders who spend so much time and expense on their tables', seems to have had an inspiring effect. Castelho Branco surrendered at discretion after four days at a cost to Berwick of only one officer and about twenty other ranks killed and five seriously wounded. It yielded stores of arms, powder, flour and tents, including those embroidered ones especially ordered for King Pedro and the Archduke Charles.

An argument now broke out between French and Spanish soldiers over the booty and in the course of it shots were fired, one of them mortally wounding an officer standing near Philip V in an adjoining field. Berwick hastened to the site of the trouble and, as he put it, 'happily had an influence' which forcefully brought the rioting troops to order. An immediate inquiry convinced him that the Spaniards, from the La Reyna (Queen's) Dragoons, were the aggressors and he ordered the ringleaders to be hanged. Spanish officers objected to this and King Philip wavered, as was his habit, but Berwick insisted that unless strict discipline was kept, peace could not be preserved between the French and Spanish troops. At a drumhead court martial, attended by French and Spanish officers, over which Berwick presided, the ringleaders were found guilty. They were publicly hanged, and, in Berwick's own laconic words, 'since then there has been nothing similar'.

As the Franco-Spanish invaders approached Castelho Branco, Fagel, who was covering it with four Dutch battalions and a few squadrons, withdrew to a wood. Berwick sent de Thouy with eight battalions and some squadrons after them in a night march, which resulted in surrounding the Dutch infantry at dawn. Fagel and the cavalry escaped to Sobrera Formosa where two more Dutch battalions were stationed. Most of the infantry were made prisoner. As the horses could not be fed, Fagel sent them by a circuitous route to join das Minas, dispatching two battalions under his second-in-command, Frisheim, towards Villa Velha. Underestimating de Thouy's mobility and speed in the mountains, Fagel withdrew to Zarcedas, leaving there a further two battalions under Brigadier-General Welderen. Surrounded by the French on 27th May, Welderen fired only one volley before surrendering, while Fagel, some four miles away at the time, was one of the few to escape, retreating with Frisheim and his remaining infantry to Abrantes. The Portuguese fled.

The way was now open for Berwick to strike towards Lisbon. Stanhope, not by nature a panicky man, wrote from there to his father, 'I see no human possibility of saving Lisbon but by a treaty, if the enemies push their advantage.' At the Allied headquarters Schomberg blamed Fagel, the Almirante of Castile, and anyone else involved, but took no effective action. Yet although Berwick's position looked formidable, he had advanced as far as he could. His swift central thrust now lost momentum, thanks to what he himself calls 'the timidity and imbecility of the Prince of Tzerclaes'. This Belgian in the Spanish service was a descendant of the formidable Tilly de Tzerclaes of the Thirty Years' War, but had inherited none of the dash or spirit of his ancestor. Even his handwriting and that of his secretary, although pretty to look at, have nothing about them of the man of action, compared with Berwick's strong penstrokes. As Berwick puts it in his *Memoirs*; 'the Prince of Tzerclaes, far from executing on his side what had been agreed, remained on the frontier of Extremadura, alleging that the Duke of Schomberg being encamped with a large body of troops at Estremós would cut off his provisions and communications with Spain.' As Tzerclaes had twenty-two battalions (four of them French) and thirty squadrons, whereas Schomberg had only thirty troops of horse (about 500 men), this was regarded as a poor excuse. Tzerclaes in fact considered retreating to Badajoz, but Berwick had sent Colonel d'Asfeld (the future Marshal of France) to keep an eye on him. Although d'Asfeld prevented Tzerclaes from retreating, he was unable to persuade him to move forward to Niza, which he should have reached by now, and Berwick had to undertake the move himself, sacrificing his threat to Lisbon.

He sent Puységur to Villa Velha to construct the bridge of boats which Tzerclaes should have built, and two days later crossed the river with his corps, leaving two battalions and a squadron to guard the bridge and 4,000 Spaniards on guard at Castelho Branco. Here a curious piece of temperament was shown by de Thouy. Berwick wished this able general to take charge at this post but de Thouy refused. According to Berwick, who respected him, de Thouy had a sort of craze of never liking to do what was offered to him, always suspecting that some enemy wished to exclude him from something better or 'lui jouer quelque pièce'. Berwick, showing surprising tolerance, humoured him and left the Spaniard, Major-General Gaetano, there instead. Berwick now moved south on Portalegre where he was joined by Tzerclaes who, far from abashed, claimed that he had done just as the great Turenne would have in the circumstances. Berwick complained forcibly to King Philip about the Belgian but so far from disciplining him, the monarch indolently kept him on. Berwick's patience was sorely tried.

Here at Portalegre, Tzerclaes showed further signs of weaknesss. It was too strong a place to attack, he protested. The town was on a hill and possessed a castle, though this was surrounded by higher hills. It was garrisoned by Stanhope's regiment (he was still sick in Lisbon), by two Portuguese battalions, six squadrons and a large number of volunteers led by the local bishop. Tzerclaes' opinion was backed up by that of an engineer, Goutet, who thought the surrounding heights too far off to be used for galling fire. Berwick would have none of this and merely ordered d'Asfeld to take the place. During the night the latter got fatigue parties to drag some of the few heavy guns to a ridge from which the town and its defences were dominated. At eight o'clock a brisk bombardment demolished a horn-work and blew up a magazine, and the governor beat the chamade. The garrison were made prisoners-of-war and the citizens paid 50,000 *écus* in return for not being pillaged. It is no wonder that Berwick appreciated d'Asfeld, for he had done in six hours what Tzerclaes thought totally impossible.

Tzerclaes' general incompetence had, by causing the French captain-general to concentrate on the situation south of the Tagus, left a void on the right bank and this was now filled, despite the heat of summer, by the efforts of the elderly but highly active Portuguese General das Minas. He called up as many militia as he could and rallied Fagel's scattered forces, scraping together a respectably sized corps of eighteen battalions of infantry and about the same number of squadrons of cavalry, all told about 9,000 men. He wanted to invade León and seize Ciudad Rodrigo, a rich and at that time ill fortified town, with, in Berwick's words, 'only a wall' to protect it, for this would compensate his Portuguese with loot for the pay they might never receive, and – a soldiers' soldier – he knew his troops. But on 3rd June King Pedro ordered him to turn south-west across the river Coa and check General Ronquillo, who according to Berwick's plan was now ravaging the central province of Beira.

By way of encouragement, das Minas took and let his men sack the little Spanish town of Fuente Guinaldo on the river Agueda before catching up, ten miles north of Peñamacor, with Ronquillo and twenty-one squadrons of largely French cavalry. Gaetano, fearing for his communications and expecting an attack on Salvatierra, had fallen back to join Ronquillo at Zarza. Berwick, thrown off balance by das Minas' incursion, had to react. 'Trusting very little', as he puts it, 'to the *savoir faire* of these Spanish generals', he sent de Geoffreville to liven them up together with a few squadrons under Colonel Richebourg. Ronquillo was persuaded to try to 'beat up' das Minas near Monsanto, and, leaving his artillery and eight battalions of infantry to guard a defile, he advanced towards the place with fifteen squadrons. Das Minas suddenly appeared with his cavalry, followed by infantry, outnumbering Ronquillo, who turned to retreat. Some of das Minas' squadrons fled, but with a hard core, mostly of his own guard, the old man continued to advance. In a pitched battle with the Spanish rearguard, commanded by Colonel O'Mahony, das Minas was wounded, only his slightly antique armour saving him from being cut down. His stubbornness and the approach of his infantry together with some field guns brought up by Colonel Richards, saw to it that Ronquillo withdrew in some disorder, and with a loss variously estimated as from fifty to 200 men. De Geoffreville, falling back on Salvatierra, where the infantry had been placed, was now involved in what Berwick describes as 'a somewhat bizarre event'. It had been raining heavily and some of his men fired off their musketoons to avoid leaving the powder to get damp. The infantry, about to encamp, thought that this meant that a victorious enemy was about to fall on them and, being untrained, fled in a panic as far as Alcántara leaving their baggage, which was then plundered by the more seasoned cavalry of their own side. Meantime das Minas summoned the French garrison of 120 in Monsanto to surrender and once more allowed his Portuguese a pleasurable bit of plunder. But, wounded though he was, he sternly marched them off next day towards Villa Velha where he hoped to be able to destroy the bridge of boats and cut Berwick off from the north bank of the Tagus.

Hearing, however, in good time of the disasters looming up on his right flank, Berwick took swift action. Merely sending de Geoffreville and Richebourg's little detachment had not been enough. No doubt thankfully, he dumped King Philip and his large retinue at Niza together with most of his infantry and his baggage, and went north by forced marches to try and relieve Monsanto. He was too late, and the wily old Portuguese general with tactical help from Richards, coolly wheeled round Berwick's front and made for the hills around Peñamacor.

All this is easy enough to write about, but it demanded leadership of some order in high mid-summer from an elderly, wounded man. The roads and tracks were few and rough and there was little water except from an occasional mountain stream. Food for men and fodder for horses was short. His men were raw levies, not trained to understand military necessities and loaded with looted goods which they would hate to leave behind. Das Minas, however, brought it off and was now ensconced in the Sierra, placing some hundreds of his levies along the hills between Villa Velha and Abrantes, defending the gateway to Lisbon and challenging Berwick. The Duke had no artillery and was strategically and tactically blocked in the northern sector, with time running out fast. A campaign hopefully begun was petering out, and all he could do was return southwards to Niza, leaving a small detachment under the Spanish Major-General de Aguilar to keep an eye on Peñamacor.

Here, one of the Portuguese Generals, São João, while foraging, gladdened the hearts of the rough Portuguese levies by falling on a weakly escorted French convoy of pack-animals laden with ammunition, bread, and above all, wine. And here, too, there took place a grisly inter-allied accident, recorded by Richards in his Journal.

'This night happened a very scurvy incident. Dom Pedro de Vasconcelos, lieutenant-general of horse, going the rounds with a party of horse to visit the advanced posts, met with a Dutch advanced guard. The Dutch sentinels, after their usual way, cried out 'Wer da?' (which is as much as to say 'who goes there?') several times, which the Portuguese not understanding attacked them sword in hand, killed downright [sic] one Dutchman and mortally wounded several others and although this horrible ignorance of theirs how to treat with an advanced guard is scarcely excusable, much less is their brutality, after knowing who they were, to strip and plunder the wounded and dead as they lay.'

Back once more at the royal camp at Niza, Berwick was joined by Villadarías who had marched north from Andalucia with ten battalions and a few squadrons, and was given with d'Asfeld the last action of the summer campaign, the taking of Castelho de Vide, to carry out. Many of the Spaniards were down with fever and only eight indifferent guns were available for the siege. The Castelho was not strong, for there were no outworks, but it possessed twenty-five heavy guns, a strong citadel and a garrison composed of Stewart's regiment and two Portuguese battalions. Berwick afterwards said, 'We would have been at some pains to master it', had the Portuguese governor been resolute, for the Spanish artillery was 'indifferent' and 'the heats excessive'. For three days the Castelho's guns were fired, doing little harm, and then four Spanish field pieces, mounted on a nearby hill, began, as Berwick describes it, to 'scratch' the wall. At this, the governor sent the English Lieutenant-Colonel Thomas Hussey and a Portuguese colonel to enquire about terms of surrender. They were told that the garrison would be made prisoners of war. At this Hussey 'began to swear and storm', saying 'he'd be damned if he would consent to this', and shouted to the English troops to fight it out. Berwick, who was present, then told the governor that if he had to fight he would put all the men to the sword and 'leave the women exposed to the brutality of the soldiers', but if the governor surrendered he would be allowed 'to keep all his equipage and there would be no plunder'. The governor agreed but the English marched him back into the town and made for the citadel. The Portuguese troops, however, threw all the gunpowder into a well and in the end, after being talked to by both d'Asfeld and Villadarías, Hussey acquiesced and Villadarías was the master of Castelho de Vide with a loss of only forty killed or wounded.

This was the last major action of the campaign. On 1st July Berwick, having razed the fortresses of Portalegre, Castelho de Vide and Castelho Branco which he could not afford to garrison, marched back to Spain. He watched das

Minas move off and then set up his headquarters at Salamanca, posting Tzerclaes at Badajoz, de Aguilar at Alcántara and sending Villadarías back to Andalucia after he had taken Marveon. King Philip went back to his queen at the Buen Retiro in Madrid. As we shall see, her welcome for him was far from warm.

Berwick's professionalism shines forth in his comments on this first campaign.

> 'Thus ended our first effort. Its results would have been more marked but for the imbecility of Tzerclaes. Through him we lost one out of the two months available for operations and were stopped on our road to Abrantes where we ought to have established ourselves; and (our bridges at Villa Velha having been removed thither) the next campaign should have carried us to Lisbon. But the Prince's remissness upset the plan by giving das Minas [he calls him Las Minas] time to occupy the mountains which divide Villa Velha from Abrantes.'

He is strict on his own shortcomings. He and Puységur should have made more allowance for the appalling roads of Spain. They had arranged for supplies to be brought up in covered wagons 'in the French manner', but these vehicles broke down and supplies were never in time or sufficient. Moreover the contractors tried to increase their profit by not baking the bread properly, so that it rapidly spoiled. He blames himself too for the heavy losses of horses. He did not 'give credit to the people of the country who assured us that it was absolutely necessary to give barley to the Spanish horses, without which they would perish. In other countries we were accustomed to feed the cavalry with such forage as we found on the ground.' Berwick's comments on Schomberg were as forceful as on Tzercles: 'The Duke of Schomberg tarried with his arms crossed at Estremós or Elvas, never harassing us nor even caring to scan our motions. During our stay in the Alemtéjo we did not see a single reconnaissance party of his.' And again: 'The prime fault of the confederate generals lay in their disposition of the forces at the breaking-out of hostilities. Instead of so placing the troops that an army corps might be rapidly formed to oppose us wherever we appeared, they distributed them on both sides of the Tagus without providing for inter-communication by a bridge of boats at Villa Velha or Abrantes. This vicious arrangement, this contempt of precaution, induced us to advance boldly.' It is interesting to note that a fellow-professional on the other side, Stanhope, makes the same comment, almost verbatim, in a letter to his father, dated May 31st: 'Inferior officers amongst us have foreseen all that has happened long since, and cried out upon our disposing the troops at no less a distance than the whole length of

Portugal, at there being no care taken to make a bridge, and to secure communication on the river, nor to provide magazines to enable the army to draw together and subsist.'

Despite apologists for Schomberg such as Bishop Burnet, Berwick's and Stanhope's views of him were clearly shared by the English Government, who removed him from command, replacing him with the Early of Galway. This would lead on a number of occasions in the Peninsula to a Frenchman commanding an English army facing an Englishman (Berwick) in command of a French army. For Henri de Massue, Second Marquis de Ruvigny, was a Huguenot who had been given the title of Viscount Galway by William III in 1692. He was born in 1648 and served as an aide-de-camp to Turenne in 1674. Louis XIV used him as a go-between to Charles II of England in 1678 and Galway (then de Ruvigny) was successful in arranging a secret understanding between the two monarchs. But he was a Protestant and after the Revocation of the Edict of Nantes he left France for ever, even though King Louis appreciated his services and his integrity so much that he offered him personal religious dispensation. He entered the English service as a major-general of horse. At the battle of the Boyne, where his brother was killed, and at the battle of Aughrim, he so distinguished himself that he was created Viscount Galway on November 25th 1692, but he had no lands in Ireland and his estates in Picardy were forfeit under the Act of Resumption in 1700. William III paid him a pension of £1,000 a year, for like his enemy, King Louis, he appreciated this selfless man. A contemporary described him as 'one of the finest generals in the army, with a head fitted for the Cabinet as well as the camp. He is very modest, vigilant and sincere, a man of honour and honesty without pride or affectation. He wears his own hair and is plain in his dress and manners.' He had no liking for party politics, was discreet, tolerant, unselfish and personally charitable, but he never learned to speak English fluently and this probably made difficult his relationship with his English confrères, some of them to put it mildly cussed. This will appear in three or four years' time. Perhaps because he was obviously not English – and knew it, though his father had taken English nationality in 1680 – he was the more diplomatic. A tough Portuguese like General das Minas, a square-faced Dutchman like Fagel, or an intolerant Englishman like Erle later on, would impose on his niceness and his gentle forbearance. The Earl of Galway was one of nature's gentlemen, and he was to pay the price for it. He would later be disgraced, abused and attacked for his efforts and would live to regret coming to the Peninsula.

He was now in retirement, aged 56 and suffering from gout, and it was Marlborough who suggested recalling him for service. He at first resisted but when Queen Anne pressed him he accepted. He was unmarried, not well off, and, having been raised to an earldom in 1697, felt he owed something to England. He was generally a popular choice. Marlborough wrote to him, 'I do heartily rejoice at the honour Her Majesty has done Your Lordship in putting you at the head of her troops in Portugal. All that wish well to the public good, I am sure, agree very sincerely with me, for without the assistance of your good conduct, and the succours Her Majesty is sending over, all our hopes on that side would soon vanish.' Yet perhaps Marlborough's judgment faltered in this case. Galway was a splendid man but may have lacked the final touch which makes a great general.

Marlborough's grave doubts about the state of affairs in the Peninsula were in fact paralleled – for reasons of politics – by even graver doubts among his opponents. For while Queen Anne was firmly enthroned, King Philip V and Queen María Luisa were engaged in activities which nearly unseated them. It is time to return to Madrid and observe the situation there.

★   ★   ★

King Philip returned from the wars to his young wife and his dilapidated court, where, as the Duc de Noailles describes it in his *Memoirs*, 'slipshod lords-in-waiting and slatternly ladies-in-waiting filled the mouldering palace [of Buen Retiro] and a fry of pestilent dwarfs, ripe for vile employment, infested the ante-rooms.'[5] Queen María Luisa was awaiting her husband, but was not in the best of moods for reasons that will appear. There are a number of descriptions of her from Tessé, from Gramont and others which testify to her strength of personality – already demonstrated by her spirited conduct of affairs in 1702 while Philip was in Italy. Physically she was small – about the same height as her sister the Duchess of Burgundy, says Gramont, writing to Madame de Maintenon. 'She has a slender waist and a gracious manner, both noble and majestic. Her eyes are of medium size and very lively, her complexion pale but good. She has a small mouth and her teeth are white though irregular. She is not a beauty but has a grace which would please any man of taste. As to her wit, the elegance and justice of her conversation is astonishing in someone of her age. She is quite extraordinary.' Her intelligence, commonsense and courage attracted everyone to her. St Simon, normally sharp about people, says, 'She had everything necessary to be adored', and Louis himself, growing accustomed to her wilfulness, came to appreciate her qualities.

She early realized that her husband was not a strong character, writing of him to Louis, 'I humbly beg Your Majesty to use all the authority you have over the King your grandson in order to accustom him to say boldly: "I wish this" or "I do not wish that", or in other words to imitate you. If he can manage this he will be a perfect prince.' But, although now fifteen, she was still in some ways a child, and, as already noted, Louis had felt it as well to provide her with a seasoned guide in the shape of the Princess des Ursins, who at fifty-nine was old enough to be her grandmother. Speaking excellent Castilian and well acquainted with Spanish customs, the princess had known Cardinal Portocarerro and Cardinal d'Estrées – the ambassador who replaced Blécourt – during her sojourn in Rome as a married woman. Anne Marie de la Trémoille, widow of the Prince des Ursins must have seemed an ideal choice as *Camarera Major*, but she was too ambitious and too sophisticated. Her letters show that she looked on Philip as a backward boy: 'I ask you! It's I who take the king's dressing-gown from him when he goes to bed and hand him his slippers when he gets up. This is fair enough. But every evening when he goes to join the queen, his great chamberlain hands me his sword and a lamp which I usually upset over my dress. It is quite grotesque.'

Furthermore, sensing her domination over the royal couple, she was tempted to intervene in government. This began with her attendance alongside the queen-regent at meetings of the *despacho* during Philip's absence – a practice which gave her an insight into the characters and weaknesses of the grandees. Soon she was so influential as to turn Portocarrero and d'Estrées against her out of jealousy, and cabals at Court began to form for and against her. Some of the French bitterly opposed her. Others, like Orry, found it helpful to curry favour with her. When Cabreras, the Almirante of Castile, changed sides in 1703, she had played Portocarrero against d'Estrées. The latter's arrogance had made it fairly simple to persuade Louis to recall him, leaving his nephew the abbé in his stead. The abbé found it convenient to pretend to be on her side, but before long he found her encouragement of Spanish courtiers and her domineering way of treating many of the French embarrassing, and secretly turned against her, he began reporting adversely about her to Versailles and complaining that he had to live a life of perpetual deception. Orry, who was her close confidant – and that of the king and queen – soon began himself writing secretly to Paris suggesting that the abbé should be recalled – on which Chammillart commented, 'This is a matter which would be most inconvenient.'

While the Princess des Ursins' efforts were almost certainly useful in turning María Luisa's charm and intelligence to account for the good of the new dynasty, she had a major weak point. At fifty-nine she was no longer the siren so much admired in Rome. But still, as a Victorian historian coyly puts it, 'singular as it may appear to some, she was susceptible in her sixtieth year to the tender passion.' Her paramour in Madrid was her '*intendant*', a large, well built, insolent ruffian called d'Aubigny, who on one occasion made highly familiar and suggestive remarks to her in the hearing of the Marquis de Louville and the Duque de Medinaceli. He was moreover sometimes seen shaving in front of the windows of her apartment. She suspected that d'Estrées was writing about her and therefore arranged with Philip that she should intercept the abbé's despatches. In one of these she found herself described as being secretly married to d'Aubigny, and in her fury was unwise enough to write on it, 'As for marriage, no!' and then let the letter go forward to Versailles. Here it came to the notice of King Louis, who was by now disturbed by complaints about her which had reached him, and decided to remove her.

One of her interventions had been an involvement in the disputes between Orry and Puységur which had in part come about because the latter was staying with d'Estrées. It was partly because of this that Louis ordered Berwick to report on the factions at the Madrid Court. Although, as we have seen, Berwick dissociated himself from all concerned and concentrated on his military duties, he could not altogether avoid involvement, for Louis felt he might have to make a clean sweep in Madrid. The princess, Orry, and d'Estrées were all suspect. But first d'Estrées was to convey Louis' instructions to Philip about the princess. Since, however, Philip and María Luisa had taken against the ambassador, Berwick was enjoined to give his backing. But he had to press Philip to join the army for the campaign in order to separate him from his wife, and then stand by to persuade him, forcibly if necessary, to obey his grandfather's instructions. So, at the Plasencia camp in May there was a difficult interlude. Berwick suggested using the royal confessor, a certain Father Daubentin, as a go-between and the latter was so successful as to ensure that Philip accepted the decision although he must have known it would cause trouble with his queen. Berwick took care to write and explain to Madame des Ursins the part he had had to play and to advise her to submit gracefully to Louis' wishes, but both he and d'Estrées were – with justice – concerned at what might be the reactions of the queen, 'a princess of infinite vivacity, sensibility and *hauteur*,.

Madame des Ursins left Madrid at once without open comment or complaint but was nevertheless determined to return, and, as the sequel shows, she would have her way, thus, in St Simon's words, 'demonstrating the address, subtlety and range of woman's resources'. The queen exploded in fury. She inveighed against all those she thought were involved, notably d'Estrées and Berwick. The latter, in his detached way, sympathised with her, considering that she had not always been treated with proper respect by those who disliked Mme des Ursins. 'There is nothing more annoying for a queen', he wrote, 'than to see someone in whom she has complete confidence removed from her.' Yet he also wrote to King Louis applauding the removal of the princess from Madrid as the only course open to him, if Philip's throne were to be saved. Philip and María Luisa insisted on the abbé's recall, and Louis acquiesced, nominating the Duc de Gramont as his successor. Madrid was now no place for d'Estrées, so he awaited his replacement under Berwick's wing, first of all at Niza and later at Salamanca. The king and queen, nursing their grievances, continued to bombard Louis with letters about the Princess des Ursins, and these did not spare Berwick. Although they did not know it, they were to some extent justified for he had written in his own hand to Chamillart for King Louis' information,

> 'Madame des Ursins and Orry do everything without consulting the King and Queen and if the latter do anything themselves they counter it later, changing everything whether it concerns the army or the Court. These two despotically give orders as they will. Orry is particularly unpopular and in danger for his life, though I think him capable and necessary. But someone should be put in charge of him. Affairs are at present in dreadful disorder. As far as d'Estrées is concerned the King and Queen are totally estranged from him and Mme. des Ursins will have nothing to do with him. I do not know who is to blame, probably both. I feel it my duty to report this.'

Louis added fuel to the flames by also recalling Orry, on whom the king and queen felt themselves dependent for the management of the royal finances.

During those summer and autumn months of 1704 the royal pair could think of nothing but their grievances, and this indirectly cost Spain Gibraltar, for, as Berwick's eventual successor would later report in a cyphered despatch to Chamillart,

> 'The King of Spain thinks of nobody but the Queen. The Queen thinks of nothing but Mme des Ursins, of the *offensant* way in which she has been removed, and of means of getting her back. The Marqués de Rivas [Spanish Minister for War] thinks of nothing but to swim between the two tides of opinion and please the court, in whose languor and subjection he has always lived. He wants to make sure that the responsibility for everything falls on us [the French]. The *despacho* thinks of nothing but of ensuring that the king should be without authority – as was Charles II.'

And Chamillart, in writing to Gramont soon after the latter's arrival in Spain, could say bitterly, 'If the Archduke Charles were in Vienna and the English and Dutch were not around we could get used to the customs of the Spanish Court, but it is infinitely painful to see such a shaky situation.' This 'shaky situation' forms the background to the second campaign of 1704 with all its unpleasant surprises for Louis, for Philip, for Berwick and for many others.

★   ★   ★

While that inconclusive first campaign was being fought on and across the border between Spain and Portugal, a second manifestation of sea power was taking place off the north-east corner of Spain.[6] Darmstadt had always maintained an active correspondence with important Catalans who were unhappy under Spanish rule. As regent for King Charles of Valencia, Catalonia and the Balearics, he had convinced himself that if he were to arrive at Barcelona with the king and an army of 20,000 men, the province of Catalonia would rise against Philip. An amphibious operation was therefore prepared, but in a half-hearted fashion. Charles did not accompany it, there were only 3,000 instead of 20,000 men, and the doubting Rooke, distrustful of Mediterranean policy, commanded the naval squadron. Moreover, the Governor of Barcelona, Don Francisco de Velasco, had taken strong defence measures and kept a close watch on the supporters of the Habsburgs.

Almost immediately after reaching Lisbon with Charles, Rooke himself left in H.M.S. *Royal Catherine* for a reconnaissance cruise in the Straits of Gibraltar, leaving some of his fleet to be refitted. On this trip he took three prizes but saw nothing of the French fleet and he returned to Lisbon early in May 1703 (N.S.). Here he found that King Pedro and Methuen expected him to cruise up and down off the coast of Portugal as protection against the French, an idea he did not relish. Moreover, he now received secret instructions from London. These would make it difficult to fulfil Pedro's wishes and equally difficult to carry out Darmstadt's proposals for Catalonia. The immediate priority in his secret orders was to go to the aid of the Duke of Savoy and to protect Nice which was wrongly believed to be in immediate danger. Alternatively, if Victor Amadeus were to undertake an attack on Toulon, Rooke was to help him. At the same time he was to engage the French Mediterranean fleet wherever he found it and, with lower priority, to attack Cadiz or Barcelona, or at least threaten them. And as if that were not enough, he was to protect English interests in Florence, Imperial assets throughout Italy, destroy a French squadron in the Straits, intervene in Provence in order to encourage Cevennois rebels, and try to persuade the Algerians to join the Allies. Rooke cannot be blamed for feeling over-burdened. Though he had been against the Mediterranean policy, this was now so firmly stated that he must needs carry it out, at least in part. He had only marines, no army landing force, for Pedro had not produced soldiers as yet and Charles and Prince George did not have any to speak of. As to leaving ships in Portuguese waters, he considered that his new orders superseded the original treaty agreement.

King Pedro did not mind Rooke attacking a Spanish port but he was angry that the admiral would leave no ships – and his anger and that of the Portuguese generals was still further fanned when Shovell, on his way later to join Rooke, took a similar line. One cannot blame the king. His country was being invaded by land and if the French chose could be attacked by sea as well. The Dutch and Imperial ministers, who knew nothing of Rooke's secret instructions, put pressure on Methuen to intervene. He himself was also in the dark though he had stoutly told King Pedro that Rooke's job was to defeat the French fleet and that the place to do this was the Mediterranean. Even Callenburg knew nothing of Rooke's orders. When the three ambassadors went together to Rooke, they found him inflexible. On 8th May, the very day that Berwick crossed the Portuguese frontier, and without waiting for confirmation from Victor Amadeus or from Richard Hill, the English ambassador in Turin, Rooke sailed for the Mediterranean.

He had a fleet of twenty-two English and fourteen Dutch ships-of-the-line and numerous auxiliaries. In his flagship, *Royal Catherine*, were Darmstadt and his younger brother, Prince Henry, aged twenty-seven years. A Valencian engineer, Colonel Juan Basset y Ramos and the Irish Colonel Henry Nugent (created Conde de Val de Soto for earlier services in Barcelona) were on his staff. An English contingent of 1,900 and a Dutch one of 400 marines were under the command of Brigadier-General Fox, who had fought the cool rearguard action at Cadiz two years before. A handful of Catalan volunteer cavalry attached to Prince George and twenty or so Spanish officer deserters from Philip's forces were also present.

Perhaps the most noteworthy figure, however, was Rooke's second-in-command, Vice-Admiral Sir John Leake, who now made his first appearance in this sector. Born in 1656 he was the son of Richard Leake, Master Gunner of England. He had joined the Royal Navy as a volunteer and had served in Irish waters, at the Battle of La Hogue in H.M.S. *Eagle*, and off Newfoundland. He had just been knighted for his services. He appears to have been a good seaman, much liked by his men, and adept at inter-service co-operation. Honest in financial matters and full of commonsense and drive, he would make a name for himself in the next few years. With him also were Rear-Admirals Byng, Dilkes and Wishart, and the Dutch Callenburg, Wassenaer and Van der Dussen.

After a call for water at Altea, near Valencia, on 21st May, they made for Barcelona. The situation in Nice was still unclear, and Darmstadt, still optimistic, thought the Catalans would rise and that Velasco could be intimidated by Rooke's powerful squadron. He was wrong. Velasco acted with some resolution. He has always had a bad press. He never had the charisma of Prince George and on one occasion in 1697 he had, when in command of Spanish troops at Llobregat, failed to come to the aid of the prince who was besieged by the French in Barcelona. As a Spaniard the Catalans looked on him as an enemy, a soldier sent by Madrid to impose Philip V's policies. He was a moderately capable man, neither better nor worse than many others. He was doing his duty as he saw it, for instance when he cut down trees in front of his palace so as to be able to get a view of any possible attack or when he pursued members of the Council of a 100 for Habsburg sympathies. The fact that Philip's current policies also involved breaking his promise to respect the Catalan *fueros* was further fuel on the flames of Catalan dislike for their viceroy. But for the moment the policy was effective.

Prince George was now on good terms with Rooke and the admirals and as Charles' representative was admitted to Allied councils of war. At Altea, where Shovell had a year earlier found that most of the population was against Philip, he landed the Valencian Colonel Basset y Ramos, who had come with Charles from Vienna, to say to Charles' adherents that liberation was on the way but that they were to await further news. With Basset were also Garcia de Avila and a Captain Sebastian Mulet, both Valencians. They seem to have had considerable effect. Prince George persuaded Rooke to send a frigate, H.M.S. *Lark* to Barcelona to deliver letters and later to take the fleet there for twenty-four hours. Richard Hill, in Turin, had a 'little fleet' as he called it, of four frigates with which he planned a diversion, but this came to nothing, though the threat it seemed to pose may have been of some value.

The *Lark* meantime returned from Barcelona with the news that the Bourbon garrison was only 1,200 strong. So, despite orders, as yet still valid, to go to Nice, a council of war agreed to see whether Darmstadt could be landed at Barcelona. Calms and adverse winds delayed them at Altea for six days, but at length Zinzerling, Prince George's secretary, was put ashore and greeted cheerfully by a crowd of Catalans. These were dispersed by Spanish horse and Zinzerling sent a message to Velasco asking him to receive an emissary. Velasco, although some of Philip's court doubted his loyalty, firmly gave Zinzerling a flea in the ear. Rooke wanted to sail for Nice but was persuaded by Prince George to cover a landing east of Barcelona.

This duly took place on 30th May, the 1,200 English and 400 Dutch marines landing with the prince. A small body of horse was driven off and crowds came flocking in with joy. But there was no general rising of peasants and Velasco brushed aside a summons to surrender sent by trumpeter. Prince George then ordered a bombardment but the ships had to be warped in and were not in position until 31st May. Meantime Velasco had heard from Irish deserters how small the landing force was, although Prince George was marching the men to and fro to give the impression of a large army. The deserters had also told the Viceroy that Rooke was meant to be on his way to Nice. By now, although Prince George had been joined by about 1,000 Catalans, when he marched up to the Angel gate of the city it remained firmly shut and after a desultory exchange of fire he ordered the local supporters to disperse and on 1st June he himself and the 1,600 marines re-embarked. Rooke was critical. He was sure that if there had been sufficient landing force, there would have been a massive insurrection and that this affair, going off at half-cock, had done more harm than good. Nevertheless the movement against Philip rumbled on, notably in the plains of Vich, with what result we shall see in a year's time. Baudrillart considers that the resistance movement gained by being forced underground. In his haste to resist a siege, Velasco had issued arms to large numbers of citizens without taking note of their names. Many pieces were hidden away, to be used next year when the Allies returned with greater force.

Now, after a desultory bombardment on 1st June, soon abandoned for fear of offending Charles III's loyal supporters, the fleet sailed for Provence. It will be recalled that Prince George had been accompanied by some eighty Catalans when he left Lisbon. Their numbers were now swollen as dissidents from Barcelona joined, some 170 of them, mostly soldiers but with some influential clerics; and one Macià Cateura had a coasting vessel, the *Santa Eulàlia* which would be most useful to George for carrying despatches and secret correspondence during the siege of Gibraltar in a few month's time.

Rooke was himself blamed for this setback by Bishop Burnet because he would not stay more than three days off Barcelona, but as we have noted, Burnet was inclined to believe anything discreditable to Rooke. Campbell, in his *Lives of the British Admirals*, refers to a debate in the House of Lords some thirty-six years later, in the course of which the Duke of Argyll stated, 'It is a story of Bishop Burnet's and those who have sat in this House with that prelate must know he was a very credulous and weak man. With regard to what he says against Admiral Rooke I know, I have heard it from those who were present, that the greatest part of it is a downright lie.' Be that as it may, Rooke does not show up so well in the sequel. On 22nd May, two weeks after he had weighed anchor from Lisbon, a French fleet on its way from Brest to Toulon was sighted off the mouth of the Tagus. Methuen was able to point out to King Pedro that it had been no threat to the coast of Portugal. An English ship, the *Charles Galley*, which had been delayed, was sent at once by him to Rooke with this intelligence and also up-to-date news that Nice and Villefranche were in no danger. The French fleet of twenty ships-of-the-line and fifteen smaller vessels was under the command of Louis' son, the Comte de Toulouse, and the Comte d'Estrées had been transferred from his Spanish post to be Chief of Staff to the royal admiral. Two days later the Allied fleet ran into a stiff gale 'which sent our English canvas flying like dirt as usual and did as much damage to yards, masts and sails as a battle'. They reached Hyères on 4th June. Here Rear-Admiral Sir Thomas Dilkes joined him. He had been sent to reconnoitre Toulon, had had a brush with six French men-of-war and had learned from captured craft that there were ten or fifteen ships in Toulon and that a squadron had sailed but not to attack Nice. Rear-Admiral Wishart, who had been detached to seek out French ships sailing individually and had been chased by Toulouse, had come up on 29th May with the news that the French commander-in-chief had been joined off Cadiz by additional ships and was now sailing under a north-westerly wind for Toulon. And on 5th June Methuen's message, sent from Lisbon in the *Charles Galley*, arrived with news of Toulouse's Brest fleet sailing past Lisbon. The *Charles Galley* was sent at once to Villefranche to land some French prisoners and to give the impression that Rooke was following and thus spread alarm.

Methuen's information exaggerated the strength of Toulouse's fleet to forty ships-of-the-line, whereas he had only twenty-six, four frigates and six fireships. Rooke was now between the main French fleet and its base but he had not yet been joined by Shovell whom he was expecting, and his only scouting ship to make contact with the enemy reported forty-two ships including thirty-one of the line. Sighting and counting, even keeping station, in those days was difficult and errors came easily so if, as surmised, Toulouse's fleet had five 90-gunners and twelve 70–80 it would, together with the vessels in Toulon have much more fire-power than Rooke's force. Nevertheless, although subsequent writers have suggested otherwise, Rooke decided to risk battle. Jettisoning what was left of the royal furniture in H.M.S. *Royal Catherine* and stripping for action, he formed line and ordered all ships' companies to battle stations, with ammunition struck up from the magazines, so that his intentions were clearly understood by the men. He then sailed into the wind to intercept the enemy, now twelve miles away. He had stated at a council of war that he thought himself the weaker, and if his account is correct this had not deterred him. But as this council was taking place the wind dropped and Toulouse at sundown was further ahead, ignoring Rooke's scouting ships and using his galleys to tow sluggish units towards Toulon harbour, some thirty miles away. As night fell they were hull down on the horizon and by morning only twenty miles from base. Rooke would not risk coming under the guns of Toulon and therefore turned for the Straits and Lisbon.

On 18th June he was back at Altea, taking in water and landing 400 marines at Prince George's request, to take Alicante's seaward forts, capture the governor, and leave word that reprisals would be taken if inhabitants of that town and others were maltreated for supplying the Allies. By 27th June he was at Lagos in the Algarve, outside the Straits and here he was at last joined by Shovell. He sent Zinzerling ashore with his despatches and received the first mails he had had from London since leaving Lisbon in early May. Belatedly, Mr Secretary Hedges cancelled the orders about Nice and Toulon and gave priority to Barcelona. Rooke was also to concert operations with Kings Pedro and Charles. He was conscious of something of a fiasco in the Gulf of Lions and had it not been for subsequent events he would certainly have faced a public inquiry. He had enabled the French fleet in the Mediterranean to be strengthened because he had not brought it to action – as a Blake before him or a Duncan after him would probably have done. Moreover the two kings had been complaining vociferously to London that he had left them unprotected at Lisbon. His fleet now numbered seventy-two ships of war and he had 3,000 marines; and clearly something positive must be done. With Toulon and Nice no longer a problem he felt able to detach a small squadron to the Azores to meet the incoming fleet from Brazil, but he was uneasy about what might be being said of him in Lisbon and London.

He had every right to be. Queen Anne had sent a soothing letter to Charles but Zinzerling found Schonenberg and Methuen at loggerheads and the Portuguese both angry and obstructive. Methuen was prostrated with gout and of course nobody had realized that an amphibious attack on Spain needed a landing-force as well as a fleet. At Santarem the two kings talked of another attack on Cadiz featuring a bombardment followed by a landing by marines. This was supported by Lichtenstein and Schonenberg but not by Zinzerling, who favoured another shot at Barcelona, or, with Prince George's blessing, a descent on Port Mahon in Minorca. Letters dated 1st and 9th July were sent from Santarem to Rooke urging him to tackle Cadiz.

His frigates reported, incorrectly, that the French fleet was off Málaga but he disregarded this, and instead cruised off Cadiz 'if the enemy arrived there to consider whether it would be advisable and practicable to force the port and insult them in the Bay'. Although the two kings had told him that the place was ill defended, a reconnaissance party found the reverse to be true. Cadiz could only be successfully attacked with a siege-train and a sizeable landing-force and he had neither. Hearing, therefore, that Toulouse's fleet was nowhere near he continued for the present to hover between Cape Spartel and Lagos 'till he should see or hear of them again'. His force was now further re-inforced by the arrival of Rear-Admiral George Byng who, with a squadron, had been exchanging prisoners of war at Cadiz, and Rooke, too experienced not to be aware that he was being criticised not only by the two kings but in the English Parliament and by the English public, just as he had been two years earlier, felt that he clearly must do something positive.

But what should this rugged but indecisive man do?

★   ★   ★

CHAPTER THREE

Gibraltar

> Major Beckmann do speak to me greatly in commendation of Gibraltar as the place which above all our King aught to have for keeping an entire command in the Straits, and which he says he might have without loss of one man's life, no cost, fortified very cheap, ... it being capable of being attacked in but one place.
>
> – Samuel Pepys, Notes on Gibraltar, *The Tangier Papers* (1935), p. 231.

I N his *Historical Essays*, Macaulay devotes ten inaccurate lines to the taking of Gibraltar by the maritime powers. Of these the operative sentences are: 'the garrison went to say their prayers instead of standing to their guard. A few English sailors climbed the Rock.' It was much more complicated than that.[1]

On 28th July, off Tetuan, Rooke held a council of war to discuss possible courses of action, and once more in the great cabin of the *Royal Catherine* perspiring admirals, Dutch and English, met to argue in the summer's heat. Cadiz, Port Mahon and Barcelona were ruled out, but only a few miles away to the north was Gibraltar, one of the possible targets mentioned in Rooke's secret orders. It was known by the Allies and of course by the Bourbons to have only a tiny garrison. Berwick describes it as being 'held by a hundred vagabonds under a weak governor'. Although there had been a survey by French engineers, nothing had been done to its dilapidated walls. During a French attack in 1693 from the sea the new mole had been covered by the guns of four warships from a squadron commanded by Rooke, fighting on the Spanish side. Its battery consisted of twelve brass and ten iron guns, and it was later found that on the entire walls there were only eighty iron guns, from 18- down to 3-pounders in serviceable condition. And although there were small arms for 1,000 men, and powder and lead were in good supply, the men themselves were not there. The record of the council does not particularise any quarrels but there was almost certainly some disagreement, for Rooke and Byng were often opposed and the

Dutch liked an argument. It was attended by Rooke, Shovell, Leake, Byng and Wishart, and the Dutch Callenburg, Wassenaer and Van der Dussen. Dilkes was absent. Here is the note:

> 'Upon reading and considering my Lord Ambassador Methuen's letters of 10th and 17th inst. with a copy of the proposals made by the Kings of Spain and Portugal, for attempting Cadiz etc. as also a letter received this day from His Highness the Prince of Hesse; it is agreed and resolved that since we conclude it is impracticable to attempt Cadiz with any prospect, or hopes of success, without an army to co-operate with a fleet: that we land our Marines, English and Dutch, under the command of the Prince of Hesse, in the Bay of Gibraltar, to cut off that town from any communication with the main[land], and at the same time that we do bombard & cannonade the place from our ships, and endeavour by that means to reduce it to the King of Spain's obedience.'

Byng was to command the naval bombardment task force, flying his flag in H.M.S. *Ranelagh*, and second in command was Rear-Admiral Philip Van der Dussen in the *Veluwe*.

Byng would be active over the next few years in the waters off Spain. He had started his naval career in 1678 as a 'king's letter boy' – an entrant with recommendations from the Admiralty, not a personal captain's appointment (then a recent innovation of Pepys), and had risen to be Rear-Admiral of the Red in 1703. He had at one time been Rooke's flag-lieutenant but they had been personally and politically incompatible. Byng would in time become Admiral of the Fleet Lord Torrington, and although criticized by some contemporary writers such as Martin-Leake, and by Colonel John Richards in his letters, he appears to have been a capable seaman. It is a quirk of history that while he was engaged in the assault on Gibraltar his fourth son, John, was born. This was the man who 53 years later was to be shot on the quarterdeck of H.M.S. *Monarch* at Portsmouth for having failed to save Minorca from the French. His execution, the result of disgraceful political buck-passing, is best known for Voltaire's description of it in *Candide* where an eye-witness says that the English shoot an admiral from time to time '*pour encourager les autres*'. Now George Byng braced himself for the attack, coming into the roadstead on 31st July. He had, in fact, been one of those opposed to the idea at the council of war, but on the day he carried it out faithfully. One can almost see him lifting his high-bridged nose, suppressed insubordination curling his lip.

The inclusion of Gibraltar as a target represented respectable and long matured strategic thinking. Cromwell had envisaged its capture, as had William

III. Samuel Pepys, when Secretary to the Navy, had written of it, too. Marlborough and Godolphin had discussed it and Charles III in a letter to Darmstadt of 5th May 1704 had pressed for it. For centuries after its first sighting, this, the northern Pillar of Hercules, seems to have been looked on by sailors as something enormous, mystical and quite useless. Phoenicians, Greeks, Romans and Vikings merely sailed past it, and it was not until AD 711 that the Moors first set foot permanently on it, finding wild beasts in its heavy woods and calling it Gebel-Tarik, the Rock of Tarik, after their chief. It was they who built the citadel on the site where it still stands, modified somewhat in the centuries that followed. It became Spanish in the fifteenth century. Charles V had extended and improved the fortifications but he had long been dead and the Rock neglected. Its woods were still being cut down in the 1690s for the repair of Spanish ships.

The grey precipice facing the Mediterranean is so imposing that it is hard to believe that the Rock is only three miles long and half a mile wide with a bay five miles long and five wide to the north-west. At its highest point, overlooking Spain across a flat sandspit, it is 1,400 feet high. The northern, eastern and southern faces are precipitous and only the western side is slightly more gently sloping. Under this stiff slope between the bay, the mountain and its own walls, nestled the little town, with two short moles giving somewhat limited protection to the roadstead, the New Mole to the south and the Old Mole to the north. The land front at the north was then protected by a light rampart, with a gate and a ditch. The old Moorish citadel and a round tower were part of the defences. Similar works at the southern end of the town, with two detached forts, the redoubt 100 yards away and the New Mole fort (*Nuestra Señora de Europa*), 1,000 yards away, defended that side. Facing the sea was a crumbling wall in which about fifty small guns were mounted, few of them fit for firing and fewer still manned. San Felipe says, 'The city could offer little defence, without guns or ammunition'. A plan, made just after the Treaty of Utrecht in 1713, shows the main fortifications as they then were.

The garrison in July 1704 was much as described by Berwick, nominally about eighty but augmented by militia and volunteers, haphazardly armed, to about 470. The governor, Don Diego de Salinas, of whom Berwick was so critical, says in his own account that he had only 56 regulars of whom 30 were 'serviceable', and that the militia 'armed as God willed' were of such poor quality that 'they began to run away even before they arrived at their posts'.

Sayer, in his history of Gibraltar quotes from Spanish sources the names of Don Bartolome Caetano as being in charge of the batteries on the Old Mole, with 200 citizens, Don Francisco Toribio de Fuentes at the New Mole with 20 militiamen and eight invalid soldiers, while Don Diego de Avila held the land port with sixty invalid soldiers and the castle was manned by a miscellaneous force of sixty-two including six dismounted cavalrymen. According to a letter to Philip, dated 5th August in the San Roque archives the local 'Home Guard' amounted to about 300 men.

The official account on the Allied side reports,

'On Friday August 1st the combined fleet hove into sight of Gibraltar. The English and Dutch had between them amassed a mighty force: sixty-nine ships-of-the-line, seven of 96 cannon, five of 80 or 84 and the rest of 60 or 70, and sixteen frigates of between 30 and 50 cannon. That same day the fleet entered the harbour and although they came under the fire of the fortress known as *Nuestra Señora de la Europa* no damage was done to men or vessels.'

Seeing Byng's squadron anchored in line abreast out of range of such guns as Gibraltar possessed and Rooke with the rest of the fleet in the bay, anchored between the rivers Palmones and Guadaranque, Don Diego at once sent messages for help to Villadarías, who was still some way off, returning, slowed down by the heats, from the first campaign. 'That same day, an hour past noon, under cover from the fire of the frigates they put ashore three thousand men from the combined armies, a cannon-shot from the Land Port.' One account gives the number as 1,800 marines and a few Spaniards as landing at Puerta Mala on the flat isthmus; San Felipe says 4,000 (based on French reports and probably an exaggeration), while Darmstadt in a letter dated 7th August to Charles claims: 'I landed with 2,300 or 2,400 men unopposed except by a cavalry troop of 50 who were soon driven off. The troops took up positions half a cannon shot away from the city.' Rooke reported landing only 1,800 but was merely accounting for his own men. In all probability Darmstadt was including troops, Spanish and Catalan, who were serving with him. Captain Whitaker, in command of landing-craft, writes of 2,000 men, which still leaves about 300–400 unaccounted for. These would appear to be the deserting Spanish officers (perhaps forty or fifty) and the more numerous Catalans who had joined Darmstadt's seventy after the abortive landing at Barcelona. Later the garrison numbers in Gibraltar were to be reported by the Quartermaster Abraham Knox as 2,600, and by December to be 900 more than the 2,000 for whom Rooke had provided rations. These 900 were 'the Prince's People and Catalonians, Spanish officers, inhabitants, prisoners'. We may conclude with George Hills that 'several hundred Catalans did in fact take part in the landing and during the whole siege served in the Catalan company and Catalan battery to which there are numerous references in all the primary documents'. To this day the 'Catalan Guard' and Catalan Bay serve as reminders of this.

Darmstadt landed with them. He had no field guns but in order to be able to attack the Land Port he took some grenadiers 'armed with crowbars and axes'. The official account says, '150 enemy horse attempted to prevent this landing', but they must have been fewer since Salinas had only a tiny force of cavalry. Sent out through the Land Port they were 'peppered with gun-fire' and driven back leaving one trooper dead. Darmstadt now took up position in some old windmills within musket range of the walls and cut off communications between the Rock and the mainland. Here he paused and sent a trumpeter to Salinas, carrying a letter dated 5th May from King Charles III demanding his acknowledgement of Charles as 'lawful king', painting a grim picture of what might happen and saying that if this should be refused the Allies would 'adopt such severities as war brings with it'.

Salinas summoned the city council and, persuading them that 'he could stage a defence, since the town was both by its natural position well guarded against attack and had been most skilfully constructed, to boot', sent back a firm reply that 'having taken the oath to King Philip they would defend Gibraltar with their lives while there was a single shell remaining in the town that could be fired in its defence'. He certainly must have realized the hopelessness of his position and probably thought of allowing himself and his meagre garrison to be forced by sheer weight of fire back to the castle, where he and they would fight to the last man. He had asked Villadarías for reinforcements and had got none, and now the city council wrote to the Marqués asking him to say that the city was determined to sacrifice itself in King Philip's service. In his desperation Salinas sounds understandably bitter. It was the time for 'severities' and he must have known how slight were the chances of all his small force sharing any kamikaze intentions. And of course, the tough Berwick may have been correct in his view of the governor.

Byng drew up his squadron in battle order in a line between the New and Old Moles. This took all day on the 2nd and most of the night, for the winds were very light and offshore and the ships had to be warped into position. Rooke had added five vessels to Byng's squadron which now consisted of sixteen English ships-of-the-line. All except *Ranelagh*, which was an 80-gun ship, and *Nottingham*, *Montague* and *Monck* (60), carried 70 guns. There were six Dutch vessels. The flagship was in the centre of the line and six vessels were to attack the New Mole, six the Old, and ten the city and south bastion. Altogether the squadron carried about 8,000 sailors and 1,490 heavy guns of which of course only half could fire a simultaneous broadside.

During the night Rooke caused a diversion by sending Captain Edward Whitaker of the *Dorsetshire* (his brother Samuel commanded the *Nottingham*) with ships' boats to destroy a French twelve-gun privateer within the Old Mole and stop it firing on Darmstadt's camp nearby, where 'the English and Dutch troops who were encamped in the fields immediately below the town defences and the walls ... had set about digging trenches for themselves as protection'. From this privateer and a French merchant ship 'more than 100 French were taken prisoner'.

By five o'clock in the morning warping had got the main units so close in that there was very little water beneath their keels, but the Dutch bomb ketches, which were oar-propelled and of lighter draft, had begun bombarding at midnight throwing in 'carcasses', a kind of primitive incendiary shell. San Felipe says there were four of these *balandras* (there were in fact three) and that 'the peasants were distraught at the novelty of the damage caused'. Meantime the few manageable guns on the sea wall fired at the ships. Most of the shot went harmlessly overhead but the *Ranelagh*'s mainmast was damaged. At this stage the fleet held its fire. As the sun began to rise on a very hot, windless day, the squadron then opened fire with greater enthusiasm than was needed. Not only did the gunsmoke hang in clouds between ships and shore obscuring the targets, but some vessels used so much ammunition that, being far from sources of supply, they reduced their stocks to such an extent as to cripple them when they came to action again three weeks later. The inhabitants began very early to run away uphill out of range, and Byng in the interests of visibility ordered that only the lower deck guns should fire, these being generally the heaviest.

There is seldom much glamour about a battle for those taking part. It is a matter of being often scared, sometimes excited, and always having to put up with noise, smell and other discomforts. During this particular action, one eye-witness, Dr Thomas Pocock, Byng's brother-in-law and the chaplain of the flagship, makes particular reference to 'the thin slimy matter covering the sea as is usual after a long calm'. This was composed of the discharge from the ships' latrines, augmented no doubt by the sewers of the town. And in the August heat the stink of this and gunpowder was disgusting.

Pocock's journal is one of the rare published documents which names a number of more junior officers in addition to the Captain, Cowe, who had taken part as a lieutenant in the reconnaissance landing at Cadiz two years before. The *Renelagh* (as Pocock spells it) included in her ship's company Lieutenants Davenport and Vanbrugh; Burn, the Master; Ball, the Gunner; Clements, the Bo'sun; Scriven, the Purser; Coleman, the Cook; and Gasceron, the Surgeon's Mate. He says little about them but he also names seven 'volunteers', precursors of midshipmen, aged from 11 to 14, including William and George Cowe, apparently the captain's sons, and records 'giving six young gentlemen sixpence apiece for learning the first six psalms' while he catechised them. He states that 1,400 rounds were fired but this must be a misprint. The official figure is 'above 15,000'. Don Diego, having been at the receiving end gives, perhaps naturally, a higher figure – 30,000. On the other hand the Lisbon account says that 'in the space of 5 or 6 hours they fired 25,000 rounds at the town and sent 500 carcases hurtling at the defence'. The log of the *Royal Catherine* gives 17,490 English and 23,500 Dutch shells and bombs. Rooke ordered cease fire after two hours but Byng, either purposely or otherwise, took no notice. Damage to the town was slight. At noon, Captain Edward Whitaker, who had joined the *Ranelagh* after his night's cutting-out sortie, was sent by Byng to order all ships to cease fire in order that the effect of the bombardment could be observed.

On reaching the southernmost ship, the *Lenox*, he and her captain noticed that the guns on the New Mole were silent. 'A sizeable breech had been opened in the first of the outlying Spanish forts.' Both were dashing men and concluded that the moment had come to attempt a landing which might well be unopposed. Captain (later Admiral Sir William) Jumper of the *Lenox* has a bastion (formerly that of Santa Cruz) named after him in Gibraltar. We have a brief description of him by the unattractive Captain Hawley who sailed with him as A.D.C. to General Erle a little later: 'He loved drinking, music and Hazard from morning to night.' But he was also a good fighting man, having always made the most of any chance. (He had lost his wife in a boating accident in 1695 at Plymouth. Perhaps it was this that gave him his carefree air.)

Whitaker reported to Byng who sent him on to Rooke to ask permission to land and ordered ships' boats to be manned in readiness. 'The Admiral sent word to all the vessels of the fleet that they should each one lower a longboat and man it forthwith with both soldiery and marines.' Flotilla after flotilla of boats then made for the New Mole. As this was taking place, and while the choking gunsmoke slowly cleared, there was an unintended diversion. Two miles south of the citadel was the shrine at Europa Point, erected and embellished by Spanish admirals, and here most of the women and children of the town had been sent for safety. Seeing English sailors about to come between them and their homes they panicked and began to run towards the town. At the orders of Admiral Shovell, now on board Byng's flagship, a warning shot was fired in front of them and they returned to the shrine, though Pocock records some of the women being accidentally killed. Jumper of the *Lenox* and Hicks of the *Yarmouth* who had mistaken the warning shots as a signal to land were first ashore and well established near the New Mole, without waiting for Whitaker to whom Rooke had entrusted the main landing party, and to whom Byng added Captains Fairfax, Roffey, Mighels and Aston. 'Three thousand men from both branches of the service were put ashore and they advanced on the said fort, and taking the breach ran up the colours of the two Nations, the Dutch at the same time capturing the next fort along, which is the second of the three that stand in a group above *Nuestra Señora de la Europa*'. According to one account the enemy resisted and 'sprang a mine' in the fort, killing and wounding a large number of the landing party, but most reports, particularly Pocock's, say that the fort was undefended and that the casualties were the result of over-excitement and carelessness. The sailors were jostling and tumbling casually into the fort, forgetting that it might contain a powder magazine. Some of them carried lighted port-fires and one or more of these appears to have been dropped near some loose powder. There was an explosion which blew up the fort, killed about 40 sailors, wounded a further 60 and sent debris flying over to sink a number of boats. 'Many of our boats were staved in pieces', says Pocock, who writes of 'the heedless courage of our seamen with lighted matches in their hands'.

There was a moment of panic. The sailors, thinking themselves the victims of a Spanish trap – 'trepanned by the enemy' – began to retreat. But Whitaker, landing with reinforcements, rallied them and resumed the attack, leaving Captain Roffey of the *Burford* and fifty seamen as a guard over the ruined fort, the *Torre del Tuerto*. With 300 seamen Whitaker now marched along the deserted seafront to a bastion, a half-moon battery dating from 1627, half a musket shot short of the southern wall, where he 'hoisted his colours', i.e. ran up the Union flag and paused. In San Felipe's account Darmstadt was with the advanced party, which given the prince's habitual boldness is quite possible (though unlikely because he would have had to take a boat from his command post north of the town), and that he hoisted the Imperial flag, proclaiming that the place belonged to King Charles III. This, according to San Felipe and Ayala (another Spanish historian writing years later) was 'resisted' by the English who ordered the Imperial flag struck and, running up the Union flag, proclaimed for Queen Anne. It seems highly improbable that such an incident took place during the initial landing. It could have happened later when Darmstadt entered and was installed as governor, with a salute of twenty-one guns. But then the log of the *Royal Catherine* records that he was left in possession. He had in the past refused to fly the Spanish flag and Wratislaw had made it plain that Allied troops would not fight under an Imperial flag. Since Charles was now King of Spain the Spanish flag would have been appropriate but it is not clear what flag Prince George actually flew. He may have used his personal standard as Landgrave of Hesse-Darmstadt. During the siege that followed both Spanish and British flags were flown but though the British government, John Methuen and the rank and file looked on the Rock as English, Rooke's instructions had been 'to endeavour by that means [a landing] to reduce it [Gibraltar] to the King of Spain's obedience' and he would not have acted in defiance of this. The only contemporary reference stated that English sailors hoisted the Union flag on the redoubt they captured beyond the New Mole, and they were entitled to do so, as Prince George would have agreed.

Later, Rooke recommended the use of Portuguese troops as garrison and Methuen encouraged this in order to involve King Pedro more deeply (he had not yet declared war on France and might revert to neutrality). Then, realizing that this was unworkable he and Schonenberg proposed an Anglo–Dutch garrison. But the Dutch refused to contribute to the cost and Methuen came to the conclusion that the place was important enough to deserve an English garrison. Prince George seems to have concurred in this. He might hold title as governor on behalf of Charles but he saw the place only as a base for the invasion of Spain, and, fearing that Rooke could not spare marines for long, asked Galway to send a garrison – even 2,500 Portuguese. He told Cabreras that 10,000 men used to invade Andalucia would be worth 30,000 anywhere else. For the next few years there would be a preponderance of English troops there with some few from other Allied armies, and nobody seemed to worry unduly. Only in the few months before the war ended would all non-English troops be sent away from the place. Finally, when Gibraltar did become British by the Treaty of Utrecht in 1713, King Philip only let it go grudgingly as we shall see. 'He yielded it to Queen Anne and she did not hold it by right of conquest'.

But to return, Byng joined Whitaker ashore during the hot afternoon with several hundred seamen. Bombardment of the town was resumed. It was invested from the south and under musket fire from Darmstadt's marines in the north. The women and children were under guard at Europa Point and most of the militia had fled. Darmstadt was now back outside the Landport Gate, if indeed he had ever left it. Byng withdrew all the seamen except those in the Redoubt and the New Mole fort, leaving a party to guard the women and children. There was now apparently a lull in the proceedings. Either the shock of the explosion, or the fall of darkness or a kind of general confusion – the accounts vary – took over. But 'the two nations did not desist from their attack' and next morning Byng joined Darmstadt.

On the evening of August 3rd Darmstadt sent in a fresh demand for surrender from the landward gate '*Puerto de Tierra*', giving Salinas only half an hour to reply. Salinas said he had to obtain the accord of the city council and asked for eight hours' truce while he did so. The behaviour of English troops at

Cadiz two years earlier had not been forgotten and in his message to Byng he asked that 'the women in his possession might be kept from the rudeness of the sailors and to release them ... The citizens were very apprehensive that some injuries might be offered them', and he offered hostages in their place. Byng and Darmstadt 'assured [the citizens] that [no injuries] had been offered any of [the women] and acquainted them with the care he had taken to protect them by the guards he had posted for their security.' Meantime Salinas had held a council of war which had unanimously concluded that 'the defence of the city and fortress was impossible in the circumstances and that they should seek honourable terms of surrender'. And sometime after midnight, a city council meeting, having heard 'how overwhelmingly superior the attacking force was to the defenders, decided that it was more pleasing to His Majesty [Philip] that they should seek such terms and surrender than that they should hold on to no purpose and occasion severe loss to the city and his subjects'.

This was conveyed verbally to Darmstadt at dawn on 4th August, according to his report to Charles III: 'He asked me to appoint two negotiators. I sent the Count of Val de Soto and the Dutch Captain Landschager, while he appointed the *Maestro de Campo* Don Diego Davila Pacheco and Don Baltasar de Guzmán, a gentleman of the city, as his negotiators.' The latter 'rode out from the town to the open ground that lies behind', but, 'as they brought no proposals in writing', says Darmstadt,

> 'I thought this was just a ruse to gain time. There were people moving about among the buildings. While I had nothing to fear if it was a ruse, I sent the Englishman Captain Fox [of the Marines] with my written terms and with the message that if they were not accepted by [midday] and if by then the landward gate had not been handed over, he could expect nothing short of unconditional surrender. As soon as he heard this the governor decided to hand the gate over. On my side I agreed to further conditions [so as] not to delay Your Majesty's acquisition of so important a fortress.'

He had 'received the delegates in with all the ceremony and magnanimity which is characteristic of his princely nature, inviting them to dine at his table. At two hours past noon the whole camp accompanied the prince to the land port', where terms of surrender were signed. As we shall note during the next few months, Prince George of Hesse-Darmstadt believed in keeping up appearances and providing a good table and wine as a lubricant to the wheels of war and diplomacy.

The terms of surrender are given in full by Ayala and can be summarised as follows: The garrisons should march out in three days' time with arms, baggage, three brass guns, colours flying, and supplies for six days. Any civilian inhabitants wishing to stay must swear allegiance to Charles III but would retain the privileges and rights enjoyed under Charles the Sufferer and Philip V. French subjects would be prisoners of war. There was to be no change in the religion or laws of Gibraltar. With acceptance of this the landward gate was handed over to Darmstadt and Byng 'conducted the ladies and others that had been in the south chapel for two days without provision, to the gates of the town, to prevent their being insulted or abused by the seamen.'

The Reverend Mr Pocock, going ashore on 6th August and walking 'all over the town' found that 'great disorders had been committed by the boats crews that came on shore and marines; but the general officers took great care to prevent them, by continually patrolling with their sergeants, and sending them on board their ships and punishing the marines; one of which was hanged after he had thrown dice with a Dutchman who had ten and the Englishman nine'. Nevertheless a number of private houses were sacked and only one church escaped altogether because its priest, Don Juan Romero de Figueros, and his curate, stayed to protect it. Byng laid the blame on Prince George's Catalans but whoever was reponsible the inhabitants were not favourably predisposed to 'the heretics'. In any case their priests told them that the French would retake the place in a few weeks. So it is not surprising that all but a handful (about seventy) decided to leave. Some 4,000 refugees from 1,200 houses left with what they could carry and sought shelter in villages and towns as far away as Ronda, Medina Sidonia and Málaga. Sixty-five Poor Clares walked through high summer some fifteen miles to Jimena and were then split up among convents in Carmona, Seville and Jeréz – scores of miles away. Some of the wealthier inhabitants who had property on the mainland, offered shelter. One of these, Don Bartolomé Luis Varela, a city councillor, preserved the city's standards and records and provided a meeting place for the council. Looking back on the Rock, he left by the roadside a tile bearing an outline of the place, a cross, and the words: 'Here I wept for Gibraltar, August 1704. Varel' It is now in the museum of San Roque together with many other articles. San Roque was given royal recognition by Philip in 1706 as 'My City of Gibraltar in the fields'. He could not call it New Gibraltar without admitting that the Rock was lost for ever. For long the poorer inhabitants squatted on the mainland, the peasants around San Roque and the fishermen near Algeciras.

About thirty families and six clergymen, including Don Juan Romero, John the Hermit, and Bartolo the Bell-ringer; a Doctor of Medicine, a mother and daughter and some with no family connections, stayed. They had a thin time awaiting them, although the official report says that many Spaniards were persuaded by Darmstadt's 'kindly and courteous treatment' to return and that it was hoped that in the light of this 'many more will be guided ... to join our glorious party and that the righteous cause which we all serve shall carry all before it in triumph'. This, of course was mere propaganda.

When Darmstadt marched in officially and the marines relieved the sailors of the redoubt and the New Mole fort, the reckoning showed that the taking of Gibraltar had cost the Allies two lieutenants, one master mariner and fifty-seven sailors killed; one captain, seven lieutenants, one boatswain and 207 sailors wounded. Most casualties were caused when the fort blew up. Spanish casualties were probably over sixty. The Allies captured 114 guns of various calibres (the official published account says only 10), 1,200 barrels of gunpowder and not much else except 200 horses. They had taken what seemed then and has long been considered an important stronghold for their Mediterranean strategy. Secretary Hedges called it 'a footing for the King of Spain in the strongest fort belonging to that country and of great use to us for security of our trade and interrupting the enemy's'. Addison called it 'The Strait's mouth and the key to the Levant'. Both descriptions were exaggerated, and Queen Anne's advisers were not all that impressed. Marlborough, while recognizing its potential strategic importance took very little interest, possibly because it was so heartily welcomed by the Tories. And as so often happens, the cost of the its maintenance seems to have been the main Cabinet consideration, not surprisingly as we shall shortly see. For, after all, it could not protect a fleet against a stronger one or offer much in the way of shelter, and was only useful to a few men-of-war at a time. It could never rival Lisbon or Port Mahon, except in position. But an envoy of the King of Morocco had been taken on board to observe this operation and had been much impressed. And the psychological effect of its capture on Louis XIV and the Madrid government was considerable, followed as it was a few days later by Marlborough's victory at Blenheim at the other end of Europe. For Rooke's reputation it was critical, since it compensated for his cautious performance in the Gulf of Lions. His political supporters succeeded in coupling it with Blenheim in mention in the House of Commons, thereby eventually harming him. Blenheim was of greater immediate consequence but Gibraltar had nevertheless a more permanent significance. It is ironical that it remained in British hands at the end of the war because the Allies failed in imposing their candidate on the throne of Spain – Charles would by then have become Emperor on the death of his brother. Had Philip been toppled, Charles would probably have insisted on his rights to what he always called 'my city of

Gibraltar'. As it was, war-weariness in Louis XIV and his grandson would cause them to yield it to Queen Anne.

But long before that it would undergo its twelfth siege and would have to be held against all comers. And that challenge would come a bare three weeks after its capture.

★   ★   ★

Since movement of troops by land took time – even if they had been immediately available – the first reaction from France was to send the Mediterranean fleet in an attempt to regain Gibraltar. Accordingly the whole French fleet sailed from Toulon avowedly to drive the Allied fleet back into the Atlantic. This was to result in what was to be the only general sea action of the war.[2]

Darmstadt's letters to Galway and King Charles in Portugal on the morrow of the capture of Gibraltar show that he regarded it not merely as something to be celebrated with *feux de joie* but as a springboard from which the Allies could enter Spain, advance on Seville and then Madrid and further the cause of his master. But Madrid is some four hundred miles from Gibraltar and however disorganized the Spanish army was, it would have been capable of holding up a few hundred Allied troops, even if they were led by a splendid fighter like Darmstadt. In any case he could only get logistic support by sea and Rooke was concerned about the state of the English and Dutch ships under his command. They had now been at sea for at least six months and needed repair and refitting. Moreover he had had trouble with the Dutch, writing on 28th July to the Admiralty, ['They] are looking home with their whole Squadron, they have sent away the Rear-Admiral with six ships ... more than one-third of their strength.' He had unwillingly let Van der Dussen go off to Lisbon in order to provide, after a refit, escort for reinforcements for the army in Portugal.

Leaving Darmstadt at Gibraltar with 1,000 marines as garrison, the admiral stood his fleet over to the north African coast. Here the ships were watered and, according to San Felipe, he attempted to persuade the governor of Ceuta to yield the place, since with Gibraltar it would enable him to dominate the straits. It had been under siege by the Moors for some thirty years and the governor, a Catalan, the Marqués de Gironella, although a staunch supporter of Philip, was justifiably worried about an attack from the sea. But the local bishop urged Gironella to resist and Rooke's approaches were declined.

The admiral had heard that the Comte de Toulouse had left his base at

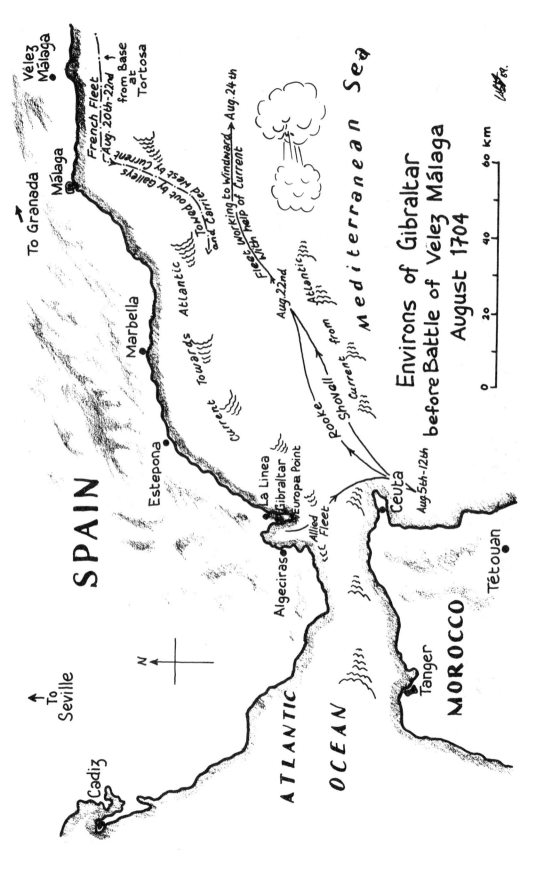

Environs of Gibraltar
before Battle of Velez Málaga
August 1704

VELEZ MÁLAGA

Action Begins. 10.a.m. 24th August 1704

Velez Málaga

Málaga

French~Spanish Fleet
51. Ships of the Line
6. Frigates
22. Galleys

Foudroyant (Flagship)
Intrépide~ Invincible~
Monarque~ Tonnant~
Mercure ~ Fier

REAR. Langeron
(Blue) French Ships + 6 Genoese Galleys

CENTRE.
French Ships + 4 French Galleys
Toulouse & Roye
(White)

Foudroyant

Foudroyant

CENTRE (white)
Rooke (Dilkes)
(Royal Catherine)
Byng. Renelagh

Van.
Shovell (White)
Leake (Balfleur)
(Royal George)

Van. Villette
(white & Blue)

French Ships
+ 12 Spanish Galleys

REAR (Blue)
Callenburg & Dutch
incl. Graff Van Albemarle & Unie

Allied Fleet
53 Ships of the line
+ 6 Frigates ~ 7 Fire Ships
Incl. Royal Catherine~Barfleur~
Warspite~ Swiftsure~ Namur~
Prince George~ Grafton ~
Royal Oak~Eagle~Kingston

Appr. Scale

0   1   2 miles

VELEZ MÁLAGA

End of Action 4.30–6.30 p.m. August 24th~Dawn 25th

French Ships towed away   Arrive Malaga Aug 27th

Wind Direction

Callenburg Claims to
have beaten Langeron

night of
24th~25th

← 24th

← 25th

Eagle–Shrewsbury
St. George
pulling out for
Lack of ammunition

Rooke

Burford
etc. pulling
out for lack
of ammunition

Arrive Malaga
Aug. 26–27th

Magnifique
Towed out by
Turcis

Shovell
& Leake
to aid
Rooke

Allied Fleet Driven off by wind
Changing to West, Night of 24–25th
Distance apart by Dawn 25th. 12 miles

←— 26th~27th Eastwards to proximity of Gibraltar

Appr. Scale

0   miles   2

Toulon and so he sailed from Ceuta on 12th August, leaving Shovell with his squadron of twelve still taking on water. He stationed himself to the east of Gibraltar in order to forestall any attack by Toulouse. On the 20th August, H.M.S. *Centurion*, scouting to the east of the fleet reported sighting French sail to windward. Her signal was first seen by Byng who reported it to the commander-in-chief. In a discussion which followed, Rooke's Captain of the Fleet, Wishart, proposed falling back on Gibraltar and anchoring there, whereas Byng recommended holding to their present station. A council of war, attended by the Dutch, decided that the fleet should continue to the east of Gibraltar, send for as many marines as Darmstadt could spare, and await Shovell. In the past, ships at anchor in a roadstead had generally been considered safe from attack but the French were believed to have fireships which galleys could tow to within striking distance. In fact the wind at this time would probably not have been strong enough to carry fireships on to their targets, but this was not then known.

One account of the battle in the French archives is fairly brief. It reports Toulouse at anchor at Málaga from the 20th to 22nd in company with the commandants of twenty-four galleys, Spanish, Genoese and French, when the Marquis de Forville, leading a squadron of the van, signalled the enemy in sight to the west. There had been virtually no wind for two days but on the 22nd a slight cloud over the sun signalled that a levanter (easterly wind) was about to blow. The French weighed anchor and with the help of the galleys moved fifteen miles off the coast, where they stayed until the 23rd. There are two opposing currents in the straits, one from the Atlantic towards the Mediterranean running along the African coast, and the other in the opposite direction running along the Spanish coast. The Allied fleet was able to take advantage of the former in working to windward, while the French fleet was at some risk as the current prevailing near the Spanish coast tended to carry them on to a lee shore. Navigation in the straits in the days of sail was made precarious by the currents. While Toulouse was working his way out that night in search of sea room, Rooke, who had now been joined by Shovell, struggled to work his fleet eastwards in order to keep the weather gauge, and with the assistance of the current his ships were able to maintain their position under reefed sails. The two fleets lost contact in the dark.

During the forenoon of the 23rd they sighted each other again and 'partly by towing, partly with the help of the wind', the French kept moving until they were, according to their accounts, in a crescent formation 'twenty miles from the enemy who were to the east'. They had a sweltering time of it for the wind dropped away. What there was of it served to provide some coolness for the Allied fleet and to enable Rooke to call in his scouting vessels, for according to his report he was only ten miles away from the French and it was time to form line of battle. Next day, Sunday 24th August, there was once more a light easterly wind and swell and this 'being favourable to the enemy carried them towards us to cannon range', says the French account. The two fleets were of approximately equal size. San Felipe writes of Rooke having 118 ships of varying size plus eight bomb ketches, while Toulouse had 108, but more reliable reports indicate that each fleet had about three-quarters of these numbers.

Toulouse had as chief of staff the Comte d'Estrées, son of an admiral who had fought alongside the English in the Third Dutch War. He had recently relinquished his post as a Vice-Admiral of the Spanish Navy. The French fleet is fairly accurately known to have consisted of fifty-one ships-of-the-line, six frigates, and twenty-two large French, Genoese and Spanish galleys. The main duty of these galleys in battle was to tow damaged ships out of the line and replacements in. The guns numbered 3,577 and the number of men was estimated at 24,775. The fleet sailed in three divisions each of seventeen or eighteen sail of the line with attendant galleys. Toulouse was in the centre, flying a white ensign (the Bourbon Colours), and accompanied by the Marquis de Roye with four French galleys. The Marquis de Villette led the van, flying a white and blue ensign and accompanied by twelve Spanish galleys under the Duque de Turcis, and the rear was commanded by the Marquis de Langeron, flying a blue ensign and with the six Genoese galleys. The fleet included a 104-gun three-decker, *Foudroyant*, the flagship, another of 100 guns and one of 88. Though the list of ships is not complete or entirely reliable, the remainder are known to have been mainly 54-gun two-deckers. It was noted by their opponents during the action that the French used their 'small frigates' to repeat signals along the line of battle because of the gunsmoke hanging around.

The Allied fleet of fifty-three ships-of-the-line, six frigates, seven fireships and sundry smaller vessels, carried 3,614 guns and 22,545 men – calculated after the event. It too sailed in three divisions. Rooke's squadron was in the centre plus those of Rear-Admirals Byng and Dilkes and with Rear-Admiral Sir James Wishart as Captain of the Fleet. The van was led by Vice-Admiral Sir John Leake, flying his blue ensign at the foremast of H.M.S. *Prince George* (90 guns, commanded by his brother-in-law, Captain Stephen Martin), with Admiral Sir Cloudesley Shovell in overall command flying his white ensign at the mainmast of H.M.S. *Barfleur* (90 guns, Captain Stewart). The rear was commanded by Lieutenant-Admiral Gerrit Callenburg in the *Graaf van Albemarle* with Rear-Admiral Wassenaer in the *Unie*, and consisted of twelve ships. Rooke had nothing larger than 90-gun three-deckers. He had no first rates and only five second rates, his own *Royal Catherine* being the smallest of these in the Navy. His two-deckers carried only 52 guns as against the French 54, and one had only 50. (A 50-gun ship was by now the smallest 'admitted to the line' and would soon be regarded as 'below the line of battle'.) The Dutch as we have seen had sent a third of their strength home to refit, and a number of the Allied ships had fired far too many rounds at the taking of Gibraltar. Moreover their cast-iron guns were inferior to the French bronze cannon. He decided to keep two of his weakest two-deckers in reserve and make full use of his bomb ketches. Although these were inaccurate in their firing because of the swell, Villette would later report that a projectile from one of them had gone through three decks of his ship, the *Fier*, causing heavy damage.

As the wind was so light, conditions between decks in both fleets were suffocating as ships' companies made ready for battle, knocking down bulkheads, watering and sanding decks so that fire would not start or feet slip, bringing up powder kegs, setting butts of sea-water, and testing reeving tackle. Below in the dark, foul-smelling orlops, often painted red in English ships to disguise blood splashed from operations, ships' surgeons and their mates pre-pared their primitive instruments and the barrels into which amputated limbs were thrown. More feared even than wounds needing this were the appalling effects in wood ships of huge jagged splinters, which had usually to be cut away leaving hideous scars.

At nine o'clock that Sunday morning according to logs of English ships, the French fleet, with the Bourbon flag, golden fleur-de-lis on white at the mastheads, lay motionless as the English van and centre approached to within a mile. Then, with a light breeze the French edged away. A gap opened in the centre of the Allied line as Rooke made for the French van. The French centre swiftly fore-reached him as their ships were fresh from harbour. His own were foul-bottomed and the Dutch, after nearly a year, still fouler with weed. The approach continued in a tense near-silence, broken chiefly by the creak of rigging and timbers, the lap of water against the hulls, the piping and calling of orders in the Allied fleet, the sound, as the moment for opening fire came, of drums and trumpets in the French. And, as a ground bass, the murmur of excited men. The French crescent formation was noted by the Allies as unusual, with a massing at either end of the line to fire 'a punch with both hands'. Rooke's line was the orthodox one, straight and close-hauled to the wind. At length Rooke hove-to alongside the *Foudroyant* and signalled his fleet to do likewise, but Byng, for reasons of his own, continued sailing his squadron until it was in action. According to the log of H.M.S. *Kingston*, second in his division, the signal 'to fall on them' was made at 10.30, by which time Leake's flagship, *Prince George*, was almost within musket-shot of Villette's *Fier*. With a sudden thunder-clap the broadsides flew out and by 11.00 all the English ships were engaged. The Dutch in the rear division were becalmed and did not come into action until later. From the start the French were affected by the contrary wind, whereas the Allied ships were steadier in the following breeze. Moreover the wind blew gunsmoke away from the Allies and towards the French.

Leake's brother-in-law, Captain Martin, is the source of one of the very few personal anecdotes recorded of this battle and passed it down to his son (and Leake's godchild). His steward, a German named Daniel Milker, refused to go below, saying 'Do you think I will leave my master?' Then he was knocked down by a cannon-ball which hit him full in the chest. It must have been a spent ricochet for, to his own and everybody else's surprise, he picked himself up, only bruised and winded. Retrieving the shot as a souvenir he annouced that as he was not feeling well he would now go down below after all. (He lived thirty years after this, retiring to Chatham where he kept a slop shop.) No other individual tales of seamen involved seem to have survived, though there must have been many of them at the time.

The French galleys, apart from their work, of towing, and of evacuating the wounded, made a feint against the Dutch but were not otherwise directly involved. The rest of the fleets were now engaged in a slogging match. The French often attempted to board Rooke's vessels, but the latter in most cases held them off at cannon or at least musket range. After an hour Villette in the French van bore out of the line because of damage, and his opponent was in much the same state, Leake and Martin both having splinter-wounds, and ninety of the crew of the *Prince George* already *hors de combat*. The ship's sails could not be trimmed as rapidly as they should be and there was no more ammunition from the middle- and lower-deck guns. Three hours later several more of Villette's ships were crippled and, as Shovell put it in his report, 'the whole of them were on the run'. But by now Rooke in the centre was heavily engaged and out-matched as his opponent the *Foudroyant* was surrounded by a concentration of French ships. As Leake's immediate opponents had been towed away he sent Captain Martin to Shovell, proposing that they should together pursue the French van, but Shovell, seeing how hard-pressed Rooke was, insisted that they go instead to his assistance. Accordingly the *Barfleur*, *Namur* and *Prince George* backed their topsails and went astern to help the commander-in-chief. San Felipe, with a touch of hyperbole, describes the sea as 'being dyed and the ships stained with blood'. Men were being blinded, dismembered, disfigured and blown in pieces. He was certainly right about that.

It was now, however, that the effect of the bombardment of Gibraltar was seen. Rooke had left England with forty rounds per gun (the equivalent of eighty broadsides). On average fifteen rounds had been fired during the current battle, leaving in principle, twenty five. But the ships which had been engaged at Gibraltar were far worse off; eight ships, *Eagle*, *Grafton*, *Monmouth*, *Nassau*, *Montague*, *Suffolk*, *Burford* and *Kingston* had nothing left to fight with and had to haul out of the line. At the courts martial which they had afterwards to face their captains were acquitted.

By 4.30 p.m. both fleets were so badly mauled that they could attempt no new manoeuvre and although firing continued sporadically until dusk, the results were inconclusive. By then, too, gunsmoke was so thick as to make aiming difficult. At 6.30 Callenburg claimed to have beaten de Langeron whose ships were towed out of battle by galleys. At 7.00 p.m. firing ceased altogether and the two fleets separated in silence as the wind and sea rose and station-keeping became difficult. No single Allied ship had been sunk, captured or burned out but few were undamaged and many unserviceable. In the Allied view the French fired too high, causing more damage to rigging, masts and spars than to hulls. The only Dutch ship lost was the *Graaf van Albemarle* which blew up two days later, probably by accident when cartridges were being filled with powder. Callenburg, who was visiting another ship, escaped. The French lost *Cheval Martin* and two galleys during the fight and later these were joined by the *Fier*, *Excellent*, *Fortuné* and *Mercure*. The casualties were heavy on both sides. Estimates from the logs of Allied ships put their total at 2,718 (2,358 English), of whom 787 were killed (695 English) and 1,931 wounded. Of the wounded about one-third died within days or at most, weeks. The average casualties in each of the English ships-of-the-line were seventeen killed and forty wounded. At Trafalgar a century later it was seventeen killed and forty-six wounded. Among those dead were Captain Cowe of the *Ranelagh* and Queen Anne's 'handsome captain', Sir Andrew Leake, who had been knighted for his action at Vigo in the *Torbay*. At Velez Málaga he commanded the *Grafton* which was very closely engaged in the centre until forced to sheer off because she had lost so many of her ship's company (thirty-one killed and sixty-one wounded) as to be unmanageable. Sir Andrew, gravely wounded, insisted, after his wounds had been dressed and bandaged, on being wrapped 'in a table cloth and placed in an elbow chair on his quarterdeck.' There he 'partook of the glories of the day till he boldly breathed his last.' Three other captains including Christopher Myngs were wounded, and as well as the *Grafton*, the *Lenox*, *Shrewsbury* and *Monck* lost over a quarter of their ships' companies. (The *Monck's* losses were due to three attempts at boarding by the French *Sérieux*.) Five others, including Rooke's *Royal Catherine* lost between fifteen and twenty-three per cent of their men. French total losses were estimated at 3,050. One Admiral, de Belleisle-Erard, and Captain de Bailly-Lorraine of the *Vainqueur*, were killed. Toulouse himself and Captains de Rélingue, du Casse, de Phélypeaux and Chateaurenault (son of the admiral) were wounded, Toulouse in three places, while Rélingue lost a leg. Two others, not named individually in the French battle order and probably captains of galleys, are listed by Campbell and Parnell.

According to an unpublished French account, 'the French galleys were occupied all night towing ships of the van in an attempt to get the weather gauge. On the 25th at dawn the wind had changed to the west in favour of the French, but to get into battle order it would have been necessary to sail towards a lee shore. A council of war decided against this.' The fleets were now nine miles apart, having spent the night carrying out repairs and in Rooke's case, trying to share out the ammunition. San Felipe says that Rooke beat up wind overnight with great skill whereas the French could not, for lack of sea room. Owing to the change of wind, the French had the weather gauge, so Rooke sent his worst-hit ships to the rear and prepared to renew action in the same position as on the previous day. The French were between him and Gibraltar and had the advantage of station, and he was short of ammunition though his opponents did not apparently know this. Had they known it they might have fought and beaten him and retaken Gibraltar. But they were worried about the lee shore, and at the council in the *Foudroyant*, although Captain de Rélingue pressed for a further attack, the courtiers advised against it since Toulouse, a 'son of France', was wounded and a number of senior officers were casualties. During the evening the wind and sea got up, there was rain, hail and thunder, and the galleys were ordered to withdraw to Málaga.

On the 27th the French galleys were in port. On the 28th some of the fleet entered and took in water, and the Genoese and Spanish galleys rejoined the fleet. Thereafter the whole force sailed towards its base in Toulon.

On the 30th Rooke put back to Gibraltar. From his journal for 24th August it is clear that he had enjoyed himself.

'This morning we were within three leagues of the enemy, who brought to with their heads to the southward ... We steered down upon them until ten o'clock or half an hour past, they being at little more than a musket-shot distance. I was forced to make the signal and begin the battle; the enemy setting their sails and seeming to intend to crowd ahead of our van. The fight was maintained on both sides with great fury for three hours, but several ships ... were forced to go out of the line, some being disabled but most for want of shot, so that the body of their fleet fell very heavy upon my ship, the *St George*, *Shrewsbury* and *Eagle* ... so that we were much shattered and disabled. It has been the sharpest day's service that I ever saw, and what was most extraordinary, every officer in the fleet performed their [sic] duty without the least umbrage or deflection; and I have never observed the true English spirit more apparent in our seamen than on this occasion ... Sir C. Shovell and other flag-officers of the front and rear say that the enemy did not behave themselves well in those quarters. I am sure those in the centre did their duty very gallantly and heartily.'

Toulouse's own 'relation' is rather disingenuous and inaccurate. 'I was left master of the battle,' he concluded, 'as we could see that they did not want to fight. We then returned to Velez Málaga ... The enemy had the windward gauge and more ships-of-the-line. The wind and sea were too high for us to use our galleys properly but they did help bring the rearguard into line. I am assured that a ship of the enemy vanguard was sunk. This makes two'. Toulouse seems to have been covering up, and he certainly mistook his enemy's intentions either deliberately or out of ignorance, for he was not left 'master of the battle'. His claims for enemy ships sunk are untrue and he makes no mention of his own losses. But his relation is positively truthful compared to the concluding paragraph of the brief French account at Vincennes: 'We owe the glory of this action to the French, since the enemy had 18 ships more than the Comte de Toulouse and a favourable wind, which gave them the advantage.'

Another French report, printed in translation by Boyer says: 'The enemy had all the advantages on their side, superiority in number of ships, the wind which favoured them and prevented our receiving from the galleys all the assistance that was to be expected from the good disposition of those who commanded them.' (Boyer. Op. cit. III. App xxv 56). But this reads like the usual disclaimer put out after any encounter by either side.

Some details had also reached Madrid a few days later and eventually found their way to Boyer. Gramont, writing to Paris of Captain Bailly-Lorraine, said:

'He fell like an old Roman. Poor man! A cannon ball taking off part of his belly and his bowels falling out, he gathered them up with his own hands and put them in again; and observing his officers and sailors extremely troubled to see him in that condition, he told them: 'he did not want their pity and bid them keep everyone to his post, and redouble their fire'. Soon after he had said this he expired.'

Other immediate reports within Spain were sparse and over-optimistic. *Legajo* 552 in the Madrid *Archivo* contains only one letter about the battle, from the Conde de Peñarrubia, Governor of Málaga, based on what he had been told by a Spanish galley captain, Francisco Alcón, and later by other skippers. On the 24th, he says, the Armadas fought from 10.00 a.m. to 8.00 p.m. between Melilla and El Peñón,and the French 'had the windward gauge' but later corrects this to say that the English had this advantage. 'It seems that 12 English ships were sunk'. Then, on the 26th, a levanter (easterly wind) arose at five in the morning, which would have favoured the French. He had been sent a number of wounded officers for whom he was arranging treatment. The Spanish galleys, he notes, had lost contact with the fleet during the night of the 24th, and the English, by 29th August made for the Barbary Coast and were lost to sight. And that is all. But there must have been a rapid dissemination of news, probably largely by word of mouth. Le Marié wrote from Salamanca on 6th September, 'I long to hear what the admiral is going to do to pursue the enemy, having beaten them and sunk eight large vessels of which one is thought to have been the English flagship, and put another eight out of action. If they [the French fleet] could put into Lisbon it would cause great consternation and might force the King of Portugal to withdraw his forces.'

In time this rosy impression would be corrected.

News of the battle reached London by mid-September, Brydges writing reasonably accurately about it from the Admiralty on 14th September. The High Tories in the Commons, in boosting Rooke's services, appear to have done him an ill turn. In Daniel Defoe's words, they 'looked on Sir George Rooke as their own. The victory at sea they look on as their victory over the Moderate party, and his health is now drunk by those who won't drink the Queen's health ... I am obliged to hear Her Majesty slighted and the sea victory set against the land victory [Blenheim], Sir George exalted above the Duke of Marlborough.' Boyer reported that 'the queen and the prince received Admiral Rook [sic] very graciously and expressed themselves very well satisfied with his conduct. However, 'tis remarkable that no publick rejoicings were made in London upon the first news of the late sea fight (which few people allowed to be a victory) save only that the guns of the Tower were discharged.' The Whigs and people near the throne had their revenge for this. A private committee of the House of Lords was set up and this judged Rooke coolly. On 6th January 1705 the Lord High Admiral, Prince George, approved of Rooke being retired and named Shovell as his successor. Rooke felt this bitterly, as he says in a letter of 22nd February,

'I will only tell you that my services of last year have been so ill-received by some and so ill-rewarded by others that I could no longer forbear gratifying my inclinations to quit command of the fleet, to which my long indisposition [gout] gave me fair pretence ... The House of Lords have been ... all this session upon the cold hunt to discover miscarriages in the fleet last summer and not feeling able to find any faults they have thought fit to say nothing. So that where I can't be marked with public censure I must not expect to be justified.'

Understandably, he was to carry his resentment to the grave, when he died in Kent of gout in 1709. His memorial is in Canterbury Cathedral.

Velez Málaga can be compared to Jutland 212 years later. Both battles were indecisive. In the case of Málaga both sides claimed victory – the French the more vociferously. After Jutland the German Navy gained a propaganda victory while the Admiralty issued a fatuous and defeatist communiqué. San Felipe says the French main fleet after Málaga did not emerge from harbour again – in fact it did so once, in 1706 in an attempt to retake Barcelona, but would not face an Allied fleet under Leake. Similarly, although after Jutland the German High Seas Fleet made a couple of sorties under Hipper, it did not seriously challenge the Royal Navy again during the 1914–18 war.

Rooke may have had his faults but his name is deservedly associated forever with the capture of Gibraltar, and the effects of that feat of arms, though less dominant on the war as a whole, put the Franco-Spanish forces in Spain itself off balance.

*   *   *

Berwick at his camp at Niza and later at his summer quarters at Salamanca can scarcely have felt much at ease. Naturally disturbed by the cabals in Madrid he had felt it his duty to offer hospitality to the Abbé d'Estrées, whose dismissal made a stay in the capital – where he was *persona non grata* – impossible. The new ambassador, Gramont, could not take over until July.[3]

As Louis' military representative and as Philip's appointed captain-general, Berwick's authority over the Franco-Spanish armies was as yet unquestioned and although his first campaign had not succeeded as he had hoped, King Louis had approved his dispositions in writing. But there were jealousies. Chamillart noted in August that 'Milord Berwick has found people envious of him. It is only his position that attracts them, for he has worthily done his job as a general.' Among the envious were Puységur and the Abbé d'Estrées's successor as ambassador, another bad choice, nearly as disastrous as that of the cardinal. Of the same age as Berwick, Antoine, fourth Duc de Gramont was arrogant, opinionated and stupid. St Simon said, 'He had nothing in his favour but his name, his dignity, and a fine figure', and according to de Noailles he was convinced that the Spanish nation 'looked on Grandfather [Louis XIV] as a god who could do nothing wrong'. Before he had even set foot in Spain in late June he began writing to Torcy giving at great length his views on that country and the Spaniards and complaining when Berwick advised him to bring with him all he needed for his comfort since nothing was available on the spot.

At length, d'Estrées took chilly, official leave of Philip and relinquished a post which he had coveted but which had become vexatious. King Louis, experienced in the ways of the world and invariably kindly to servants who had not succeeded in their jobs, treated the abbé generously. Young, good-looking, and far too fond of the ladies, he could scarcely be offered a bishopric, even in a church which was greatly under the king's influence (himself not particularly prudish). Instead d'Estrées was awarded the Cordon Bleu, a distinction rarely accorded to anyone so young or to any ecclesiastic below the rank of cardinal. We do not hear of him again in Spain.

Gramont was determined to be Louis' senior representative in Spain in military as well as political matters. In Berwick's words, 'he had taken it into his head to govern that country as despotically as Richelieu and Mazarin had formerly governed France'. Although a dragoon, his military experience was fairly negligible (twenty years later he would, however, be a Marshal of France), but he considered it his duty to give instructions to Berwick. There was friction from the start and when Gramont reached Madrid from Salamanca in July, he began at once to throw his weight about, as Berwick knew he would.

The news of Gibraltar reached Versailles within a day or two of that of Blenheim and together they clearly upset the normal calm of the *grand monarque*, for in a letter to Philip dated 20th August he exhibits a rare fit of near-panic.

'I am deeply disturbed to learn of the capture of Gibraltar, though I think it will be difficult for the enemy to establish themselves strongly in a place with no port and without a safe roadstead, and one which they can only sustain from the sea. It is essential that you prevent them from establishing themselves in Castile or Extremadura. They will use every effort to maintain any cities they may take. You must examine whether without weakening your army too much you can withdraw troops from your frontier. If so you would do well to make up a detachment strong enough to recover Gibraltar as soon as possible. If you can't you must postpone such an expedition until later and meantime the Marquis de Villadarías with his troops and those you send him from Madrid can prevent the enemy from penetrating any further.'

This letter was worrying for a young man who was uncertain of himself and in awe of his grandfather. It was in any case asking too much – the protection of Castile and Extremadura as well as the possible recapture of Gibraltar – of the Franco-Spanish troops available in the Peninsula. And it encouraged Gramont's ideas of grandeur. He too had heard by mid-August of the fall of Gibraltar and on 1st September came the news of the hammer-blow of Blenheim, which he considered much more important since it forced the French 'entirely out of Germany and to defend the frontiers of Alsace'. While still at Salamanca he heard of Toulouse's 'victory' which in his view 'would only serve to keep the Catalans in subjection for the rest of the year and provide a reputation for the Comte de Toulouse'. His tone suggests some acerbity towards this 'son of France'.

Berwick was soon under pressure himself from Versailles, Chamillart writing on 2nd September to say how necessary it was to re-establish Philip's armies and that he had himself written to Gramont and to Rivas, now the Spanish Minister for War, about how this should be handled, 'for you cannot rely only on King Louis' troops'. This was scarcely tactful in a letter to a man who was greatly disenchanted with his position and who, long before Chamillart's missive could arrive, was at loggerheads with Gramont. The latter, taking King Louis' instructions about Gibraltar literally, put pressure on Philip to order Villadarías to retake the Rock, and himself wrote to Berwick 'at the King of Spain's command' pressing for a strong detachment to be sent to help Villadarías. The political situation in Madrid was the more ticklish in that Gibraltar and Blenheim had served as a considerable encouragement to pro-Austrian circles, including the Dowager Queen Mariana, who was Charles III's aunt, in nearby Toledo.

Berwick's reaction showed a proper sense of military priorities. He knew that the Allies were assembling a considerable force. Their plan, which he described as a good one, was to leave the south side of the Tagus alone, since there they would have to tackle Alcántara, Marveon, Albuquerque and Badajoz. That sector was far from Madrid, and in concentrating between the Duero and Sierra de Gata, their attack would be far closer, 'only fifty leagues across good and plentiful country, so open that it was scarcely possible to stop the progress of an army except with a force of about equal size'. The only fortress in the way of such an attack was Ciudad Rodrigo which could not be defended and Berwick's force consisted of only eighteen battalions 'reduced to nothing', none of them having more than 100 men, and thirty-seven squadrons 'in the weakest condition'. All the rest, apart from 500 in the garrison at Ciudad Rodrigo, were with Tzerclaes in Extremadura.

That worthy was adding to the panic in Madrid, complaining of danger because the Portuguese had replaced their regulars with militia, assuming that the enemy were massing against him, and demanding reinforcements. Berwick discounted this, writing to Chamillart about Tzerclaes' feeble behaviour during the first campaign. 'The apprehensions of this general are chimerical.'

Berwick knew he would be faced by the Allied troops 'assembled under the princes at Coimbra (with the image of St Anthony of Padua)' and that they had announced that they were making for the frontier. The Madrid court, advised by the jealous Puységur that Berwick would not be faced by a large force, 'considered him a visionary', and it would be some little time before they found that he was right.

Meantime, although Gramont had written 'by the King of Spain's command', Berwick peremptorily refused to detach any forces to Villadarías. On 4th September he wrote to the ambassador, 'I am a man of honour and uprightness and as a soldier I must speak frankly of my complaints on the way you have behaved towards me. In the matter of the war it is I who am in charge and I *must* be consulted. You seem not only not to consult me but, as in this case of Gibraltar, even to hide from me what you are doing.' This was, in Berwick's words, 'disagreeable to the ambassador, who, seeing no other way of succeeding in his designs, resolved to try and put somebody in my place'. In reply, Gramont withdrew his instructions and apologised, but henceforth he began to represent Berwick to Philip and the queen as a singularly stubborn and insubordinate officer determined not to obey Philip's orders, and to recommend that he be dismissed. Puységur did nothing to oppose this, no doubt (in Berwick's retrospective view) hoping that he would have more authority with another general. Rivas seconded Gramont, probably, says Berwick drily, 'in order to put everything into confusion', and other Spaniards, 'who do not like opposition', were of the same mind. Gramont himself hoped to have one of his friends, probably Marshal Bouffers, to replace Berwick.

In a matter of days María Luisa, remembering Berwick's involuntary involvement in the removal of Mme des Ursins, made Philip ('persecuted on my account', says Berwick) write to his grandfather suggesting that only a Marshal of France could satisfactorily fill the post of captain-general and that one such should be sent to replace Berwick. As Berwick later pointed out, this was a frivolous concept, that a captain-general is of the same order as a marshal, and that it would have been perfectly simple to have awarded him a marshal's baton if necessary. He apologised to Chamillart for bothering him with all his political troubles. 'I know that all these factions must bore you but as this affair affects my honour I hope you will pardon me for wasting your time.' He did not know that Philip's letter to his grandfather was being treated as a matter of urgency. María Luisa had proposed that Berwick should be replaced, not by one of Gramont's friends, but by Marshal Tessé, an old friend of King Louis and on close terms with the queen's sister, the Duchess of Burgundy. Her preference for him was stimulated by the belief that he would influence grandfather Louis to agree to the return of Mme des Ursins. She, and therefore King Philip, could think of nothing else but this. Gibraltar, the threat on the Portuguese border, the state of the armies, the lack of finance, none of these appeared to matter.

The sequel to this bitter, vulgar domestic squabble, with all its political reverberations took months to evolve and will be examined later. Its effects on the military situation were near disastrous. Berwick during all this was on the rack. He wrote to Chamillart on 6th September hoping for the return of Orry (who was kicking his heels in Versailles, having spent weeks waiting for an interview with King Louis or one of his ministers). At least Orry might find ways of paying the army:

'I haven't one single *sou* to pay the troops though they are due three months' pay. I doubt if the Spanish infantry can ever be reconstituted and in any case French infantry are far better . . . I would be happy with French infantry and Spanish cavalry. If the English and Dutch send additional troops to Portugal I doubt if we can in our present state undertake even a siege, let alone a battle. If the enemy are not reinforced it may be easier.'

And again on 12th September: 'By torturing myself and scraping I can get enough to hold the army together for fifteen days . . . I have been asked by King Philip to take care of Old Castile, otherwise there would be [inconvenience].' To Philip he wrote, 'As to your orders to send troops to the Marquis of Villadarías to help chase the enemy from Gibraltar I hope this is no longer an order. The enemy [fleet] having been beaten by the Count of Toulouse, he will be in a position to provide the help needed, and after we have retaken Gibraltar you will see what I intend from my letter to Villadarías.' He, like others, seems to have been hoodwinked by the French claims of victory at Velez Málaga, or possibly he just found it a convenient argument with which to back his refusal to reinforce Villadarías.

By 19th September, while still concerning himself with a variety of small problems such as that of dealing with officers' valets who left their masters (he had just received a reply from Chamillart about this), he was able to give Versailles his order of battle for dealing with the threat from across the Portuguese border. He had six divisions, encamped from early September at Castros, four leagues from Ciudad Rodrigo. The Spanish cavalry was nearby and the rest were ready to march to join him, and in a few days all the infantry would be with him.

By now the Spanish Court was 'seized by so much fear' that they sent orders that he should remain on the defensive and not risk an action. A second, more panicky note ordered him to retire as the enemy advance. He replied firmly that as the River Agueda was the only position at which the enemy could be stopped and prevented from marching on Madrid he absolutely must oppose them there. Despite positive orders from Philip, Berwick considered that if he did not oppose the crossing of the river, Spain would be lost to the Bourbons. 'It is much better to hazard a battle with some hope of success than to abandon a position and forfeit everything without striking a blow ... a shameful and infamous measure.' Berwick's integrity and soldierly qualities were at their best in this perilous situation. He did not know it but within two days of his taking up this stance, King Louis would be writing to him ordering his recall to France as a result of Gramont's and María Luisa's pressure on Philip, who at this time was being less than *animoso*. That integrity and soldierly spirit will be seen to shine even more brightly during the tense weeks that followed.

Das Minas together with Galway had by the 21st September reached Almeida. Galway's position was that of adviser to the Portuguese, since King Pedro insisted that the command must be in Portuguese hands. The two generals now awaited the arrival of Charles III and King Pedro, who had announced that they wished to be present. Berwick at about this time arranged with Galway to exchange 100 English prisoners of war for 100 French sailors captured at Gibraltar. By such a contact, and by intelligence gained from deserters, he now had a more accurate assessment of the strength of the forces facing him, and their state of preparation. He knew, for example, that the Portuguese had given orders that bread for six days be issued. In a letter of 23rd September he announced the arrival of the two kings at Almeida, 'which means they have a design to undertake ... I will not risk the Crown of Spain in a battle but will carry out a *guerre à l'oeuil* and you can be sure that I will omit nothing.' He added that he had 'every trust in the Spanish troops'. This was scarcely true. In a letter of the same date to Chamillart he complains about the attitude of the Madrid court and how he has had to 'oppose their designs ... Things always go wrong when the man in charge is given no credit or confidence ... I will do my best but I hope they [the Allies] will not cross the Agueda in spite of their superior strength'.

Of that numerical superiority there is no doubt. Das Minas had some 20,000 men, 3,000 of them cavalry, these being mostly English and including Harvey's and the Royal Dragoons. With these he intended to cross the frontier, take Ciudad Rodrigo and obtain some plunder. But he was over-optimistic. His troops, poorly victualled and clothed for the most part, were unfit for a hard campaign. Galway, seeing their condition, tried to dissuade das Minas but, as a mere adviser, was over-ruled, after some fierce arguments. Accompanied, then, by the two kings, and of course by the statue of St Anthony of Padua, they reached the Agueda and by 2nd October had camped in a leisurely fashion on the left bank, where they had to wait for their bread. The convoys carrying this were under attack by Spanish irregular raiding parties. On the night of 29th September Berwick had caused some alarm by attacking the pickets of their advance guard, 'making a lot of noise with trumpets'.

The Allies expected desertions from their Spanish opponents, but there were none, and the peasants in the area remained quiet. This stiffening of morale was attibuted by some to the distribution by Philip of a medal showing his rival's head with the sarcastic motto, 'King Charles by the grace of the HERETICS, the Catholic King'. But it seems probable that the medal was issued later.

Berwick occupied the fords over the river, placing entrenchments on the right bank, keeping his main force of infantry in the rear poised for manoeuvre and his cavalry ready to scout the plain. this meant that the Allies could not cross without risking a battle which, as Galway had told them, they were in no position to offer. Between 2nd and 7th October, while they awaited their bread they moved along the left bank, followed by Berwick along the opposite bank until they reached the bend on which Ciudad Rodrigo lies. This, as it gave them a choice for the next move, forced on Berwick a difficult tactical decision, and it was just at this very moment that he received King Louis' personal letter of 21st September telling him that he was to be replaced in command. The timing could not have been worse, for the military situation was intensely critical and required the greatest attention and awareness.

Yet Louis could not help the fact that letters took about a couple of weeks from Versailles, nor could he know that the recipient would be in battle when it arrived. His letter is a masterpiece of gentleness, appreciation and firmness. As it helps to show why he was well served it is worth quoting in full:

'My cousin, affairs in Spain having become more difficult since the taking of Gibraltar and with the archduke and the King of Portugal strengthening themselves day by day with the succours sent them by the English and Dutch, it is impossible to keep the war going if those who have command of the army are not acting in perfect harmony and are not of the same sentiment. The equality [of status] between you, Villadarías and Prince Tzerclaes has been causing me disquiet. The King of Spain has reinforced this disquiet by telling me that what you are engaged in at this conjuncture is so important that it is necessary to have a general to command the captains-general. He has asked me to send a Marshal of France, saying that there will be no difficulty in his being obeyed. The way you have served me in that country, your probity, uprightness and your good conduct in everything have given me no reason to believe that the king, my grandson, should have any wish for a general who would suit him better than you. But he has nevertheless explained matters in such a way that I am obliged to recall you to France and send Marshal Tessé. You will go to Madrid at about the same time as he arrives and advise him of all that he needs to know. You will then come [here] to me and will receive every mark of the satisfaction I have in the service you have rendered and of the esteem which I have for you.'

However courteous the letter, even a strong-minded recipient might have been forgiven for voicing resentment and even for taking some action to show this. But Berwick apparently kept it almost completely to himself and continued to concentrate his efforts on foiling the expected Allied attack. In his *Memoirs* he did mention a person (unnamed) to whom he had shown Louis' letter and who advised him to attack the enemy, presumably to show Philip – and Louis – who was in charge of military matters. But, said Berwick, 'I did not think myself justified in honour and confidence to hazard improperly the general affairs for a private pique. It was sufficient for my reputation that I had thwarted the enemy in their grand design.' A despatch from Philip, also arriving at this time, authorised him to fight. He had thwarted but not defeated the enemy and he now had to cope with threats of crossing either above or below Ciudad Rodrigo, so

'Simply because I had to, I divided my army, half of it a full half league from the other half and with the town between them. I had 6,500 infantry and 3,000 horse and the enemy 18,000 foot and 4,000 horse, which made the splitting of the army the more dangerous, but I had to dispute the passage of the river, and this move was my only recourse. I placed my cavalry on a small height parallel to the river so that the enemy could not reconnoitre without driving our people off and this they hesitated to do. Two days after this I sent General de Thouy with 2,000 infantry and 1,000 horse towards their camp on my left. They edged their way cautiously and de Thouy added some pickets in support. [Meantime] I took 200 horse, and splitting them into ten troops to make them look more numerous edged along the ridge of the height as though to fall on the enemy flank. They halted and retreated.'

There is some confusion about the date of the next critical engagement. The Anglo-Portuguese reports place it on 7th October. In his *Memoirs* Berwick says it was on the 8th 'at first break of day'. His letter to King Louis is dated the 6th and reads as if it were written on the same day as the encounter. One to Chamillart dated 8th October refers to a delay in despatching because 'I was being attacked'. Berwick was under great stress at that moment and, quite understandably, he propably forgot which day was which. The most likely date is the 7th. The fullest account is in his *Memoirs*, the others being brief, breathless notes:

'As it was impossible to cross the Agueda above Ciudad Rodrigo except near the Abbey of La Caridad, where six squadrons could pass abreast, I supported the right of my infantry on this convent and extended the rest to a small house on high ground commanding the plain into which the enemy would debouch after they had passed the ford. The left wing of my cavalry I placed to the left in two lines and six squadrons with General de Geo-ffreville on an eminence still further to the left. These could fall on the enemy as soon as they attempted to form up on emerging from the water. I placed four cannon here and scattered the rest over ground with a good command of the river and the plain. The cavalry right was to the right of the Abbey and two regiments of dragoons were in reserve.'

At nine o'clock (not break of day) the English artillery train began to fire on the French entrenchments. (It was commanded by Colonel John Richards). But the cannon were silenced by the response from Berwick's guns. The Portuguese then drew nearer but were themselves driven back by the French guns. One report says this retreat came about because a cannon ball knocked away the upper part of the statue of St Anthony of Padua, which caused such alarm that the Portuguese could think only of flight. 'We were like this,' continues Berwick, 'until three or four in the evening. They they returned to their camp and I sent our troops to re-occupy the terrain they had left. I count on it that in a few days they will return to their own country because of shortage of supplies. Their convoys have to come via Alfagete for safety, a great detour.' The Allies withdrew completely at length on the 12th, reaching Almeida three days later. Here they stayed till the end of the month, when as the rains became continuous 'they separated entirely'.

It was only after this tense encounter that Berwick replied to Louis. Giving a brief account of the fight, he went on, 'I received you Majesty's letter after dinner yesterday [6th or 7th, see above] telling me to hand over to Marshal Tessé and to tell him everything he needs to know. I will execute this order most punctually and will thereafter come to France with diligence.' There was more vexation to put up with from Madrid. Berwick had been accused of meddling, but as he explained to Chamillart on 8th October, 'I did not write direct to the King of Spain suggesting he should come and be at the head of his troops, but only to Gramont, as I did not want to seem to be interfering in other people's business. I have enough to do with my own.' He also had his troubles with Tzerclaes who 'kept writing to Madrid that the enemy were about to fall on him'. He explained that his refusal to carry out orders from Rivas and Gramont was because he 'did not wish affairs to fall again into the same disorder as before. This is the reason for my recall, telling the truth! I am worried about my reputation and would be desperate if my conscience were not clear. I should much appreciate some public mark of King Louis' satisfaction so that my honour is not the victim of the incapacity of others...'

He may have been mollified, when it reached him, by a letter dated 8th October from his monarch approving all his military actions, saying that Tessé had left and assuring Berwick that he would be pleased with the job the king had in mind for him. 'I could not be more content with your services in the country where you are.'

By the 24th Berwick was on his way. Soon all the *tripotage* would be for Tessé to deal with. The latter was 'very much my friend' and it would not be fair for him not to be installed without a briefing. So Berwick went back to Madrid to await him.

Jean-Baptiste-Réné Mans de Froulay, Comte de Tessé, was now fifty-three, twenty years older than the man he was replacing. Following St Simon, many historians describe him as a lightweight. 'His sweetness of character and affability made him liked, while his frivolity and his stuffiness – often to be seen – made him little thought of.' But he had fought, from the age of seventeen, in Germany, the Netherlands and Ireland. Two years before, he had defended Mantua for six months until relieved by Vendôme. He had often been wounded, and had been made a Marshal of France in 1703. His memoirs are sprightly and Louis XIV thought well of him. Indeed, as will be seen, in his letters to his king and the king's ministers sometimes in his own hand, an impatient scribble, he did not hesitate to speak his mind, about Philip, about Spain, and about fellow-Frenchmen. He will be seen in action on a number of occasions and coping with the kind of problems which had beset Berwick, though with less patience.

Now, on his way to replace Berwick, Louis sent him on a detour to Toulouse in order to see Madame des Ursins who had decided to wait there while the political pack was shuffled, rather than go to Rome as ordered. In a letter to Louis dated 20th October, he described what must have been a somewhat uncomfortable interview with Madame, 'who has great influence with the Queen of Spain', and is full of protestations of loyalty to King Louis. He quotes her verbatim: 'If I am a criminal, then condemn me. If I am innocent, my pride demands justification.'

Making no recommendations, Tessé then moved on to Madrid, complaining of bad roads and worse horses. Here Berwick gave him what information was needed – he had heard from Louis, congratulating him on his action on the Agueda – and Tessé was also the recipient of a letter dated 31st October from Tzerclaes, at Badajoz. Berwick, said the panicky Belgian, 'has probably not given the full picture'; there was every sign that the enemy were about to attack Valencia de Alcántara. This, Berwick remarked robustly, was rubbish. Then he was off. Louis, meanwhile, acknowledged Tessé's letter about Madame des Ursins but said she 'has not given me any reason to be certain of her good intentions or of the zeal which she assured you she has for my service.'

Tessé, after only a couple of weeks, found the atmosphere at the Buen Retiro Palace 'with its cabals and confusions' even worse than he had been warned. He told Louis frankly, in a letter of 12th November, that Philip was 'almost incomprehensible. He is not precise in his words and is slow, almost lazy about taking decisions, and far too worried that the slightest mistake in a king is a crime.' The queen, he said, had an agreeable face and a taking manner, together with dignity. For her, Louis was 'the only person in the world she has a passion to please' and she spoke with tears in her eyes, saying she would never be consoled about the absence of Madame des Ursins. In the course of this audience she also showed her wilfulness. Tessé in his memoirs (Berwick quotes him), recorded that the Marshal naturally asked if the queen did not have reason to be satisfied with the campaigns Berwick had carried out, to which she replied that he was much esteemed and had rendered great services. To further questions she replied equally favourably. 'Then', asked Tessé, 'why did you have him recalled?' The answer was, 'What would you have me say to you? He is a great, dry devil of an Englishman who always goes on in his own way.'

Berwick's recall was thus due to a whim, and when he saw Louis at

Versailles in early December the king asked him why he though his grandson had requested the recall of so efficient a general. Sticking firmly to his avoidance of politics, Berwick answered, 'Since Your Majesty does not know the reason I am content, for it is evident that you are not dissatisfied with my conduct.'

Louis believed that Tessé and Gramont would work in harmony but it was only a few days before they were in disagreement, and Tessé was at army headquarters away from Madrid, sickened like Berwick by the intrigues. But the ambassador felt that in the absence of Madame des Ursins his job was to govern the king and queen. No doubt he told them of Louis' haughty reply about the *camerera mayor*'s removal: 'I determine everything myself and nobody should dare to suppose that the facts which I accept are contrary to the truth.'

Gramont had also been partly instrumental in the recall of Orry, and in a post-mortem on the fall of Gibraltar did not hesitate to blame him for that debacle. Gramont then changed his tactics. Instead of bullying María Luisa he tried flattery, begging her to use her influence with her husband. With a show of humility she asked 'how a girl of fifteen could presume to touch affairs of state?' At the same time she made sure behind the scenes that every transaction passed through her hands. She told Rivas, Gramont's creature at the head of the *Despacho*, that she placed no confidence in him, and she stirred up opposition in all quarters.

The luckless ambassador wrote unhappily to Versailles that the administration was in chaos, the intrigues of the Austrian faction growing, the army short of supplies, and suggested that Louis should write to the queen enlisting her help. Louis did so, praising her judgement, expressing affection and asking her to 'break her rule of not meddling in her husband's affairs'. This was only in part a pretence on Louis' part, for at this time he also wrote to Tessé that he had been pleasantly surprised by his descriptions of the queen. 'Her wit is well above her age and she has a great deal of power over the king and does much to help his government.'

She was not moved. As Tessé noted, 'she seems determined to lose her crown rather than fail to obtain the return of the Princess des Ursins'. In the end Louis realized that he would have to give way. He permitted Madame des Ursins to stay on in Toulouse rather than go to Rome, though he also wrote to María Luisa saying she must accept Gramont's advice in affairs of State. The ambassador's initial reaction was delight, and he wrote that 'the hydra's head has been cut off.' But in the face of the queen's intransigence and the favourite's charm, his position was untenable. Collecting the Order of the Golden Fleece as a parting gift from the king, he wrote to Paris asking permission to take his *congé* from Spain 'for reasons of health'. Louis found it necessary to offer the Princess des Ursins the choice of a new ambassador if she would return to Madrid. But she now said she was unwell and did not feel up to resuming her strenuous duties. It is possible that she had begun to form a preference for Versailles. Indeed, unkind rumours said that she was hoping to replace Madame de Maintenon in Louis' favours. But her reluctance was soon revealed as a ploy. She helped select a new ambassador, Amelot, later to be Comte de Gouray, a professional diplomat of humble origin, who had served Louis well in Venice, Lisbon and Switzerland. San Felipe describes him as 'a wise and prudent man, a former member of the Paris parliament and by no means ignorant. But as he was thrown abruptly into the management of a country he did not know, he at first did not act in keeping with what the Princess [des Ursins] intended, which was to place in his hands all the authority carried by the Spanish minsters.' He was to have, like his predecessors, a most difficult time of it. Then, too, with an abrupt change of mind, Louis sent Orry back, as Madame des Ursins had asked him to organise the royal finances.

Weeks later, having waited for winter to be over, the princess was on her way back to Madrid. Her return was a triumph. Six miles outside the city she was met in person by the king and queen who were only with difficulty prevented from committing the unthinkable solecism of taking her into their carriage. San Felipe says 'she was received by the monarchs with demonstrations never seen from a sovereign to a subject.'

By then it was July 1705, and in the meantime the situation in Spain had gone from bad to worse for the Bourbons. Gibraltar had fought off a siege and Barcelona was about to fall into Allied hands. It is time to take up the military thread again.

★   ★   ★

The seizure of Gibraltar in early August 1704 and the foiling of the naval attempt under Toulouse to recapture it later that month were major coups for the Allies,[4] but although Darmstadt considered it a springboard for advances into Spain the Allied hold on the Rock was most tenuous. The threat it offered to Andalucia was nothing like as great as was thought in Spain or France. Le Marié might fear far-ranging cavalry attacks and King Louis that the Allies might take and fortify Spanish cities against his grandson, but this was merely a reaction to a severe and unexpected blow. Darmstadt just did not have the strength to do more than hold on to the place and his ability to do even that was doubtful. He and his allies could not know of the chaos in the Madrid government, of the squabbles in high circles there, of the panic behind the dispatch of Villadarías and all the men he could gather to Algeciras, of Louis' plans to assist or of the deep affront which many Spaniards would feel when a Marshal of France and French troops were sent to help. Nor could they know of the impulse their victory had given to the raising of regiments in Spain – or of the ineffectiveness with which this policy was carried out.

As early as January 1704 there had been proposals for calling up numbers of men and many appointments of brigadiers, colonels and captains had been made, including that of Daniel O'Mahony as colonel of a regiment of Irish dragoons. But by May little or nothing had actually happened and correspondence was chiefly taken up with money difficulties or with relative minutiae such as an order that all cavalry officers were to provide their own mounts or a note from Berwick to de Thouy on the suitability of French horse in Spain. De Bay, to emphasize money problems, wrote from Badajoz (he was captain-general of the forces in Extremadura) giving his numbers (1,113 horses, 977 pistols and 1,104 sabres – and he is short of all these). The fall of Gibraltar goaded the authorities into speedier action. Regiments were named: La Reyna, Asturias, Hordena, Rosellon Viejo and Neuvo, Milan, Santiago, Montenegro and so forth. But still, although numbers called to the colours increased, the administration continued to lumber and creak, and training took time, so that little enough could be done about Gibraltar itself straight away. Much of the time the defenders were heavily out-numbered and knew it. What they did not know was how appallingly difficult their opponents were finding the operation, or how the use by Leake of sea power to keep supplies arriving at the Rock depressed the spirits of the besiegers, dampened as they were in any case by the terrible weather which persisted for weeks.

A near-contemporary engraving, made in 1713, gives a clear picture of what the place looked like when Darmstadt, meagrely supplied and with a tiny garrison – even including the men Rooke had left with him – set to in mid-August to put the crumbling defences, not notably improved by Byng's bombardment, into some sort of order. He knew that there must soon be an attempt to recapture the Rock, and indeed the forward elements of the siege army were already on their way.

Looking towards Spain, the Landport curtain wall ran from the Old Mole, where there was a battery, eastwards up the hillside, to part of the old Moorish citadel. Two hundred yards in advance of this was another but weaker wall running from the north face of the Rock to the Round Tower. A trench called the King's Lines connected the Round Tower with the Landport wall.

Darmstadt placed a light battery on the edge of the precipice above so as to provide plunging fire on any attacker reaching the advanced wall, and cobbled together the rest of the landward defences as best he could. It was recorded that,

> 'He spent all his days in the works and most part of his nights in the Covertway. He was the soul of the garrison and scarce ever allowed himself two hours of continual rest either by day or night ... discharging at once the different parts of general, soldier, engineer, gunner, carpenter and pioneer which was a mighty encouragement to the officers to do their respective duties.'

As well as his letters, a diary of the siege gives an account of his problems and of how he kept up morale in the motley garrison. Leake's sailors were paid one *real* (then 3d) for daywork and two for nightwork and there were of course arguments about overtime. Marines were hardy and adaptable though discontented. Regular troops were less willing though the Dutch were more amenable than the English. But all had to be alert all the time as well as to maintain walls, batteries, mines and guns and to bring up shot and powder. Darmstadt insisted on feeding the men as well as he could and providing drink and money. And he was well supported by Admiral van der Dussen (when later there), by the Dutch Colonel Tullekens and by Zinzerling. He flooded Schonenberg and Lichtenstein with appeals and kept up a brisk correspondence with Leake and Galway. As well as what could be sent from Lisbon he obtained food and drink from Morocco and the Algarve by his feluccas as well as from passing naval and merchant vessels. He kept open house for his officers, offering wine and brandy – though he complained that the English officers were eating him out of house and home. All this cost him about 8,000 dollars a month – he had also to keep his Lisbon staff going and the Catalans, Spaniards and others who had come with him, and as the weeks wore on, to increase bonuses for special jobs and daily payments.

He had little cash and was in debt when he started, the 12,000 crowns provided by the emperor being long since exhausted. But he was able to make money on the side by trading goods brought in by felucca. He got part of the money promised by the Portuguese and as the English and Dutch had so far paid nothing he made no bones about drawing on their account. Captain Fotherby of H.M.S. *Lark* lent 5,000 dollars, to be charged to ambassador Methuen – who later found he had to settle a large number of bills. (Although grumbling, he did so.) So, with captured sugar from Martinique, fish from Newfoundland, wine and brandy from across the Straits, the prince encouraged the work of the siege.

Encouragement was needed. By November the Round Tower was in ruins and the main wall full of gaps and as winter came in it was found that the winds made the moles and the roadstead unsafe for ships. Easterly winds could gust up and carry away masts and westerly winds meant movement out into the Bay and a threat there from enemy guns. The garrison itself was small. Parnell gives a figure of 2,442 initially: 1,900 English marines under Colonel (Acting-Brigadier) Henry Fox, who had been at Cadiz and Vigo, with Lieutenant-Colonel Jacob Borr as second-in-command; 72 English seamen, 400 Dutch marines and 70 Catalans and some Spaniards. The number of Catalans may however have been 250 or more, since some had joined the prince after his brief landing near Barcelona. They and the few local inhabitants capable of bearing arms were under the command of Darmstadt's brother, Prince Henry, and the Valencian Colonel Basset y Ramos. They almost certainly manned the battery at the *Salto del Lobo* (Wolf's Leap), which is still called the Catalan Guard, and equally probably took part in the defence of the city walls.

There was frequent disasaffection within the garrison. Well might the prince write to his master, 'I am surrounded with enemies within and without but hope that God will bring me through it all.' There is something warming about his simple, faithful, convert's optimism. Yet he was not out of reach of material assistance. Leake had been detached by Rooke at Lisbon two hundred miles away with a winter squadron and was due to be joined by Rear-Admiral van der Dussen and a small Dutch contingent. Almost all the vessels needed careening to clean their bottoms of weed and some needed other repairs, but they were there.

Leake's instructions from Rooke were manifold: To provide convoys for merchantmen going to England and to 'annoy the enemy' and guard the coasts of Portugal and Spain. But above all he was 'to keep always some clean ships to cruise off that place [Gibraltar] to discover the enemy's ships'. If the King of Portugal did not relieve the garrison within three months Leake was to supply it with provisions and as soon as it was relieved he was to take as many marines as he needed and send the rest back to England. Rooke had asked King Charles and King Pedro to undertake the garrisoning, but not surprisingly nothing had been done and the Admiralty now advised Leake that the Queen's Government had decided to take on the responsibility.

Little has been written for a couple of centuries about Sir John Leake. His principal biography was published in 1750 in a limited edition of 50 for the Leake family, It was written by his nephew and godson, Stephen Martin-Leake, Garter King-at-Arms, and is inevitably rather biased. The 1920 reprint was edited by Geoffrey Callender, who although critical, generally accepts the author's views and attributes the relative obscurity surrounding Leake to four factors: the admiral's personal modesty: the 'pan-Churchill cult': the 'Peterborough tradition' and the 'Stanhope myth'. Of the last two figures we shall see something in the course of this study, and Marlborough inevitably dominates the scene, overshadowing all others.

Of the admiral's modesty there is no doubt. A most self-effacing man, he had turned down the post of Master-Gunner of England which his father had held. He had twice refused a knighthood, only accepting when Queen Anne insisted, for fear of offending her. When Prince George of Denmark died, Leake would carry out the duties of Lord High Admiral but refuse the title and perquisites. He would refuse any imperial marks of gratitude for his work in the Mediterranean and decline an English earldom at the end of his active career. He was the antithesis of Peterborough (with whom he would serve in 1705 and 1706), and he would probably have regarded Nelson as a publicity-seeker. He was now nearly fifty, stocky, and 'of full habit of body', his face open and florid. His eyes, under a broad forehead and thick eyebrows were described as 'proving', and he always spoke his mind, avoiding hair-splitting. At meetings he would listen while something was declared impractical and then, after agreeing that it was so, would seek means nevertheless of making it work. He was always plainly dressed, disliking 'pretty fellows with Steinkirk cravats, buckram-lined coats and waistcoats smelling of bergamot', and he normally stood with his feet apart, a habit which comes to sailors.

Velez Málaga had destroyed any possibility of a full-scale naval expedition to recapture the Rock and it was now a matter of a formal siege from the landward with supplies and if possible troop reinforcements to be provided by sea. The disgrace of losing that tiny but symbolically important scrap of land was so keenly felt throughout Spain that its recapture by Spanish forces was a matter of honour. Having lost it themselves they were fiercely anxious to recapture it themselves.

The general closest to Gibraltar was Villadarías, Captain-General of Andalucia who had at once been ordered to march there with 8,000 men. His advance guard of 600 cavalry and 500 foot arrived on 24th August and began to prepare for operations, and he himself with the main body was eventually in place by 3rd September. He had three Spanish lieutenant-generals, de Ossuna, de Aguilar and de Alvarez and his considerable siege train of 40 guns and twelve mortars was commanded by Don Bernardo Renaud Eligazarai. He was *in situ* before Rooke had even sailed for home, and he was intent on retaking the place before any major assistance could arrive from his domineering allies.

Although under no illusions as to the difficulties, he felt fairly confident, but to fail would be a further bitter blow and his anxieties show in the voluminous correspondence with which he bombarded Madrid. For the next seven months he wrote daily, at great length and sometimes four or five times a day, and his scores of letters in the Madrid *Archivo* are fascinating reading. He used over and over again the phrase, 'Divine mercy will aid us in the recovery of this place.' As the months passed, and the unusual weather drenched him and his men, the defending batteries repeatedly damaged the walls of crumbling trenches dug in the sand, and men were killed, went sick or deserted, this phrase became almost an incantation until at the end he even gave up this refrain in his disappointment.

After the main French fleet had slunk back to Toulon, King Louis had ordered the fitting out of a squadron, not to challenge the Allied fleet but to convoy French troops and material to assist Villadarías. This squadron, consisting of fourteen ships-of-the-line, seventeen frigates and a large number of transports, was commanded by Rear-Admiral Jean Bernard, Baron de Pointis, aged fifty-nine and although a reasonably steady seaman, somewhat lacking in drive.

By 21st September the convoy was at Málaga, where de Pointis in the *Magnanime* wrote to the governor apologizing for not paying his respects, owing to the bad weather which had already set in. He also wrote a memorandum on his intentions about disembarking troops and supplies at Gibraltar. He was supposed to land 3,000 marines, 500 seamen-gunners and 500 cavalry together with quantities of material, but he now considered that the most he could manage would be a total of about 2,000 men. He was worried about the distance he would be offshore, and that he was short of boats, which would delay matters. Moreover, the bad weather might persist, and he was himself also short of food. He would therefore put the men on half-rations and instead of their daily allowance of a pint of wine they would be given a *chopine* (a pint mug) of wine and water half-and-half 'in order to avoid the disorder and drunkenness which would be inevitable'.

The convoy reached Gibraltar Bay on 4th October and had discharged by the 8th, before sailing swiftly to Cadiz where de Pointis' orders were to wait and intercept Allied supplies sent from Lisbon to the Rock. Also landed was an engineer, Colonel Richards, and a few frigates were left in Gibraltar Bay for communications. Had de Pointis but known it, he might have taken Gibraltar. Darmstadt, tense with excitement, was relieved when he saw the squadron sail away. The Bourbons had missed a great chance.

De Pointis and Villadarías did not work well together. Even allowing for the vagaries of the sea the admiral appears to have been lethargic. When later taxed by the general with letting some Allied vessels pass he said he had been becalmed at Rota near Cadiz, and asked how many vessels were involved. To this Villadarías replied snappishly,

'You know better than I that some four warships of 50 or 60 guns and 22 merchant vessels came from England with the wind, whereas you at the same time were becalmed. It is a further proof of our misfortune that the enemy is favoured by the wind. We must have recourse to heaven and implore help from there.'

In all, as Villadarías began the siege in earnest, he had about 11,000 men facing a garrison of just over 2,400. As soon as de Pointis arrived, Darmstadt sent by his private felucca to Lagos for onward transmission – with a copy by the frigate H.M.S. *Lark* (Captain Fotherby) – a vibrant letter to Leake telling him the news and going on, 'I desire the favour of you to . . . make all the speed you can and as you shall judge most proper for the public service and the relief of this place.'

No doubt Leake wished to respond at once with aid, but his squadron had only just arrived in Lisbon, was incomplete and still in poor condition, and neither reinforcements nor supplies could as yet reach him from England. On 30th September the *Tiger*, one of the few 'clean' ships had arrived from scouting off Gibraltar to report an enemy squadron near the Rock. Galway from army headquarters reported that French army prisoners had said the whole French fleet under the Comte de Toulouse was besieging Gibraltar. Dutch privateers reported 13 enemy sail-of-the-line off Ceuta.

Of Leake's ships his flagship, the *Nottingham*, was having all her lower masts shifted, the *Panther* and *Centurion* some of theirs. The *Leopard*, *Antelope* and *Roebuck* were unrigged and careening. He had shifted his flag temporarily to the tiny *Swallow*, and then to the more commodious *Yarmouth*. The *Swiftsure*, *Monck*, *Assurance* and *Vulture* (fireship) were available but insufficient. And van der Dussen and his five ships were still on their way with a convoy from England.

The Portuguese dockyards were lackadaisical. Even gunners' stores were short in his ships – 'not 25 rounds of shot per gun nor 10 cartridges'. With help from the Methuens he obtained 200 barrels of gunpowder, barely sufficient for one broadside for the squadron, but shot had to come from England. He wrote to Their Lordships 'acquainting them of the vigorous proceedings of the enemy' and of his shortages. But the Admiralty had anticipated his problems, at least in part, and ten days before they could have had his despatch, the *Pembroke* and *Canterbury* arrived with instructions permitting him to keep the four and the new arrivals to replace his two worst ships which were to be sailed home. Four months' supplies for Gibraltar were on the way.

For the meantime he sent the *Leopard* to scout between Oporto and the Burling Islands and the *Antelope*, newly careened, and the *Tiger* to the Straits, taking with them some provisions for Gibraltar to be 'thrown into that place should opportunity offer.' If these two should gain any intelligence, *Antelope* should remain off Cape Spartel while *Tiger* brought back the news. In the event they parted company and went prowling, one turning up later with a Spanish prize laden with wine and brandy and the other with two French prizes inward bound from Newfoundland. Leake sent the *Antelope* off again in company with the *Roebuck* in the same search for intelligence, the former also to deliver a letter to Darmstadt:

> 'I am making all possible dispatch to get the ships of my squadron ready for service and have detained the four ships which were under orders for England to strengthen us, so that when the convoy arrives from England, which is expected every minute. I hope to be in a condition to see Your Highness at Gibraltar. But if I should be so unfortunate as not to be in a condition before the garrison is straitened for provisions, I will find some way to push in a ship in the night with provisions, and in order thereunto am loading one which sails very well, so that if the guard upon the New Mole should discover in the night a ship approaching that place, with four lights placed where they may best be seen, they may be sure they are friends.'

Darmstadt was under severe stress, like everyone else, for it was now that he wrote to Charles about the first of at least two plots. A Spaniard had been caught communicating with the enemy. He was tortured and confessed and although priests persuaded him to take everything back, he was hanged. A Colonel González and a (probably Huguenot) Colonel d'Husson, together with some friars were named as principals, but for lack of evidence all Darmstadt could do was keep an eye on them. Confrontation might do more harm than good. Charles, who had now moved to Belém and was frustrated by lack of action, wrote through Lichtenstein advising a court-martial with 'independent' members of Court and punishment with both 'severity and clemency', but there the matter rested until later in December.

An indication of the tension under which Leake was working is given by a quarrel he now had with ambassador Methuen. Just before Velez Málaga Leake had complained that the Dutch ambassador seemed more successful than Methuen at getting supplies from the Portuguese. Now there was an argument between them about the French prisoners taken by the *Antelope* and *Tiger* who were still under guard aboard and, in the crowded little ships, were suffering from sickness. This term probably covered everything from scurvy and the pox to yellow fever contracted in the West Indies, and Leake, anxious to protect his crews, wished to put all the prisoners ashore, saying 'he should never consent to make Her Majesty's ships gaols, to the prejudice of his own men'. Methuen said they should remain on board but Leake won the argument.

It was not until 30th October that van der Dussen arrived with the convoy from England and Leake could think of sailing for Gibraltar. It was just in time. On November 2nd a letter from Darmstadt advised that the French squadron had beaten away to windward leaving six frigates offshore and that the enemy appeared to be about to begin the siege.

According to published Spanish accounts Villadarías was disturbed at even the small amount of supplies the garrison had received. He pressed on with siege works amid what an anonymous diary (preserved in an unpublished letter of Gramont's) called, 'terrible wind and rain ... it is to be hoped that the hurricanes do not finish us off'. The trenches were of sand, vulnerable to rain and gunfire alike. Villadarías' own letters bear this out, though he was at this time not unconfident. On 29th October he reported, 'A breach has been opened and I hope we shall have a favourable success ... God willing we shall succeed.' By 2nd November, however, he was less sanguine. Rivas in Madrid was nagging him about slow progress and he replied, 'We are doing all we humanly can with the forces available to us ... There are many flights and desertions, so much so that I have to place armed horsemen on the roads and offer three pesos for any deserter they catch.' Even this had so far had little result so he now felt that 'the only remedy is dire punishment. Perpetual service in the galleys is the only answer.'

On November 3rd: 'Rains are falling more heavily than I have ever experienced.' On November 4th: 'Money is now causing me great loss of sleep.' On 6th November he wrote, 'I am doing all I can to obtain the surrender of Gibraltar before the enemy can receive succour ... Last night in trying to hasten the construction of batteries we made such a noise that the enemy must have [even] heard the hammering of our carpenters.' On November 8th and 9th: 'Firing with a battery of thirty pieces is breaching the ramparts and the curtain wall', but he was beginning to be short of supplies. On the 11th he made a complaint about the poor quality of his troops and of the appalling weather, wind and rain. From now on the tone of the Marqués' letters becomes almost uniformly despondent.

*　　*　　*

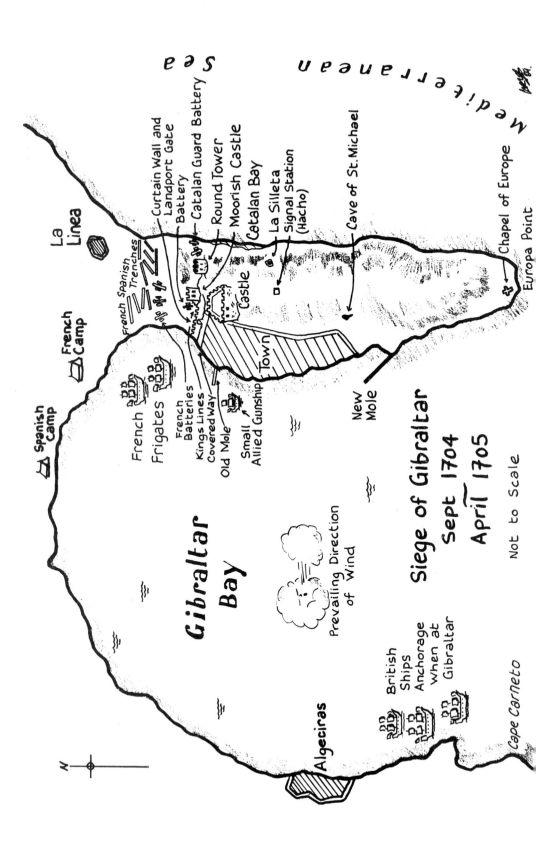

Mediterranean Sea

La Linea

French Spanish Trenches

French Camp

Spanish Camp

Curtain Wall and Landport Gate
Battery
Catalan Guard Battery
Round Tower
Moorish Castle
Catalan Bay
La Silleta
Signal Station
(Hacho)

Cave of St. Michael

Chapel of Europe
Europa Point

French Frigates

French Batteries
Kings Lines Covered Way
Old Mole
Small Allied Gunship

Castle

Town

New Mole

N

Gibraltar Bay

Prevailing Direction of Wind

Siege of Gibraltar
Sept 1704
April 1705

Not to Scale

British Ships
Anchorage when at Gibraltar

Algeciras

Cape Carneto

Meanwhile, immediately on receipt of Darmstadt's letter, Leake held a council of war on Saturday, 3rd November, and it was agreed that even if not enough powder was available the squadron should sail on the 5th. In the event, his flotilla left on the Tuesday. In order not to be recognized Leake struck his colours off Cape Spartel and then ordered all the 'clean' ships to sail on ahead in order to trap any French vessels. Of those left by de Pointis only one frigate, *l'Etoile*, escaped temporarily, to be chased and captured by the *Swallow*. The rest were run ashore and set on fire by their crews.

Leake had arrived in the nick of time, in appalling weather it is true, but the naval service is accustomed to that. Renaud Eligazarai's batteries were making only slow progress but Darmstadt had lost many men and of those still alive many were sick. On the other side, Renaud said, 'Had this fleet not arrived we would have gone ahead, though desertion and sickness were reducing our numbers whereas the Allied fleet is supplying gunners and workmen.' He hoped for an attack on this fleet by the squadron at Cadiz. As far as the Franco-Spanish force was concerned, 'it is a terrible problem to get the men to be active. The fresh troops who have arrived are untrained and the marines, although they may be all right at sea are not suited to this work.'

The Marqués knew that if he did not succeed he would be supplanted or put under the command of a Frenchman. He felt he had to do something and he therefore planned a pincer movement. He had already considered 'going up the hill' on 23rd October. Now he collected 3,000 men whom he intended to land at the New Mole to the south of the town and at Europa Point, synchronising this with an assault on the breach in the Landport curtain while at the same time 1,500 men would attack over the steep eastern side of the Rock where the defenders would be off their guard. The uphill assault was intended for the night of November 10th but was postponed until the 11th, the Allies being kept occupied by bombardment from a battery of 50 guns and 12 mortars. Captain Bennet, just arrived, was much impressed.

On further consideration, Leake's presence made it necessary to abandon the amphibious plan but at nightfall on the 11th the recently promoted Colonel de Figueroa led an advance party of 500 Spaniards forward to scale the eastern face, so as to attack Darmstadt's uphill battery. A Gibraltese goat-herd, Simon Susarte showed them an almost unknown track which led to the summit. Using ropes the party reached a place called *La Silleta* (the Little Saddle) halfway between the southern end of the ridge and the centre and descended to the Cave of St. Michael just below, facing west. Here they awaited in hiding the arrival of the main body of 1,000.

They waited in vain, for it never came. Left on their own and with nothing to eat, Figueroa's men lost their nerve and choosing surrender rather than starvation quitted their hiding place. It is probable that they were first spotted by the Catalan Guard in the battery at the *Salto del Lobo*, when they reached a signal station called the *Hacho* an hour before daylight. Darmstadt sent Colonel Borr with 500 marines, accompanied by Prince Henry and some 300 Grenadiers with Catalan support to attack them. There was a brisk engagement in the course of which the prince was wounded in the shoulder, some 200 Spaniards were thought to have been killed and 190 were captured, including the colonel and 35 officers.

Darmstadt wished to follow up the successful scrap on the mountain with a sortie against the trenches but Leake had too few men to help. For Leake there was the gnawing anxiety of de Pointis' intentions. A merchant ship reported sighting sixteen ships at Cadiz and two English prisoners-of-war escaped from there reported that de Pointis was preparing to sail. A Spanish deserter from Villadarías' forces told Darmstadt that his opponents were beginning to think that only an attack by de Pointis would serve to recapture the Rock and that 1,000 French marines had been withdrawn from the assault force and sent to Cadiz for this purpose. He also said that the French and Spanish besiegers were at each others' throats and only kept apart by threats of punishment. A hand-drawn map in the Vincennes *Depôt de Guerre* shows the French and Spanish encampments as separated, the former being a few hundred yards from the siege lines.

Leake's scouting frigates kept watch outside Cadiz and Tangier and to the east of the Rock and he kept getting reports confirming de Pointis' growing readiness. On the 30th he moved his squadron to Point Carneto on the west side of the Bay from which he kept up his feinted landings night and day. Then on December 4th an easterly gale sprang up. Leake's flagship, the *Nottingham* and several Dutch ships lost their anchors and cables and the *Panther* was nearly driven ashore. Leake, seriously worried about his ships' safety, proposed to stand well off to the west.

At a combined council of war, Darmstadt and the soldiers begged him not to. Although the enemy's rate of firing had diminished, the garrison was now down to 900 fit men.

Heavy rains had now begun again and the discomfort of the besiegers markedly increased. At least the defenders had solid quarters to return to between spells in the line and although Villadarías' bombardment continued unabated, the relatively low power of early eighteenth century explosive – it was only gunpowder and the projectiles were largely solid roundshot – meant that well-built structures could take a lot of punishment.

For the Spaniards and French (more of whom were beginning to arrive) it was far worse. War and heavy rain are both a source of mess and disorder. When they come together as they now did in the Bourbon encampments the result is a multiplication not a simple addition. Rain washed away the sandy covering of unquiet corpses and turned the primitive latrines into foetid ponds. Late-season flies busily carried infection from these to camp kitchens, hospital tents, messes and sleeping quarters.

Food was short, the task of maintaining the siegeworks heavy, and clothes and boots were not available. On November 29th Villadarías complained that 2,000 pairs of boots and 2,000 shirts he had ordered had never arrived. There was no uniform available even for the highborn Colonel Marqués de Paterna Zal de Sevilla. Only 98 sets of uniform had been sent. He had hoped for 1,895 soldiers and 180 officers as reinforcements, but there was as yet no sign. He gave an analysis in detail of his present strength. He had begun with 8,294 men, including militia and was now down to 3,774 in spite of de Pointis' contribution. Battalion ration strength was 100–130 men and 30 officers, about one-fifth of what it should be.

Recruitment was a nightmare.

'The recruits arriving are useless or else recaptured deserters, mostly the former. When I reprimand the officers who bring them in they say they have been told to bring in any kind of person (and those unarmed, naked, unshod and without even hose) ... Yesterday (November 30th) there arrived a few infantry captains with 59 men of whom 30 were deserters and 16 quite useless, being mere boys. The trenches are inundated ... I have ordered them to be made wider as otherwise we lose people in them ... The enemy bombardment knocks the trench walls in. Last night (December 11th) we had 20 men killed and wounded ... Only Divine mercy can help ... 160 recruits have come in. They are fit for nothing but to work as labourers – to which I have put them.'

Every now and then a deserter from the garrison provided him with news, some encouraging, some not. He heard that Nugent (Val de Soto) had been mortally wounded, together with many others, including Prince Henry of Hesse-Darmstadt and that things were bad for the Allies. On the other hand an Anglo-Dutch fleet was reported to have arrived in Portugal early in December.

This was accurate, for on 14th December the first genuine news arrived in Gibraltar with a vessel from Lisbon carrying three experienced officers, the Scotsman Colonel Lundy, and Lieut.-Colonels Rieutort and d'Harcourt, sent by Galway to assist Darmstadt.

In a letter brought by them Methuen advised Leake that Galway had been impressed by Leake's and Bennet's representations and was now embarking 2,500 of the 3,000 fresh troops sent from England. These, under the command of Brigadier-General John Shrimpton of the 1st Foot Guards, with Lord Donegal as second-in-command, were a battalion each of the Guards, Donegal's, and Barrymore's, and a Dutch contingent of 400 under Colonel Waes, and they were due to sail at once. The Dutch contribution was due to van der Dussen's strong representations to Schonenberg and Fagel. The Portuguese proposed 500 whom Galway intended to place under his Huguenot friend Montandré, a naturalised British citizen, but they were apparently not ready in time.

The wind had by now swung to the west and Leake would have difficulty in beating to sea if he were needed to rescue the Lisbon-Gibraltar convoy from a grab by de Pointis from Cadiz.

On 10th December the convoy left the Tagus, escorted by four frigates *Antelope* (Captain Legge), *Roebuck*, *Newcastle* and *Greenwich*. On the 17th off Cape Spartel they sighted a squadron of 22 ships. Believing them to be Leake's, Legge ran towards them under a light wind, making a private recognition signal. Upon this they struck the Allied colours, hoisted the French and put on all sail to attack in a crescent formation. It was de Pointis' squadron.

A fresh breeze from the south-west enabled Legge and some of the convoy to escape southwards – one transport being captured. The *Roebuck* and four transports ran for Lisbon, but on the 18th the *Antelope* and nine transports reached Gibraltar, followed two days later by the *Newcastle* and seven more. The *Roebuck* was commanded by Captain Kempthorne and it was only by using sweeps and towing with ships' boats that they were able to catch the wind and get away from the enemy. Their return to Lisbon caused much alarm there. On the 24th the *Greenwich* arrived at Gibraltar with another company of Donegal's and on the 25th the weather at last permitted Leake to return close in to the Rock. It was agreed between him and Darmstadt that he should sail for Lisbon to refit and revictual on January 3rd 1705, for although the garrison was now much stronger it was considered nearly certain that there would be further attacks and that the winter squadron's help would again be needed.

Faced with the need to find a replacement for Nugent (Val de Soto) as governor and aware of the adverse reception which had greeted his appointement, Darmstadt now proposed to Charles III that Shrimpton, with whom he considered he would get on well, should be 'Governor and General of this fortress so that we may all go towards the same goal'.

Since there was an objection from London, 'the queen not dreaming for a moment that the civil power should be in the hands of any subject of hers', Darmstadt therefore retained his powers as representative of Charles III in overall military and civil control, giving Shrimpton a commission as Major-General in Charles III's service. This strongly suggests that at least at this stage England was not claiming sovereignty over Gibraltar.

Heartened by the reinforcements and by letters of encouragement from Lisbon and driven by his natural aggressiveness, Darmstadt now began making sorties, levelling trenches and burning the fascines, gabions and other wooden assault equipment of the besiegers. Meantime Renaud, short of ammunition, ceased firing his large battery and reduced the rate of fire of the others.

On 23rd December a sortie 170 yards from the palisades caused considerable destruction and Leake returned temporarily two days later. His council of war vetoed a landing but he agreed to remain for a little while though he had to send to Lisbon for supplies. He did however arrange for three frigates to go to Morocco for supplies, two of them to remain afterwards at Gibraltar and said he would fetch the 1,500 Portuguese from Lagos as soon as he had sufficient ships careened. On 31st December a major sortie of 400 men drove the Spaniards and French out of their lines at a cost of 35 casualties including six officers.

Captain Bennett gives a breathless impression of what life was like in Gibraltar that Christmas time:

'When the fleet left us the Enemy had a design to make a general Assault and only wanted to know if our Mines was charged, but the Messenger they sent was taken by the Centry [sic] and so the Marquis of Villideras [sic] did not think fit to put his design into execution, however we had our whole garrison at arms on the Breaches night and day and hourly expected an Attack and all our fear was for our succours in Portugall ... By what Providence I know not, we had 2,200 good men landed a Day after, the rest were either taken or gone back, but a Drummer which return'd from the Enemy's camp who was sent by us says: that the Enemy report they have got 11 companys of Lord Barramors [sic] Regt, three of Donegall's, six of the Dutch and 200 Recruites. We shall endeavour to have them exchanged for the Prisoners we have ...

The next day after we got our succours we made a sally with 200 men and into the new works Broughth [sic] near us and only had 4 men killed and eight wounded. To revenge which the Enemy next day fired the

Facines at the Round Tower by two men we thought were Deserters and so returned safe. I am afraid of having the whole Line of Communication burnt and no other remedy than to fling stones and what else we could get to put it out and during all the Enemy fired furiously with their cannon and small shot at our men and as we had many high rocks hanging over us their Ball did great damage in breaking the stones and I have received many wounds by it on the face and head, but none of any danger excepting my Eye cut, hope it will be well soon.

The enemy has flung no Bombs into the Town these 5 or 6 days but formerly sent over 170 or 180 in a night, we believe it is for want of powder. Their cannon by often firing are almost spoiled and many of their vents so large they have no force to send their Balls. We hear that there is not above 2,500 French left and 800 Walloons and about 5,000 Spaniards, the rest are destroyed or died of drinking new wine and the great fatigues; by their securing the front of their Batterys we believe they will turn the siege into a Blockade ... Our fleet sails to-morrow for Lisbon, I have nothing to tell you only that I have enjoyed great fatigues and for this six weeks never went to bed a night.'

Since the garrison had been increased by nearly 200% of effectives while the besieging force had been reduced in fact to 3,700 by sickness and casualties, there was, at the turn of the year, a perceptible shift in the balance towards the Allies.

Tessé wrote to the Prince de Condé that the English maintained them-selves at sea as easily as 'your swans at Chantilly'. By the 1st January 1705 so little progress had been made that King Philip decided to make a new effort to 'bring this place, which is so important, under his obedience', and sent orders to the Baron de Pointis to close the Straits with a squadron to prevent supplies reaching Gibraltar for a long siege.' Again, on 4th January 1705, he wrote to Tessé on his gold-edged paper, asking him to send every man he can spare to Gibraltar. 'Our only aim must be towards recovering it, and as far as all the rest is concerned we must remain on the defensive. Once we have got this thorn out of our foot we shall be in a better position to attack Portugal.' King Louis was equally deter-mined not to let the Allies gobble up this 'terrible morsel'. 'You know how important it is,' he wrote to Tessé on 15th January, 'to make ourselves masters of Gibraltar and the inconvenience caused if it remains in enemy hands.'

In London where public interest in Gibraltar was now also intense, although news took weeks to get through by sea in winter weather, there was optimism. The *Newsletter* of 3rd March declared, 'The government is as resolute to preserve Gibraltar as the Spanish court is to take it.' And that resolution had already been clearly indicated by a vote in the Commons for supplies for 40,000 seamen and 8,000 marines for 1705, plus £100,000 for the 'ordinary' and £40,000 for the ordinance stores of the Navy.

There was thus determination on both sides. This was flawed on the Franco-Spanish side by indecision, by the continuing court factions (it was in January 1705 that Gramont advised Philip and María Luisa of Louis' decision to allow Madame des Ursins' return), by perennial shortage of money, and by differences at all levels between French and Spanish soldiers. Tessé, indeed, complained that the Frenchmen he was sending to the Gibraltar front were being delayed by the Spaniards, who having themselves lost the place did not relish its being recovered by their allies. On the Allied side there was relative harmony at higher levels, though Darmstadt and Shrimpton would later fall out, but the technical difficulties of reinforcements and supply were still of major importance.

In the third week of January the balance tipped again with the arrival of General de Thouy and 4,000 men, mostly French, to strengthen the besieging force. With him also arrived the news that Tessé was coming to take over the higher command. Villadarías' pique was such that he decided on a further assault before Tessé arrived. His engineers had pushed forward to within 10 yards of the Round Tower and made a breach in it wide enough for 30 men abreast, while there was also a 'practicable' breach in the curtain wall. A reconnaissance of the Round Tower by 50 men on February 2nd had been driven off with some loss but, as Villars et Lugein reports on the 7th ('let me tell you what has happened today'), Villadarías ordered a concerted attack 'on his own responsibility'. It was timed, according to the Allied report, for dawn when the Allied night guard of three officers and 60 men was relieved by the smaller day guard of one subaltern and 30 men.

The Allied guard was uphill, while the Round Tower was held by Colonel Borr and 240 men. During the night of the 6th Villadarías sent about 300 grenadiers up the hill in front of the wall to hide and wait till dawn. He sent six companies (600 men) of grenadiers and 100 dragoons from O'Mahony's regiment on foot into the approach trenches. The infantry in the rear, according to English reports, were Spanish and numbered about 1,000. Villars et Lugein described sacks of earth, gabions, fascines, and powder and ball being sent forward for distribution. The whole force was under de Thouy's command.

At dawn, at a signal 'of three bombs together' the grenadiers of the left assaulted from uphill and those on the right also went in. The French account says, 'The besieged held fire and waited for our grenadiers before opening heavy fire'. It was however less calculated than this according to Brigadier-General Shrimpton in his report to Marlborough. The assailants came 'over the hill as far as the Fort Gun Battery forty paces from the Castle breach which [was] very easy to enter and the last opposition on that side' (the Allied right). It was not a question of 'holding fire'. The Allied reserves had been asleep and had only just been wakened by the three bombs going off. They were still mustering, half-dressed, fumbling for their arms, and probably still half asleep, for they had been through an exhausting few weeks.

But the way was not open to the attackers from uphill. A small detachment of seventeen men of Seymour's (The Queen's) Marines was there under a Captain Fisher and their presence held up the French grenadiers' advance for a few minutes, just long enough for the rest of the defenders to come up. Fisher was overpowered, wounded and taken prisoner with his men.

'The grenadiers on the left', says Villars et Lugein, 'pushed them back following their retreat as far as the Communication Trench' (the King's Lines). Attacked from above with rocks and grenades and with his rear threatened, Borr retreated, climbing with his men inside the Landport curtain. 'This helped the attack lower down which was vigorously pushed by the Spaniards,' Villars et Lugein continues.

But by now 500 of the Guards and others, including twenty grenadiers of the 2nd Guards with Lieutenant-Colonel Rivett and under command of the Huguenot Colonel Moncal, came forward. Some approached the scene from the town, lower down, and others uphill from the covert way, which for some reason the assailants had not attacked.

There was then a sharp struggle, lasting perhaps ten minutes in the dim light, men slithering and grappling and stabbing on the damp limestone, while, according to the French account, there was 'half an hour's continuous firing, cannon, musketry and even stones thrown on flank and front. The grenadiers having lost almost all their officers began to break and it was impossible to stop them.

The garrison pushed them back through the Fort Gun Battery, through the King's Lines and through the Round Tower, which had been occupied by them for less than an hour, 'The enemy', says the French report, 'then put up their flags and opened heavy fire to which our artillery responded'.

Villadarías' attack had penetrated to within forty paces of the breach before Moncal's and Rivett's stand, but had not been carried through because the 1,000 supporting troops failed to come up. Had they done so it is possible that Gibraltar might have been taken. The Bourbons, despite further desperate attempts would hereafter never come nearer to success. 'Villadarías', says Villars et Lugein, 'had meant to send the men in again and had even given orders for this but de Thouy made him understand that he [de Thouy] was responsible for King Louis' troops. Fire ceased for one and a half hours to enable the dead and wounded to be removed. Thereafter there was no further assault and no further losses.'

The French alone had by now lost 53 dead and 73 wounded. The Spanish losses are not given. The Allies lost 27 killed and 120 wounded, and claimed a total of 70 officers and men killed, 200 wounded and 35 prisoners from among the attackers. 'We await Tessé,' said Villars et Lugein, in conclusion, 'and the king's ships with (we hope) guns and men. We cannot fire any longer as we are so short of powder.'

Tessé, arrived with 3,000 French troops two days later, and at once formed the opinion that though 'The French and Spanish both did marvels, this place cannot be taken by them, nor are the breaches in a state for an assault'. He felt stranded, 'in these pools of water, on this tongue of land' – the description is de Thouy's while 'de Pointis sends nothing, and nothing is coming from France or from Barcelona'.

On 16th February, 'If we are going to continue the siege Your Majesty *must* order the squadron here.' His hopes were temporarily raised by seeing ships offshore. They might be de Pointis'. But no, they were English. 'I vow,' he concluded, 'that I am riven with doubts.' When de Pointis arrived on 26th February, unloading was impeded by the garrison's guns and the proximity of the Allied fleet.

Tessé's correspondence grew even gloomier. On 16th March, he wrote to Chamillart from 'the camp before Gibraltar'. He had had no letters. 'Gibraltar is the end of the world, and a place which perhaps nobody in France know about.' Its climate is appalling. 'I have had eight days when the weather was so bad that you wouldn't put a dog out of doors.' The climate was the bringer of disease. 'Have flames burn this paper', wrote Tessé to Madame la Duchesse de Bourgogne, his friend and María Luisa's sister, 'before you open it. I assure you it comes from the most evil air in the world, where death and contagion hold the worst company anyone could find.'

Then came the news of a setback at sea. In Villars et Lugein's words. 'Sir Lacke' (as he calls him) had arrived off Gibraltar, 'surprising de Pointis who had only five warships with him. He cut cables and after a five hour fight during which [the French] repelled boarders sword in hand, in the end they ran ashore at Marbella. Here [de Pointis] was obliged to burn them after saving the crews.' The other six [ships], separated by a storm, reached Toulon safely. 'This will make it unlikely that we shall recapture Gibraltar this year, but Marshal Tessé is continuing the siege.'

This is not of course an eye-witness account of the little action off Marbella, for which it is necessary to return to Leake. In late February he had still been in Lisbon, short of all kinds of supplies, even surgeons' stores, and awaiting the arrival of Rear-Admiral Wishart from England. The state of the Dutch ships was still bad. The copper sheathing, having come adrift from the hulls, acted as a drogue. Worrying still about de Pointis he ordered each ship to put on board a month's supplies, although there was then only enough in store in Lisbon for forty days for his squadron and the fortress.

Then Rear-Admiral Sir Thomas Dilkes arrived on 10th March from England with five third-rates, *Revenge*, *Warspite*, *Bedford*, *Expedition* and *Hampton Court*. He also brought a commission of promotion for Leake to Vice-Admiral of the White and Commander-in-Chief of Her Majesty's fleet in the Mediterranean. Leake struck his blue ensign and hoisted the white in the *Hampton Court*. These arrivals brought the total Allied fleet up to twenty-three English, four Dutch (two were still unready), and eight Portuguese. Here the Methuen Treaty caused trouble, since if Portuguese forces were involved the whole squadron had in principle to be under Portuguese command. Leake would have none of this and after an argument obtained agreement that the Portuguese captains should be 'private' (i.e. not sailing under the Portuguese flag) and would serve under his command.

The wind being fair on 17th March he sailed for Gibraltar with the usual orders for rendezvous off Cape Spartel. During an otherwise uneventful voyage he found, in a practice manoeuvre, that he had to allow half an hour extra for the Portuguese ships to follow orders.

Then at 5.30 on the morning of the 21st he was on the point of entering Gibraltar when he spotted five sail-of-the-line stealing away past Europa Point. He gave chase. De Pointis, now with only those five ships, *Lys* (or *Lys Vaisseau*) (84 guns) *Magnanime* (74), *Ardent* (60), and *Marquis* (60), *Arrogant* (60), first made for the African coast but was out-sailed and stood over towards Spain. Weather had slowed down his delivery of supplies and the rest of the fleet had, as we have seen, been blown away in storms which had delayed his departure.

At nine in the morning Dilkes had the *Revenge*, another English and a Dutch ship within gunshot of the *Arrogant* and she struck her colours. The *Ardent* and *Marquis* were taken by Dutch ships and the *Lys* and *Magnanime* were run ashore, the latter so hard that 'her masts came by the board' and only part of her hull remained above water. She had been given a couple of broadsides and many of her company, including de Pointis, were wounded. Leake then looked in at Málaga but found only a single merchantman there, the rest of the French squadron being already on the way back to Toulon.

The French had not sought a battle and de Pointis in his report was defeatist. 'It was my good fortune that bad weather separated so many ships. Otherwise the more I had, the more I had lost.' Leake was critical of his own captains. Of course, the French as usual fired high and the *Hampton Court, Revenge* and *Warspite* all had damage to masts and rigging, which made manoeuvre difficult. But this was, he said, no excuse. They should have laid aboard the *Lys*. And as for the Portuguese, 'Those that durst get anything near did more harm than good, and one of them mistaking the *Pembroke* for the *Lys* gave her a broadside but it did little damage.'

This skirmish effectively meant the end of seaborne aid to the besiegers of Gibraltar. It also meant that the waters of the whole eastern coast of Spain were now hostile to the French; and Richard Hill, the English ambassador to Savoy, reported to London, 'All the ships of war that were in the road of Toulon are hauled into harbour and nothing durst look out for several days.' Darmstadt had a gold cup made as a memento for Leake and wrote,

'I expected with great impatience this good opportunity to express my hearty joy of your great and good success you had at your second appearing off this place, which I hope hath been the final stroke towards our relief, the enemy having since five days begun to withdraw their heavy cannon; being the effects only to be ascribed to your good conduct and care . . .'

For Tessé things looked worse than ever and he wrote to Louis XIV on 21st March, 'In these cruel circumstances I felt I must send '*le petit Renaud*' not only to describe what has happened here – he has been here all along – but to give you an idea by word of mouth of the general state of affairs, on which Your Majesty may not be fully informed.'

As a Marshal of France he would, although at present away from the centre of affairs, have had a fairly shrewd idea of Louis' preoccupations after Blenheim. That battle, although it did not end the war, had altered its balance. Until the summer of 1704 Louis had had the initiative on land. Since then, although many still considered that Marlborough had merely had a fluke of luck and been carried to victory by Prince Eugene, Louis knew that he would have to react to a number of possible threats along the frontiers of France and Spain, and must be on the defensive. he could be threatened from Flanders by 60,000 men under the Dutch General Overkirk, by Marlborough with 60,000 men on the Moselle, by a force of 30,000 under the Margrave of Baden on the Rhine, by

30,000 men in Italy under Prince Eugene and by over 15,000 in Portugal under das Minas and Galway. He had managed by March 1705 to recoup the losses of Blenheim, raising by compulsory recruitment and drafts from the militia a total of 200,000 men under arms – though slightly short in cavalry, for horses in France were dying of some disease. But he could not go on at this rate, and in any case the Allied forces now numbered 250,000. He could guess perhaps that Marlborough's choices would be limited by the attitudes of the Dutch, the Margrave and the Austrian Empire. But he could not be certain and he had to play for safety. Moreover neither he nor anybody else could be sure of where the amphibious forces of the Allies would attack in Spain.

He must therefore have been relieved when '*le petit Renaud*' gave Tessé's word of mouth recommendations which, as is clear from the marshal's subsequent correspondence, were to raise the siege of Gibraltar. He sent Renaud straight back to Madrid to convince his grandson. On 12th April, 'You will have heard,' he wrote to Philip, from Renaud

> 'about the siege of Gibraltar. I wish in the light of what he has told me that you had given orders to abandon the enterprise as you could not hope for success since you lack everything needed. I order that Marshal Tessé shall raise the siege at once. I am sorry to have to take a decision which I would have wished you to take yourself.'

In fact, on the very day that his grandfather wrote, and therefore at least a fortnight before he could receive it, the hapless Philip had himself decided that the siege should be converted into a blockade. Villadarías' letters to Madrid no doubt helped bring about Philip's decision. On 5th April the former reported that his manpower now totalled only 1,438 including officers and drummers. The weather was so bad that all these were sick. On the other hand two Italian deserters from the Rock (perhaps planted on him) told him that 'the enemy Armada had 15,000 men and even without disembarking from it there were 3,000 men in Gibraltar'. Listlessly Villadarías went on writing his daily budget of bad news. 'I will continue sending despatches until His Majesty tells me otherwise.'

On 16th April Tessé received orders from Philip to leave Gibraltar to Villadarías and march away towards Extremadura where 'I have need of you on the frontier'. De Thouy wrote at about this time demanding to be recalled from Gibraltar, and a French engineer of the king's, de Rosman, in a report to Paris, said that the failure at Gibraltar was due to 'bad intelligence on the part of the generals, to a shortage of troops, and to the failure of de Pointis.' On his way home, Tessé wrote a masterpiece of complaint to Louis. 'We have failed before Gibraltar for lack of method and planning, of foresight and of all that Your Majesty knows better than I or anyone else knows to be necessary. The misfortune of your ships was due to lack of knowledge in Madrid.' The Spaniards (once more) were useless and Philip 'indolent, uncertain, and entirely governed by the queen . . . Put in Spain a king who desires to be master, to talk, to work, to take decisions, or who chooses a chief minister and gives him full authority.' Villadarías stayed on in Gibraltar for a few more weeks, now writing less frequently, sending through to Mejorada depressing lists of officers and men many of whom were sick.

So, after seven months of desperate fighting on both sides, Gibraltar was in the hands of the Allies, holding it then and for the next six years on behalf of Charles III. On 18th April Leake, convinced that he had done all he could and under orders to provide convoy escorts, sailed back once more to Lisbon. On 4th May, New Style, which is 23rd April (St. George's Day) Old Style, Prince George of Hesse-Darmstadt reviewed the garrison and after the parades there were *feux de joie* in the evening. He himself had been the saviour of the Rock, though without Leake – and without Tory support in London – he probably could not have succeeded. His cavalier attitude to money was certainly of importance in obtaining credit but he would not have been able to continue this without much help from Methuen (about whom he complained). The ambassador had pledged his personal credit, had spent £1,644 on communications boats by the end of 1704 alone, and was owed over £3,000 by May 1705. Darmstadt received £6,000 from the English government but owed Methuen £1,485. The latter had bought stores and medicines and financed Captain Joseph Bennet, the engineer. And his son Paul paid out £536 for the Portuguese at Lagos and £1,125 for bills on his visit to Gibraltar. Here, too, he not only smoothed over Darmstadt's discontent with John Methuen but intervened successfully to keep the peace between the prince and his English officers, who 'were all now like dogs and cats together' and wishful to take things easy, whereas Darmstadt was insisting on improving the fortifications in accordance with a plan Bennet had drawn up.

He had received many letters of congratulation; from Ormonde, from Godolphin and from Galway among others, though the last-named was careful to attribute much of the success to the fleet.

Perhaps it was an unconscious freak of history that Darmstadt's celebrations took place on St. George's Day. He considered that he held the place for King Charles of Spain, and so – then – did his Allies. But by 1711, particularly when King Charles became Emperor of Austria, and more still by 1713, the Rock had become British, *de facto*. It has since suffered two other sieges, notably the Great Siege of 1779–83 when the defenders under Governor Elliott were the Marines – by that time the *Royal* Marines, the successors of Captain Fisher and his seventeen men.

For the Allies, for King Louis XIV, for King Philip V, and for all those involved in Gibraltar in 1704/5 it had indeed been 'a terrible morsel'. It was still to be difficult to digest eight years later at the time of the Treaty of Utrecht – and nearly three centuries afterwards.

CHAPTER FOUR

Struggle for Barcelona

The most mistrusted and neglected *métier* in Spain is that of war.

— Tessé to Philip V, 2nd April, 1705

The trouble with Barcelona is that once or twice in every century an army from Castile is obliged to conquer it.

— remark attributed to Franco

On 10th February 1705 Monsieur Chamblay produced another annual forecast at Versailles 'The English and Dutch', he wrote,

'intend to gather a large corps in Portugal and Marlborough himself will go to Lisbon to command the King of Portugal's armies. These will be almost entirely of infantry. There will be little cavalry since horses are scarce.'

ALTHOUGH right about the shortage of horses, for the rest he was, as St Paul put it, seeing in part and therefore prophesying in part, and he was wide of the mark on one point. Even if Marlborough had wished to go to the Peninsula — and he may well have at times — he could not do so for he was at the high centre of Allied strategy, carrying the twin burdens of foreign policy and commander-in-chief in the field as well as the responsibility for raising and maintaining England's armed forces. He could not have operated from so remote a situation. Indeed he could in an emergency return swiftly by boat down the Rhine to his headquarters at The Hague. But it is too easy to be wise with hindsight, and M. Chamblay was doing his best.[1]

Writing soon after the event, San Felipe's introduction to 1705 is sombre. 'The century, the war, and its misfortunes were all moving the same way.'

The Allies, who had been successful at Blenheim and in Flanders, were determined on winning the war. For Philip the only course, if he wished to continue, was to depend even more on France for military, economic and political support, and this is the policy he adopted willy-nilly, though his subjects resented and disliked their French allies increasingly as the months went by.

As far as the Peninsula was concerned the maritime powers, provided they were prepared to produce the means, had a considerable choice of targets. Though as 1705 dawned they were not yet certain of Gibraltar, they had good hopes and by March could be nearly sure. They provided men, money and munitions for attacks in co-operation with Portugal on Spain's western frontier. And there was the possibility of a successful landing somewhere on Spain's long coast, Barcelona perhaps, or Cadiz, despite previous failures. Barcelona was particularly favoured because of reports sent to London by an English agent in the area, Mitford Crowe, who was in close contact with influential Catalans.

The optimism of the maritime powers at this stage is thus understandable. The despondency in France and Spain is equally so. Correspondence already quoted from Gramont and others shows severe disillusionment in every sphere, and when Amelot came to replace Gramont towards the end of May 1705 he, too, soon succumbed to frustration in his dealings with the monarchs and grandees, particularly those on the *Despacho*, writing, 'Most of the time is spent discussing *bagatelles* which are quite unworthy of being raised before a King of Spain ... The Spaniards are no help. We don't know where to turn for money...' The new ambassador, and when she returned, Madame des Ursins, pressed Philip to get rid of many members of the *Despacho* because they were incompetent. Some, like the Marqués de Jamaica, thought only of their trade with the New World, the source of their riches. Mancera was old and decrepit, Medinaceli 'had the vapours'. Others were 'extravagant and bizarre'. Yet, Amelot says, Philip was popular with the ordinary people and the bourgeois, and had little to fear from the grandees.

As 1705 wore on, and until late in 1706 letters from Madrid and from various sectors in the field became even more dejected, descending, as we shall see, into panic as the Allies achieved – however flukily – success after success. Although some inkling of the atmosphere in Spain did reach the Allied commanders they could only guess at how bad it was and as will be seen below over-estimated it at times. Moreover they too were in frequent disagreement and indulged themselves in arguments and delays. Had they not done so they would probably have won all Spain at this time. As it was, fright, squabbles and lack of money on the Bourbon side were to be more than compensated for by over-confidence, jealousies, disagreements and sheer incompetence among their opponents. These two counter-balancing combinations of failings can be clearly seen during the spring campaign of 1705 on the Spanish-Portuguese frontier.

On the Allied side, too, security was weak and intelligence efforts in Spain and Portugal, primitive and lacking in gadgetry as they might appear in the late 20th century, favoured the Bourbons. What was discussed in London and The Hague was of course communicated to Lisbon and had there to be considered by a large number of people, not all of whom were in sympathy with the Allies. The pro-French faction in Portugal was still strong. As we shall see in 1706 its activities would enable Berwick to keep a step ahead of his opponents in the field. In 1705 a Madame d'Elvas was taking particular care of French prisoners and 'working hard for the service of the king [Philip]'. Amelot says she was 'highly valued by the French' and suggested sending her 50,000 livres to enable her to try and arrange peace with Portugal. King Philip's confessor, Daubentin, was in direct contact with her. However, the Dowager Queen Catherine of Portugal (widow of Charles II of England and King Pedro's sister) stepped in (while acting as regent for her sick brother) and ordered the arrest of Madame d'Elvas before she could receive this douceur.

It is not surprising in these circumstances that a good deal of information about Allied plans was available to their enemies. One of Tessé's letters, written in early April to Chamillart, before he had even left the Gibraltar sector, is revealing. He was, as usual, in a complaining mood. His rival, Marshal Vendôme – himself involved before this in Spain and due to return one day – had been writing behind his back to Philip V describing him (Tessé) as dangerous, difficult and untrustworthy, and he wished to put the record straight. Then he cites at great length 'a well-informed and well-intentioned man whom I retain close to Milord Galloway [Galway].'

This spy, whom Tessé is careful not to name, provided what reads almost like a verbatim account of the 'Council meeting in London before Queen Anne, Lord Marlborough and the Chiefs of the Admiralty', presumably based on a document leaked in Lisbon.

London had discussed three proposals. First, Marlborough had proposed sending 100 men-of-war into the Mediterranean 'in order to burn the King's ships at Toulon'. Marlborough insisted that this was possible (it would indeed be done later in the war and would in fact be included in last-minute secret orders to Lord Peterborough and Admiral Shovell, the joint commanders of the Allied amphibious expedition later in 1705 – thereby further confusing an enterprise doomed to confusion) but 'the Navy officers said it could not be done as it would require easterly winds' and the queen and Marlborough had to accept this for the time being.

Secondly, an 'enterprise against Barcelona' was proposed in view of the 'strong memories' there of Darmstadt, and of the Catalans' love of their privileges (*fueros*). 'The Council are holding to this project.'

Thirdly, 'Cadiz is poorly armed and there are many English and Dutch merchants who have lived there for more than a century and would rise against the Spanish government in order not to be deprived of their goods.' A feint could be made towards the harbour through the *Puntales* by the Navy. This might cost four or five ships. A general present at the meeting said it would be possible to attack at the same time from the sea, using barges and ladders 'as there is only one sentry post on this side of the city'. The loss of Cadiz to Philip would, it was considered, bring over the whole of Andalucia to the Allies.

The Admiralty was preparing a memorandum on Cadiz but were against the Barcelona proposal 'because the defence works there are considerable, including the demolition of houses; and the punishment being meted out to supporters of Charles III [in the city] would make the project difficult'.

This deadly but useful informant had many but not all of his facts right and his remarks about Cadiz were sufficient to spur Philip to prepare that place against attack.

While London considered plans for later in the year, discussions in Lisbon concentrated on a Spring campaign, and these were obfuscated by personalities and nationalities. First of all the pressure of the various embassies affected the command. Methuen pressed for Galway to have supreme command and indeed thanks to his own seniority and his contacts with King Pedro he obtained his appointment as *Mestre de Campo* before Schonenberg could achieve such an appointment for Baron Fagel. Probably as a result of pressure from Cabreras, the Admiral of Castile, the king also appointed the Conde de Corzana to a similar rank. There were thus three *Mestres de Campo*. Though the rank suggests field marshal, it was equivalent to anything between a brigadier and a lieutenant-general and all three, the Huguenot, the Dutchman and the Spaniard were subordinate to the Portuguese Galveas who was in his eighties.

The Portuguese army numbers 12,000 (admittedly mostly raw recruits), and it possessed an artillery train of 20 heavy guns, seven mortars, 24 field pieces and 80 smaller calibre cannon. Such was the protocol in the Portuguese army that the big guns had to go first and when as often occurred the oxen drawing them broke down, the whole train was held up. Colonel John Richards had now obtained a Portuguese commission and jointed the train at Estremós. His account of the confusion obtaining among the Portuguese is depressing, coming as it does from a professional. The cavalry were in poor shape, short of mounts. The supply arrangements were haphazard, carried out by groups of peasants rather as if going to market. Carters were in short supply and carts were easily upset. Half the mortars were useless and there was no timber to make gun platforms. No foreigner might take the lead, and the Portuguese insisted on passing ahead of the English and Dutch even if the latter were so positioned that they had to wait because of this.

Of course there were more Portuguese than Allied troops. Galway's English force only numbered 2,500 foot (Portmore's, Brudenell's, Stewart's, Blood's and Duncanson's) for he had generously sent considerable reinforcements to Gibraltar. Of the total cavalry only 200 of Harvey's had horses and the Royal Dragoons and Conyngham's had to be left in Lisbon for lack of mounts. In general the English troops were suffering from the climate and food of Portugal. An officer of the Royal Dragoons wrote to the colonel of his regiment, Lord Raby, 'Pray God you never see this hellish country. Everybody is weary of it. I heard General Wyndham swear the other day he believed they'd starve our horse first and then us.' Such was this 'forgotten army'. Hugh Wyndham, for example, was now nominally a lieutenant-general and had been a major-general for a year but he was still being paid only as a brigadier. He and Brudenell had now been joined by a third, a genial Irishman, Henry Conyngham. The chief engineer was Colonel Carles and there was a small train of five 5-pounders under John Richards' assistant, Albert Borgard. The Dutch contingent, under the pessimistic Fagel, numbered 2,300. Methuen was ill, and Cabreras apparently had high blood pressure and was at odds with everyone. Galway did his best but Fagel and Corzana disagreed with him. The three of them could not even agree on their respective seniorities and had to compromise on a feeble arrangement whereby they took command week and week about. Had Berwick been in command of the opposition he would have made mincemeat of them, even if his own forces were at a low ebb. As it was, Tessé, chastened and disconsolate after his experiences at Gibraltar and permanently disillusioned with the Spanish court, did the best he could with what was at his disposal. It was to be just enough.

The threat from across the western frontier was causing panic in Madrid; Gramont, awaiting his chance to leave, wrote, 'We are in a desperate state, expecting an attack between Estremós and Elvas – where we have devil of an infantryman, and there are no recruits coming in.' Philip appealed to Tessé on 25th April, 'You will see from the enclosed letter from de Bay [in command at Extremadura] that the enemy is assembling before Estremós. There is no time to lose. Go straight to Badajoz. Do not obey my grandfather's orders but come at once to be at the head of my army.' At least Tessé, though short of troops, had under him in the various sectors a group of experienced and effective generals, including d'Asfeld, Puységur, de Geoffreville and de Légal, and he, as a Marshal of France, was their accepted chief so that what he ordered was carried out. This was quite different from the Allied command arrangements.

On April 24th the Allied armies straggled, rather than marched into Spain and on May 2nd reached the little fortress of Valencia de Alcántara. The garrison here numbered 700, commanded by Alonso Madariaga, Marqués de Villa Fuerte. It was Fagel's week of command and as Galway was later to report to Harley in London: 'The greatest oppostiion I meet is from Mr. Fagel who is supported and encouraged in it by the adverse party to the Alliance.' Now, during those early May days, Galway was ill and Fagel was determined to control the Portuguese train. Looking on Richards as a creature of Galway's he insisted on his Dutch master-gunner setting up the batteries while Richards and Major Borgard were forced to stand and watch. A small hill outside the town was occupied, and the siege works, begun on 3rd May, were complete enough for the batteries to open fire on a bastion on 6th May – though Richards thought this fire was of poor standard and that sounder reconnaissance would have produced a better battery site. He was no doubt feeling bitter at being brushed aside.

Storming a breach in this period was only attempted when it was considered 'practicable' which was defined as being when sufficient stonework and earth had eroded into the ditch to enable assaulting soldiers to climb through with ease using both hands for their weapons. The first assailants were often called the Forlorn Hope, and were usually volunteers.

On 8th May a force of 900 English, Dutch and Portuguese grenadiers made the assault on the breach which was after bombardment thought 'practicable'. They were supported by a second wave of Duncanson's English, de Noyelles' Dutch and two Portuguese regiments.

The attack was immediately in trouble and the grenadiers were falling back in confusion, but Duncanson led up his men with colours flying and drove the garrison into the keep. Villa Fuerte made a resolute defence, sustaining five assaults and fighting hand to hand until, wounded he was forced to surrender. The garrison was sent to Lisbon under escort, and the Portuguese then pillaged the town. San Felipe says, 'The Spanish [inhabitants], naked and without arms were tied up and brutally treated, and the Portuguese took their horses and fled.' Richards notes with regret that the churches were sacked (Fagel makes no comment) and says that he posted engineers as guards but that these had been called away to some other duty, leaving the Portuguese rear echelons and camp followers to plunder. Earlier, at Codiciera, the English and Dutch had been involved when they found liquor and began to loot, although a party of priests had been promised protection from pillage. Galway shot the first looter he saw but the damage was done and although from now on most of the pillaging was done by Portuguese (who in their own view were only taking revenge on the Spaniards for what *they* had done a year earlier), the odium was of course attached to the heretics.

Duncanson, mortally wounded, died soon aferwards, Borgard's left arm was shattered and Captain Fletcher of Brudenell's had been killed in the approach trenches. Borgard was invalided home and replaced by a Huguenot, Lieutenant-Colonel Manclère.

Encouraged by this modest success, the Allies next made for Albuquerque, another fortress on a hill which was surmounted by a keep and garrisoned by 800 Spaniards. The intention had been to march to Alcántara, some thirty miles on, but transport was short and the enemy still held Marvão near the lines of communication. At the same time, although das Minas had retaken Salvatierra and its 360-strong garrison and reached Sarca, this was on the other side of the Tagus and there was no means of crossing the river, since the pontoons although ordered months before in Lisbon and the Netherlands, had – not surprisingly in the general confusion and incompetence – failed to arrive. Hence Albuquerque as target. A small fortified town, its occupation would cut the enemy's communications with Badajoz. It was Galway's week of command and he began the attack on 16th May. The outer part of the town was rapidly stormed by the Portuguese, but the Keep was high and well built and cannon had no effect.

This appears to be because after Richards had agreed a site with Galway and cut a way through to it through vineyards, the generals changed their minds and the only Portuguese battery available was badly placed. Richards brought up heavier guns but began to run out of ammunition – as might have been expected from the chaotic logistics of this Allied force. Bread was running out too and speed was essential. So the Portuguese drove one mine under the Keep and the English engineers, under former Captain, now justly promoted Lieutenant-Colonel Joseph Bennet who had come from Gibraltar, drove another. Bennet received a musket wound, and the mines were not used, as Richards had by now opened a breach in the wall of a church close by, through which an attacking party was able to reach the church tower. This gave a clear view into the town and provided a site from which light guns could pepper the place. However, before these could be hoisted into position, the garrison surrendered with the honours of war. This meant no pillaging, which was unpopular with the Portuguese. It was now 21st May.

The Allies began to bicker again about the next objective. Fagel wanted to march on to Alcántara, Galway still preferred Badajoz. The former target was further off and it was rumoured that das Minas had had to retreat from Sarca to

Peñamacor. Fresh instructions were sent for from Lisbon, since the march to Alcántara was still officially ordered. Galway began to shift artillery towards Badajoz in anticipation, though Fagel objected. At length Galveas gave Galway discretion and the Allies marched to occupy a bank of the Guadiana, where the Spanish army was defending the opposite bank. But by now Tessé had arrived from Andalucia and had been joined by 6,000 infantry and 2,200 horse from the Gibraltar sector. He took over from de Bay who had hitherto been in command, and sent de Thouy with most of the foot and eight squadrons of horse northwards to watch what das Minas was up to in Beira. That elderly general had already, as rumoured, abandoned Salvatierra and gone into summer quarters.

Tessé's march had led him through Merida and Sarca. Although – or perhaps because – it had been exhausting, it had not stopped the flow of his correspondence. For example, from Merida, to Chamillart, 'How could any ambassador succeed with a King of Spain who is crazy about his wife and tells her everything? Gramont is well out of it. And poor Father Daubentin, what business did he have getting himself into that mess?' And, a few days later, from Sarca, before he left it, and written mostly in cypher:

> 'The confusion and abandon in the army and everything to do with the war goes on . . . I have only carried out the precise orders of those who are now "throwing a cat at my legs". The King and Queen of Spain are a miserable brothel [sic] . . . There is no infantry. Only half the cavalry officers are in post. The cavalry have no saddles, boots or pay. There are no wagons or mules. The enemy are fools if they do not drive us right back to Madrid and plunder it.'

The enemy *were* fools, or at least they did not know or take advantage of the situation of their opponents. The quarrelling Allied triumvirate moved their siege train to Campo Maíor, sent for additional siege *matériel* from Elvas 12 miles away, and by June 5th were camped four miles from Badajoz between the Guadiana and the Caya. Here Tessé crossed the Guadiana to threaten their flank. The additional siege train had not arrived and the summer heats were on them but Galway and Fagel, for once in accord, still wanted to attack Badajoz and would probably have taken it and opened the way to Madrid. but now the Portuguese refused again. They also refused the alternative of attacking Ayamonte and devastating Andalucia, because the way there 'was rough, dangerous and wild'. So the decision was referred to King Pedro by Galveas.

Meantime Tessé had reinforced Badajoz with cavalry, and the River Guadiana had fallen to its low summer level which meant that in theory he could fall on the flank of the Allies who were now unprotected. They little knew how far he was in spirit from such an act of boldness, being themselves desperate for their own reasons, as well as divided. As long ago as March, Galway had insisted that the campaign depended on mounts for the cavalry. These had been promised back in 1704. The emperor had been asked for 2,000 and King Pedro had even suggested a means of transport for them, the Setubal boats which took salt to Holland. But as usual the Empire failed to produce and Methuen and his opposite number in London, da Cunha, arranged for 1,300 Irish mounts, which arrived on June 1st at Lisbon. Although Methuen said only 60 had died on the voyage and only a further 53 were unfit, and arranged for them to go to the royal stables on arrival, they were eventually found to be mostly below standard. (Not for the first or last time the copers were at work!) And in any case Schonenberg and Fagel mislaid between them the instructions for their shares. By the time this was sorted out it was too late. Moreover, lack of money – and of forethought – had resulted in Galway being short of mules as well. He needed 2,000 and King Pedro was meant to supply them. But he had no money, so Methuen advanced him £7,000 to cover the cost. All this took time.

Charles III, poor young man, had been suffering the frustrations of the damned in his quarters at Belém. He wanted desperately to go to the front but could only go with King Pedro. And the latter had suffered a stroke and the aftermath left him in an acute state of bloody-minded melancholy. He let it be known that if he could not join the army, Charles should not either, even though the young man had said he would go with a suite of only ten or twelve. Methuen and the Allied generals sympathised with Charles and tried to raise money either in London or from Portuguese merchants to pay for him to go to the front, but it was no good. Pedro, now approaching his end, would not budge. An eye witness, whom we shall later meet, describes vividly the sad state into which King Pedro's earlier excesses had brought him. 'He spoke always to strangers by an interpreter, for the palate of his mouth was so much damaged that even the Portuguese that were admitted to a great familiarity could not understand him without great difficulty.' It was the more creditable that not only John Methuen but his son, Paul, who posed as something of a dilettante, were able to communicate with this once vigorous but now pathetic creature and sometimes obtain decisions from him. Now, however, there was nothing to be done. Queen Catherine had given up her attempts at intervention. João, Prince of Brazil, Pedro's heir, was too young to take a line. In the end the summer heats provided an excuse. On 13th June orders were sent from Lisbon to go into summer quarters and the three contingents separated, the English to the Andalucian frontier, the Dutch to the Tagus – where de Bay would watch them – and the Portuguese back to the Alemtéjo.

An opportunity had been missed. Galway, in despair, wrote to London, wishing he could pack up and leave. His wish was not granted.

He – and London – did not know it, but Tessé's spirits were at an even lower ebb. He 'would not trust any Spaniard even with the defence of a steeple'. He had detached thirteen French battalions to de Thouy to make sure of that sector. But, (in cypher), 'We have a general upset here. There is no army, no troops, no money. King Philip each day is made to sign everything that is harmful to his service. I would not be surprised if he were to sign his own death warrant.' Even while Galway, Fagel and Corzana were waiting for orders from Lisbon, Tessé at Badajoz was consumed with worry. 'The affairs of the Monarchy,' he wrote to Chamillart on 14th June, 'and even King Philip personally are in imminent peril.'

Perhaps, if Monsieur Chamblay had been wrong and Marlborough, with his marvellous grasp of essentials, had been able to be on the Spanish-Portuguese frontier that Spring, the Allies would have thrust aside their opponents' feeble defences and reached Madrid. They would have, over the next year, another major chance, but although their efforts were to be graced by occasional flashes of brilliance, that chance too would be missed. We are approaching the watershed of the war.

★   ★   ★

Disappointed in his hopes of going to the front, King Charles III was awaiting in Lisbon the arrival of the expeditionary force for an amphibious enterprise. While he waited, he heard the news that his pious, incompetent father, Emperor Leopold had died, on 9th May. Leopold totally lacked judgment of both affairs and men, choosing always as advisers those whom everybody but he could see were mere hangers-on, and was obstinate in retaining them. Charles' brother Joseph, King of the Romans, was now Emperor and he himself was the Imperial heir, since Joseph had no son. But for the present his ambitions still lay in Spain.

The expedition was to be jointly commanded by Admiral Shovell, who has already figured in this account, and Charles Mordaunt, known in after days as 'The Great Earl of Peterborough', who was also commissioned as commander-in-chief. This nobleman was a most colourful figure, but it is difficult to place him, for he attracted both among his contemporaries and among subsequent observers the extremes of liking and loathing, admiration and mistrust.[2] His contemporaries, after an initial period of enchantment, usually fell foul of him sooner or later and while still being fond of him were glad to have him out of the way. He was the sort of person to whom it was impossible to be indifferent. Many writers have described him as having no judgment and less virtue; of being vainglorious and without commonsense; full of undigested schemes, wayward, selfish, ungovernable; morbidly addicted to novelty, excitement and fickle amours; a coward, liar and thief who did not mind being thought a knave but made sure to enhance his reputation at the expense of better men. But there was another side. A woman whom he had wronged said even so that to vileness of soul he allied a sort of knight errantry, and it is not therefore surprising that some writers should describe him as a kind friend, a magnanimous enemy, an able diplomatist, a fine orator and wit, a brilliant general and a fabulous hero. Jonathan Swift, who liked him but described him as 'a hangdog I dearly love', also called him 'the ramblingest lying rogue on earth'. He was the son of John Mordaunt, Lord Mordaunt and Avalon, younger brother of the then Earl of Peterborough a royalist who had narrowly escaped execution under Cromwell, and of Elizabeth Carey, daughter of Lord Monmouth. Born in 1658, he was christened Charles and was now (in 1705) about 47. He would live to the ripe age of 77.

In 1675 he had succeeded his father as Lord Mordaunt and in 1697 his uncle as third Earl of Peterborough. In 1686 he had quarrelled with James II's court and gone to Holland, whence in 1688 he was prominent in helping William of Orange's incursion into England. He was present at the battle of Beachy Head in 1690 but soon after got into trouble by criticising William's campaign in the Netherlands and was dismissed from court. Out of office he is reported as dividing his time between amatory and political intrigues. In particular he was suspected of complicity in a plot led by Sir John Fenwick to kill William at Turnham Green. Sent to the Tower, he ratted on Fenwick and then tried to persuade him to implicate Marlborough. Stripped of his Privy Councillorship, he was nevertheless released from imprisonment in 1697. Taking no further public part during the rest of William's reign, he appears to have been totally unmoved by his dangers. Macaulay says of him that he had one of those minds on which the deepest wounds heal and leave no scar.

In 1677, at the age of nineteen, he had married, impulsively and for love, a Scottish girl, Elizabeth Fraser. Although he was consistently unfaithful to her until she died, they had a number of children. The eldest son, Lord Mordaunt, served gallantly in Flanders in Forlorn Hope, and wished to marry Marlborough's favourite daughter, Mary. The duke, describing him as 'a raskell', would have none of it. Another son we shall meet serving as captain of a ship in the Mediterranean. Later on Peterborough married again, this time to Anastasia Robinson, a singer whose portrait depicts a lady with prominent teeth, and who was one of Handel's favourite voices. After her marriage, Peterborough forced her to give up her profession, though the marriage was for long kept secret.

Although he had been present at Beachy Head, his military experience prior to 1705 had been sparse. In 1674 he served as a volunteer in an expedition against the Algerian coast, where he must have met a Lieutenant Cloudesley Shovell, who then led a cutting-out operation and who was now as an admiral to be his fellow commander-in-chief. In 1678 Peterborough had shipped as a 'passenger' (volunteer) in a vessel called H.M.S. *Bristol.* He infuriated the chaplain of the ship, the Rev. Henry Teonge, by proposing to preach a mock sermon while the latter was ill with influenza.[3] It took some courage for an impoverished parson to oppose a rich young sprig of nobility, but he had his captain on his side. He records having

> 'found the zealous Lord with our Captain, whom I did so handle in a smart and short discourse that he went out of the cabin in great wrath. In the afternoon Lord Peterborough set one of the Carpenters' crew to work about his Cabin. I, by the Captain's order discharged the workman [it being Sunday], at which the 'Reverend' Lord was so vexed that he borrowed a hammer and busied himself all that day in nailing up his hangings. But, being done on the Sabbath day and also when there was no necessity, I hope the work will not be long-lived. From that day he loved neither me nor the Captain.'

Peterborough transferred to H.M.S. *Rupert* a few days later. In 1680 he served briefly in Tangier.

After so little military experience and none in high command it is no wonder that his appointment caused ribald comment in such places as Wills's Coffee House, wits comparing it with Caligula's making his horse a consul. Public opinion, limited as it was to the upper classes, favoured the idea that Prince George of Hesse-Darmstadt should hold the Royal Commission, but he was now a Roman Catholic and therefore excluded automatically.

It is even more astonishing that Marlborough, who after all had at that time almost total control over major military appointments, should not have vetoed one who had tried to implicate him in a treasonable plot. This is the more mysterious since Marlborough gave his views on Peterborough in a letter to his

Duchess Sarah, the recipient of much of Peterborough's sprightly correspondence. But she had found him amusing, and knowing him to be short of money had suggested that he be given some post. Her judgment of people was impulsive, and though tough she was very kind-hearted. In one particular case – that of Abigail Hill – this was to be to her own eventual cost. Of the new commander-in-chief, Marlborough wrote:—

> 'What you say concerning Lord Peterborough and his fair Lady is certainly very just for there is nothing that may not be expected from them. I have observed, since I have been in the world, that the next misfortune to that of having friendship with such people is that of having any dispute with them, and care should be taken to have as little to do with them as possible.'

Such advice cannot be followed here. For whatever reason Lord Peterborough was from mid-1705 to mid-1706 to be deeply involved in the Spanish sector of the war, and contrived to leave behind him what Geoffrey Callender has called 'the Peterborough Legend'.

This rests mainly on four sets of documents: his own letters to many people; '*A Journal of Lord Peterborough's Proceedings in Spain*' written by his secretary, Arent Furly (or Furley), godson of Isaac Newton, mathematician and Master of the Mint; an account written at Peterborough's request by Dr John Freind, a physician who accompanied him to Spain; and a book first published in 1728, '*The Military Memoirs of Captain George Carleton*'. Peterborough himself wrote a memoir in three volumes, which may have been the source of Freind's and Carleton's works, but his second wife, Anastasia, burned the papers after his death either because she was shocked by them or to avoid legal actions should they be published. Peterborough's letters, where they survive, are racy, amusing, untrustworthy, and sometimes openly treacherous. He was clearly a rapid thinker, and later on, while on an embassy to Austria, employed no fewer than nine secretaries. Furly's Journal is a fairly dry record. Dr Freind's opus was written to please his master and is therefore suspect. Carleton's *Memoirs* are another matter, and represent a mystery. There was indeed a Captain George Carleton who served in the Peninsula. When his Memoirs were published he would however, on sure evidence, have been 76. Though we shall later come across an anonymous holograph record written by an ex-trooper aged eighty which is nevertheless lucid, it cannot be certain that Carleton was anything but senile by 1728, (he was dead by 1730) and it is at least probable that he was short of money and was persuaded for cash to lend his name – and any notes he had for embellishment – to someone. The *Memoirs* are well written in the style of a picaresque romance but internal evidence suggests that they were not those of a soldier. The literary style is vivid but the military terms are unprofessional. Parnell's demolition of *The Military Memoirs of Captain George Carleton* is savage. He talks of

> '(1) the ironical and unmilitary manner in which the lively stories are related, containing as they do many expressions ... which could never have entered the mind of a trained officer, (2) the numerous clerical, Latin and classical allusions..., (3) the impiety and indecency of many of the religious references, and (d) the frequent mention of Irish persons (and especially Irish priests).'

Parnell's target is Peterborough, whom he describes as a cowardly deserter. He considers it certain that Peterborough paid for the publication and that the writer of the published version was probably Swift. But like so much to do with the earl there is in fact no certainty, only a strong probability that the *Memoirs* are almost completely bogus.

So, for the great expedition of 1705 we have two ill-assorted commanders, a long, lithe, able admiral of humble origins and a highly-strung, unreliable little earl. Somehow they had to work together and to cope with alien allies and a military and political farrago. From what is known of them it was bound to be Shovell who provided commonsense while Peterborough in his erratic way contributed *élan* from time to time. In May 1705 they were preparing at last to sail for the Peninsula.

Months before this, in November 1704, Admiral Mitchell, a member of the Admiralty Board, had gone to The Hague to confer with the Dutch Government and his naval opposite numbers there. He saw Pensionaries Heinsius and Buys, the States-General, and finally the heads of five 'admiralties' who together ran the naval affairs of the Republic. After no doubt stately discussion – affable, too, for the affairs of the Allies seemed to be going well – it had been agreed to form a joint force of 40 ships-of-the-line and 5,000 troops from England and twenty ships and 2,500 foot and cavalry from the Netherlands. The precise objectives were left for later decision and time was needed for the logistic preparation. This, then was the force that was awaiting Peterborough and Shovell at Portsmouth and for which Charles was waiting in Lisbon. The Dutch army contingent was to be commanded by General Willem van Schratenbach, with Colonels van Palme and St. Amand. The Dutch squadron was commanded overall by Vice-Admiral Philip van Allmonde (or Almonde) with Rear-Admirals Wassenaer and de Jongh, and the vessels included were four 90-gunners (550 men), a 70-gunner, four 60-gunners, two 50-gunners and a number of smaller units such as transports, fireships and bomb-ketches. They were to rendezvous at Lisbon with the British home fleet, sailing with British ships from St. Helen's and also with Leake's and van der Dussen's winter squadrons.

For Peterborough, taking public office required that he should kiss hands on being restored to the Privy Council and moreover attend Holy Communion. This, perhaps with a wink at his cronies, he did. He arranged loans and mortgages on his estate at Dauntsey in Wiltshire to provide cash for personal expenditure and sent a servant into the Netherlands to buy 'Tay, chocolate, rum, claret, Rhenish, burgundy and sturgeon'. At length, towards the end of May 1705 he reached Portsmouth. There had been a delay in sailing, which 'surprised' Whitehall, but the expedition finally weighed anchor from St. Helen's on the last day of the month and reached Lisbon on 20th June to find Leake's winter squadron and van Allmonde with his Dutch ships there. The Allies' confidence was reflected by 'All the accounts we have from Spain or of it from any other place seem to give a very hopeful prospect.'

But what prospect? The commander-in-chief and the naval commander had been given official instructions, leaving considerable room for discussion with King Charles, King Pedro, Darmstadt and the Dutch. These orders gave priority to an attack on Cadiz or Barcelona, the former preferably being left for the return voyage. If opportunity arose the expedition was to help the Duke of Savoy, but not to the detriment of other plans. Above all, the interests of King Charles III were to be advanced.

As far as Barcelona was concerned the orders were coloured by what had happened in Catalonia since Darmstadt's abortive landing in 1704 and by the activities in Genoa of Mitford Crowe, to whom reference has been made and to whom a special mission had now been entrusted to deal with Catalan affairs. Crowe had long been familiar with Barcelona and had been a business partner there of the British Consul, Shallett, who in his day had helped Darmstadt pawn his jewels to enable him to leave Catalonia at the end of his vice-royalty. Crowe seems to have been a capable and canny man, known to Godolphin and Galway, and even able to stay on good terms with Peterborough. With his special knowledge of Catalonia, that individual and fiery province, he had at Godolphin's request for a report, written optimistically to London late in 1704 of the possibilities of a rising there in favour of Charles, so long as he would restore and uphold their *fueros*. The people were, he wrote, largely anti-French, many were believed to be pro-Austrian and certainly favourable to Darmstadt. Many of the nobility and gentry would rally to the Allies and the Principality could provide an alternative starting-point to Gibraltar and a recruiting ground for mercenaries, since for a long time there had been bands of irregulars there known as *Miquelets*, armed countrymen whose ancestors had fought the Moors, had fought the Turks, had dominated parts of the Eastern Mediterranean, and who, when there was nothing better to do, fought each other. At one time they had been in two factions, the Nyerros (pigs) and Cadells (puppies). We shall frequently meet them later. In 1704/5 they were extremely active in and around Vich, Urgell, Manlleu and Cardona. When Crowe himself was appointed overtly to run a trade mission but in fact to negotiate with Catalan 'nobles, gentlemen, magistrates and any other officers, military or civil', his chief Catalan contacts were however now dubious about a general rising, though there were some who felt otherwise and who had recent direct experience.

Porta, from his deep studies of Catalonia during the period, is able to give the names of many of those concerned and their backgrounds. He points out that it is incorrect to suppose that all Catalans or all Barcelonians were in favour of a rising or even pro-Austrian. Some – particularly among the nobility – were pro-Bourbon. He gives their names including that of Honorat Palleja and a number of clergy, though many of the latter were pro-Austrian, and three major Catalan Institutions, the Council of a 100, the *Diputació* of the Province and the *Braç Militar*, had been similarly inclined, in order to fight for their *fueros* against the impositions of Castile. Governor Velasco had in 1704 taken repressive measures, in some cases; for example those of the writer Feliú de la Penya, de Kies the Dutch Consul, Ramon Vilana y Perlas (later Secretary to Charles III's Council) and many others, sending them to prison. Each of the institutions through its committee of six represented respectively either the nobles, merchants and citizens of the city, or the clergy. Under these repressive measures they could not be relied upon to act before an Allied landing, a fact of which Darmstadt, whose main contacts they had been, was uncomfortably aware. The Dutch press was full of the measures taken in Barcelona, under orders from a Madrid which was suspicious of the place.

Yet there were many individuals who were keen to stand against oppression. While the pro-Bourbons – known as *Botiflers* – held up their heads under Velasco, there were numerous bourgeois families in Barcelona and members of city guilds who were staunchly pro-Austrian. One family in particular, that of Dalmau, would later be prominent in action right to the end, but there were plenty of others. These would suffer considerable vicissitudes within the city as Velasco, using Spanish and Neapolitan troops, kept matters in control, but they would in time – together with some of the upper classes and the clergy – offer diplomatic and military assistance on a considerable scale to the Anglo-Dutch-Imperial Allies. If, particularly towards the end, their objectives did not always accord with the aims of those Allies, it should be borne in mind that the Catalans had, like everyone else, their own desiderata, their own deep-seated hankering for autonomy and this was the prime reason for their activities. In the end, alas, they were to be left on their own.

Crowe, however, was enthusiastic in his efforts for they chimed in with his love for Catalonia and his personal ambitions. His negotiations were with two young men. The first of these, aged 23, was Antoni de Peguera i Aimeric, leader of the *Braç Militar*, who had escaped dressed as an abbé when Velasco clamped down in May 1704. A bright student, he preferred to think of himself as a soldier. When he reached Genoa however he made little impact on the British Ambassador, Blackwell, or the Consul, Kirk. The Dutch Consul, Bosch, was suspected by the local police and although in principle helpful could do little. So Peguera went on to Vienna, where he was well received, with the backing of the Duque de Moles, a Neapolitan Spaniard, and Charles' ambassador to the Emperor. Moles introduced him to George Stepney, the British ambassador, who wrote in turn to London strongly in favour of the young man. This to some extent offset Emperor Joseph's preference for Darmstadt against his own brother.

Peguera had, in order to impress Crowe with his seriousness, visited Catalonia and returned with a second young man, Dr Dominic Perera, an able lawyer who came with full powers to negotiate, reporting an incipient rising in Vich and the taking of the town of Cardona by the rebels. The latter was significant since it was the seat of the only extant duchy in Catalonia and was now – thanks to the marriage of its holder, a woman, to the Duque de Medinaceli in a sense a Castilian foothold. By 20th June 1705 Crowe had signed the 'Pact of Genoa' with these representatives of Catalonia. Young they might be but they were vigorous and effective. The full terms of the pact included a guarantee by Queen Anne of the Catalan *fueros* on behalf of Charles III, and a promise to send money, as well as supplies and munitions, while the Catalans in turn promised to raise 6,000 men to be ready to help an Allied disembarkation (but to be armed and supplied by the Allies). They would of course declare for King Charles. They insisted, however, that ancient privileges permitted the Catalans to refuse obedience to any king unless he were actually present in the Principality. London at this stage had come to look on Barcelona as a smoke-screen for an amphibious attack on Toulon. Ever since Victor Amadeus of Savoy had switched to join the Grand Alliance he had been under pressure from London to co-operate in a land and sea attack on this important French naval base, and now the Savoyard Minister in London, de Briançon, had promised that Victor Amadeus would oblige. This news resulted in a most secret order to Peterborough and Shovell, issued a day or so after their official instructions, saying that as soon as confirmation of Victor Amadeus' intentions was received from either Victor Amadeus himself or Richard Hill, the British minister in Turin, the attack on Toulon was to be given top priority.

Secrecy was of course essential, but these orders, contradicting as they did the official ones, were to result in a good deal of argument, indecision and bad blood during the next few monts, for in the Allied councils the British commanders could not admit to having secret orders.

Galway was disillusioned with the whole concept of the frontier war. He had groaned at the divided command and at Portuguese sloth and ineptitude. He still found Fagel a difficult colleague. And, as a Huguenot Frenchman himself, he was influenced by his contacts in southern France. So he now proposed attacking Languedoc, which he knew to be full of Calvinists, financially supported by Swiss followers of Jean Calvin, who could be armed and would rise against Louis. There were at least 10,000 such rebels active in and around Nîmes, Orange, Montpelier, and elsewhere in Provence, led by valiant men 'full of zeal for their religion'. Béarn, Foz, and Aquitaine as far as Bordeaux would join in the rising and soon there would be similar movements in Normandy and Brittany. The Duke of Savoy, a neighbour of the Swiss, had been drawn in and would carry out a concerted attack on the Dauphiné. As well as English and Dutch money sent via Switzerland there would be finance from the Jews in France who were in touch with their co-religionists in the Netherlands. All French troops of any value were, said Galway, on the Rhine or in Flanders and his proposal would fatally weaken the French effort in Spain and bring about the downfall of the Bourbon monarchy there.

But he had been out of England for some time and was in any case no longer closely associated with the inner centre of government there. He was of course not privy to Peterborough's and Shovell's secret instructions. Moreover his disillusionment with Portugal and with campaigns in that sector was known, so his proposals, which were suspect for this reason, were ruled out.

This was just as well, for Marshal Berwick had been sent to Montpelier in March that year to scotch rebellion there. The area had for three years been a hotbed of insurrection. In 1702, two men, Roland and Cavalier, had led disturbances, their Huguenot followers being called *Camisards* because they wore shirts over their ordinary clothes so as to be able to recognize each other by night. Roland had been killed fighting but Cavalier had fled to Switzerland and from thence to join the Duke of Savoy. (He later entered the English service, to end up as Governor of Jersey where he died in 1740.) Two Marshals of France, Montreuil and Villars, had tried unsuccessfully, by force of arms in one case and by negotiation in the other, to break the insurrection. Berwick, although not by nature bloodthirsty, was determined to extirpate the trouble. He was swift to trap the leaders. Three hundred of those involved were 'delivered to punishment'. Some he had burned alive, others broken on the wheel, justifying himself by the crimes of which he believed them guilty. Although perhaps 200,000 Huguenots (a French estimate) lived in the region and were encouraged in rebellion by the English and Dutch, the removal of the ring-leaders effectively dowsed any possible rising.

At the same time, Berwick watched carefully for any sign of Allied preparations for attacks on southern France and set up a system of fortifications and signal posts along the coast and on the Rhone to ward off any moves by the Duke of Savoy. He would himself have liked to go back to Spain but was instead sent to capture Nice, then one of the strongest cities in Europe. Later in 1705 he would do this, providing a further instance of his military talents. But for the present it was enough that he at least ensured that the Allies could not easily invade France from the south and that Galway's proposals, despite the low state of morale among both French and Spaniards in Spain, would have had no chance of success.

Moreover, if Berwick had had his way, the next Allied proposal, which we are about to examine, would have been abortive. He spent much of the spring and summer urging Chamillart to send 12,000 French troops from Roussillon, Provence and Languedoc into Catalonia, replacing them in France by militia. There is little doubt that even with a few French dragoon regiments and an artillery train from de Quinson at Perpignan, the outcome at Barcelona would have been different, particularly if Berwick himself had been allowed to command. His view of the Viceroy of Catalonia was not very complimentary: 'a faithful subject but a man of little courage', who needed backing up. But Chamillart was either too idle or too blind to see this and, in Berwick's bitter words, 'by his incapacity he pushed France to the edge of a precipice from which she only drew back by a miracle'.

None of this was, of course, known to the Allies at their meetings in Lisbon.

The next proposal they considered, then, was for a much stronger landing than that of 1704 at Barcelona. This was backed by Peterborough who realized that it was geographically close enough to Toulon to enable him to switch the attack if necessary in accordance with his secret orders. To the surprise of some, Darmstadt, who had been strongly in favour of a landing in Catalonia, had as we have seen recently adopted instead a proposal for Valencia which was of course closer to Madrid in distance. His earlier arguments in favour of Barcelona still stood, however. Most Catalan nobles and many citizens had taken an oath to Charles. Velasco, the Viceroy was 'a man of little authority and detested'. Barcelona was no stronghold (though had he not personally defended it successfully in 1697) The Conde de Cifuentes, now escaped and in Aragon, would help produce an army. The priests, except for the Jesuits and a few bishops, were pro-Carlist and rumour said that they had even gone so far as to refuse to confess or absolve those 'who did not detest in their hearts the Bourbon domination'. Pro-Austrian nobles were wearing as a sign of their allegiance a yellow sash. Once Barcelona fell there was little between it and Valencia in one direction, only Gerona between it and France in another, and only Lérida, an ancient place incapable of resistance, between Barcelona and the Kingdom of Aragon on the way to Madrid. While the Council was meeting, Darmstadt (in Gibraltar) was still worried about a premature rising. However, in the end, since Peterborough was apparently in favour of Barcelona, he was to concur and to sail with the expedition – to his death.

★   ★   ★

Despite occasional references in correspondence between Madrid and Versailles there is relatively little in the Madrid *Archivo* about preparations to improve the defences of Barcelona or Catalonia as a whole. This may be because thanks to the rebellious attitude of the population of the Province, mails just did not get through or it may have been slackness on the part of the Viceroy, Velasco. And of course in the early part of 1705 Bourbon efforts in Spain were haplessly concentrated on the attempt to recover Gibraltar, to secure Cadiz against attack and to protect the border between Extremadura and Castile, and Portugal. Moreover even with a recruiting drive under way little could be done from within Spain and reinforcements for Catalonia would have to come in from Roussillon or Naples and other Spanish possessions in Italy.

One of the *Legajos* (Number 272) contains some letters, usually brief, from Velasco to Rivas and his successor Mejorada. As early as 1st January 1705 Velasco reported hearing from a Colonel who had been a prisoner-of-war in English hands that there was talk of an Allied landing in Catalonia. He was looking to his defences and believed that gunpowder could be produced at a rate of 300 *arrobas* a month by the powder mills of Catalonia. Yet he asked for ammunition to be sent from the Gibraltar sector, a somewhat futile request in the light of what was going on there. He said little more until 10th February when in a short letter asking for infantry reinforcements he added: 'I am per-suaded that before the enemy fleet could get into these waters enough reinforce-ments will have come from Naples and Milan.'

Believing that the Conde de Cifuentes had much influence in the area he tried to meet him but the Conde was ill and in any case no doubt too fly to be drawn into discussions, and on 11th February Velasco reported that he could not make contact. Later in that month he ordered artillery from Majorca and reques-ted two months' supplies of grain and other foodstuffs.

In April he began to write twice a week or more to Madrid, nearly always complaining about shortages of men (he had to send troops to Tarragona and other cities as garrisons). The fortification of Montjuich was receiving attention, but now he found he could not get gunpowder and asked for it to be sent from France. However, he had changed his views on Allied intentions and now thought that if there were to be an Allied expedition it would go to Nice rather than Barcelona. All in all, Berwick's view of him seems justified. He was doing his best but it was not enough. Unfortunately much of his later correspondence appears to be missing.

However, there exists a continuous series of notes from the French intend-ants and other responsible officials which provide – until the capture of Barcelona – some account of military efforts there and an insight into the atmosphere in Catalonia.[4] Much of the information on Barcelona comes via de Quinson, the lieutenant-general governing Roussillon, who was based at Per-pignan, just across the border, and of the intendant, d'Albaret, responsible for disbursement of cash. These two were in continuous contact with Velasco. Occasional letters from him still filtered through to Don José de Grimaldo, and to Mejorada in Madrid, and provide some further colour. And there are scraps of information in letters to Versailles from Gramont and his successor as ambassador, Amelot, which reflect the Franco-Spanish views on the progress of the war.

Barcelona, although a fortified city, was not of the same quality as the great strongholds in northern France, Flanders and the Netherlands. It had a popu-lation of 35,000 or so (including a large number of religious) – the whole population of Catalonia was somewhere near 500,000 – and the citizens had suffered severely in the siege of 1695–7. Around it, where there are now suburbs or industrial quarters, there were a number of small villages set in attractive garden country where fruit and flowers grew well. Its sea-front was well inland from the present, which has been expanded enormously with recovered ground. Although the map of 1697 published by Sanpère y Miquel shows moles and there is reference in some accounts to one with a battery in the centre of the waterfront and two more to the west, a French map of 1697 shows that these had not been built and were only planned. In 1705 the city was split into two well defined sections, the old city and the Raval separated by the Ramblas (which is now a main street). The curtain wall, Vauban-like in intention, was weak on the western side though this was to some extent compensated for by the dominating rocky hill of Montjuich, 1,200 yards from the wall, and 750 feet high.

De Quinson was scathing about the population – 'the ecclesiastics are the worst' – and noted that desertions went on all the time. By mid-April his news was 'uniformly bad'. Velasco was fortifying the citadel of Montjuich and erecting palisades at the ends of all the roads leading to the ramparts. 'The people of Vich are disloyal and disobey the Viceroy.' By the end of that month Velasco was apparently counting on it that 'those people' (the Allies) would not stay long, but de Quinson was not so sure of this.

Although so much of Velasco's correspondence is missing, he himself appears still to have been doing his best as spring became summer. But his hold on the rural areas was becoming more and more tenuous as pro-Austrian sentiments spread through the people of Vich, Urgell and the Balearics. Ring-leaders such as the three Puig brothers, the Moragues and the Cortadas were summoned to Barcelona but only one – Josep Mas i Torre de Roda – went. He was imprisoned. The remainder were able to escape even when search parties were sent after them, and to take refuge in the mountainous, difficult country. Here they awaited news from Perera in Genoa. Velasco tried desperately to extinguish the fires of what he clearly recognized as a widespread armed rising. He appointed a three-man committee under Llupia Agulló-Pinós. From Vich they wrote to confirm that what in effect was taking place was a full-scale rebellion in favour of Charles III. Meantime de Quinson admits that things are still much the same in Barcelona. 'Revolt is only awaiting the arrival of an enemy fleet. The Viceroy has arrested a few people including a priest and a merchant called Amador Dalmau.' The area around Vich is 'a hotbed of rebellion and the leaders of the revolt are spending so much that they must be receiving financial aid.' As an official summary of the high summer of 1705, put it, 'Everything seemed to conspire this year to assure the loss of Spain.'

*   *   *

On 24th July the English troops including the Royal Dragoons, and a body of Spaniards 500 strong and called the King's Guard, were embarked. On the

28th, Peterborough together with Charles III and his court boarded H.M.S. *Ranelagh*. By now Peterborough who had loathed them from the start was openly referring to them as 'the German crew'. The Conde de Assumar, the Portuguese envoy, was with them, and Paul Methuen. Some vessels had already sailed for Gibraltar, and Sarsfield at Cadiz reported 'an Allied fleet' passing on July 13th and some ships 'looking in' on the 19th.

By 3rd August the whole Allied armada, united with Shovell and the main part of the fleet, was at Gibraltar. Peterborough had entertained Charles and 'the German crew' lavishly while in transit, no doubt using the Rhenish burgundy and sturgeon he had bought in Holland. The expense was of course considerable and the ceremony stifling. Next day Charles went ashore in state and was proclaimed lawful sovereign of Gibraltar. Weighing anchor on 5th August the armada was delayed for days by a brisk easterly wind. Renaud, still before Gibraltar, reported that the armada had moved into Gibraltar Bay, but his letter, dated 14th August, could add no more.

De Quinson, on tenterhooks at Perpignan, had heard that the fleet was now in the Mediterranean and reported it to Versailles. He was having to send expresses to Versailles, Madrid and also to the Duke of Berwick in Languedoc, and was forced to ask Intendant d'Albaret to defray the increasing cost of communications as the threat and the tension rose. D'Albaret was also asked to provide the money required for paying the militia 'on the same scale as in the last war'.

Every few days de Quinson reports further disturbing developments. The garrison at Rosas is very weak though that at Gerona is a little stronger, but more troops are needed from Roussillon. At Vich three of the gates have had to be kept closed in order that the others may be properly guarded. Restlessness is increasing in Catalonia but Velasco – still apparently 'a man of spirit and zeal' – should not be blamed, for many people are not doing their duty. De Quinson has been told that 1,200 Neapolitan troops are on their way to help garrison Barcelona. Then the number is corrected. It will only be 500. D'Albaret has his own tales of woe. He has arrested a Neapolitan monk who was travelling to Barcelona to seduce some Neapolitan troops already in the garrison. The rebels of Vich have tried and shot a man from Barcelona believed to be plotting to kill their chief, and they have had word from Darmstadt that an Allied fleet of 80 vessels is on its way. The same rebels have made their bishop hand over 16,000 *reals* under threat. There was in fact no bishop at the time. Antoni Pasqual had died a year earlier, but rumour and counter-rumour abound in such circumstances, as anyone who has lived through a war will confirm.

At last the Allies were on the move when the wind changed and by 11th

August had reached Altea Bay where they anchored for three days in order to take on water. Here they sent three or four *caballeros* ashore, according to Amelot, to encourage the population to join King Charles' cause, and the king began to receive many local notables, come to kiss his hand. The Province of Valencia had heard of Darmstadt's reputation and people were attracted to the Austrian interest. Peterborough began to issue broadsheets to the effect that he had come 'to deliver the Spanish nation from the hateful yoke of Frenchmen and foreigners.'

Charles himself issued a formal manifesto, dated 15th August 'aboard the *Gran Bretaña*' (H.M.S. *Britannia*). Beginning with a recital of his titles it proceeds in stately Spanish to set out his claim to the kingship and then to state categorically that he has only come 'to restore the Spanish monarchy and save the country from the servitude to which it has been reduced'. He promises 'his royal benignity to all loyal vassals'.

A copy of this reached Valencia whence it was forwarded by the viceroy to Grimaldo on 1st September, with the comment that it was a 'seditious paper'. It helped to stimulate a broad popular movement in Charles' favour throughout the southern lands of the Kingdom of Valencia, as the Allied fleet slid by, landing agents and bribes. San Felipe and another almost contemporary chronicler, Miñana, who were trying to please the court of Madrid, wrote of the situation in the Kingdom of Valencia as though it were an agrarian revolt, but the Valencians had been restless for a decade or more. Now they were against 'the French' which was probably a loose term including those who were pro-Bourbon.

While the fleet watered at Altea, many of the people flocked to greet Charles and Darmstadt with presents and offers of adherence. But Peterborough's secret instructions, to make for Toulon and a land and sea attack in concert with the Duke of Savoy, still held so far. It was while at Altea between 10th and 16th August that he received a batch of letters that deepened his quandary, when the frigate H.M.S. *Lyme* arrived with the details of the Genoa pact, some letters from Mitford Crowe, from the Dutch Consul at Genoa and from Richard Hill, the English minister in Turin. Although the Genoa pact and Crowe's letters were such as to encourage the Allies to attempt the Barcelona landing, they were still contradictory to Peterborough's secret orders about Toulon. Yet these in turn were now rendered futile by what Hill wrote.

There had been a misunderstanding in London, said this Minister, and de Briançon should never have promised on his master's behalf to participate in an attack on Toulon. The duke, so far from being able to provide men, was in dire difficulties for Turin itself was under siege. And even if he had had the men he would not have been prepared to send them through the enemy-held passes to Provence. 'His Royal Highness is not and cannot be in a position to assist your Lordship in the Toulon project,' wrote Hill. His first letter on the subject was dated 1st July and was followed by two others, of the 12th and 19th repeating the situation, and he also wrote directly to Shovell in the same sense. So far from attacking Toulon, Victor Amadeus believed he needed help himself to prevent Nice and Villefranche falling into Bourbon hands.

Peterborough wrote furiously to Hill, beginning his letter while at Altea, and concluding it a couple of weeks later when off Barcelona: 'Your letter has changed the whole sense of the war and will send elsewhere the two thousand men intended to help the Duke of Savoy.' He still hankered after Italy – now with only the purpose of going to the aid of Victor Amadeus. He veered towards a proposal made in July by Darmstadt of landing at Valencia and marching to Madrid. Nevertheless he appears in the end to have fallen in with the rest of the council of war when it met at Charles' request on 13th August for there exists a short note sent by van Allmonde the next day to The Hague:

> 'The King sat at a table apart. In polite but nevertheless definite language he spoke of the need to go ahead with the plan to disembark in the neighbour-hood of Barcelona. He said that his subjects, the inhabitants of the King-dom of Valencia had given ample signs of good will towards him. He was sure that those of the Kingdom of Catalonia would not be less disposed to throw off the reign of the Duke of Anjou [Philip] and submit themselves to his dominion. He was sure that with the powerful aid of the English and the Republic [the Netherlands] the undertaking would be a success.'

There seems to have been unanimous agreement.

Present at this meeting were Peterborough, Admirals Shovell, Leake and Fairborne, Generals Conyngham, Donegal, Charlemont, Stanhope, Gorges, and the Dutch Admiral van Allmonde and General van Schratenbach as well as Darmstadt and Lichtenstein. And Peterborough must have realized that these would have communicated the decision to their subordinates. Thus, according to a contemporary note, 'This broke His Lordship's former measures and obliged him, contrary to his inclination, to frame designs upon Catalonia.'

At mid-day on 22nd August, Shovell brought the fleet to anchor three miles east of Barcelona and within sight of the city. A cursory bombardment of the seashore drove off a small force of cavalry which had appeared and next day a party of 200 grenadiers was landed in heavy surf at Badalona on the mouth of the River Besòs and took up a covering position while a further 3,000 troops went ashore during the next five hours, the local country folk providing planks and in their enthusiasm even carrying soldiers ashore on their backs. Shovell in order to assist lent a party of 1,150 marines from his squadron and on the 24th the Royal Dragoons landed. By the 25th the Barcelona garrison, perhaps some 5,000 strong altogether, including Popoli's newly arrived Neapolitans, was faced by up to 8,000 Allied foot and 1,800 horse who had come ashore, many of them at Sant Andreu between Barcelona and Badalona. Darmstadt landed with the first wave which marched to a village called Sant Marti a mile north-east of Barcelona, with their left resting on the sea. A road junction called the Covered Cross was occupied, and a force of *Miquelets* turned up as promised. Darmstadt, who had been the first to land, and had been greeted with pleasure by the locals, began without opening siege works, to place the whole force in a position to invest the city.[5]

Velasco, whose assistants were Popoli, the French Marquis de Richebourg and the Spaniard Aytona ('men', says San Felipe, 'of undoubted loyalty and courage'), did nothing, 'for he was short of troops and many of those he had were in favour of the Austrian cause.' But an informant of d'Alabret's claimed that 'Velasco, although thought to be out for the glory of making a stout defence, instead of wearing modest practical clothes is going about in a gold coat with diamond buttons'. The noblemen who were disposed to Charles III 'deceitfully kept quiet but pushed their affairs ahead', says San Felipe. Meanwhile '6,000 rebels and bandits – a mob of the worst types in the principality, only there to seek in rebellion pardon for their misdeeds – came to the very gates of the city. Here they flew the Austrian flag and encircled the place so that supplies could not be brought in from the surrounding country and the inhabitants suffered hunger. Velasco asked the magistrates for money but they impudently refused to provide it. All was corruption. Some citizens and noblemen went gladly out to raise the province, for the open country was all for the new king. Some walled cities out of evil intention hoped for the arrival of enemy troops to whom they would open the gates.' D'Albaret passed on snippets of news as they came in.

'There are not more than 9,000 men disembarked and the Archduke is still sleeping on board ... Darmstadt is telling the rebels that there will soon be 20,000 soldiers and 60 large cannon ... He talks of sending 40 companies of *Miquelets* into Roussillon ... There is talk of the Allies making for Port Mahon [in Minorca] ... The priests and monks are leading the revolt.'

But soon: 'The poison of revolt and brigandage in Catalonia has become so strong that we have hardly any communications.'

During all this, insulated by distance and time, Philip was relatively undisturbed. His grandfather, in Paris, was even more remote. Late in July, after lecturing his grandson ('You must have sufficient forces to enable you to hold your head up against the enemy. It is not good to have to avoid them, and if you cannot win you must at least not give your manoeuvres the appearance of continual flight...'), he wrote, 'The embarkation of the Archduke is the last attempt the enemy will make before abandoning their designs on Spain.'

He was deluded, but while he could not know it, all was not well in the Allied camp. Charles III had indeed landed and 'everybody in Barcelona, monks, women and children had gone to see him'. Priests celebrated Mass at a portable altar. The city was encircled. But no siege works had been begun and Charles is understood to have forbidden a bombardment, though twenty-six large cannon and fifteen mortars were already ashore, for fear of alienating his prospective subjects. He could describe himself as the Catholic King and give formal audiences to the ambassadors of the various crowns who had come with him – the Duke of Moles, soon to be representing the emperor; Paul Methuen for England, and de Assumar for Portugal. He could fly his flag. The people could run to see him. He could as 'their natural Lord' issue awards and decorations. He and Darmstadt could send letters and manifestos. So could, and did Peterborough. But the fact remained that the general rising had not taken place, and Barcelona was still held for the Bourbons. Moreover as nothing was going as planned there were again severe disagreements between the various Allied commanders, and the expedition was at stalemate.

Peterborough began to say impatiently that they had come 'on a bootless errand'; Darmstadt had promised and so had London that Barcelona would be found ill fortified and poorly garrisoned, that the inhabitants would rise and open the gates and that there would be 10,000 Catalans to cover and support the landing. What was the true situation? Instead of 10,000 fighting men there were only as many 'higglers and sutlers'. The garrison was 7,000 strong – about equal to the numbers he had brought. He began to exaggerate. The fortifications were *very* strong. The ground in which siege works would be dug was soggy. If a battery were placed 500 yards from the walls and a breach made it could only be stormed under heavy fire. There were not enough men to bring up fascines and gabions or serve the battery. Since France was only 140 miles away the garrison was likely to be easily reinforced.

He gave no weight to favourable factors. Barcelona, as we have seen, was not in fact strongly fortified. Velasco, the Viceroy, had made little or no attempt

to stop the Allied landing or to sally and counterattack. There was sure information that his position was uncertain in the extreme. Good intelligence put the
garrison at not more than 5,000 of whom many were disaffected. Even if the
Allied army were only about double this figure there were now a few thousand
Miquelets capable of auxiliary service. For manual labour there were hundreds if
not thousands of local civilians who were willing to lend a hand. (Of course they
wanted pay, but although this request was backed by Darmstadt, Peterborough
turned it down.) But above all there was the fleet of about sixty of the line,
manned by 20,000 sailors and carrying 3,500 guns.

Within the city Velasco, with the help of his Spanish and Italian regulars
was still in control. Men of good family were under house arrest. A curfew was
enforced with night patrols, cannon were placed at street corners. But beneath
this thin meniscus he knew that pressure was building up. The list of 'rebel'
families quoted by San Felipe – Centelles, Pinós, Savallá, and the rest, does not
represent anything like the number of true pro-Austrians. In his perplexity
Velasco redoubled his repressive measures.

Had the Allies been more resolute they would have succeeded earlier but
they could not at first know of the true position, nor of the panic gripping the
Madrid Court and – through the reports from Perpignan and elsewhere – the
concern at Versailles. They certainly had some indications but mistrusted these.
And there was no good generalship there, capable of taking a chance. Charles
and Darmstadt might press that it would be humiliating, having come so far, to
withdraw without even trying something, but they had themselves no army,
and while Shovell and the admirals were for an offensive, Peterborough was
commander-in-chief.

And he it was, claiming that a siege of Barcelona was impracticable and that
if it were attempted there could be no retreat, who favoured inaction, calling
council after council while the disembarkation proceeded. High words were
exchanged. Shovell and the admirals – and some of the generals – sided with
Charles in favour of an assault. A contemporary report shows why the decision
was made at least to stay on in the area. The debate lasted four hours at the end of
which Charles himself spoke for half an hour,

'resuming [summing up] the whole debate. He answered all the objections
that were made against the siege and treated every one of those who had
made them, as he answered them, with particular civilities. In the state in
which his affairs then stood nothing could be proposed that had not great
difficulties in it. All was doubtful and much must be put to hazard. But this
seemed less dangerous than any other thing that was proposed. Many of his

subjects had come and declared for him to the hazard of their lives. It became him therefore to let them see that he would run the same hazard with them. He desired that they [the English and Dutch] should stay so long with him till such attempts should be made, that all the world might be convinced that nothing could be done, and he hoped, till that appeared, they would not leave him. He added that if their orders obliged them to leave him yet he could not desert his own subjects.'

Ably argued and forcibly and movingly delivered by a twenty-year-old with little experience and practice, this speech persuaded his Allies at least to stay with him, though not necessarily on his terms.

Peterborough appeared to yield a little. A battery of fifty guns might be landed and if possible the place would be carried by assault. But he qualified this by limiting the time. As joint commander-in-chief he bore admiral's as well as general's rank and, using the former, he pointed out that it was a general rule in the Navy not to stay in the Mediterranean beyond the first half of September, since the weather was treacherous and squadrons returning to England were in danger of gales or fog in the Channel. The Spaniards had a saying:

'Junio, Julio, Agosto y Puerto Mahon
Los mejores puertos en el Mediterráneo son',

while the English put it more prosaically:

'There are only three safe ports in the Mediterranean,
June, July and Port Mahon.'

The first were past and the last was in Spanish hands. Peterborough took no positive steps. Colonel John Richards records that the earl instructed him 'merely to amuse' Charles by a show of activity, and at the same time conveniently 'forgot' to order Petit to erect the battery works.

At a further meeting Shovell repeated his order of priorities: Barcelona, Cadiz, some other spot on the Spanish coast and only if all these failed, Italy. Peterborough continued to prevaricate. He would prefer to attack Valencia if the king and Darmstadt would agree. If, on the other hand, Barcelona were unsuccessfully attacked, Darmstadt would get the blame, for, said Peterborough, 'His Highness is regarded in England as prodigal of soldiers' lives.' Moreover, if it were known by the men that the generals were against an assault on the city they might mutiny.

He was still hankering after Italy, writing to the Duke of Savoy, saying that his most earnest wish was to concert operations with him and that to succour Savoy was the preferred object of the expedition, better by far than attempt to take a town of which his forces could only encircle a fifth.

While he was still adopting this stance, however, trenches had been opened on the eastern side, English and Dutch soldiers working alongside Catalan labourers. The latter wanted 5 *centims* a day but as Peterborough was not paying a day rate to his men he refused, though while soldiers had pay (on a different basis) and rations, the peasants had nothing. It was a slow process and as late as 2nd September Velasco was able to get a message out to Perpignan and Berwick could send in two officers to see what was happening.

Small engagements took place, the Allies taking a convent on the outskirts. Some forty Spanish soldiers deserted from the Gate of l'Angel during the night. Velasco decided to expel some of the dissidents but as those who left early were insulted and fired on, few followed them. He cannot have been much encouraged when a letter he had sent to Madrid was returned to him because it had been wrongly addressed – to the Duque de Medina Sidonia not the Duque de Montalba. Bureaucracy was as rife as ever. He received demands for provisions from the city Council of 100. A couple of deserters from the Allied camp came in and told him of the preparations being made. He forced some of the city's labourers to work on the fortifications. He hanged a few men found wearing the yellow sash and thus showing pro-Austrian feelings. And so it went on desultorily, while the Allied generals bickered and delayed.

★   ★   ★

Although there was growing disaffection among the grandees in Madrid, Aragon was loyal, thanks in no small way to the archbishop of its capital, Saragossa. Early reports of its secession to Charles were panicky. In fact the archbishop, Antonio Ibañez, and a majority of its noblemen were staunchly for Philip. His prolific correspondence, of which there are dozens of examples in the Madrid *Archivo*, show him to have been very much of the Church Militant, and a great deal more practical and energetic than most of the military hierarchy. Always chronically short of money he made no bones about pressing for *donativos* in his diocese, and as early as 12th September (just before the capture of Montjuich) he was concerned about the importance of holding the line formed by the rivers Cinca and Ebro which meet at Mequinenza near Lérida, and scraped together 400 men from within Saragossa and from Barbastro, seventy miles to the north-east of his capital, sending them to Lérida as reinforcements 'until the Royal Troops arrive', for there were reports of tumults in that city.

Lérida itself (in Catalan Lleida), with its high citadel, the Suda, was an obvious key point in the defence of Aragon. Almost exactly halfway between Barcelona and Saragossa, in a commanding situation where communications had always crossed, it had long ago been fought over by Caesar's and Pompey's legions and had been occupied for four centuries by the Moors. Now it was again to be a battleground, and two years later its cathedral, with the tall octagonal belfry, a little like a masculine version of the lantern at Ely, would be converted by Philip into a fortress.

On 29th August, 1705, Prince Henry of Hesse-Darmstadt arrived there with a regiment of German cavalry to take it, well before the fall of Barcelona. The bishop, another militant prelate, wrote to Grimaldo in Madrid reporting its loss. Like the Archbishop of Saragossa he was firmly loyal to Philip and excused both himself and the governor who 'could do nothing for lack of succours'. He asked, too, for money to help recruitment.

A whole bundle of letters can be seen in the Madrid *Archivo* reporting sedition in Balaguer, Cervera and elsewhere. Inland from the coast Caspé, Alcañiz and San Mateo fell to bands of mixed *Miquelets* and regulars. Igualada had been occupied by the rebels. In desparation the Commander-in-chief in Valencia, General José Salazar, was ordered to Aragon. He, together with *Maréchal du Camp* Luis de Zúñiga had just left Almansa, and a day-by-day account of their marches exists. They invested Denia unavailingly and were by September 8th on their way to Gandia, sending all their cavalry ahead into Catalonia. On their way de Zúñiga had forced the rebels in Molinet to surrender. Villagarcía, the Viceroy of the Province of Valencia wrote to Grimaldo about pardoning repentant rebels and only punishing the hardened ones, but it was no time for half measures. He was, however, in a better situation than heretofore, supplies having arrived on 28th August, though he was 'disconsolate' at having to send men to Barcelona as it left him short.

Other reinforcements were being rushed north-eastwards through the harsh summer heats. Colonel Cornelius O'Driscoll at Almansa reported the arrival at about this time of three regiments at two-day intervals. There were 999 muskets with bayonets, 986 sabres and 120 'stones' available at Almansa for them. But as the Possoblanco regiment had come from Cadiz and O'Mahony had marched his from outside Gibraltar, they must all have been exhausted. Another Irish regiment, Dillon's, was also reported on its way, and the French regiment de Maine was also ordered to the sector.

It was all a matter of stop-gaps and barrel-scraping, and it was not enough, though the squabbling between the Allies was such that even the tiny efforts of the Bourbons could have prevailed. That they did not do so was due to a temporary cessation of bickering in Allied headquarters.

By some obscure instinct de Quinson in Perpignan put his finger on a possibility that nobody else had mentioned and which appears only to have occurred at the last possible moment to the Allied command. On 21st September, before he could have any idea of what was going on, he began a letter to Chamillart saying that he was concerned that Barcelona was threatened 'from the heights'. To that letter he added a later PS, saying that he had just heard rumours that Darmstadt had been killed in an attack on Montjuich. He was right.

★   ★   ★

As dawn broke on Monday September 14th 1705 an assault party of 400 English and Irish troops, including some dragoons, commanded by Lieutenant-Colonel William Southwell of Rivers' Regiment and backed by a support group of 400 English, 100 Dutch and 100 Spanish musketeers under Lieutenant-Colonel Thomas Allen of Brudenell's, was waiting to attack Fort Montjuich on the hill 750 feet above and 1,200 yards to the west of the city of Barcelona. Prince George of Hesse-Darmstadt and the Earl of Peterborough were there, the former as a volunteer the latter in command. The Irishman, Colonel John Richards, was there too. Half a mile or so away downhill was a main reserve of 300 dragoons and about 1,000 infantrymen together with some small mortars and fieldpieces, all under Brigadier-General James Stanhope.

The assault party had been divided into a Forlorn Hope of thirty shock troops under an un-named Lieutenant and a back-up group of fifty under a Captain, with the remainder in the rear as a reserve. They were awaiting the signal to break, without any preliminary bombardment, into the bastion of the fort nearest to the city (i.e. on the east side). They were a little later than intended for they had come by a roundabout route from east of the city by a night march over unfamiliar ground. Their guides had been unreliable and the last part of the route from Sarriá had been over very broken territory. About 200 had gone astray and missed the rendezvous and the remainder had been much spread out when they arrived two hours before dawn. So it had taken time to sort the force out in the dark and in the silence imposed by the need for surprise.

Written twenty years after the event, Carleton's account says that Peterborough had insisted that a night or dawn attack would be too risky and that the men needed to rest after their long approach march. Perhaps, but Colonel Richards in his journal says somewhat critically that they had all lost their way, 'the musqueteers going in one direction, the grenadiers in another and the generals a third, and all wrong'. The result in any case was that they would soon be spotted by the fort's sentries if these were alert, but such a situation was inevitable since this bold stroke had been decided only a day or so before. There had been no time for rehearsal and, although Carleton says that Peterborough had reconnoitred in advance, accompanied by a single staff officer (Richards), this had been at least ten days earlier.

While the task force endures the tension of waiting for action it is time to examine the genesis of the affair, for it has long been disputed by those who like and those who dislike Peterborough. There had been those councils of war over a period of nearly three weeks. One had produced a decision that a siege of Barcelona was impracticable, another that an attempt should be made but only for a limited period of eighteen days. There had been one at which Peter- borough signed an agreement in favour of a siege and sent Stanhope to Shovell asking for naval reinforcements, only to come himself aboard the *Britannia* the same day, change his general's hat for an admiral's and cancel the request. *The Full and Impartial History* concludes that 'he did not vote for undertaking the siege at all and yet had a mind the experiment should be made at the hazard of other admirals in his absence'.

This pamphlet claims that Peterborough 'had little inclination to con- tribute to the reduction of Catalonia', whereas 'the Prince of Hesse [was] continually advising His Majesty to press the siege'. It is not surprising that communications between the two generals had become sterile and that Charles himself was convinced that Peterborough was not to be trusted. The king had, after all, impressed everybody with his determination at the four-hour-long council meeting he attended, and might reasonably have hoped for some consis- tency on the part of the English commander-in-chief. But this was not in Peterborough's character, 'changing his plans and his friends as readily as he shifted his shirt' (Trevelyan). He was now determined on re-embarking all siege material and troops.

Darmstadt had expressed his and his monarch's view in a letter dated 8th September (six days before the assault on Montjuich) to Shovell, whom he had clearly come to trust and who had missed that critical council of war.

'His Catholic Majesty, being in the greatest trouble in the world to find my Lord Peterborough again resolved to leave this enterprise hath his only recourse to you; His Majesty declaring that, if His Lordship persists in his resolution to go away, His Majesty finding that without reason his crown and so good subjects shall be sacrificed, is resolved to stay with them. This I must acquaint you with, in hopes that you will never permit such a cruel abandoning, and to take your measures accordingly. The king begs it of you as the last [i.e. greatest] favour, and intreats you in the most submissive manner, to find out a way, that His Majesty may not be the sacrifice of fools and knaves.'

At this stage then we find Peterborough still determined to break off the Barcelona operation while Charles and Darmstadt are equally determined to stay on whatever happens, and Shovell, though bound to leave the Mediterranean before too long in order not to risk his fleet, is still prepared to help. He was apparently a rock of steadiness in the eyes of the anxious young king, far from home and seeking means of fulfilling the mission entrusted to him, and those of the resolute, impetuous, outspoken Darmstadt.

Later that same day, Darmstadt wrote again to Shovell, by hand of Captain John Norris, R.N., Captain of H.M.S. *Britannia* and Shovell's acting liaison officer with the Court, hoping that Peterborough would not begin 'a sudden embarking' and asking the admiral 'if it could be done, being the resolutions of the council of war, to land as soon as possible all the guns and everything necessary to hinder any resolution to the contrary'.

Norris, born probably in 1660, is less well known than some of his contemporaries though when he died in 1749 he was an Admiral of the Fleet. He had been lieutenant of H.M.S. *Edgar* in 1689, serving under the then Captain Shovell. In 1698 he had been suspected of treachery for failing to attack St John's, Newfoundland, but let off by the influence of Russell, Earl of Orford (to whom he had attached himself). At Cadiz in 1702, when in command of H.M.S. *Orford* (named after Russell), he had got himself into trouble on board Rooke's flagship the *Royal Sovereign* by having a dispute with its Captain, Ley. Norris 'beat Ley, threw him over a gun and drew his sword upon him on the quarterdeck.'. This time the Duke of Ormonde got him released from arrest. Ley died soon afterwards, but Norris' career continued. He served as a captain under Shovell at Velez Málaga. Peterborough disliked him, calling him 'a governing coxcomb' and it is strange to find him doing liaison duties with the earl. But Shovell obviously appreciated him and found him a serviceable subordinate two years later in 1707.

Darmstadt's letters, as always, though couched in a formal English which was not even his mother tongue, convey deeply-felt and energetic urgency.

Next day, the 9th, he wrote again, saying that the king, finding it impossible to abandon subjects who showed so much zeal for him and who would be ruined if deserted, had asked Peterborough to propose some other expedient such as a march to Tarragona 'keeping the Dutch with us', followed by winter quarters in Tortosa or even Valencia. Shovell's assistance was requested for 'the only expedient left to preserve some hopes of being put into the possession of the crown of Spain'. Some reports suggest that the volatile *Miquelets* were threatening, if the Allies did not capture Barcelona, to kill any of their troops still remaining as well as local supporters of Charles 'in order to earn pardon' from Philip V.

On the 10th Darmstadt wrote to Shovell saying that Peterborough had 'at last' agreed to the march and went on to ask that while this was going on the fleet should take Majorca, Minorca or Ibiza, 'where no resistance can be made', and leave there 'some winter squadrons'. He further suggested 'before we leave this place', that Shovell should 'throw some shells and cannonade the place where they build their gallies, and there to summon the town; and then to make some attack with boats and with ladders by the country people . . . all which I leave to your best consideration'. The letter ended with a very warm message of thanks for all that Shovell had done and an acknowledgement that the king would 'always owe to him the good success of this undertaking'. On the same day Charles wrote to Peterborough personally formally accepting the offer to march to Tarragona, 'seeing there remains nothing else to support me in Spain', and leaving to the Earl 'the dispositions and particulars of the march *and of further designs to be formed* (my italics). It is possible that Peterborough had hinted at some special plan, though in the account written at his request by Dr Freind it is explicitly stated that the Earl, 'because of the misunderstanding' between him and Darmstadt 'even concealed that design [the attack on Montjuich] from the court'.

At all events, on 13th September, after three weeks of indecision, some resolution had evidently been made, for Darmstadt, hearing that Captain Cavendish (H.M.S. *Antelope)* was about to sail, sent a letter to Shovell to stop the sailing, 'some particular service being resolved'. The letter ended, 'My Lord Peterborough desires me to write these lines and *hopes that this night's business will make us all easy'* (my italics). Shovell's own correspondence, containing an exact though brief journal of the siege, also indicates that something unusual was about to be undertaken at this time. It can only have been the venture against Fort Montjuich. Darmstadt's letter of the 13th clearly indicates that Peterborough, with whom he had for some time not been on speaking terms, was actually with him as he wrote. But which of the two was actually responsible for planning the taking of Montjuich as a key to Barcelona?[6]

It would have riled Peterborough to know that in the French and Spanish accounts of Montjuich his name is not even mentioned. Freind's and Carleton's accounts on the other hand insist that it was Peterborough who took the initiative, the former going out of his way to depreciate Darmstadt's relevance. 'That brave prince indeed had two [sic] great a share in the danger of this undertaking but as he had no command in the army so he was not in the least concerned in this design.'

It is certain that deserters from Barcelona came daily to the army and brought intelligence including probably the information that Monjuich was not well guarded, since it was believed by Velasco that the Allies were not strong enough to attack it. Richards mentions two reconnaissances in which he himself was involved. One of them, on 3rd September, took three hours from Peterborough's headquarters but there is no mention of Montjuich. The other, on the 17th, was after the fall of the citadel. On the other hand there is a strong tradition, referred to by Parnell and Francis, of a conspiracy within the garrison of Montjuich. There was certainly a meeting between Darmstadt and Peterborough, for there was an eye-witness of it who is to be trusted, and that was Colonel John Richards. The march to Tarragona had been agreed, he says. Then

> 'It was the 13th of the said month that my Lord Peterborough was pleased to communicate to me certain information which he got from divers deserters from the Citadel . . . [those deserters again].He ordered me to the Pr. of Hesse to appoint a time of conference with him. It was resolved to attack. I was the only person present at this conference.'

Later he says:

> 'Notwithstanding the former resolution of a march, my Lord Peterborough being resolved of the ill state of Montjuich . . . *he proposed to me the surprise of it this night by escalade, and afterwards the Prince approving thereof.*'

Elsewhere Richards' writings are critical of Peterborough and, if there had been no behind-the-scenes deal, this makes his evidence and Peterborough's claim the more credible.

Yet there is still another piece of evidence, this time in Abel Boyer's *History* to which some weight must be given. Here it is clearly stated, in a book published the next year and *dedicated to Peterborough*:

'*The Prince of Hesse proposed the attacking of Montjuich*. The Earl of Peterborough having taken a view of Fort Montjuich and of the Town on that
side and maturely weighed His Higness' Reasons . . . *not only concurr'd* with
the Prince and granted him the 1,000 men he desired but likewise decided
to support His Highness himself with some men more and some dragoons.
The better to conceal His Design from the enemy, the cannon, stores and
baggage were drawn off to be reimbarked and 'twas given out that the
Army would march by land to join the fleet at Tarragona.'

Now it seems extraordinary that if Peterborough really wanted – as it would
appear – to grab the credit for the assault, he should have allowed such a
statement to appear in a book actually dedicated to him. Admittedly he was still
abroad, either in Spain or on his leisurely way home, when it came out. But he
does not seem to have issued any contradiction at the time, though Swift later
included Boyer in his extensive gallery of rogues.

★   ★   ★

Most battles are confused affairs to those taking part and Montjuich was no
exception. The accounts of it vary according to the teller.

It is certain that the assault did not begin until the sun rose to show the
attackers the fort looming over them, and occasional shots indicated that they
had been spotted. Caraccioli knew in fact that an assault would made made that
morning for some *Miquelets* had told him of the Allies' march. Since the outer
walls of the fort were in poor condition and provided vantage points for the
attackers he ordered the garrison to man the interior wall which was in good
condition and commanded a well-cleared glacis. The first wave of the attack
scaled the outer walls and tackled the defenders who were camped in tents. The
defence was driven into the keep and the attackers built a breastwork of stones to
protect themselves. The scaling ladders were now found to be too short to
enable the advance party to reach the top of the inner walls and they retired
behind the breastworks. At this the dragoons present retreated in turn just as
Peterborough and Darmstadt came up. According to St Pierre, the two generals
ordered the dragoons forward again. They then agreed to divide their duties.
Peterborough, in Richards' words, 'seeing the way things were likely to go,
turned aside to give the necessary orders for the advancing of more troops

perticularly [sic] a reserve commanded by Brigadier Stanhope'. This involved riding downhill to where Stanhope was waiting.

The force under Stanhope's command had the dual rôle of reserve for the assault and of preventing reinforcements being sent uphill from the city. It consisted of about 300 dismounted dragoons and 1,000 foot and may also have contained a further few hundred Catalan volunteers under Antoni de Peguera, acting as colonel of militia. A further 100 Catalans were with the attacking force. These were probably Darmstadt's personal guard which he had brought from Gibraltar.

Meantime Darmstadt, observing that communications between the city and the fort were still open, had decided to lead the forward reserve to cut them. He was accompanied by his brother, Prince Henry, and a Dutch colonel. In doing so, to Richards' amazement, Darmstadt 'absolutely mistook the way, which a body would think scarcely possibly [sic] for a man of his caracter [sic] and that had commanded 6 years in the Town'. Darmstadt's route took him and his men past the Grand Gate of the citadel, where, says Richards, 'We were all seen from head to foot whilst we saw nothing more of the enemy than their hatts'.

Firing was heavy and it was now that a musket ball hit Darmstadt in the thigh just by a wound he had received at the siege of Bonn sixteen years before. A main artery was cut but he refused to withdraw, merely allowing a surgeon to tie up the wound and bleed him – which seems an odd remedy to apply to someone who was already haemorrhaging. One account says that a cannonball landing nearby wounded him again, this time in the shoulder, but this is unconfirmed and it is more likely that the wound in the thigh was enough. Richards says touchingly, 'His glass being runne out of late cut the thread of life of the bravest man in the world, and that by a very slight wound.'

The Spanish report says, 'Such was the effect of his [Darmstadt's] death that nobody could think of anything but retiring'; that is precisely true. The defence had recovered from its surprise. The governor of the fort, Caraccioli, seeing only a small number of attackers gathered some four hundred of his men together for a sally. It was warmer now and the air was full of powder-smoke and dust. Richards records that 'the want of water was extreme' and this did not help. The senior Allied brigadier present, Lord Charlemont, an inexperienced officer, ordered a retreat and then, as the enemy did not pursue at once, halted it and ordered a renewal of the assault.

This was met with heavy musket fire and a new, panicky retreat began which officers were unable to stop even with swords drawn. Richards says 'they fled with greater consternation than I ever saw [in] Englishmen'. Had the defenders sallied in force they would soon have overcome the weary, diminished assault party. Meantime Peterborough, on his way downhill, had been advised of the sorry situation at the fort and could hear heavy firing from that direction. He therefore turned and spurred uphill again. Now the Earl met the retreating men when they were 'half a musket shot' – about fifty yards – from the fort, and showed considerable resolution. Despite his diminutive size he dominated the proceedings, falling, says Richards, 'into the horriblest rage that ever man was seen in'. Seizing a half-pike (used for carrying a regimental colour), he called on the men to follow him. They did so and were back, according to Carleton, at their posts 'before Caraccioli knew they had left'. Richards describes the move as 'very rash', since the enemy were now plainly seen sallying from the city. It was now seven o'clock.

Between Barcelona and where Stanhope was posted there was a Chapel of Sant Bertran, 'on the croup of the hill' says the Spanish account, which, poorly defended, had just been captured by a party of *Miquelets*. Velasco and the Duke of Popoli saw that their enemy was not in retreat. However, they sent a couple of hundred grenadiers riding on the cruppers of Spanish dragoons to reinforce the garrison. The arrival of this force provoked shouts of '*Viva el Rey*' and the defenders opened the gates. Richards thought 'they made a motion to lay down their arms' and that it was a ruse.

Although Velasco was cheered by the defence of Montjuich, the fort was now surrounded. Yet the besieging force was not strong enough to take it. Peterborough 'continued quiet in the outworks', attempting to attack but 'with no great hopes of succeeding' during the next three days. 3,000 naval ratings were landed; two seven-inch mortars were set up; but the stalemate continued until the 17th, which dawned with rain and little wind. At three in the afternoon, a lucky hit from one of the mortars set off the fort's ammunition, which was stored in the chapel, there being no proper magazine. The explosion killed Caraccioli, who was at dinner next door, and a number of officers and men, and caused a large breach in the walls of the keep. Colonel Southwell now approached, sword in hand, with some English and Dutch troops and a number of Catalan irregulars. There were believed to be about 300 Allied prisoners of war in the place. If so, they outnumbered the garrison, for when Colonel Mena, the deputy-governor, hung out a white flag and offered unconditional surrender, it was granted to only fifteen officers and 27 men.

After the capture of the Fort, Damstadt lay in state in a small convent-chapel whose monks had prepared him for burial. He was fully dressed, bewigged and hatted, his sword in his right hand, his ribboned walking-stick in his left. While a priest murmured the Office of the Dead, Catalans mingled with English and Dutch soldiers to pay their respects to a man who had earned these by his qualities of personal gallantry, energy, charm, intelligence and fortitude. On 14th February 1706 a packet boat was reported taken by a privateer after three days, 'chase and a five hours' fight. She was carrying 'the Prince of Hess his hart [sic], to have been sent to Germany'. The ship went ashore near St Malo and Reuss, the prince's secretary, was taken prisoner on the beach, still holding the casket containing Darmstadt's heart. Liselotte (King Philip's aunt) and Sophia, Electress of Hanover, were both related to Darmstadt and tried to obtain release of the relic. But, exalted as they were, these two ladies failed, even in exchange for a Canadian bishop. Eventually, in 1711, the heart was exhanged for twenty naval officer prisoners-of-war, and buried in the Evangelical Church at Darmstadt with the Protestant members of his family. The casket is still there but the coffin and a memorial erected in Barcelona disappeared over a century ago.

The taking of Montjuich had two results. The immediate – though temporary – one was an improvement in co-operation on the Allied side. Peterborough's mind was no longer on Italy. The longer-term effect was that Barcelona was no longer tenable by Philip's forces. The Allied army remained on the north-east of the town facing the wall between the New Gate (Portal Nou) and that of Sant Pere. Meanwhile Shovell and his Dutch colleagues gave renewed evidence of their commitment to the capture of the city although they were well past the normal date for sailing homewards. Unlike the capricious commander-in-chief they were determined to take the risk in order to assist in gaining the capital of the Principality of Catalonia, and indeed to do even more than they had hitherto. Already as we have seen, 2,500 English and 500 Dutch seamen had been landed under their own officers below Montjuich and some heavy guns put ashore. Now more were to be made available. Barcelona was to be submitted to a full-scale siege and this would involve heavy bombardment.[6]

The Archive of the Crown of Aragon in the viceregal palace in Barcelona contains the minute books of the *Diputació General* of Catalonia from 1704 onwards and these give a picture of what was going on within the city. Early minutes are rather like those of a borough council in peacetime, meeting twice a week to distribute money and take municipal decisions. Normally these were signed by four or five men, Pedro de Oliver, Braço y Durán, Colanell, Monfort and Novelly Nadal. The capture of the city is also covered by a diary apparently written in the same hand. Both seem remarkably placid, recording, 'The enemy army of England and Holland continues its siege of this capital by sea and land and has attacked the fort of Montjuich', and continuing laconically to report the bombardment, the St Antoni Bastion in danger, and so on until 8th October. Then the 'enemy', gradually becomes the 'ally' and within three weeks the

Diputació decides to present H.M. King Charles III with a regiment of 1,000 men. One feels oneself in the presence of an extremely smooth machine which nothing will stop. They even go on paying themselves attendance money throughout. And all the correspondence is included with each appropriate minute. Certainly they make little reference to Velasco, and they were probably in touch with the enemy-turned-to-ally throughout. These meantime were making serious efforts to bring matters to a close.

Shovell warped in bomb-ketches to shell the south-east of the city and landed more heavy guns. There were no horses to tow these so they were manhandled into position by parties of seamen, no doubt glad to be able to set foot ashore, and by enthusiastic locals. Fifty-eight guns were soon sited, although in somewhat primitive battery works. The earliest and largest was a battery of forty guns at the Torre del Marmer, some 400 yards from the scarp between the recently-built demi-lune of Sant Pau and the bastion of the Sant Antoni Gate. Richards was in overall command of the train but as he had other duties, much of the work was undertaken by Colonel Petit. Soon not only the army's but the ships' cannon were at work. The first night 100 shot fell on the city but subsequently the bombardment became fiercer, the bomb-ketches alone throwing in 400 shells a night. Charles spent much time both ashore and afloat watching the guns. On one occasion he asked for eight bomb-ketches to give a simultaneous salvo and shouted with pleasure at the noise. It is plain from ships' logs that it was not only the city walls that were under attack. It was the morale of the defenders that was being assaulted and a contemporary note says that the bombardment 'occasioned a great consternation among the people'.

Velasco himself experienced discomfort and more. The very first night he was sleeping at the house of a Bourbon sympathiser which was among the earliest to be hit. He fled in some disarray and a street patrol which stopped him would not at first believe that this blackened and dishevelled figure was the viceroy. His palace was set on fire and when he asked the Council of 100 to send to put it out they pointed out that he had forbidden anyone to circulate.

In the countryside around the uprisings began and though he may not have had accurate information, Velasco must have guessed it was taking place. At Vich one Francesc Bernoia who had fought at Gibraltar had obtained formal accession to the Allies. In Ampurdan, Gerona under de Beck was threatened by a force commanded by Jaume Birolà, a Catalan soldier who had also fought at Gibraltar. The garrison of three companies fled and de Beck surrendered. The chief places in the Duchy of Cardona proffered obedience when called on by a priest, Joan Malaver, sent by Darmstadt before he was killed, and accompanied by only thirty men. Cardona itself surrendered after a perfunctory discharge of guns by its forty-strong garrison. And so the movement continued, in the Pyrenees, to the west of Barcelona at Balaguer, Lérida, Cervera, Fraga and elsewhere. A force of some 2,000 *Miquelets* ranged as far as the Aragon border. Figueras, which had a garrison of only seventy men was taken by a force of 500 cavalry and some infantry. Urgell, San Feliú and Manresa declared for King Charles, and to the south one of the five Nebot brothers, Joseph, took over Tortosa and invested Tarragona. Shovell sent H.M.S. *Antelope* (Captain Cavendish), a couple of frigates and the fireship *Phoenix* to help and Tarragona surrendered. Only Rosas on the frontier with France refused to surrender but de Quinson reported that he could only supply it by sea. A Neapolitan regiment which had reached him without provisions or money (the Castel d'Ayola) he sent via Port Vendres to reinforce the Rosas garrison. Amelot on 30th September reported that Lérida had gone without a fight and that Orry was rushing to Saragossa with money to pay the troops there.

In the city, shelling continued and some of the more valuable religious statues were collected and placed in the crypt of the Church of St Eulàlia. Shots fell on the town hall and the cathedral. Whatever might be the feelings of the city's inhabitants the enthusiasm of Catalans outside for Charles III grew daily and he declared that once the city was taken he would set up a provisional court there rather than return to Lisbon. As an indication of his intentions he established an ecclesiastical Junta of prominent churchmen who had emerged from the city. Velasco sent out a request that the Duchess of Popoli and the Marchioness of Aytona should be allowed to leave the city. Peterborough refused tersely. Their husbands, he said, should not have stayed and kept them in the city.

1st October was Charles' birthday – he was 20 – but there were no celebrations. Instead the bombardment was intensified and Peterborough set up his tent near the batteries, so as to be at hand day and night. Numerous casualties were caused in one of the Allied batteries when a lucky hit sent up six powder barrels. Peterborough now appears to have fallen ill briefly but on the 3rd, preparations began for an assault. Velasco decided to let women, children and old and sick people leave and then mined the breach opened by the bombardment and set up a breastwork. However, a couple of lucky mortar shells exploded the mines, and the citizens of Barcelona, believing this was the signal for the expected Allied assualt, took up the arms which Velasco had given them during Darmstadt's abortive landing a year before, and which they had since kept hidden. These included 689 musketoons, 138 crossbows, 103 muskets, sundry arms of other kinds, forty-five *quintals* of powder and forty-four of shot. With these they began to fire on Spanish soldiers and a number were killed.

Although on 4th October de Quinson was reporting to Versailles that Barcelona was 'still defending itself well', it was in fact on that very day that Peterborough sent in a message under trumpet to Velasco saying that he could expect no relief and giving him five hours to submit or the city would be stormed and sacked. (Parnell, unable to let the earl have any credit, attributes this to Lichtenstein.) Peterborough seems to have felt short-handed for he now exclaimed that if he had 2,000 men ready he could storm the place. The men were in fact available on the other side of the city away from the breach, and in addition he had now some thousands of armed Catalan volunteers, but these he seems still not to have considered. Velasco replied that five hours was too short a time for such a decision but that if no relief arrived within four days he would agree to a capitulation.

Armed riots at the street corners within, casualties among his soldiers, and the threat from without left him no alternative and when the bombardment began again he agreed to an exchange of hostages. Stanhope was sent into the city in exchange for the Conde de Ribeira. But Velasco refused to consult with the citizens, preferring as a professional soldier to treat only with English and Dutch professionals. He prepared a long list of points to be discussed and sent these out. In particular he insisted that any matters concerning the Catalan institutions 'would be discussed with the Commons *after* the Allied army has entered the city'.

At six p.m. on the 5th Peterborough gave the draft capitulation to Charles III and discussions of the many points took a couple of days. Eventually on the 7th they were sent back under trumpet for Stanhope to hand over to Velasco. When after three hours there was no response, Peterborough sent in a further warning and at last Stanhope came out accompanied by the Marquis Richebourg, who had full authority to treat.

The same day some further thousands of Catalan volunteers arrived, a portion only of all those now taking up arms all over the Principality, and showed the enormous 'zeal and love which this nation has for His Catholic Majesty'. On the 8th, a rainy, windy day, two thousand men were sent to Gerona, so strong was the certainty that Barcelona would soon fall, and eventually on the 9th, 'a day of strong winds, rain and hail' the Capitulation's forty-nine detailed articles were each marked *accordé*, and the document was signed by both Peterborough and Velasco.

The exodus of Velasco and his associates and garrison was fixed for 14th October. By then the city had been severely knocked about, some 50,000 rounds having probably fallen on it. The number of casualties is not known. The day dawned stormy and wet. Although the capitulation had been signed by

Peterborough and Velasco wished to surrender with colours flying to regular Allied troops, the situation within the city was tense. A rumour had spread that Velasco was going to take with him all those who were in gaol, in particular political prisoners who were pro-Austrian. Led by the Council of 100 the inhabitants began to attack the prisons, and the inmates – such as Feliú de la Penya, who has left an account – began to take their own measures for escape. Bells called to arms. Velasco had received early that morning a request from an English officer for the liberation of the prisoners but had refused. Now, threatened as he thought with death, he took refuge in the Convent of Sant Pere. The crowd, not finding him at his Palace, made for the sea wall to open communications with the fleet. Everywhere there were cries of 'Long live our Country! Long live King Charles III!' Other volunteers marched to the breach between the gates of Sant Pau and Sant Antoni. Popular vengeance was being exacted from the *Botiflers*. The number killed or hurt was small for many had fled, but some were burned in effigy and their houses sacked and set on fire. In de la Penya's account, whose breathlessness is that of one who was actually involved.

'Peasants wearing the yellow sash called: 'To arms and let us free the prisoners. Long live Charles III.' A woman, Geronyma Peyró, told her son Antoni to collect a gang and free the prisoners. Her husband, Thomas, also did well, disarming 70 Neapolitan soldiers ... Afterwards some companies of English troops and the generals came in and took the keys. Peasants sacked the houses of Philip's supporters. There was an earthquake and a hurricane.'

This seems to fit in with the English accounts. These do not record an earthquake but the elements were clearly being dramatic. The Royal Navy reported 'a waterspout, which had hardly ever been known there', on 3rd October, attended with a hurricane and a surprising whirlwind. Men on shore were forced to catch hold of anything near them to prevent being blown up into the air, to the great astonishment of the beholders. And on 5th and 6th October there was 'a violent storm of wind which drove several of the fleet and did great damage, and was attended with such violent thunder and lightning that several of the seamen on board the *Prince George* were struck senseless for a considerable time, not only upon the deck but in the hold of the ship.'

Stanhope is reported to have alerted Peterborough who now swiftly led in English and Dutch troops in order to save the lives of Velasco, Popoli, de Aytona and the others with them. On the other hand the Barcelona authorities – the Council of 100 and the Commons – were apparently anxious that the governor should not be attacked and it is claimed that they sent word to Peterborough at the Gate of the Angel. He was there, according to this account, with Schratenbach, Stanhope and Richards and eventually they made their way to meet Velasco and his companions who, guided by a chaplain at the convent, had left their shelter by a garden door and avoided the mob. Schratenbach describes the governor as 'a small dark man, trembling nervously as though he was going to be eaten'. He and his companions were then conducted out of the city. It appears that the Dutch and English soldiers behaved well, did not plunder, and avoided major troubles with the Catalans. But, with shot flying in all directions the situation was ugly for some time and Stanhope wrote afterwards that he had been in greater danger that afternoon and evening than at any time during the siege. Eventually the tumult fell and regular guards were put on houses of prominent Bourbon supporters. Peterborough gave quarters in camp to Richebourg, de Aytona, Popoli and his family, and a number of other noblemen. The Neapolitan guard remained loyal, apparently shouting, 'Long live King Philip, who is in Madrid.' They were composed 'of scions of the most illustrious houses in their kingdom'. Passports were issued to a large number of noble families and many ecclesiastics, inquisitors, Jesuits and others who wished to go to Madrid.

Some 2,500 of Velasco's garrison had gone over to the Allies and he asked that the 1,200 'unarmed and naked' guard should be shipped with him first of all to San Feliú near Palamos and then when that fell into Allied hands, to Málaga. According to St Pierre, the viceroy was for safety escorted by a strong guard on board the flagship *Britannia*. Here Shovell received him coldly, 'it being an affront to the King and himself to send a man so tyrannical and odious to the people to make use of an apartment fitted up for the King'. It was 'thought fitt to have him removed into another ship ye next day'. He, the Popolis and the rest now had a couple of weeks to wait aboard, probably in some discomfort.

A council of war was now held at which 'it was thought fit to comply with [Charles'] resolution of venturing his own person with the Catalans. The Earl of Peterborough should continue with the prince with the land forces and as many of the marines as could be spared from the service of the ships.' Shovell, it was agreed, should sail at once, 'the season of the year being far spent'. He and the Dutch Admiral van Allmonde were to return home, leaving a winter squadron at Lisbon under Leake and Wassenaer. Four English and two Dutch frigates were left at Barcelona. Velasco and the rest were to be dropped off at Málaga by Shovell on the way. From among the disaffected men in the garrison at Barcelona who had transferred their services, Charles formed a regiment of 500 dragoons as his personal guard.

The honeymoon atmosphere (alas only temporary) can be seen in a letter in which Peterborough comes out well, which Stanhope carried home to God-olphin:

> 'The commendations he [Charles] gives to the troops, the officers and Brigadier Stanhope in particular all that is but their due. And I believe no body in command ever met with such a spirit in troops with such discipline and cheerful obedience in officers and soldiers. There never was a greater trial of their submission nor a higher proof of English humanity than to enter a place [amid] pillaging by others and not to commit the least hostility but to employ themselves in saving at the same time the town and their enemies ... I owe too much to these troops to see them injured and oppressed.'

On 23rd October Shovell, van Allmonde and the combined fleet weighed anchor, a month and more later than was usually acceptable. Some of the squadrons, those destined for Lisbon, sailed a couple of days later. On the same day – or possibly the day before, as accounts differ – Charles entered formally on horseback into the city, making a triumphal entry. He had formally received the Council of 100 and the Commons, and also the *Braç Militar* and had, through them, sent orders for the whole Principality to be put in a proper state of defence and particularly Barcelona city. Charles' entry was accompanied by salvoes from the guns of the fleet and by songs, for example,

> Viva, viva, Carlos viva!
> Since you give us liberty!

or a ninety-seven-verse *'Song of the Birds'*.

A mass was celebrated in the packed Church of Santa María del Mar which was alongside the viceregal palace where he now set up quarters. It was noted that those who had audience of him were now more respectful than hitherto. The king's Catholic zeal was quite genuine as we have observed at Lisbon. Driving in his coach one day through the fruit market here in Barcelona an English observer describes the king as seeing the Host being carried to the bedside of a dying woman. Leaving his coach he knelt in the street and then, taper in hand, followed the procession. By then, of course, Barcelona was quiet.

The fact that Barcelona was calm and orderly was due not only to enthusiasm for Charles, dislike of the Bourbons or memories of Darmstadt. It is only fair to Peterborough to say that he had been conciliatory and shrewd in his dealings with the population, showing a discretion and judgment quite alien to the impetuousness which had marked his parliamentary career and most of his relationships in private life. Moreover the city's official institutions were potent factors for peace and order and no doubt took advantage of the continued presence of their Allies' regular soldiers.

In Madrid a postmortem on the loss of Barcelona sombrely gave the reasons for it. The grandees and merchants felt that the French were taking away the trade of the Indies, and Spanish ports were being starved as French ship owners would not go to Spain. French artisans and workmen were flooding into every Spanish town and taking away jobs. The mood of Spain was anti-French, even without the knowledge (carefully concealed by Louis XIV) that he was turning a blind eye to the Dutch trading with Spain. King Philip's despair showed in his letters to Versailles.

'It is a matter of nothing but the loss of all Spain. We are under pressure on two sides and cannot get out of our difficulties without prompt help from France ... It is seven o'clock at night [on 15th October]. Esteban and other officers have just reported Alcañiz and Saragossa taken, Sir, you see us in a terrible situation. Think, I beg you, for a moment of my state. I am going to the Palace to see what orders I have to send tonight.'

Madame des Ursins, writing a little earlier to the Duc de la Feuillade was less worried about Barcelona: 'The enemy cannot do us as much harm there as they could in Andalucia.' Tessé, battling on the western front, was also inclined to be sanguine, after a successful defence of Badajoz against a siege raised within a couple of days of the fall of Barcelona.[7] In the first week of November, after reviewing the overall strategic picture, he concluded that affairs were still 'a toss-up' (*croix on pile*). The internal contradiction of the Bourbon predicament was deepening: resistance required French resources; French intervention provoked Spanish sensibilities. In practical terms, there was no choice but to rely on French help. 'We must have it', wrote Tessé to Chamillart on 28th November, 'or risk losing Spain, which is hanging by a thread'.

CHAPTER FIVE

1706: The Year of the Dragon

The result, good or bad, of the siege of Barcelona, will make all the difference.

> – Amelot (writing in ignorance of events at Barcelona) to Chamillart,
> 21st May, 1706.

Advantage is a better soldier than rashness.

> – Shakespeare.

Never on the world stage has Fortune played so many rôles. She showed favour to those who foresaw adversity and was tough on those who expected favour. It was the wisdom of Providence, teaching men to make good use of hope and fear so that the one does not exalt nor the other humble the spirit more than is right.

> – San Felipe on 1706.

WHEN Lord Peterborough marched southwards away from Barcelona in early January 1706 his governing emotions were jealousy of Cifuentes and others who had been appointed grandees and hatred for the 'German crew'.[1] His only important sympathiser at court and council was probably Mitford Crowe, who had briefly returned to Barcelona as English minister. Stanhope, with whom the earl was still on good terms, had not yet left London. Charles III blamed Peterborough for the festering relationships that existed at headquarters and Burnet comments that the earl 'had not much of a forbearing or forgiving temper in him'. His spleen was further roused on 29th December 1705, when Charles appointed Cifuentes Viceroy of Valencia, to supercede Cardona. On 30th December he wrote to Godolphin, 'To send a man of his [Cifuentes'] character ... before he [Charles] had bestowed the least sign of favour or honour on any of the most ancient and noble houses of Catalonia ... would prejudice the cause of King Charles on

Valencia.' In fact Charles withdrew the appointment, for Cifuentes did not go with Peterborough and when the latter reached Valencia city Cardona was still there.

The council of war held by Charles on 30th December must therefore have been a sultry affair. It is important to consider what was known to those present of the military situation and the enemy's movements.

The Allies did *not* know that Philip was intending to join his army for the reduction of Valencia and Catalonia or that Tessé himself was due to move north-eastwards. They did not then know of the huge forces and supplies for a decisive siege of Barcelona. Amelot, noting the easy recapture of Morella and Monroyo, observed that the re-establishment of Philip's authority would not be '*une oeuvre à longue haleine*' (a long job) and that the king should stick to his decision to be with the army. But Council *did* know that Hans Hamilton had in mid-December sent from Tortosa a Spanish-speaking officer of Barrymore's, Lieutenant-Colonel John Jones, with 30 Royal Dragoons, 300 Catalan *Miquelets* and 700 Valencian irregulars to try and secure the Allies' flimsy hold on the passes at Monroyo. Jones, although described by St Pierre as 'a very good officer and a very stirring man who hath done good service', failed in this instance for instead of marching swiftly westwards he set off southwards along the coast to Castellón de la Plana and arrived at Monroyo too late to forestall O'Mahony. Too weak moreover to challenge the Bourbons in the plains, he had made for San Mateo, a small walled town some twenty-five miles from the coast and installed himself there. A captured letter of his, which is included in de las Torres' correspondence (in the Madrid *Archivo*) describes the inhabitants as showing 'great fidelity' in surrendering. It was accompanied by a proclamation by 'Don Juan Jones, sergeant-major-commandant on the frontiers of Aragon and Catalonia for King Charles III (Whom God preserve)' ordering the citizens of San Mateo to show their obedience and promising that their goods would be restored.

Jones' small force was surrounded immediately by greatly superior numbers under Torres. He got a message away by a devious route to Tortosa asking for help and his precise situation was certainly known when Charles' council of war met on 30th December. It was there agreed, no doubt with pleasure all round, that Peterborough should leave at once with 1,000 Spanish foot and 300 English horse to Jones' relief, and it was promised that more men should follow.

As he left, Peterborough may have known from correspondence with some ladies in Valencia, including perhaps the Marquesa de la Casta, that the Allied position in that city was tenuous, and it is quite certain that, ambitious and restless as he was, the mere relief of a relatively unimportant town like San

Mateo would not be enough to satisfy him and that he had his eye on the whole Kingdom of Valencia.

Torres with about 7,000 men was intending to base himself at Moncada, near Valencia whence, according to San Felipe, 'Parties [would go] out against the rebel places, laying waste the countryside and burning the villages. It was all destroying Spain, but such was the sickness that fire and sword were necessary. The count [Torres] carried out this task with firmness; some said cruelly, but at least with justice.' His first job was to try and eliminate Jones' garrison at San Mateo. Starting from Morella he had made at once for this little town, forcing on the way a pass guarded by 400 *Miquelets* and arriving on 27th December. He advised Madrid that he would attack the place next day 'giving no quarter if the inhabitants cause it to be taken by force'.

The town had itself no artillery but it could not be taken without siege guns, and Torres had none. So both sides settled down to an exchange of musketry, coupled on the besieging side with mining. Torres captured two monasteries outside the walls. Colonel Jones left a record, *The Journal of the Siege of San Mateo* (London 1707) which recounts how Torres was joined at the new year by O'Mahony and on 1st January a mine was driven under the town's Barcelona Gate, but it was flooded out by rain. Another, laid on 2nd January, was also flooded, this time when two resolute defenders (un-named) crept out of the town and let out water from a large tank belonging to a mill. In his *Journal* Jones reports that when he ran out of ammunition he persuaded the citizens to sell their pewter pots and dishes and to let these and even the church organ pipes be melted and cast into bullets while he also erected makeshift parapets made of woolsacks. Called on by O'Mahony on the 3rd to surrender, he refused.

We have a record from Torres covering the next few weeks. On the 3rd he wrote to Madrid saying the enemy had twice attacked him.

'They have a company of the Queen's [Dragoons] and the best *Miquelets* from Tortosa, Viñaroz and other places. I hope soon to make myself master of this place. We are not far from the walls and have built galleries to take mines and blow the wall up. Yesterday [2nd] I was reinforced with 500 infantry and 200 horse, all militia ... If the place does not surrender at discretion we will put all the soldiers and *Miquelets* to the sword ... I hope to fill His Majesty's galleys with rebels.'

The reinforcements probably came in with O'Mahony and an attack of a sort was made at midnight (on the 6th?) in the course of which three or four of the besiegers were killed and ten or twelve wounded. On the 7th Torres himself left San Mateo, according to his record of his march. O'Mahony remained in charge of the siege and on the 7th again demanded that Jones surrender. Although bread was running out in the town the call was refused, and probably in pursuance of orders from Torres O'Mahony himself began to raise the siege in order to follow his commander. At any rate by the 9th the Bourbon forces were moving off. The official reason given by Torres to Madrid was, 'There were great rains which dampened the mines under the wall', but he probably had another reason for moving. Arcos' march to Valencia via Requena was intended to recapture that city but he was also under instructions to take over as Philip's viceroy and commander-in-chief, and Torres, who had been apprised of this, wanted to meet Arcos and sort the situation out. As we shall see, a row was building up on this matter. By 8th January he was, according to his report, near the coast where he was joined by the Regiment of Navarre; by the 9th he was at Salvadella and by the 12th at Villareal where he was rejoined by O'Mahony. There does not appear therefore to have been any sudden panicky withdrawal from San Mateo, merely a decision not to waste time and men on reducing a relatively unimportant place held by a small but active garrison. Peterborough, having set out to relieve San Mateo, no doubt felt that he must report success come what may. But the end of the siege owed little or nothing to his inter-vention.

On arriving early in the morning of 12th January at Albocacer, a small town in the hills, south of San Mateo, Peterborough received an express des-patch from Charles III in Barcelona. Some of its contents were certain, others less so.

> 'The Duke of Noailles is entering with near 8,000 men in Catalonia, from the side of Roussillon; the body under Prince Tsercles [sic] Tilly in Aragon is four or five thousand pressing upon all the places near Lérida; the Duke of Anjou [Philip V] with Marshal de Thessé [sic] is forming a body of ten thousand men near Madrid which will soon be in motion; besides the troops under the duke of Berwick on the side of Portugal.'

This last was conjecture for Berwick was not yet appointed to go to Spain and would not leave Montpelier until mid-February. But rumours were no doubt flying. Charles told Peterborough that he had in these circumstances countermanded his order for a thousand foot and three-hundred horse to join the earl (they had nearly reached Tortosa) and recalled them to Barcelona. There was also a request that Peterborough should himself return to Catalonia, but he was allowed latitude.

Peterborough was furious and immediately called a council of war of all his officers, who now included, as well as Killigrew and St Pierre, Brigadier-General Gorges just promoted. St Pierre wrote an account of it to his colonel,[2] Lord Raby, who was then English ambassador in Berlin. Peterborough described the idea of returning to Barcelona as 'mad' and gave three reasons for his own intentions. First: Valencia was on the way to Madrid and could be supplied by sea. Second, the kingdom had plenty of horses and mules and his troops needed remounts. Third, the situation in the city of Valencia was dangerous and Torres was known only to be awaiting reinforcements led by the Duke of Arcos in order to attack it. The minutes of the council state:

> 'All the officers of the Allies and of the King of Spain [Charles] were unanimously of the opinion not to advance further on the plains towards Valencia but to attempt Peñiscola merely from Viñaroz, a proper post to expect the troops that are coming to join, which post was not far from Tortosa, but that His Lordship might employ his forces to the relief of Catalonia and pass ye Ebro if occasion required; as likewise to assist Valencia as soon as reinforced.'

In other words Peterborough was alone in his views. He stuck to them, however, determined to secure Valencia and preferring freedom of action. He could, it is true, claim that by doing so he would draw off forces who would otherwise attack Charles. He agreed under pressure that the infantry (who were exhausted) and any officers who did not wish to go with him should return to Viñaroz, where they could be victualled by sea or return to Barcelona, but insisted that he and the 170 or so Royal Dragoons would pursue Torres and make for Valencia. All the officers, it is recorded, were opposed but were unable to persuade him against this. St Pierre says, 'We did what we could to dissuade him but to no purpose. I offered to go with him but he would not let me go because I was too wise to go with him. With what I have', wrote Peterborough 'I march straight to Valencia. I can take no other measure, leaving the rest to Providence.' He now had a potential force of about 1,500 regulars and 3,500 irregulars.

Morale among the Bourbon forces may not have been very high but Torres was determined to concentrate near Valencia city and on the way to try and teach the rebels a lesson. On 12th January while Peterborough was holding his council of war the Spanish general arrived at the small walled town of Villareal just inland and south of Castellón. In his report he says, 'This place refused to surrender but I ordered General Amezaga, and Brigadier-Generals del Sello, Vinterfeld and Mahoni not to attack without orders from me.' Apparently, however, one of Vinterfeld's officers was shot from the walls, so this Brigadier and his Walloon Guard

> 'penetrated the gate. There was much fighting for two and a half hours. Priests came out into the streets carrying the Host. Our men at first respected this and the Cross. But then others fired, killing some officers and men and retreating into a church. Women and children who had retired there were trapped. Their cries would have melted stone. We released many Frenchmen from prison where they had been maltreated. One hundred and fifty of the enemy in the church tower surrendered at discretion. Altogether more than 700 died in the fighting and 800 to 1,000 were buried in this town and in the neighbourhood.'

On the 16th Torres led a reconnaissance party of 400 horse towards the capital. He was ambushed in a pass, his van opposed and his rearguard attacked. In this 'embarrasing position' he decided to withdraw to Moncada, where he made his preparations for the recovery of Valencia. 'In order to facilitate any attack', he reported, 'and to show the world that the king's troops are not barbarians I have sent a note to the City and Deputation of Valencia'. He promised that King Philip would be benevolent if people behaved themselves. 'Those who do otherwise will give an account before the Tribunal of Heaven of the atrocities and monstrous consequences of war.'

By 20th January, Torres was poised for the assault. He had positioned O'Mahony at Murviedro to halt Peterborough's relief column. Only the arrival of the Duke of Arcos with reinforcements was now wanting. Yet that expected blessing, when it came, proved a curse. Torres immediately fell out with his new superior and left for Madrid in a huff. At a critical juncture, the Bourbon strategy for the recovery of Valencia was left without informed overall direction.

Peterborough claimed that he tricked O'Mahony into surrender, and Arcos into retreat. The truth seems to have been that the defenders of Murviedro were hopelessly outnumbered and the duke hopelessly ill informed. On 2nd February, O'Mahony wrote to Arcos from Murviedro

> 'The enemy has appeared before this place, six squadrons dressed in red, two battalions of English with red colours and one with white, as well as the Nebot cavalry and 5,000 peasants. I judge this place not to be tenable unless we were to be sent 500 foot. There is not a moment of time to lose so I feel obliged to withdraw with the garrison leaving with chagrin a place of the highest consequence for the King and many wounded officers and men

whom I cannot transport. I think this the most important post in the Kingdom of Valencia and it would be well worth abandoning the blockade of Valencia for a few days and sending [the forces] here. Give me your views about this because there is not a moment to lose and [such a] march must be made all night.'

Then there is an addition:

'My Lord Peterborough has just sent me a Colonel and a Captain to demand my surrender. I have sent a Captain of my [Irish] Regiment to find out whether he is the person he says he is. I have only three hours' worth of ammunition and I therefore think it better to capitulate for the sake of the town and the wounded rather than wait while by marching by our left [*i.e.* round Murviedro] they cut me off from you. However I hope to make my retreat even if I am obliged to pierce through them. I will observe their movements and pursue whatever course is best.'

Arcos did not lift the blocade and send troops to Murviedro – indeed he would scarcely have had time – and O'Mahony negotiated a capitulation, 'very advantageously', as Amelot reported, preserving his entire force and material.

However it was procured, O'Mahony's withdrawal left the besiegers' flank exposed. Arcos had to fall back, allowing the English relief force to be welcomed in Valencia 'with infinite applause'.

★   ★   ★

Meanwhile, 150 miles to the north, Tessé was advancing slowly towards Barcelona. He had arrived at Saragossa on 21st January. On 22nd, his vanguard was checked at Barbastro, but he was marching almost due eastwards and reaching out with his left hand to make contact with the reinforcements due to come with the Duc de Noailles from Roussillon.

During the halcyon weeks in Valencia, the Earl of Peterborough seems to have given very little thought to Charles's situation in Barcelona.[3] Indeed, Amelot perceived this: 'It is hard to understand what purpose that general can have in mind, leaving the archduke in Barcelona with only tiny forces.' When Peterborough did give it some thought, it took the form of a very peculiar letter to Charles, dated 13th March,

'I confess, Sir, that I would have Your Majesty in the present conjuncture take a resolution as extraordinary as that which brought you before Barcelona. I would have Your Majesty embark in some ships I have prepared for that purpose and with a fair wind endeavour to gain the first land you can in Portugal and then put yourself at the head of our 25,000 men (in good condition) on the borders of that Kingdom. The enemy have now but 5,000 men in arms in that part of Spain and with this change of affairs in our favour I doubt not that Your Majesty will soon arrive in Madrid. Meanwhile I would venture to maintain Catalonia and Valencia and possibly open the way to Madrid [from here]. This, Sir, were perhaps the finest stroke in politics that any age has produced, as also the least expected and it might even give the quickest relief to Catalonia, which would not be so vigorously attacked if Your Majesty were in person elsewhere.'

Peterborough's suggestions were a fantasy. But reality was now beginning to catch up with him. Soldiers cost money and so does pleasure. Bad relations with the court at Barcelona meant that he could expect little financial help from them – even if they had had the wherewithal. He was dependent on what came from England. A letter to Godolphin, dated 29th March, endeavours to shift any blame on to others.

'The first money I touched came two nights ago. Judge, my Lord, our severe trial – information of a flow of enemies from all parts, without a letter in near five months, without any assistance of men or money, without grounds for hopes ... with a most wretched minister influencing a young King, frightened out of his senses; the Prince of Lichtenstein, assisted by a mad Spaniard, the Count of Cifuentes, having with German pride and ignorance baulked and disgusted the Catalans, our only hope. His wretched policies ... have retarded all the means of raising money or levying men.'

Perhaps with a feeling that things were really going badly, Peterborough now committed himself to what would certainly have been thought of by Charles as treachery. On 30th March, the day after his letter to Godolphin, he wrote to Victor Amadeus, Duke of Savoy:

'May God preserve his Majesty [Charles] but it is my duty to Your Highness that in case of his death I shall give Spain to him who has the right to it ... The most fatal event for the public will be a captive King of Spain. The game will be difficult and delicate and I can only say I will do my best. For your interests, Monseigneur, will always be paramount and Your Royal Highness cannot wish for a more devoted or faithful servant.'

Amelot could never have known of this of course, but on 23rd March, his comment of a few days earlier, 'I cannot understand why Milord Peterborough has stayed quietly in Valencia while the archduke is in peril', adding in cypher, 'It makes me think that he is not a man of war and is light-minded ... One cannot conceive why he takes no measures to fulfil his commitments.'

★   ★   ★

While Peterborough dallied in Valencia in the spring of 1706 the war in Spain as a whole was building up to a direct confrontation between the two claimants, who would at one time be separated by only a few miles, each full of doubts and fears, each alternatively determined and undecided. Either side, given a little more confidence, a little less divided counsel, a little more luck, might have won, and the history of Europe would have been changed.

To Charles and his small garrison in Barcelona the enemy must have appeared to be both confident and menacing. Had he but known it, as we do, they were full of doubts. On 14th February Amelot, for instance, committed a real *cri de coeur* in cypher.

'Things in Spain are in a state which leaves everything to be feared, nothing to be hoped for. The people here are gangrened to the marrow of their bones. If the King were one day to decide for peace I believe he would do so at any price. It is no longer a matter of honour or of sustaining the monarchy intact. If Spain is lost as seems all too likely, France is in great danger. It is not fear that makes me speak thus, for I am resolved to face up to whatever happens. But I believe it is my duty to warn the King [Louis] of what I think and see.'

On February 23rd, however, King Philip left for Tessé's camp, 'accompanied by a large number of magnates' and by the 28th Amelot confessed that he was 'breathing more freely because of the arrival of more French troops [de Noailles' and de Légal's] in Catalonia and the reinforcements promised for Extremadura.' Philip in stately progress was met at Saragossa by San Esteban de

Gormaz, the Viceroy of Aragon, and eventually joined Tessé at Caspé on the Ebro some eighty miles to the east of Saragossa. The marshal's 12,000 men were spread along the river banks but two bridges of boats were built and the king and the army then concentrated at Fraga.

Here he published a General Pardon, intended to bring the Catalans over to his side. It had no effect. Amelot and Queen María Luisa, far away in Madrid, were more bellicose. Instead of an amnesty, the walls of Barcelona, Vich, Gerona and other towns should be razed. And here, too, there was disagreement in the council of war. Tessé wished first to besiege Lérida, Monzón and Tortosa so that in case of trouble in taking Barcelona his flanks would be protected. He was a disillusioned and timid man and was doubtful even then of success. But the majority of the generals, particularly the Spaniards, disagreed. 'It did not appear possible to them that Barcelona could do otherwise than surrender. Its garrison was small and they did not think it could be rapidly relieved. Speed was of the essence and if Barcelona fell, the rest would be plain sailing.' Tessé at length wearily accepted this, still doubtful about the outcome.

The army now advanced to Igualada, twenty-five miles west of Barcelona and Philip sent out a number of notables – Gironella (formerly Governor of Ceuta), Argansola, and others – to exhort the population of the Province to take advantage of the General Pardon and throw themselves on his mercy. This move, too, failed.

'Day by day hatred grew for the person of the king and for the Castillians ... Peasants burned forage and anything that could serve to feed the army, drove their cattle into the hills and poisoned the water. Women and children sheltered in the forests. Anybody who could bear arms joined Cifuentes who went around dressed as a *montagnard*.'

Prince Henry of Hesse-Darmstadt at Lérida, closed the mountain passes when the army had marched through, cut off supplies from Aragon and made communications with Madrid difficult. Allied outposts were however brushed aside by the vanguard and at length Philip and Tessé reached the river Llobregat, just outside Barcelona, on 3rd April. Here they were joined from Roussillon by about 9,000 men (21 battalions and 5 squadrons of cavalry) under de Noailles and de Légal, together with some artillery. A signal was sent to the Comte de Toulouse who had left Toulon on 3rd March and should have been bombarding the place for a month before any help could reach it by sea. But two great storms had blown up 'which did so scatter their tartans [transports] and disable their ships of war that, as some were cast away and others much damaged, so they all lost a month's time'. Only therefore as Tessé arrived was Toulouse's storm-tossed fleet of twenty-five ships-of-the-line, eight frigates, ten galleys and 184 transports anchored off Barcelona and his three bomb-ketches moored close inshore, although a few vessels appear to have arrived earlier and given the garrison the feeling of encirclement.

Charles was thus confronted by Philip, surrounded to landward by an army far bigger than his garrison and now cordoned off to seaward by a huge fleet. His 1,400 regulars – 300 English Guards, 400 Spanish horse and 700 infantry – were being reinforced. Peterborough, the commander-in-chief, was miles away – perhaps fortunately – so Charles appointed Lichtenstein as Minister of War and Uhlfeldt as Governor of Barcelona but took overall command himself. The garrison of Gerona (1,800, consisting of Charlemont's and two Dutch and a Neapolitan battalion) could not have stopped de Noailles. Its commander, the Dutchman Schratenbach, had died, and Lord Donegal who had taken over was ordered to bring his troops in. They found some boats, dropped down river and, dodging Toulouse's cordon, crept 80 miles along the coast. Wills in soldierly fashion sent a dismounted detachment of Conyngham's Regiment by similar means via Mataró and Killigrew in Tortosa sent Hamilton's Regiment, 400 strong, by forced march, using mules. They arrived just as Tessé reached the Llobregat. 1,500 *Miquelets* scrambled in somehow and 5,000 citizens of Barcelona formed themselves – not for the first or last time – into companies. Meanwhile the engineer Colonel, Lewis Petit, who had served at Gibraltar, filled in breaches in the walls, mounted guns, constructed a sickle-shaped 'lunette' in front of the gates of the citadel of Montjuich and otherwise fettled up its defences. Between this high citadel and the city he demolished the little fort of Sant Bertran and ran an almost continuous trench, strengthened with palisades. Donegal, with 500 English and Dutch and 200 Catalans was put in to hold the citadel.

It was all pretty meagre and survival depended entirely on the Winter Squadron arriving from Lisbon in time. Yet now Charles showed fortitude and tenacity, and within Barcelona itself the atmosphere was vastly different from what it had been six months earlier. Then, according to San Felipe, 'churches had been vandalised and the Holy Sacrament defiled by heretics. Even King Charles, though a zealous Catholic, could do nothing, for the troops obeyed only Peterborough and he obeyed nobody'. So 'rape, robbery and violence of all kinds' seem to have been the pattern of life. Now by contrast the volatile citizens were for the most part enthusiastically loyal to Charles. Priests and monks preached fiery sermons. Even the Capuchins tied up their beards and took up muskets while the mendicants ceased to beg and began to handle spades.

At a council of war convened at the end of March 'they debated long and pondered deep' on what could be done and actually recommended that Charles 'should seize the opportunity to get out of the city while he still could ... especially in the light of the many several siege engines and other horrible inventions which it is the practice to use in war against those who resist a siege'. Charles at first agreed to go, 'sending Mitford Grove [Crowe] to Valencia to ask Peterborough to come to lend assistance'. Peterborough merely ordered some cavalry to go from Valencia. Charles even wrote three letters to the citizens saying how disinclined he was to leave. Then as the enemy approached he decided to stay. To explain this he let it be known that he had seen a vision of the Virgin and two angels who had told him he had nothing to fear as long as he stayed in the city.

All this might have seemed hopeless bravado, but Philip's situation was in fact far from satisfactory. His 21,000 regular troops had no communications to the rear and were entirely dependent on the French fleet for supplies. Cifuentes and his *Miquelets* by the thousands not only ringed them round but swooped in on them from the hills like birds of prey. Lines of circumvallation constructed to protect the army from attack during the siege were almost valueless, for Cifuentes, working closely with Prince Henry (at Lérida) carried out frequent night attacks. One night he took 700 sheep from the French commissariat park. On another he swooped in on Sarriá, where Philip had his quarters, grabbed the monarch's plate and personal belongings and so nearly captured the king himself that he was forced thereafter to sleep on board Toulouse's flagship.

Moreover the Bourbon command was riven with jealousies, divided as to tactics, and riddled with pessimism. Tessé's view in a letter to Chamillart on 8th April, was 'Either we shall take Barcelona or we shall not'. He had had more than enough of Spain, and although virtually his entire force was French he was half-hearted as he began to open siege works with the aid of Lieutenant-General de la Pará (who had attacked the place unsuccessfully nine years earlier) and *le petit Renaud*. He was four weeks behind schedule, thanks to Philip's delay and the time taken by reinforcements from Roussillon. Toulouse, shaken by the storms, had, since the battle of Velez Málaga, no intention of challenging the Allied fleet again. Indeed, it had been agreed in advance that if and when they turned up he should leave.

As Montjuich was well garrisoned, Pará had to set up forward approaches and it was not until April 12th that he had two 6-gun emplacements at work against it. (He had asked for 15 days to reduce Barcelona but had been allowed eight.) These killed many of the English and Dutch defenders and a breach was opened on the western side of the fort. Then the new 'lunette' fell into Bourbon hands, a five-gun battery was mounted in it and Donegal only just managed to beat off an attack by the Marqués de Aytona on the 15th.

Downhill outside the city, siege work was impeded by sallies from the defenders who briskly attacked the trenches, de Légal and other French senior officers becoming fiercely involved in the fighting. Philip was reported as visiting the siege works to encourage the troops. He criticised Pará's placing of a battery in a position called the Serpent's Tongue, near the bastion of Sant Antóni, whereupon the engineer, wishing to improve the siting, went up himself to within musket range on the 17th. He was hit either by a musket ball or a fragment of roundshot 'in the lower part of the belly' and died a couple of hours later leaving Renaud in charge. Wooden equipment was set on fire by the defenders and the wind fanned the flames. Renaud sited the siege guns better and in due course 'the angle of the rampart of San Felipe and a large part of that of San Ignacio began to fall. The besiegers got into the covered way and made a lodgement there because the English did not defend it as well as they should have.'

Meantime Toulouse's bombardment from seaward was at first having only a slight effect, for the inhabitants were able to take refuge in church crypts and cellars, emerging at intervals to man the less exposed fortifications or serve in hospitals and canteens. Nevertheless their morale began to falter as the days passed and there were many who now began to blame Charles as the source of their misfortunes. 'There were some mutinies raised and some of the magistrates killed in them. But the king came among them on all occasions and both quieted and animated them.'

Divided counsels and timidity had led Tessé to order the taking of Montjuich first. This was a tactical error which compounded the delays in starting the siege. The citadel could not hold out for ever but Donegal was a determined soldier and hung on for three weeks. On the 21st, at 7.00 p.m. Tessé, considering the breaches practicable, ordered de Aytona to assault on a large scale. At the most exposed breach Donegal faced the attack with 500 men (the remaining Dutch and English guards and Charlemont's Foot), but the Catalans at another point were overpowered and retreated into the keep. Donegal lost 300 of his men, including his second-in-command, Colonel Wray and Colonel Russell of the guards, wounded and taken prisoner. He came face to face with de Aytona in person at one point and 'acting the part of a good grenadier' killed several Frenchmen. He was twice offered quarter but refused it, dying at last from a musket ball in the head. The survivors asked for a truce to find his body and when this was agreed 'paid him funeral honours after their fashion', as San Felipe puts it. They then held out for four more days, only a handful surviving to surrender the citadel. When the siege was over Charles wrote to Queen Anne to praise Donegal. This was entirely right, for the twenty-two-day stand at Monjuich had further delayed the main attack on the city and this in effect, though it could not be known at the time, was to save it.

San Felipe states that the fall of Montjuich caused great consternation in Barcelona. An attempt by Cifuentes to send in twenty-six boatloads of supplies had failed and on 25th April 'on a dark night, Charles, on the advice of Lichtenstein and Peterborough, decided to leave Barcelona'. With three open breaches the place had become untenable. But nothing happened. There was no assault on the city, and the Allied fleet was approaching all the time. Word of its movements was coming in from Governors of Spanish ports as it progressed inexorably round the coast of Spain. Leake was about to do once more what he had done at Gibraltar a year before, demonstrate the efficacy of a well handled fleet in breaking the siege of a place on the coast.[4] Amelot heard on 25th April that the fleet had entered the Mediterranean but hoped that 'they will arrive too late to save Barcelona.' By the 29th, however, Leake had reached Altea and by 6th May, Tortosa, where he was bombarded with despatches from both Peterborough and Charles. The former sent four. The first two ordered that all except 1,000 men were to be put ashore at Viñaroz, the 1,000 going to Barcelona. In the third the earl said the 1,000 were to be sent in all haste to Barcelona 'to save the crown of Spain'. In the fourth he reported that he was himself at Sitges, then a fishing village 15 miles short of Barcelona with 1,000 English marines and 400 Dutch infantry, waiting to send them in under protection by Leake's fleet. But a letter from Charles, dated 4th May, reached Leake by fast frigate on the 6th. It asked him

'To come at once without stopping or disembarking the forces elsewhere as some other persons [Peterborough] may pretend to direct you, for they can nowhere be as necessary as in this town, which is on the point of being lost for want of relief ... Sir, you will see the condition we are in by our letters and I hope you will come as soon as possible to save us; of which you alone shall have the glory.'

It was an exact parallel of the situation with Darmstadt at Gibraltar over a year earlier – even almost to the phraseology of the letter. Leake did not hesitate. Once more disregarding Peterborough he wrote to Lichtenstein:

'I do assure Your Highness that had not contrary winds prevented us, the place had been relieved three days ago and, if it please God suddenly to give us a fair wind I doubt not I shall be before Barcelona by the time this reaches Your Highness' hands, with forty-eight sail of ships-of-the-line and 5,000 succours.'

Off Tarragona the admiral briskly ordered that when they were within three leagues (10 miles) of Barcelona each captain was to sail independently and to lay himself alongside a French ship. All sail was crowded on and Leake still expected a battle as he reckoned without Toulouse's restraining orders. The French Admiral received news of Leake's approach by a fast Genoese scouting ship on the evening of 6th May and gave his instructions. Shaking their topsails the French fleet left quietly for Toulon during the night. There was to be no repetition of Velez Málaga and in effect Charles and Barcelona were now safe. On 12th May, Tessé broke up camp and fled, abandoning 150 or 160 brass guns.[5]

The raising of the siege of Barcelona was coloured by a natural phenomenon which caused much comment at the time. Stanhope wrote:

'I cannot omit mentioning that this morning a little after nine, when their rearguard was about a random cannon shot distant from the town there happened a very great eclipse of the sun, which our side were extremely pleased with, and have taken it as a happy omen, threatening ruin to him who takes the sun for his device [Louis XIV]. Whether the enemy have taken it for an evil presage I cannot tell.'

The eclipse was total and lasted three hours, during which time candles had to be lit in Barcelona in mid-morning. And according to San Felipe it had seldom been so dark. 'For three hours one could see the stars. It was so dark that the troops could not march and did not know where they were.' Philip's horse 'stopped several times, frightened ... but the king's courage prevailed. Those who flattered King Charles', he continues, 'made the most dire predictions about Philip. And the Spaniards believed in these for they began to feel the effects.'

The peculiar astronomical conjuncture had been predicted and was known in Spain as 'The Day of the Dragon' – hence criticism of Tessé for deciding to leave on that day. At the time, news of the failure at Barcelona coupled ten days later with that of Marlborough's victory at Ramillies must have sent a shiver down the spines of many on the Bourbon side. Amelot writing to Chamillart was 'in total ignorance about Barcelona'.

★   ★   ★

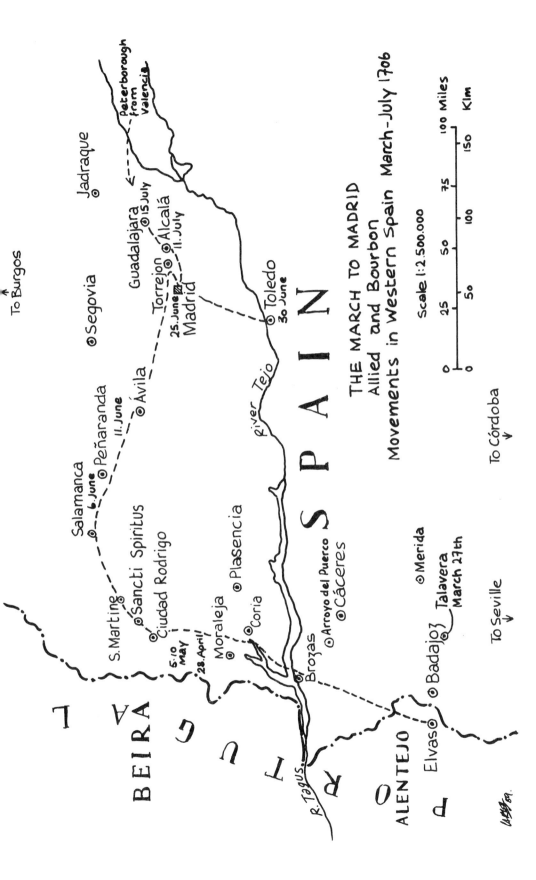

THE MARCH TO MADRID
Allied and Bourbon
Movements in Western Spain March-July 1706

Scale 1:2.500.000

To Burgos

Jadraque

Peterborough from Valencia

Guadalajara
15 July
Torrejon
25 June
Alcalá
11 July
Madrid

Segovia

Peñaranda
11 June

Ávila

Salamanca
6 June

Sancti Spiritus
S. Martino

Ciudad Rodrigo
5-10 MAY

Moraleja
28 April

Plasencia

Coria

River Tejo

Toledo
30 June

S P A I N

Arroyo del Puerco
Cáceres

Brozas

R. Tagus

To Córdoba

BEIRA

PORTUGAL

ALENTEJO

Elvas

Badajoz
Talavera
March 27th

Merida

To Seville

One sentence of Stanhope's in his letter of 21st March to Galway summed up the situation as it seemed to the authorities in London: 'The whole contest for the Spanish monarchy seems to be brought to a crisis, and will depend upon this summer's operations in these parts' – *i.e.* on the Portuguese frontier.

As yet nobody could guess what the outcome would be as Charles and Philip confronted each other in Catalonia, but it was rightly recognized that the western frontier zone was furthest from France, therefore least easily reinforced, and at the same time close to Madrid. Galway needed no telling. As soon as Tessé and his French troops began to move towards Catalonia in December 1705 the Huguenot started pressing for the Anglo-Dutch-Portuguese forces to cross into Spain and make for Madrid. But he could give no orders since das Minas was Generalissimo and the Portuguese adhered rigidly to their primacy under the Methuen Treaties. As a Protestant he had to be tactful in his dealings with the strongly Catholic Portuguese. The most Galway had been able to achieve by February 1706 was an earlier mobilisation than usual. He was elderly, unwell, and in a post which carried responsibility for failure without credit for success – and which he longed to leave – but he stuck it out.

By the time he received Stanhope's letter he had, with the help of pressure on King Pedro by the equally failing John Methuen, got the Portuguese to agree in principle to march into Spain – but no further than Alcántara, just across the frontier, and the Allied armies were encamped about Elvas just inside the border. Pedro's willingness was largely due to the arrival of wealth from Brazil. The Rio fleet came in at the end of May escorted by H.M.S. *Gloucester* and *Expedition*, and the Bahia and Pernambuco fleets, a huge convoy of 200 vessels also came in safely. They had been intercepted some fifty miles off Cabo de Roca (at the mouth of the Tagus) by Dugay-Trouin, the St. Malo privateer, and he had chased them with his 54-gun *Jason* and two other swift privateering ships. The convoy was escorted by six Portuguese men-of-war but the Frenchman isolated twenty of the merchant ships and one man-of-war, and boarded and captured the latter. He had to abandon her but carried on a running fight right into the Tagus estuary until his ship was damaged and he had to turn back and make for Cadiz. Although the Portuguese lost a man-of-war the convoy arrived *in toto*.

As a result of this, King Pedro was the richer by sixty or seventy pounds weight of gold from Rio alone and may have felt the more able to agree to the military advance into Spain. Das Minas insisted on primacy of command and not only on account of the Methuen Treaties. Of the 19,000 men in the army (San Felipe says 30,000 but this is far too high), the majority were Portuguese. Of the thirty-five battalions, forty-two squadrons, thirteen field guns and the train only

200 cavalry and 2,000 foot were English and altogether 2,000 Dutch. Galway's senior officers included Major-General O'Hara as chief of staff, Brigadier-Generals Floyd and Brudenell, Carles as chief engineer and Borgard, recovered from his wound, as commander of the train. Counts Frisheim and van Dohna commanded the Dutch. The Portuguese generals were São Vicente, Sonra, de Atayda, Fronteira, de Atalaya, Manoel, O'Farrell, Montandré and Mascarenhas.

The Allies knew that the Bourbon troops opposing them were inferior in numbers and almost all Spanish. With his commitments in northern Europe and the reinforcements sent to Catalonia, Louis had been quite unable to send the troops requested by Madrid for the frontier, but he had taken a step which was to have a major effect on the war both in the military and political sense. He too had realized that there was a crisis in the Peninsula and now turned once more to the young general who had served so well there two years earlier and had since then done brilliantly in Provence. He decided to send the Duke of Berwick back to Spain and in order that this time there should be no arguments about seniority, he appointed him a Marshal of France before he set out. Berwick was to be worth many battalions and squadrons.[6]

On 21st February he wrote from Montpelier to Louis thanking him for the promotion and saying cautiously. 'If good will can accomplish [victory on the frontier] it will be done ... but I fear that by the time I get to Madrid the Portuguese will have made great progress.' The letter is proudly signed for the first time: '*Le Maréschal Duc de Berwick'*.

Berwick then wrote to Chamillart describing his problems and adding, 'If I can't make headway against the Portuguese and if they get to Madrid the affairs of the King of Spain will be in great peril, even in danger of overthrow ... I will of course work in concert with Madame des Ursins and Amelot.' In his *Memoirs* he is withering about Chamillart's reaction. 'He made a pompous enumeration of the Spanish troops that were to compose my army and signified that fifteen battalions of French troops would be sent to join me. I later learned that he never had any intention of executing this.'

On 26th February he left for Spain, having written to Amelot about preparations for the campaign. The news of his appointment was greeted with relief and pleasure in Spain. He was at Bayonne by March 4th and reached Madrid on 11th March.

Not unexpectedly the Spaniards failed to do as promised. Orders from Madrid were 'insufficiently positive' and the ministers 'though completely ignorant of war always acted according to their own views. The number of independent generals along the same frontier was a pernicious circumstance.'

Hijar, Viceroy of Galicia, held on to the troops he was supposed to send and Villadarías kept his at Cadiz, to meet an Allied attack. 'As they were attacking Barcelona', snorted the marshal, 'it was unlikely that they would besiege Cadiz.' In short, he wrote, 'I had as much to contend with in Madrid as with the enemy' and, in a justified comment on the Portuguese, 'If I had had to do with people of intelligence or activity Spain would have been lost [to us].'

Das Minas was now encamped between Caya and Campo Maior, one and a half leagues from Badajoz. Berwick arrived at Badajoz on 27th March in order to ensure that the garrison he had thrown in despite de Bay was properly clothed, armed and fed and in a strong position, but realized that 'if the enemy advanced boldly 'he would have to retreat across the Guadiana at Mérida'. He was still worried: 'The more I consider the situation of King Philip's affairs on the frontier the more I am convinced that without a considerable body of troops it will be impossible not to succumb.' In this his view was thus the mirror image of Stanhope's. Yet, unlike the ever-grousing, timid Tessé, the new marshal having made his point developed a policy which enabled him not only to keep his army in being but to tempt and coax his opponents into overstretching themselves. Gradual retreat was the only possible course open to him and he adopted the tactics of putting his infantry into major strongholds as garrisons to hold up the Allies and threaten their rear while keeping his cavalry as a *masse de manoeuvre*. One reason for doing so was that the infantry was largely made up of militia and unsuitable for the open field. He was subjected to much criticism both at the time and afterwards for not making full use of his infantry and for retreating, but a year later the end would be found to have justified the means, and in the interim he would have sufficient military strength to back his judgement in advising Philip and his queen to hold on in Spain against all odds and thus to keep their kingdom. His cool, realistic, cautious grasp of essentials, so reminiscent of his uncle Marlborough's, was to be the rock on which the throne of Spain rested and against which the Allies would beat in vain.

In order to avoid being shut in at Badajoz Berwick now withdrew eastwards to Talavera, fifteen miles off, sending for de Fiennes to join him with ten squadrons and de Geoffreville with whatever he could collect − 'but this amounted to only three squadrons of dragoons'. This move drew the cautious das Minas after him, crossing the river Salor in early April. Berwick had intended to stand his ground but was so heavily out-numbered that he had to retreat to a line between Brozas and Arroyo del Puerco.

On the way there was a brisk action. Berwick had sent his reserve under Brigadier-General Don Domingo Canales to a position on the other side of a ravine and placed his foremost cavalry to face das Minas. The old Portuguese general pushed forward rapidly but the Spaniards retired to the cover of a wood and here Berwick decided to make a stand. At first the Spanish cavalry fought off the attackers but they were charged by the few English cavalry and Dutch dragoons and retreated. The use of a wood as a battleground was unorthodox in a cavalry action and das Minas suspected that he might be ambushed in it by infantry. He did not know that Berwick had virtually none. He therefore advanced with great caution. Even so it was only 'the resolute countenance of four French squadrons led by de Fiennes' which saved the day. It was, in Berwick's words, 'a small affair'. He had lost about 100 of his none too large force and his opponents about the same, including the Portuguese General São Vicente. Das Minas, who had narrowly missed being made prisoner, was somewhat chastened and withdrew to camp at Brozas.

Berwick retired – as he hoped – on his reserve. But Canales was not where he should have been. Instead of forming up on the other side of the ravine he had stationed himself a mile away where there was fodder for his horses and Berwick, after sending out search parties, eventually found him 'at ease' there. 'If', said the marshal tersely afterwards, 'the enemy had pushed me vigorously my embarrassment would not have been slight', for 'as we thought of nothing but retreating our regiments were thrown into confusion.'

On 9th April das Minas and Galway however invested Alcántara. This, although a fort was not a good one 'having neither ditch nor covered way nor outworks', but it had imposing bastions and walls and the Allies had little artillery with them. Berwick had ordered the governor, Major-General Don Diego Gasco to carry out a holding operation. At first he should fight on until a practicable breach had been made and then capitulate on 'honourable terms'. Then, if the enemy would not accept this, he was to leave via Trajan's bridge to the right bank of the Tagus where the enemy had only two dragoon regiments and the rough thorn-covered country would make pursuit difficult; he should thereafter move by night northwards along the river Alagón to Moraleja. He would have had at least the two hours' start and could have got away. If this move proved impossible Gasco was 'to sustain an assault rather than to consent to yield and be made a prisoner of war'. Berwick, in order to emphasize these orders, had gone personally with his cavalry to Las Ventas, four leagues away, as though threatening to relieve the place.

'My orders', he wrote, 'were not observed on a single point. Before even a breach was made [Gasco] beat the *chamade* and surrendered as prisoner of war' with all his 5,000 men. 'He consented without the least dispute to everything they required and yielded the town on 14th April.' Alcántara was a main depôt and perhaps unwisely had been used as a store for 70 guns, 5,000 muskets, 200 horses and quantities of grain, oil and wine, as well as 12,000 sets of clothing. It had cost the Allies about 50 men, mostly at the taking of a convent before they had begun the siege. The garrison had consisted of the four battalions originally there and a further six put in by Berwick, and 'the loss of so many men', mourned Amelot to Chamillart, 'at the beginning of the campaign is terrible ... The loss of Alcántara can hardly be attibuted to natural causes.' He added in cypher, 'Don Miguel [sic] Gasco deserves to have his head cut off when he leaves prison [in Lisbon] which will be in six months – as well as all the other officers down to captain.' Madrid was just beginning to realise the full dangers. Berwick, falling back on Plasencia, commented, 'The loss of Alcántara ... threw me into a very distressful embarrassment. Particularly by the fault of the Council at Madrid, and the disobedience of the captains-general it was impossible for me to oppose a sufficient force to the enemy.' The Allies were masters of the Tagus and could move wherever they pleased. Orry proposed raising ten battalions of militia with which Berwick should offer battle. 'This was not enough', said the marshal coldly, 'to tempt fortune with. I thought it better to hold our ground as well as we could until we had a considerably body of troops with which to undertake major operations.' A further panic-stricken suggestion from Madrid was that he should draw the French garrisons from Pamplona, San Sebastián and Fuenterrabia. This, too, was rejected 'for it was of the utmost consequence to us to preserve those places, the loss of which would have totally shut out all the succours we hoped for from France.'

Berwick was keeping his head, rightly believing that the Portuguese would not advance far until they had news of what was happening at Barcelona. The Portuguese army, as he knew, would not like leaving untaken fortresses in their rear for they preferred not to take risks. Nevertheless they were under pressure from their English ally and paymaster. Aware that he would be blamed for lack of success, but unable to shift the stubborn das Minas, Galway had recourse to ambassador Methuen who had access at any time to King Pedro, and put heavy pressure on him. A copy of Methuen's *aide mémoire* of conversations with the king in mid-April tells the story.

'I find myself obliged to represent to Your Majesty in the name of the Queen my mistress that, since it appears now to be in Your Majesty's power by marching immediately towards Madrid to make a revolution in Spain; if any other resolution than that be taken, the Queen my mistress will look on it as the loss of the greatest occasion that could be wished. If the army should be otherwise employed this spring than in marching into Spain towards Madrid, I am commanded to retire the English forces in Portugal to be embarked on the fleet which I expect next month, and in that case I am likewise commanded not to continue the payment of the subsidies for the pay of the troops of Your Majesty according to the Treaty.'

This blunt warning compelled King Pedro to send peremptory orders to das Minas to act on all occasions in concert with Galway. It was Methuen's last and potentially most potent strategic effort. Six weeks later – and two weeks after Galway and das Minas had entered Madrid – he was dead of the gout. He was probably one of the most effective ambassadors of his day and as representative of the paymistress towered over Waldstein and Schonenberg, his imperial and Dutch colleagues, thus arousing their jealousy. In general his work was appreciated by his compatriots, as we have seen, though Lord Halifax's epitaph on him, in a letter eight months later to General Lord Rivers, was critical. Describing the Lord Ambassador as 'an old rogue', Halifax went on, 'I have always thought he was the ruin of our efforts in Spain. He was truly the minister of Portugal not of England . . . He diverted the war from being made in the West Indies which would have enriched us.' But surely Methuen was only carrying out his government's orders. And Halifax's last sentence is characteristic of his avarice. He was not unknown to sacrifice principle for gain.

After Alcántara, das Minas prodded by Galway pushed slowly onwards. On 24th April, taking Moraleja and Coria on the way, he reached the outskirts of Plasencia, Berwick's current headquarters. In order to avoid being plundered by the Allies the peasants in the area are reported to have been willing to supply meat, oil and wine. Berwick retreated, accompanied by the bishop, the *corregidor* and many leading inhabitants, and made for Massagona on the River Tietar. Plasencia fell to the Allies on the 28th.

The Allies knew little or nothing of Berwick's movements and were apparently unaware of how short he was of troops and supplies. They had captured good stocks of provisions at Alcántara, and although they had squandered these they were in a fertile corn-producing region. The Portuguese in particular, as das Minas admitted, were chiefly concerned with getting their own back on the Spaniards, and spent much of their time on plundering – particularly churches. They were to continue to delay even when they reached Salamanca five weeks later and it took all Galway's insistence and a further threat from Methuen in Lisbon to get them moving again.

Berwick now called up eight battalions from Badajoz and then, ordering the fords of the Tietar to be entrenched, pretended that he would resist there, hoping to force the Allies to take another road and thus enable him to gain time, which was about the only resource available to him. He had by now come to the conclusion that the Allies were determined to make for Madrid and had already begun to consider the best course of action for the queen regent, María Luisa. While still at Plasencia he had writen on 22nd April, 'If the queen has to leave Madrid she should come and be with the army. It is the only possible thing.' Amelot felt that somewhere further from the guns would be safer:

'The enemy is on the high road to Madrid. If they come via Ciudad Rodrigo we must in two or three days think of placing the queen in safety ... Berwick proposes that she should join him and reanimate the troops by her presence. This seems to me to be over-bold ['*gaillard*'] for the general is in a weak position and obliged to make precipitate marches. I do not see, frankly, how such an idea has entered his head. I have not mentioned it to the queen or Mme. des Ursins.'

From his un-named Portuguese contact Berwick knew that his opponents were in fact less determined than they should be. Galway wished to march straight to Madrid but das Minas halted. His troops were after all only militia. His officers needed to recoup the cost of the campaign so far at the expense of the Spaniards. There were strong fortresses to the rear threatening their communications. And there was still no news from Barcelona. At length Galway, persuaded old das Minas to move sideways and northwards to attack Ciudad Rodrigo which although further from Lisbon was only a few days' march from Madrid.

Ciudad Rodrigo, described by Berwick in a letter to Louis as 'the worst place in Europe, if indeed it can be called a place', was surrounded only by walls dating from the middle ages. It had no outworks, no moat, no covered way and its garrison was only one regular battalion and about 2,000 militia. Nevertheless, although it could not be expected to offer much resistance the fact that the Allies were moving towards it was considered good news by Berwick, 'for if they had advanced they would have been masters of all Spain'. Allied movements were slow. Lack of supplies and the fidelity of Spanish peasants to Philip, had, according to Amelot on 19th May, inhibited them. Berwick reported their slow transit via Plasencia (12th), Galisteo (13th), Coria (14th) and to the head of the Sierra de Gata (15th). A spy from the enemy confirmed that they were going to Ciudad Rodrigo, 'which is only natural. It would be difficult to stop them.'

Ciudad Rodrigo surrendered on 26th May on terms which although described by Berwick as honourable were severe. The militia were forbidden to take up arms ever again and the regulars for six months. The siege, futile for the Allies, had bought time for Berwick and time was of the essence. He fell back once more, this time to Salamanca, a university city and quite unfortified. Here he received two pieces of bad news. The first was of what a contemporary, the Duc de Feuquière, called 'the shameful raising of the siege of Barcelona by Marshal Tessé'. The second, a few days later, was of the Battle of Ramillies. The first meant that Berwick was at once faced with a crisis on the spot: What was to be done about Philip and how could the queen's safety be arranged? The marshal guessed that the young king would be concerned above all to hasten back to his wife, but by what route? They were all dangerous. And then, assuming that the two were together in Madrid what was to be done? The capital was full of ditherers giving contradictory and often unrealistic advice.

The second item of news must at the time have been quite as ominous. Berwick would know that Villeroy's defeat by Marlborough would threaten Flanders and northern France and provide one more example of the invincible qualities of his uncle. Not only would it encourage waverers in the Peninsula to transfer their support from Philip and the apparently unsuccessful Bourbons to Charles and the more fortunate Habsburgs and maritime powers; it could also mean that King Louis' ability to provide support to his grandson in the way of troops and money might be gravely curtailed.

To Berwick, as to many others in Spain and France these few weeks were the nadir of the Bourbon fortunes, but he seems, to judge from his correspondence, not just from his *Memoirs*, to have kept his head. The total change that began to take place over the next six weeks, and which continued therafter is due in no small part to this. Other factors were: King Louis' determination to reinforce him with troops and arms no longer used for besieging Barcelona; the fact that he was to all intents and purposes the only person in Spain whose authority was tacitly or overtly respected by Philip, María Luisa and all concerned; the lack of unity in the Allied camp facing him; a lack of determination on the part of King Charles, coupled with disagreements among his own courtiers, let alone with Peterborough; faulty liaison between Barcelona and Galway; the steadfastness of María Luisa in a situation which was both dangerous and uncomfortable; and an unexpected but welcome access of spirit on the part of King Philip.

★　　★　　★

Little is recorded on the Bourbon side of Tessé's nightmare, headlong retreat after the Day of the Dragon. Stanhope wrote of 'barbarities' committed by this beaten army, but there were no doubt similar barbarities committed by the

Miquelets as they fell on the rabble fleeing via Roca and Prats de Molio, for apart from the *matériel* and supplies abandoned at Barcelona (they also included 10,000 pairs of boots which would now have come in handy) and the 2,000 wounded he left to Peterborough's mercy, Tessé lost a further estimated 4,000 men during the retreat. He himself must have been at a low ebb.[7]

The terms 'nervous breakdown' and 'battle fatigue' had not been coined in the early 1700s but the conditions they describe certainly existed and affected as they still do not merely some junior officers and rank and file but also and not infrequently those in high command. It seems likely that in May 1706 Tessé was in similar case. He had been in Spain for almost eighteen months of nearly complete military disaster. He had been outwardly affable with the Spaniards, using his secret correspondence as the only vent for his true feelings about them. He was in any case accustomed to a more gentlemanly form of warfare. He must have known that he had lost his nerve at Barcelona – itself a symptom of breakdown, and welcomed the retirement to which he was soon summoned. He was incapable of deflecting King Philip from what had become his over-whelming obsession: to re-join the queen in Madrid. The queen was equally impervious to Berwick's advice to withdraw to the safety of Burgos.

'The king', Berwick wrote, 'was so eager to be with the queen that he would listen to nothing else.' The queen and the *Despacho* had not written to the king as Berwick had asked. 'In spite of my advice they did countless things out of their own heads, and usually these were blunders which I had afterwards the trouble of rectifying.'

All this is not hindsight on the marshal's part, contained in his *Memoirs* though it is. Not only was he at a time of life when perception and recollection are clear but his day by day correspondence – of which there are copies at Vincennes – confirms it. As an older married man and one conscious of his crushing responsibility he found Philip's uxoriousness tiresome, though it was understandable in a lonely young man in his twenties.

So, on 6th June Philip reached Madrid with de Noailles. Wrote Amelot to Chamillart. 'There were great demonstrations of joy as he passed through. This evening [7th] there were *feux de joie* and illuminations – which had been got ready to celebrate the recapture of Barcelona and could not [now] be better employed.'

Yet, as the fireworks sparkled in the warm, sharp, dry night skies of Madrid, and glad as the royal couple no doubt were to see each other in the pink-walled Buen Retiro Palace, it was soon clear that Berwick was right. They could not long stay there. Apart from anything else, money was so short that the king was forced to borrow against revenue for 1707 and 1708. He considered drawing from the churches, to which he had a right in emergency, but the curés would not part with the money. The grandees and other nobility were asked for a free gift but while they expressed their loyalty in words they produced very little cash. The unpopular Orry had been hard at work but had reported no success. The rich Duque de Infantado gave 1,000 *doblons*, another grandee 440 *reales*, others provided some silver plate or 12 horses and 12 men, or 2,000 *pistoles*, 1,000 ducats, and even smaller sums. The queen herself had gone, as regent, to the town hall and appealed to the city fathers, but had only managed to raise a fleabite – 6,000 *pistoles*. Cardinal Portocarrero was supposed, said Amelot, to draw from the deposits of two of the richer churches (*San Justo* and *San Paulo*) but he had not done so, and representations by the king and queen, Madame des Ursins and Amelot himself had been ineffectual. This is not surprising. The cardinal was elderly and sulky. He had openly complained a year or so before that Philip was by-passing the *Despacho*. Since then the king had fallen even more into the hands of the French – and Spain with him.

Such feelings were only at the extreme of a range of sentiment among the nobility. The Duc de Noailles who was in Madrid at the time told in his *Memoirs* of a Spanish lady who described the attitude of the grandees as a whole as being like that of a wary devotee who, in order to keep in with both sides, offered a candle to St Michael and another to the Devil.

Philip, weary no doubt after his tribulations at Barcelona and on the retreat, and his long roundabout ride from Perpignan, was now faced with gloomy meetings of the *Despacho*, the council of war and other tribunals. They all wished to get away. Some said the king should retire to Andalucia, others to France. It was decided on 17th June that the court should move at once to Guadarrama, and many of the noblemen, as Amelot reported on 21st June, went to their estates. Even old Mancera, who was ninety-eight, left Madrid. The place was 'like a big empty village'. The queen left on the 18th and at last the king on the 19th. Amelot wrote to Louis:

'It was essential not to upset the [ordinary] people's love for him. So he left at 3.30 in the morning when nobody was about, accompanied by 420 bodyguards. He joined Berwick on the 21st in the morning at Funcaval and promoted some of his general officers'

before moving on to Sopetrán, where Amelot himself joined him four days later. From here Philip moved to Torrejón (now Torrelajuna) and the ambassador reported that the queen's jewels (*pierrerie*) were on their way to Paris. It might be a question of selling them to get cash. Berwick reported to Chamillart:

'The consternation of our troops is great and it is difficult to persuade them that it is the king's intention not to leave them but stay with them. Desertion has already begun and will increase because we have no money to pay them. When I asked Orry [who was by now at Guadalajara] how much money there was he said 620,000 *livres*, which is a drop in the bucket.'

The very agents handling what cash there was had to be paid to let it go.

It was a bad time for the queen. A letter quoted in de Noailles' *Memoirs*, and written to Madame de Maintenon, gives her own story:

'I arrived at Burgos yesterday evening [5th July], much fatigued with rising before daybreak, overpowered with the heat, almost stifled with dust, and having rested only in the most wretched and ruinous hovels. In one instance a wall fell down and put many people in great danger. From this you may judge of the rest. We hoped on arriving here to be more comfortably lodged but have so far been greatly disappointed. Notwithstanding these hardships we shall not complain if the King can but prevail over his enemies. But alas scarcely a day passes without bringing us news of some fresh disaster.'

And now the Allies entered the capital. Even though Berwick had known all along that this must happen, 25th June was a depressing day for him, for Philip and for those who were with him. On that day an advanced guard of cavalry under the Marqués de Villaverde marched in and after due preparation Galway and das Minas made what was intended to be a triumphal entry. Had Charles been with them it might have been. As it was the *Madrileños* were cold and sullen in their reception probably because for the Portuguese it was an hour of glory, as they were in the capital of a country of which seventy years earlier they had been vassals. It probably did not matter too much to them that there were no shouts of acclaim, no girls waving, no welcome except from a few urchins in the street. And even these, when das Minas ordered that money should be thrown to them to raise cheers, merely shouted 'Long live Charles III – as long as he still gives us money.' However, there was no doubt plenty of plunder and a temptation to relax while they waited for Charles. The generals took up quarters at El Pardo, a royal hunting lodge six miles outside the city and the troops were camped along the River Manzanares.

★   ★   ★

Routes Taken by Philip and María Luisa May–July 1706

FRANCE

SPAIN

Atlantic Ocean

Mediterranean Sea

Bayonne

Perpignan

Barcelona

Tarragona

Tortosa

Lérida

Saragossa

Calatayud

Pamplona

Tudela

Soria

Aranda de Duero

Burgos

Valladolid

Ávila

Segovia

Madrid

Alcalá de Henares

Guadalajara

Aranjuez

Toledo

2nd June

25th May

12th May

5th July

18th June

19th June

5th June

N

Scale 1:5.000.000

0   20   40   60   80   100 Miles

0   40   80   120   160 Kms

.... María Luisa

—·—·— Philip

Charles failed to appear. There have been numerous explanations for his fatal delay but the fundamental problem has not hitherto been sufficiently emphasized. Stanhope, in a letter to Godolphin on 19th May, a week after the raising of the siege of Barcelona, put his finger on it: '*The truth is [Charles and his Ministers] have not a shilling, the siege having drained them of what little they had before*'. This shrewdly points to the seed of the trouble from which, watered and fertilised by political and personal frictions would grow the failure – ultimately to prove fatal to his cause – of the Allies' candidate to seize the opportunity offered by Galway's march to Madrid and the salvation of Barcelona. It was a robust seed, as can be seen by Stanhope's letters over the next few months which parallel the constant references to money shortages in the Bourbon correspondence, but it might have been less so if the Allies had had on the spot a single-minded and determined equivalent of Berwick. As it was they had Charles and his court, General de Noyelles, Stanhope who although a man of growing stature was too junior, and Peterborough. If Prince George of Hesse-Darmstadt had lived he might perhaps have unified the command. Indecision, bickering, changes of plan, but above all financial exigency were now to decide the progress of the war. It was to last for seven more years but with hindsight it can be said that whereas in mid-May 1706 Charles had the crown of Spain in his grasp, by late July that grasp had slipped – for ever as it would turn out.

There are three main Allied sources of information on this, Peterborough's correspondence, Stanhope's, and the minutes of meetings of the Allied councils of war, which have not apparently hitherto been consulted by English historians. Those for this period are in *Libro* 985d in the Madrid *Archivo* and record the discussions at considerable length, each individual's views being noted. The council met with varying frequency, sometimes daily but usually weekly and the numbers present varied, though a quorum seems to have been five. The most constant in attendance were Lichtenstein, de Noyelles, Stanhope, the Portuguese ambassador de Assumar, and Zinzerling. The last-named usually wrote the minutes. In one or two cases his rough drafts in a difficult hand are bound in with the fair copy. Charles occasionally attended but when he did not he read the minutes with care and he (or after his marriage and when he was absent on campaign, his queen) made marginal comments in holograph or wrote *me conforme* (I agree) and initialled this, in slightly childish writing and heavy black ink. When they were available the generals and admirals also attended – Galway, das Minas, Frisheim, Shovell and the rest and on some occasions there were between twenty-five and thirty present. Later the council discussed matters concerned principally with politics, finance, and supplies and military affairs were dealt with by a sub-committee which Charles called the *Junta*, but military and naval operations were so enmeshed with politics, money and supplies that there was frequent overlap. The council certainly did its best but unfortunately it usually did not see the wood for the trees. This was the case from the start.

There is little doubt that Charles was very short of cash. Legendre in Roussillon heard at this time that 'the city gives him 300 *pistoles* a day for his food'. Much of this found its way into the pockets of Charles' *entourage*. These, according to Stanhope, were not only mistrusted by Peterborough and others but by the Catalans who

'think that his ministers have no mind he should go to Madrid, foreseeing that their ministry would not be long-lived there. But I believe that they refine too much who will attribute any foresight to men who, I think, have never shown any, and who have used all possible means to alienate the affections of this people, to whom their master owes so much.'

That ministry was also bedevilled by personal disagreements and rivalries within itself. General the Comte de Noyelles, angling and conspiring for an independent command, set himself against Peterborough. The former argued for a march from Barcelona to Madrid via Saragossa, the latter via Valencia. The consequent delay was attributed by rumour to a secret dalliance of the archduke's. The final decision – in favour of the 'tedious and hazardous' way through Saragossa – was procured by need. According to Stanhope, the archduke had been told that taking this route through Aragon would

'bring the money, to make him independent. And those who have private ends to answer have to such a degree improved the misunderstanding that is between my Lord Peterborough and His Majesty that he will venture the not going to Madrid at all, rather than be carried thither by my lord.'

By 15th July Charles and his entourage had reached Saragossa where they were received 'with all demonstrations of joy'. They would still be there nine days later, lapping up the insincere plaudits and grabbing for cash with a fervour that turned the population totally against them the moment they left. The citizens had been persuaded to contribute 'voluntarily' to the cost of the archduke's journey to Madrid. Stanhope noted caustically in a letter to Hedges, 'We seem to have been seized with a lethargy ever since the relief of Barcelona.'

Yet a decision was now forced on Charles, for Galway's quartermaster-general, a Colonel Dubourgay, had arrived on 20th July after a dangerous journey of four days from the Portuguese camp near Guadalajara, where there were now only 4,000 horse and 10,000 foot – far less than Charles had expected. Berwick's force, moreover, 'at Atienza nine leagues from there', was believed superior in cavalry, to total 9,000 and to be receiving reinforcements. The Portuguese were anxious to go home and Berwick was thought to be about to offer battle, so Galway was pressing ever more forcibly for Charles to come quickly.

On this the archduke sent three of his four battalions ahead and decided to march himself on the 24th with the remaining battalion and 800 horse, such an escort being essential as they would pass within thirty miles of Berwick's camp. Stanhope estimated that the march, via Deroca and Molina, would take ten or twelve days. He was worried that the Portuguese might go home. 'This junction might have been made with the greatest of ease and security imaginable a month ago if the first resolution [of going via Valencia] had been followed'. Now everything was so uncertain that he did not know what to do for the best. 'I wish some angel would instruct me.' As they marched more news came in, uncertain but ominous, of French reinforcements but although the march was made safer by the roughness of the country, this also meant that they could neither get much intelligence nor give Galway any – even of their own movements.

Before leaving Saragossa, Charles had sent an express to Peterborough in Valencia instructing him to join, to which the earl replied that he would come but with only 1,300 horse and 3,000 foot as the rest were needed to cover Valencia and Cartagena. He was apparently considering at that time a fairly long stay at the Allied camp, for although when he set out he took with him in fact barely more than an escort, he ordered his heavy baggage, plate, clothing, food and wine worth about £8,000 to be sent after him. He was in a crotchety humour when, on 4th August, he met up with Charles and his court at Pastrana due east of Madrid and twenty miles from Guadalajara, where two days later they joined Galway and das Minas. The total Allied force was now a little less than 18,000 men. The Portuguese, who had been strongly posted near Jadraque on some heights had withdrawn, and Berwick, still threatened, pushing forward to camp on the plains of Marchomalo a bare five miles away. He intended to send de Légal as soon as he arrived to Alcalá. Thus, with growing conviction – aided no doubt by further precise information from his un-named Portuguese contact in the Allied camp – he effectively showed his opponents that their way back to Madrid was going to be blocked.

In the city only a few Spanish grandees remained to await Charles or came out to his camp. They were chiefly those who, like the Conde de Galveas had not been given by Philip the posts they wished. A few others were old and confused like the Duque de Infantado, whose brother-in-law, Lemos, had declared for Charles. He himself had no intention of committing himself but his sons, in rebellion against parental authority declared for Charles. Some were so uncertain of the situation that they blundered into Berwick's camp thinking it was Charles' and were promptly arrested. Among those who hesitated between going to their own estates or showing a firm commitment to Philip was that grandee of grandees the Duque de Medinaceli, whose estate lay some sixty miles to the north-east beyond Guadalajara. With the rival armies interposed between him and his home he decided to move, but by slow states *'chicas jornadas'*, says San Felipe, towards Burgos. His experiences at this point seem to have encouraged him to think of starting a peace party.

Das Minas thought he had only quit Madrid temporarily and had left behind him his pontoon-train, stores and 500 *pistoles* for clearing up the Buen Retiro Palace. (He never saw these again.) And he had thought it sufficient, too, to entrust the city to a guard of a handful of irregular horse under the Conde de Amajuelas. He had had to admit that he and Galway had received a chilly welcome. And to make matters worse – if San Felipe is to be believed – Charles would also have learned that during their stay in the capital the Portuguese had been subjected to a novel form of subversion. Apart from being knifed or mugged in the *calles*:

> 'The women of the town, out of loyalty and public spirit took it upon themselves to finish off this army if they could. Going in groups to the Portuguese tents these strumpets, scented and larded with make-up introduced to the soldiers a disease which is known as the most dangerous.'

As a result of this unorthodox display of patriotic fervour, San Felipe reports 6,000 Portuguese soldiers in hospital, but the number is probably an exaggeration. Nevertheless, on the day that Charles reached Guadalajara Berwick boldly sent the Marqués de Mejorada, a member of Philip's *Despacho* and Minister for War, accompanied by General António del Valle and 500 horse, into the city. Their welcome in Madrid was tumultouous. 'We could describe many examples which would hardly be believed', says San Felipe. 'So great was the excess of joy that the people seemed to have gone mad.' The *Madrileños* proclaimed Philip King and burned at the Puerta del Sol the public acts promulgated on Charles' behalf by Galway and das Minas. The unfortunate Amajuelas and his two or three hundred horse, who had withdrawn to the Buen Retiro, short of food, surrendered after a few hours. Amajuelas, 'an illustrious man of high quality', who had hoped to make his fortune by supporting Charles, was sent as a prisoner to France. With him went a number of others whom Berwick in a despatch to Chamillart on 10th August names

> 'the chief villains – 100 of them officers from this army . . . Del Valle gave this *canaille* a shameful capitulation. As you will see King Philip has just arrested them and sent them via Pamplona to France . . . Please order the Marshal de Montreuil when they reach him to put them in some dungeon (*cachot*) from which they cannot escape.'

The rank and file were probably sent to the galleys but there is no further information about them.

A number of grandees in the city were tried and banished by Ronquillo – Lartegui, and others who had accepted the Austrian standard. A couple of bishops such as Mendoza of Segovia who had come in disguise to greet Charles, were sent prisoner to France, but on the whole Philip was remarkably – and wisely – lenient. Bishop Mendoza had clearly been out of step with his flock for the inhabitants of Segovia now forced the Portuguese garrison to surrender and other towns and cities in Castile followed suit. Toledo had already done so, and although the Portuguese General de Atalaya remained in the Alcázar, with its proud motto – *Ne Plus Ultra* – carved on the walls, the dowager queen and Cardinal Portocarrero had shot their bolt. Philip was magnanimous here too. The queen-dowager was sent under an escort of 100 horse led by the Duque de Ossuna to Bayonne, where she remained for thirty years, more a prisoner than a queen, only returning to die at Guadalajara Palace. Portocarrero was old and had done the state some service. Moreover he was the primate of Spain and as such could not be too severely treated, so Philip pardoned him. Nevertheless he had to hand over a large sum of money for repairs to the city of Toledo which was severely damaged by the Portuguese. When they left they blew up the Alcázar, probably by accident but perhaps on purpose.

As communications with Portugal were cut neither supplies nor, more importantly, money could get through to the Allies. A convoy from Portugal had been seized at Salamanca, and although recovered by the Portuguese governor of Ciudad Rodrigo (who fined Salamanca for its disaffection), there was no chance of its reaching Guadalajara. So Charles and his 'German crew' and the mixed bag of troops – English, Dutch, Spanish, Portuguese and Neapolitan – were in a lamentable situation, oppressed by a harsh climate, short of money and supplies, and more than usually prone to sickness – quite apart from whatever Madrid's ladies of easy virtue had implanted in them. Morale drooped and desertion increased. 'The whole country', wrote Stanhope,' [is] very much against us ... The country of Castile is daily falling from us and we can only reckon ourselves masters of the ground we encamp upon.'

The situation was immediately considered at councils of war and *Juntas* on 7th August and 9th at the Palace of Guadalajara.[8] At the first there was a lengthy argument about supplies. Galway, de Noyelles, das Minas, Stanhope, Lichtenstein, Peterborough, Cifuentes, de Assumar, Mascarenhas, Fronteira and Oropesa (the renegade grandee) were present. There was also discussion of the naval situation, and the possibility of leaving a fleet in the Mediterranean – but this, it was noted, depended on England's intentions on future operations in the Peninsula, on which information was to be sought.

At the meeting on the 9th Peterborough flung in a bombshell, referring apparently to the orders he had received from his queen on 6th July to go to Italy. He had long sensed that real trouble was on the way in Spain and wished no further part of it. He had for months been at loggerheads with Charles and his court – understandably, no doubt, if Stanhope, the straightest of men, is to be believed. The earl might have started earlier for Madrid but had as we have seen dissipated his forces away from Valencia. For what it is worth when a year later his conduct was questioned by the House of Lords, five of his colonels – Hans Hamilton, Bissett, Edgeworth, Allnutt and Pitt – and his secretary, Arent Furly, stated unanimously that it had not been possible for him to march sooner. But this was perhaps to be expected.

Whatever the background, he was determined to get away. The minutes are relatively urbane. His lordship was to go with the fleet but it was noted that he was anxious still to be of assistance. He proposed to raise a loan in Italy for the archduke, who agreed that he should use as security the Spanish crown domains. He was asked to return as soon as possible having done so, and to capture Port Mahon in Minorca, 'so as to protect the coasts of Valencia and Catalonia from enemy attack'. It was also decided that 'some ships should be left in Andalucia to threaten Cadiz so that troops from thence should be prevented from joining those of the Duke of Anjou.'

It is quite probable, from the erratic earl's customary behaviour, that he hoped by thus stirring matters up to impose his strategies and opinions on his colleagues. He had hoped for overall command but Galway and de Noyelles were 'much ancienter officers than he was', though Galway offered to serve under him. He must have been humiliated by the alacrity with which Charles agreed to his going and the unanimity with which the council approved his departure. Reading between the lines it would seem that they could not wait to be rid of him.[9] He left Guadalajara on 11th August.On the 13th he reached Valencia where he heard that he had lost all his baggage. Sent from Valencia

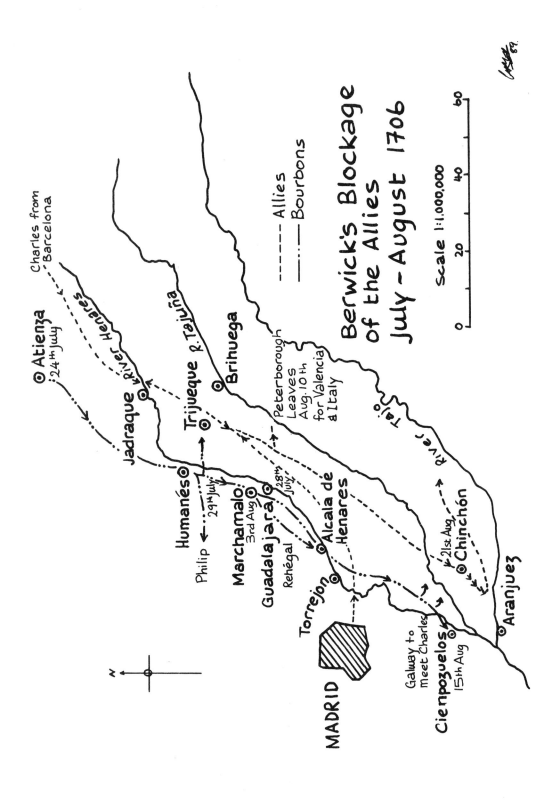

Berwick's Blockage
of the Allies
July – August 1706

Scale 1:1,000,000

Allies
Bourbons

0   20   40   60

Atienza
24th July

Charles from
Barcelona

Jadraque

River Henares

Trijueque

R. Tajuña

Brihueca

Humanés

Philip

29th July

Marchamalo
3rd Aug

28th July

Guadalajara

Rehegal

Alcala de
Henares

Torrejon

Peterborough
Leaves
Aug. 10th
for Valencia
& Italy

River Tajo

Chinchón

21st Aug

MADRID

Galway to
meet Charles

Cienpozuelos
15th Aug

Aranjuez

Battle of Almenara
27th July 1710

N

R. Noguera - Ribagorzana

← To Alfarrás

Approach of Cavalry followed by Infantry & Guns

Deep Valley

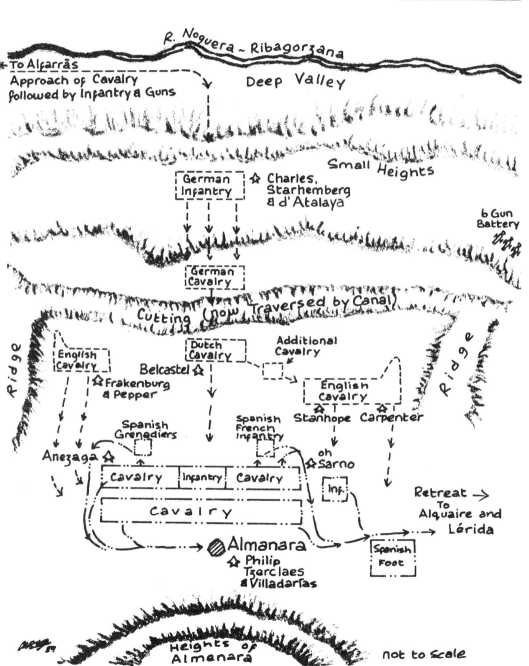

Small Heights

German Infantry — ☆ Charles, Starhemberg & d'Atalaya

6 Gun Battery

German Cavalry

Cutting (now Traversed by Canal)

Ridge

English Cavalry

☆ Frakenburg & Pepper

Belcastel ☆

Dutch Cavalry

Additional Cavalry

English Cavalry

☆ Stanhope   Carpenter

Spanish Grenadiers

Spanish French Infantry

oh Sarno ☆

Anezaga ☆

Cavalry | Infantry | Cavalry

Inf.

Retreat →
To Alquaire and Lérida

Cavalry

Almenara

☆ Philip Tzerclaes & Villadarías

Spanish Foot

Heights of Almenara

not to scale

towards Guadalajara it had only reached Huete, a tiny place about half way. Here it was the object of a raid by a young Spanish cavalry colonel, Don Juan de Zereceda, who carried out a daring attack on the earl's grandiose caravan. He had with him 150 Spanish cavalry and dragoons. It was common practice for an emblem to be worn by the troops to distinguish one side from the other. At this time the Austrian badge was a bough in the hat and when Zereceda's party entered Huete they wore this and shouted: '*Viva Carlos III!*', which deceived the Allied escort. Ridden down, seventy of these were killed and the rest made prisoner. 'I bear all other losses patiently' wrote Peterborough to Stanhope, 'besides my barbs [Barbary horses] and cheeses.'

During the next two or three weeks it is difficult to establish what he was up to. He claims to have gone at once to Alicante to hasten the capitulation of his 'ancient adversary' O'Mahony, who commanded the place for the Bourbons but this is uncertain. Leake had already been besieging the place for a month and it was only on 4th September that O'Mahony asked for terms and not until the 8th that he marched out. That Peterborough did however go there is evidenced by a letter from him quoted in Coxe's *Life of Marlborough* and dated on 4th September from Alicant Road, to the Duchess of Marlborough. It is that well known one which describes Spain as 'the most disagreeable country in the world ... Their officers the greatest robbers and their soldiers the greatest cowards. The only tolerable thing is your sex, and that attended with the greatest dangers.'

He left a mess, a lost opportunity which would prove fatal to the cause he was meant to serve and an Allied command still split by wrangles to which he had contributed. De Noyelles, as yet unable to have his own command, was not prepared to yield to anybody else and did his best to undermine Galway. Das Minas still continued to insist on his seniority, but at the same time, although lines of communications with Portugal no longer existed, he hankered after taking his rough and unreliable troops home. And Galway himself was there only out of a sense of duty. Even without Peterborough, the bickering went on. The initiative had already begun to pass to Berwick, patient, professional, unhurried, and dominating the Bourbon scene.

$$\star \quad \star \quad \star$$

On 15th August Berwick marched towards Cienpozuelos in a rich valley due south of Madrid and between the city and the Allies, and this forced his opponents to decide what they were to do. They were clearly going to make for the Kingdom of Valencia, due east, and not for Aragon, for 'after an all-night march in difficult country they crossed the Tajuña [a tributary of the Tagus]. 17th August to Chamillart: 'The enemy are taking the road via Chinchón for Aranjuez. I have chased them again. Our marches seem to have decided them to stay where they were [*i.e.* not return to Madrid] particularly as they have no subsistence.'

Now there was a pause in movement by both armies. Intercepted letters told Berwick and Amelot that Lichtenstein was deeply concerned about domestic arrangements for King Charles, and that the Allies were short of money and food. Though he was now confident Berwick's worries were manifold. Much of the Bourbon army was composed of local militia and these would not be adequate, 'as the English and Dutch are sending reinforcements and we will only be able to hold on if we are fortunate and receive reinforcements [ourselves]'. During the weeks that followed, the marshal would need every bit of his judicious mixture of daring and caution and of the diplomatic toughness which enabled him to resist impetuous pressures from Philip, the now emboldened Amelot and the Spanish generals to seek battle.

In the Allied camp indecision now reigned for a month or so. Undated notes of discussions at Chinchón refer to shortages of food, questions of hostages and the imposition of fines on Castile 'for its disaffection'. But there really was no chance of recapturing Castile, and they should have known it. Even if it had been possible in a military sense the attitude of the inhabitants was more favourable to Philip than ever before.

Some indication of the confusion can be obtained from the ten-page minutes taken by Zinzerling of a meeting on 20th August of the Allied council. Charles was there and Prince Henry of Hesse. By way of introduction, Charles noted that he had brought troops from Catalonia and Aragon to a junction of forces at Guadalajara and politely thanked das Minas for what he and his Portuguese troops had done. He then asked for a decision: should they go via Sigüenza and through Aragon (back to Catalonia) or cross the Tagus and, taking the Guadarrama pass, recover Madrid? Galway alone wished to take the second, more daring, course and so (with reservations) did Stanhope who was present. But the majority were more concerned with communications with Portugal and with holding on to what they thought they could be sure of. In this atmosphere of doubt it was agreed that there should be daily meetings, but no record of these seems to have been kept, and indeed decisions must have been difficult to reach. We can find the reason for this in a letter from Stanhope to Godolphin dated 25th August, from Chinchón. The army was penniless. Stanhope suggested that, instead of the English and Dutch subsidy being paid via

Lisbon 'where the ministers have so ordered it that the troops received no pay all this summer and are consequently forced to live with great licentiousness', the money should be sent to the queen's general (*i.e.* Galway) and issued by him. This would make the Portuguese more amenable to discipline. King Pedro had not in any case provided all the men he should have been paying for under the Methuen Treaty and the Portuguese should not be in a position to insist on overall command. Moreover, 'the war being made for the King of Spain and in his country, his general should have the command.'

It was a sensible proposal but it was lost in the morass of Allied disagreements. By the time it reached London circumstances had anyway forced the Allied army to move eastwards, lengthening their lines of communication and marching to the tune of Berwick's strategy. The marshal was blamed by his Spanish allies for avoiding battle and merely snapping at the heels of his enemy as they marched towards Valencia, but he was right. As Montesquieu, writing in tranquillity far from the scene observes; 'he conducted them thither by one march after another, as a shepherd leads his flock.'

The opportunity of reigning over Spain from a court in Madrid was now lost to Charles for ever. He would briefly return to the capital later but the pendulum had begun its as yet invisible swing against him. His generals still had hopes, as they continued what Berwick described as 'this campaign of a most singular kind from the diversity of events'. The Cabinet in London shared these hopes, for communications being as they were they had no sound reason not to. They were groping after success through the use of a Mediterranean naval strategy. The fleet had after all taken and then saved Gibraltar. It had presided over the capture of Barcelona and later so dominated its French naval opponents that Tessé had lost his nerve and failed to recapture the Catalan capital. The sea, was to continue to be an almost uniformly sympathetic element.

★ ★ ★

By early 1706 the Navy's role in the war in the Peninsula had begun to be established as a policy.[10] As early as possible in each year a large fleet of ships-of-the-line, auxiliaries and transports would set forth from Portsmouth and other traditional fleet bases carrying troop reinforcements, supplies and cash. But a change in dates was also beginning and before long it would become the pattern to get fresh troops to the Peninsula during the winter to give them time to acclimatise themselves before the spring led through a few brief weeks of campaign to the 'great heats' of high summer, to sickness, disease and desertion.

On the way to the Mediterranean the fleet had usually called in at Lisbon to effect changes of ships and land reinforcements for the war on the frontier, replenished Gibraltar and made for Barcelona, but the situation was changing. The war on the frontier had shifted eastwards, to Madrid and beyond. The Portuguese ally was taking the money but not providing the troops. And there was strong pressure, not only in London itself, but from Charles and the English generals on his staff to establish long-term facilities in the Balearics so that a winter squadron could be based inside the Middle Sea – as had long since been envisaged by Cromwell and William III. Now the move began in all seriousness.

At one of his first councils at Barcelona on 20th May 1706, Charles, convinced by the reports he had had from the Balearics, had asked Leake to undertake an expedition there. Perhaps the admiral should have done so but he politely advised the young king of the problems of the undertaking. On 1st July Leake rebuffed another plea from Charles to the same effect. Only after the capture of Alicante freed the fleet for marginal engagements did the admiral return to the archduke's request. On September 19th 1706 Leake stood some twenty miles off Ibiza and sent ashore a local notable, Don Francisco Balançat, who had brought news to Charles that the island was prepared to declare for him. Next day, 20th, the fleet sailed in to be greeted with salutes and an offer of submission by the governor. Charles was proclaimed king, a government set up in his name and an obligatory four days spent in official celebrations. Then on 24th September the fleet sailed for Majorca.

This, the largest of the Balearics, with its harbour under the guns of the Castle of San Carlos, was a prize worth having. Wonderfully fertile, its central plain, protected by two chains of tree-covered hills from the off-shore mainland winds, produces cereals, vegetables, figs and all kinds of other fruit. The port is not so easily defensible as Port Mahon in Minorca, particularly if there is treason about, and Leake was well aware that there was a strong pro-Carlist faction in the island, since many of the nobility were Catalans. Indeed he had with him Don Juan António Bojadars, Conde de Saballá, who had brought messages of loyalty to Charles in Barcelona and had been nominated as his viceroy. Saballá had inherited large estates in the island and his following included the senior judge, Sola, the Director of Finance, Balbona, the Truyols family, and many others, of whom San Felipe lists a number. They were supported by many less eminent men and had elected one of the Truyols family, Salvador, as *Caudillo* or leader.

Philip's viceroy, the Conde de Cerbellón, knew of this plot and did his best, aided by some of the score of pro-Bourbon nobles including the Cotoner family, to contain it. But he had little chance, particularly as the majority of the ecclesiastics were pro-Carlists. The tough disciplinarian, Archbishop de Alagón had just died and his acting successor, Bishop de la Portilla had little authority over the priests of Majorca.

So, when Leake arrived on 24th September with some forty-eight ships, he lay just out of range and sent Saballá in a felucca to demand surrender, fairly certain that it would be forthcoming. The immediate reply, carried by one of the Cotoner family, was a refusal. During the night Saballá met one of the chief pro-Carlists, Zaforteza, but nothing happened and next day all was quiet. So Leake 'threw in a few shells' to liven things up. On the 26th Cerbellón, accompanied by a few horse, reconnoitred the city and heard voices shouting both for Philip and Charles. 800 pro-Carlists occupied the outer port. Cerbellón retired to the castle and then to the palace. Some of his supporters wished to take on the rebels but an attempt to fire on them from the castle walls failed because the gun carriages had been sabotaged. A small force of cavalry under Don Gabriel de Verga was beaten when Verga himself was shot by a rebel. When Leake moved in once more and threatened bombardment, Cerbellón sent the Conde de Montenegro and three other local notabilities to the admiral to arrange a capitulation. Notice of this was published on the 27th and greeted with acclaim, for the majority, who wished to stay on under Charles' rule could do so and the others could leave. The small French garrison of the Castle of San Carlos, seventy or so, one of whose officers had been killed, marched out on the 28th with the 'honours of war' and together with some loyalists were sent to Rosas. Charles was proclaimed king on his birthday, 1st October. *Te Deums* were sung, there were fireworks, and Saballá, the new viceroy, wined and dined the admirals. Arrangements were made for Cerbellón, his family and the remaining pro-Bourbon loyalist nobles to leave on 8th October for Almeria.

Leake was now under pressure to go further. There was still the prize of Minorca, with Port Mahon, its legendary safe port. There was also the far bigger island of Sardinia, then a Spanish possession. Captured correspondence from Cagliari suggested that the Marqués de Jamaica, its viceroy, was wavering. A member of the Bourbon *Despacho*, he had never been much thought of and was believed to be chiefly concerned with his own possessions. Incidentally, the chronicler San Felipe, whose monumental work has been and will continue to be consulted for this book, was now directly involved in Sardinia. Born Vincente Bacallar at Caller in 1669, he was by 1706 a major figure in the island, governor of Caller since the days of Charles II, The Sufferer, and second in importance only to the Marqués de Jamaica. Educated in Spain and trained as a soldier, he had married into the Cerbellón family. An admirer of Louis XIV and a firm supporter of Philip's he must certainly have been concerned about the threat of Allied naval strategy.

For the moment he need not have worried. Leake wrote duly to Lichtenstein and Stanhope to announce that Majorca and Ibiza were in Carlist hands, but he was short of sailors and only just able to man his squadron. He was almost out of supplies. He had overstayed his time in the Mediterranean. And he now received orders dated 20th August to sail for England, detaching eighteen ships-of-the-line under Byng at Lisbon for the winter service. He had been away over two and a half years and had fought three hard and successful campaigns. It was – as his Allies had acknowledged – largely thanks to his blend of drive, commonsense, seamanship and diplomacy that Gibraltar and Barcelona were still in Allied hands and that further footholds had been established at Alicante, Cartagena, and in the Balearics. He had been prepared throughout to take risks. He had been co-operative and accommodating. Had the season not been so advanced he might have added Minorca to his score. He was received on his return by the sick, prematurely aged Lord High Admiral, Prince George of Denmark, who summoned Leake to his sick-bed and gave him a diamond ring worth £400 and a gold-chased sword. It was one of his last official actions. The queen made Leake a present of £1,000.

*   *   *

Back on shore frustration bred internal arguments on both sides as high summer faded for Berwick, the calm shepherd and for the 'hectic flock' on which he bent his efforts.

In the flock Peterborough's departure from Guadalajara on 10th August had removed almost the sole unifying factor. They had virtually all loathed him – Stanhope being the only major exception. Now they settled down to continue their disagreements, understandable and no doubt in their way enjoyable, but not conducive to war-winning with a diminished force and limited options.

King Charles wanted to fight a battle with Berwick and in this he was backed by his Spanish generals. Cifuentes, Galveas, Corzana, Mondejár, Nájera and Oropesa all took this view. Das Minas did so too, provided he could then return to Portugal. But Galway, who now openly blamed the Portuguese in his letters for their dilatoriness, pointed out that a return to Portugal (which place he had in any case come to loathe) was impossible. He would prefer to go back to Madrid or if that could not be done, to march as rapidly as possible to the Kingdom of Valencia where re-grouping and re-mounting were possible, food abundant, and the inhabitants still friendly. There was, he said, no chance of subduing Castile, and supplies were running short. De Noyelles still wanted his independent command but there were few trained German troops, so he contented himself with undermining Galway. On 11th August the move to Chinchón took place, for at least here there was ample food in August.

Berwick's professional caution had so far been amply justified.[11] Thanks to him Philip still had an army in being. Thanks to Louis' reinforcements that army was now nearly twice as strong as its opponent, but it was still the only major Bourbon force in Spain. Money as usual was short. Even ladies-in-waiting at court had been dismissed not only because of their fondness for intrigue but as an economy. In Andalucia Villadarías had begun to be hated because of his 'injusticies and avarice'. But money was so short that he had now to retain the duty on tobacco in that kingdom in order to pay his men, and send French warships away from Cadiz to avoid the cost of maintaining them. Soon the only way of raising more money in a desperate situation would be to permit trading with the enemy. There was talk of selling wool and fruit, using Spanish or neutral ships as frigates in order to buy salted meat, cordage and other ships' stores. The possibility was also considered of trading mercury, of which Spain had the world monopoly, using six armed French ships to carry it.

Much of the discontent focussed on Berwick. Philip and María Luisa were after all the *monarchs* of Spain. He was, despite his English birth, now a Frenchman, grander by far by reason of his royal blood even than the French ambassador. Stern, proud, careless of popularity, and a stickler for service, he continued to come in for much carping. Here were the Portuguese and Dutch in disarray and bound to march in disorder to the east. Why not set on them? It was wrong of the French to disparage the Spanish soldiery, for look at those brave and dashing officers, de la Paz, Zereceda and Caballero who thought nothing of attacking Allied detachments against huge odds – and bringing hundreds of prisoners.

Berwick brushed this aside, telling Philip in writing and in great detail the sound reasons for his policy. It did not reduce his unpopularity but he stuck to his guns. He covered Madrid and Toledo against any Allied movement from Chinchón and he would march parallel to them if they moved eastwards, using the partisans to harry their rearguard and cut off stragglers, but a battle he would not undertake unless he could be sure of the result.

The Allies hung about at Chinchón, undecided, for twenty-six days until early in September the rains began and they had to move. They had missed the chance of an attack on Berwick when he lay with his weak force across the Henares in July, when even the Portuguese were in good spirits and would have joined in cheerfully. The enthusiasm with which das Minas' guard in new uniforms of yellow doubled with black, and the Spanish and Italian regiments had greeted Charles had long since evaporated under the heat and sickness. They had taken to looting again, some of the officers themselves joining in this, on one occasion while Galway himself slept in his coach to give a good example of staying in camp rather than find attractive billets in a town. The fact that he had a coach when carts were in short supply was probably due to the fact that he was unable in his debilitated, wounded state to ride far. The last two carts were indeed to be lost on 11th September, the oxen drawing them falling into a deep in a river crossing.

Then, with three weeks' supplies collected they broke camp on the 9th and crossing the Tagus at Fuenteduenna, marched eastwards by long stages, towards Valencia. The diary of a Huguenot officer who was present tells of the hardships and difficulties though with occasional touches of lyrical description – fields of thyme, rosemary and serpolet. Most of the time the enemy was too active for comfort. Colonel Wade found himself near Villanueva on one occasion with only twenty-five men facing eight squadrons and with a further twenty-five in sight until aid was sent. Galway led them approximately along what is now the N111, through Palamares del Camp to cross the river Júcar – by now widening, at the bridge of Olivarez some ten miles from Valverde. The country hereabouts was lush, the season was rainy, and the exhausted men no doubt dreamed as they ended each day's march of ten or fifteen miles in the heat, of the even richer, balmier terrain of Valencia, where fruit would be ripe and a man could slake his thirst with the season's new wine and find obliging feminine company. But all the while Berwick was just behind them and to the south, making for La Roda on what is now the N501. After leaving Cienpozuelos he had skirted Aranjuez with its lovely royal palace and by the 12th had reached in his turn Uclés, behind and still between his opponents and Madrid.

Here he realized that if he were to be effective in keeping the Allies on the move he must speed matters up. 'Our marches . . . had removed us so far from our provisions that we were much embarrassed as to how we should proceed. Yet it was vital not to give them time to recollect themselves.'

He still had with him King Philip and 'a multitude of people who were expensive to us and might embarrass our motions'. These included Amelot, still in his military, aggressive mood, and large numbers of grandees, many of whom were no doubt hanging around the monarch, anxious to give evidence of their

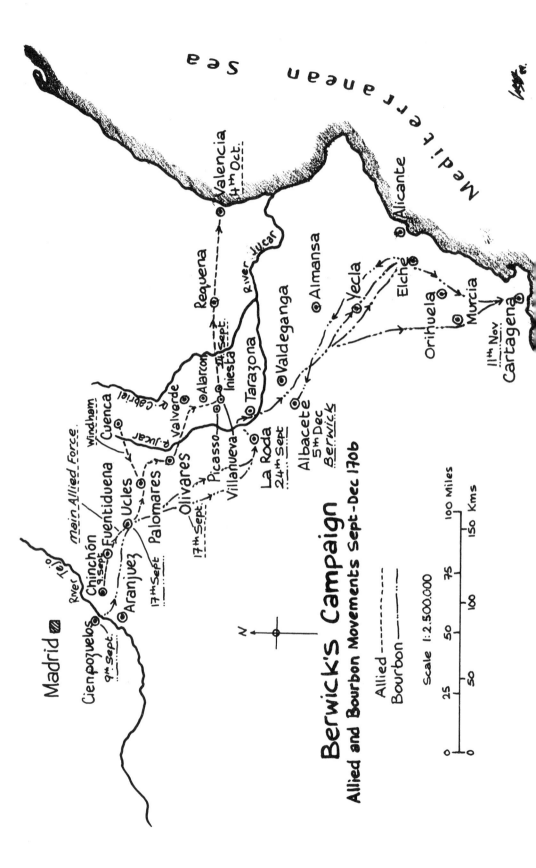

Mediterranean Sea

Madrid

River Tejo
main Allied Force
Cienpozuelos
9th Sept.
Chinchón
9 Sept.
Aranjuez
Fuentidueña
Windham
Cuenca
Ucles
17th Sept.
Palomares
Olivares
17th Sept.
Valverde
R. Jucar
R. Cabriel
Picasso
Villanueva
La Roda
24th Sept.
Alarcón
Iniesta
2nd Sept.
Tarazona
Valdeganga
Albacete
5th Dec
Berwick
Almansa
Requena
Valencia
4th Oct.
Yecla
Elche
Alicante
Orihuela
Murcia
Cartagena
11th Nov
River Jucar

N

Scale 1:2.500.000

Allied --------
Bourbon —·—·—

0 25 50 75 100 Miles
0 50 100 150 Kms

Berwick's Campaign
Allied and Bourbon Movements Sept - Dec 1706

loyalty – hitherto in some doubt. Despite his caution there might be an opportunity for battle, so for this reason, 'I besought His Catholic Majesty to return to Madrid, where as it happened the state of affairs required his presence.' Philip left gladly, no doubt hoping for a swift reunion with his queen.

After this Berwick, lightened of many a *bouche inutile* and relieved of the protocols of court, was still conscious of the fact that if a battle offered on favourable grounds he must fight it or lose his influence on his Spanish colleagues. He intended to cross the Júcar below Alarcón, some twenty miles to the south of Galway and to attempt an attack in the plains before they reached the river Gabriel. But he wanted to conceal his intentions and supplies were still scarce, so he adopted what he called a 'singular manoeuvre'. One brigade of infantry he separated off and sent by one route and the rest of the troops, mainly cavalry, by another, all to meet seventy-five miles away at La Roda, twenty miles from Albacete. Leaving de Légal with 1,000 horse to harass the enemy rearguard, Berwick himself marched with the main cavalry. Galway camped at Villanueva de la Jara, so Berwick did likewise at Picasso on the Júcar, ten miles away. Here he calculated how long his infantry brigade would take to reach La Roda and pushed his cavalry tirelessly so as to try and catch the Allies. He reached Quintanar in daylight but found his quarry had decamped during the night for Iniesta and heard that they were intending to cross the Gabriel at Valdeganga.

Stanhope certainly believed that Berwick meant to attack: 'They followed us close to a little river by Iniesta, which we passed in very good order and drew up a battle on the side of it.' About 3,000 of Berwick's cavalry had arrived at about eight that morning. 'We had', said the marshal, 'hastened our march and all our dragoons pushed forward to attack their rear, which was composed of twenty squadrons and ten battalions.'

He could still have attacked, for Stanhope in a letter dated 5th October to Mr Secretary Hedges admitted 'It is certain that they had it in their power to have fought that day [24th September] and with great advantage, the ground being very favourable for horse in which they very much outnumber us.' But Berwick had no infantry with him until the late afternoon and he did not wish to risk fighting with cavalry alone. Moreover that day the infantry 'had marched seven long leagues without water and in very hot weather'. Then the autumn night fell and he stood his army 'under arms until we had daylight enought to manoeuvre'.

By daybreak, Galway had slipped away and across the Gabriel. Berwick's skirmishing dragoons killed or took some 400 men and a number of wagons, but there was no chance now of catching the main force which was well inside the

Kingdom of Valencia, 'except a garrison which is left in Cuenca and another in Requena, the only two places we have left in Castile' said Stanhope. Berwick's troops might be tired but he himself was indefatigable and determined to retain the upper hand. While his men rested briefly he made his dispositions for the rest of the campaign season. His first target was Cuenca which he knew to be weakly fortified, and where his intelligence informed him that there was a garrison of only 1,000 foot and a regiment of horse. In fact it was even weaker than it sounded for de Noyelles had advised Charles, against Galway's wishes, to leave the Spanish Major-General Ahumada there with the remnants of regiments from five different nationalities: German, Neapolitan, Dutch, Portuguese and Spanish. Berwick dispatched Lieutenant-General Gabriel de Hessy with seven battalions of foot, 800 horse and the only heavy guns he had – three 12 pounders. He calculated that this should suffice and it did. The defending force was disillusioned, weary and in retreat, mourning lost comrades, divided, by differences of religion, language, traditions, even feeding habits. It held out for only ten days, surrendering on 9th or 10th October (the recorded dates vary), its 1,000 men, including Ahumada and the Dutch General Van Palme, being made prisoners-of-war.

It would have been a matter of satisfaction to Berwick to recapture Requena as well but geographically it was far closer to Valencia and he no doubt supposed rightly that it would figure as a strengthened outpost in whatever line the Allies decided on as winter quarters. On the other hand he had cornered them. Castile was now almost entirely pro-Bourbon and his own intended winter line was round to the south-east on the frontiers of the Kingdom of Murcia. Whereas Valencia was largely Carlist in sympathy, Murcia was strongly devoted to the Bourbon cause, thanks in considerable part to the bishop, Don Luis António de Belluga. This militant prelate, now in his mid-forties, was to live to be eighty-one and become a cardinal. Now, said Berwick, 'he called on me loudly for assistance.'

After the capture of Alicante and Cartagena the English had overrun Orihuela, a town without even a complete wall, and Elche, the former fifteen and the latter sixty miles from the provincial capital, and on the road thither from Alicante. The capital, Murcia, was itself now under siege. Berwick therefore sent the Spanish General Medinilla with four battalions and nine squadrons of horse to assist the bishop, and the Allies raised the siege of Murcia. The bishop then went into the attack and with Medinilla's force and some 2,500 irregulars took the place. There seems to have been some unrecorded spite about, possibly between the bishop's clergy and those in the place, for although by now there were no English there, 'the inhabitants alone, spirited up by the monks, defended it . . . The town was therefore plundered and numbers of the people and the monks destroyed.' Medinilla had lost 150 men and no doubt tempers were high. Orihuela although unwalled did possess a citadel and from Alicante an English force of 200 had been sent to occupy it. These, says Berwick tersely, 'were fallen on [on the way] by our cavalry and put to the sword, except for fifteen prisoners'.

Retreating on Alicante, General Gorges left Colonel Bowles and a small force of 300 foot, 150 of Killigrew's dragoons and 900 armed peasants at Elche. Short of supplies, Berwick sent de Geoffreville to attack the place. Bowles refused to surrender to de Geoffreville and Berwick had to bring up his main force, whereupon two days later Bowles capitulated. But, says Berwick, Elche, 'one of the prettiest and richest places in Spain, suffered much on this occasion. It was partly plundered, contrary to my orders, but we obtained from it 80,000 sacks of corn and 20,000 gold *pistoles*'. De Geoffreville was sent to Villena, on the border between Castile and Valencia, and a little later the Marshal pushed d'Asfeld to nearby Yecla with four battalions and fifteen squadrons 'to prevent the enemy molesting our quarters in La Mancha'. Similar detachments were posted between the rivers Júcar and Gabriel to defend that side of Castile 'and keep open our communications with Molina'.

But there still remained two ports, Alicante and Cartagena. Berwick, after his exceptionally long campaign did not feel strong enough to atack the former. In fact, had he known it, he might perhaps have done so, for Stanhope, now in Valencia, was deeply concerned about it, and about the general situation there. Writing to Marlborough on 11th October he said; 'We are at present in the greatest confusion and I see more likelihood of its increasing than otherwise. If we had fewer generals and more troops, the game were sure.' And to Secretary Hedges: 'The queen's troops here are reduced at most to half their complement. The departure of the fleet when the troops were in the field has made it impossible to recruit them.' A fortnight later, he thought nothing but a power-ful diversion could save Alicante 'from ruin'.

Not knowing this, however, Berwick decided to concentrate on besieging Cartagena; 'a city of influence with a large population, a rich and beautiful harbour and as it was in my rear I had to take it for reasons of safety'. This required much preparation. For one thing there was the availability of water. 'Singularly enough I was obliged to have made a great many buckets, for in the plain around the city there was no water save what came from wells; conse-quently, without a liberal supply of pails, battalions and squadrons would have been a-thirst.' He was moreover short of artillery, 'the chief obstacle to attempt-ing conquests'. On the 13th Berwick put his field guns (8-pounders) on a hill nearby but they were silenced by 'the great fire' of Cartagena's guns. He tried sending in an escalade of grenadiers under O'Mahony but this was repulsed, and it was only when the big guns arrived under Lieutenant-General de Rigollot that he was able to open trenches, place batteries and to begin to fire on the 17th. A breach was made on the same day and the garrison capitulated that evening. Berwick granted no conditions but made them surrender as prisoners-of-war. Three galleys in the harbour escaped and with them the Conde de Santa Cruz who had returned from Barcelona as governor. Berwick captured seventy large cannon and three mortars. He had lost only 200 men despite the heavy fire of the artillery. Leaving O'Mahony as governor of the place, the marshal now finalized his arrangements for winter quarters, with de Hessy now at Orihuela and d'Asfeld at Yecla. He placed his headquarters at Albacete and himself left for Madrid on 5th December, satisfied that his opponents were now hemmed in at Valencia and unlikely to attempt anything new.

It was altogether a gloomy outlook for the Allies in Spain. In Aragon Prince Henry of Darmstadt had managed to hold on to most of the Province. In November the French Lieutenant-General de Pons advancing from La Mancha to Calinocha was surprised and routed by a body of Austrians and Spaniards under Major-General Santiago with a loss of 400 men. But on the other side of Aragon, Tzerclaes coming in from Navarre had captured a number of undefended towns while General Salazar had relieved others. Further south, General de Bay had returned to Extremadura and recaptured Moraleja from its Portuguese garrison, and in December with only 1,800 horse and foot he took the Portuguese at Alcántara by surprise and stormed the place by escalade. So there was little enough to show for a long and wearisome campaign. The tide had fully turned against Charles. Berwick's retrospective summary is judicious and not particularly cocky. It has often been quoted but is none the worse for that:

'Thus ended this campaign, one of the most singular on record from its diversity of events. The beginning threatened us with the prospect of total ruin of our affairs; but the sequel became as advantageous as it was glorious to the arms of the Two Crowns. At first the enemy being masters of Madrid, no army to check their progress, the king obliged to raise the siege of Barcelona and retire to France, all these circumstances seemed to decide the fate of Spain; and without doubt had the enemy known how to avail themselves of the conjuncture and had pushed their point, the archduke would have been king; nor would there have been any hopes of recovering the kingdom for his Catholic Majesty; but the gross faults committed by the archduke's generals, together with the unparalleled fidelity of the Castilians gave us the time and means of regaining a superiority and of driving the enemy out of Castile.'

The war would go on in 1707, for this was the will of the English government. The victory at Ramillies seemed in London to mean that victory was possible everywhere. In both houses of Parliament, national pride and readiness to spend money were clearly visible in replies to the Queen's Speech. In the Lords the vote was for 'the restoration of the whole monarchy of Spain to King Charles the Third,' and the Commons were 'determined that no specious pretences of peace shall divert us from our steady resolutions of enabling Your Majesty to improve in all places the advantages of this successful campaign'. Things might have gone less well in the Peninsula than in Flanders but there would be no peace without Spain.

CHAPTER SIX

'The Wine is Drunk': The Battle of Almansa

> Full twenty miles we marched that day
>> Without one drop of water,
> Till we, poor souls, were almost spent
>> Before the bloody slaughter.
> Brave Galloway, our general,
>> Cried, 'Fight on while you may!
> Fight on, brave-hearted Englishmen!
>> You're one to five this day.'
>>   – doggerel about Almansa, quoted by Trevelyan.

A T eight o'clock in the morning of Easter Monday, 25th April, 1707, the roar of a great gun was heard in the plains just south of the small town of Almansa under a hill about 200 miles south-east of Madrid and seventy-five miles south-west and north-west respectively of Valencia and Alicante. In fact it was almost certainly not a gun but a powder-barrel fused and set off as a signal from Marshal the Duke of Berwick recalling foragers to return and form up for what has been called 'one of the most important battles of the Eighteenth Century.'[1] Berwick is reported to have remarked that Almansa was 'a second Ramillies'. On the Allied side, the military, in the shape of Marlborough, Galway himself and Stanhope, although shaken, were swift and soldierly in their reactions and the result was to negate in part Berwick's brilliant feat of arms. Almansa was a disaster for the Allies but it did not at once decide the War. Why? Before reaching that Easter Monday when the powder barrel summoned the foragers in the morning, it is as well to place the event in focus.

Berwick's return to Madrid from Albacete on 5th December 1706 co-incided with the arrival of news that Louis XIV was prepared to reinforce the last campaign's success, however modest, in the hopes of obtaining some positive gain in the Peninsula. Wrote Amelot to Chamillart; 'Whereas five years ago King Philip had neither troops, arms nor artillery, his servants were unpaid and hungry guardsmen scrambled with the poor for soup doled out at convent gates, this is now all changed'. There was still a chronic shortage of money but the king was now living reasonably comfortably and at least his Spanish troops were a little better cared for than they had been.

There was, moreover, another potent factor in the situation, unmilitary, domestic, and unknown alike to Louis when he wrote and to the Allies. It was something which would enhance the growing affection and respect with which 'El Animoso' and his queen were now regarded by the bulk of their Castilian subjects. María Luisa, back in Madrid after her hard and uncomfortable stay in Burgos, was pregnant with her first child. When this was confirmed by the doctors she went, as was the custom, to the Church of Our Lady of Atocha, in procession through sanded streets lined by soldiers in full dress, between houses hung with tapestry, while trumpets sounded shrilly and the Madrileños cheered. Madame des Ursins, writing to Madame de Maintenon, was probably only exaggerating mildly.

> 'Infinite numbers of people sang the praises of the king and queen. Some wept with joy and asked heaven that their Majesties should have fifty children, to last for ever. Others laughed and made funny faces. Some were so transported that they were crazy enough to say that they loved the queen more than God.'

Charles, the Allied candidate, was not even married as yet and an opinion poll taken in Spain at the end of 1706 would, for this reason alone, have shown him trailing badly, everywhere but in Catalonia and Valencia.

While Berwick was in Madrid and the Bourbon army settled into its winter quarters, Charles and the Allied army were wintering in Valencia after their strenuous but eventually botched campaign of 1706. After their ignominious withdrawal eastwards from Madrid they no doubt found the atmosphere of Valencia relaxing and agreeable but, in spite of the Allied success in Flanders, there was little to cheer them in the situation in the Peninsula.

It is true that there was some cash to spend, for Charles actually received over 300,000 guilders from his brother, the emperor. Valencia, too, was a royal city and, in warmly welcoming him, voted him 50,000 *reales*. The people were less nationalistic, less conscious of their *fueros* than the Catalans, whose privileges in any case he had slighted, despite the promises made on his behalf by Mitford Crowe in the Genoa Pact. Here in Valencia there were few of the nobility, most having fled, and Charles actually called together the *Cortes*, which was something Philip and his predecessors had never done. The ordinary folk of the city were

Movements Leading to
ALMANSA
April 1707

Valencia
Reinforcements after Cancellation of Desent

Reinforcements from France

Albacete

←To Madrid

Chinchilla

April 24.

April 14.

Montelegre

Almansa

April 25

Fuenta de la Higuera

Jativa

Denia

Ontinyent

Caudete

April 24.

Alcoy

Yecla

Villena

April 18-19

April 14.

Elda

Altea

– – – – – **Allies**
– · – · – **Bourbons**

Alicante

Elche

Sea

Murcia

Cartagena

Mediterranean

Not to Scale.

profiting from the visits of the English and Dutch fleets and the m oney that these spent.

The archduke rode about the city, showed lavishly his devotional enthusiasm in the cathedral, and in his spare time shot wildfowl in the lagoons. The Protestant troops caused little trouble and the occasional lapse, as when two English officers seduced some nuns, was hushed up. Yet Charles must, as a young man, have felt impatient with the way things were going, with the interminable arguments of all those middle-aged and elderly, difficult men about him.

As the new year opened discussions became concerned with the new campaign and were even more discordant. Peterborough returned in early January, bringing £100,000, borrowed without authority at an exhorbitant rate of interest. The money was welcome but the earl, while making up somewhat with Charles and continuing to be popular with the ladies, merely added confusion to the Allied councils which began in earnest on January 13th. He attended these only as a 'volunteer' for the slow mills of government were grinding in London and in mid-January he received a letter from Sunderland, now Secretary of State and determined to break him. The letter was stern, relieving him of his command and directing him to return home.

After a couple of meetings Charles gave instructions that each member of the council should put his proposals in writing. These are all recorded, mainly in French, and a fine picture they give of divisions of opinion, aired and discussed over a further series of meetings. Finally Charles seems to have decided that an aggressive policy was required and that an attempt should be made to do everything at once – even if it involved splitting the available forces. News had come in of the death of King Pedro of Portugal and of the loss to de Bay of Alcántara but these seem scarcely to have been taken into account. Indeed, an amateurish programme was adopted for all the wrong reasons: Orihuela, Elche, Cartagena and Murcia were to be captured. The Duke of Savoy and the emperor should be asked to send troops to Spain or at least to invade France and General Pedro Morvas was nominated to go to Italy and arrange this. An army corps should make for Navarre via Aragon or La Mancha, depending on enemy movements. Catalonia must be fortified. The Portuguese troops should stay where they were. Madrid was of central importance but to hold it and Castile required that Aragon, Catalonia and Navarre should first be taken.

By the time these conclusions had been reached, Peterborough was out of the way at last. He sailed on 14th March for Italy in H.M.S. *Resolution*, commanded by his second son, Henry Mordaunt, and escorted by two frigates. They fell in with a French squadron, unexpectedly at sea, and in the engagement the

Resolution was knocked about, forced to beach, and burned. Henry, wounded in the thigh by a cannonball, recovered somewhat, only to die a few weeks later of smallpox. His father had transferred to the frigate *Enterprise* and was soon on his way back to England, spreading trouble wherever he went.

★　　★　　★

To judge from his *Narrative* and from replies he gave some years later in the course of a House of Lords Inquiry, Galway was depressed. Council after council had urged a swift march to Madrid. The army had in any case eaten all its stores in Valencia, could not subsist there much longer and must 'break into Castile'. But first they must destroy the enemy's stores in La Mancha. Berwick's force was at that time believed to be 'not much greater in strength' than Galway's and das Minas' together. there were indications that he was to get reinforcements, but no certainty. Intelligence was scarce and unreliable.

So, wearily and and probably with hidden misgivings, Galway ordered his forces to assemble. Erle marched the newcomers to join him, together with Mountjoy's, Gorges' and Allnutt's. Losses from disease had made it necesssary to combine Farringdon's, Southwell's and Breton's regiments under Montandré. A similar motley crew marching from Alicante was ambushed by Zereceda who took about 400 prisoners. Amelot reported that the prisoners were wearing uniforms of three different regiments – a sign of weakness.

The weather itself frowned on the marching troops. 'It was, above all, very cold and wet . . . especially for those that were reduced to lie in the field.' They had, moreover, 'to cross the country with many difficult passes and an incredible scarcity of provisions for both men and horses'. At length on 30th March they were assembled at the great camp. According to a contemporary account; 'The whole army consisted of about 4,500 horse and 11,000 foot.' A further 6,000 were spread around in garrisons – 1,200 at Alicante, 350 at Elche, others at Gerona and so on. Together on the last day of March, they concentrated at Caudete, the men moving in two columns and the baggage in a third. Caudete is a small town in the centre of a plain, some twenty miles south of Almansa and ten miles from Yecla and Villena, in both of which places Berwick was known to have set up considerable stores of cattle, dried fish, wheat, barley and wine.

Finding Yecla abandoned the Allies fell thankfully upon the stores. Berwick had withdrawn some twenty miles to Montalegre and it was decided to attack him there, for his retirement suggested (incorrectly) that he was weak.

So after a two-day feast they marched away on 3rd April in the evening, without noise, leaving only two battalions to secure the camp. They were carrying as much as they could in the way of provisions for horses and men 'out of the plentiful magazines in this place.' The rest was ordered to be burnt.

Their next objective was Villena, fifteen miles to the east; described in the French account of the campaign as 'a small town with an old, badly fortified castle', it was thought by the Allies that it 'would have greatly annoyed our convoys' from its hill top, and must therefore be taken. So Galway and das Minas moved to encircle it on 18th April. Thereafter their intention was to advance into Aragon, turn the head of the Tagus and march downstream towards Madrid. Having observed Berwick's tactics the previous year Galway assumed that the marshal would not risk a battle.

> 'There were then no thoughts of coming soon to a battle, for the Lord Galway gave leave on the 20th to the Queen's Royal Regiment of Dragoons, to go as far as Denia [some 60 miles] for their clothing and to refresh their horses; and ordered Brigadier Carpenter with all the new landed dragoons, English and Dutch to go into quarters of refreshment above ten miles off, to try and recover their horses which were almost dead by the fatigues of the sea, their long marches from Alicante and the scarcity and difference of forage, having instead of hay and oats only straw and barley (the feed of the country) which was not thought good enough for the large English and Dutch horses.'

Berwick looked on Villena as ground-bait to fool Galway. The Allies thought it had a garrison of 500. In fact it was only 250 regulars and about 150 townsfolk. But Berwick had selected as governor a man whom the Allies described as resolute. He was a Captain Grosseteste of the Regiment of Charolais and when summoned to surrender he 'returned a proud answer'. On this 'some field-pieces were ordered to fire ... but as they did little damage the engineers were commanded to work with the miners'. Summoned again to surrender, Grosseteste gave the same bold reply and Galway was forced to settle down to a formal siege – a distraction it would have been better to avoid.

Berwick was comfortably placed, watching his enemy's moves from his headquarters first of all at Montalegre (5th April) as Galway marched to Fuente las Higueras, to Sorina, to Caudete, to Yecla. Then on 14th April, expecting an attack on Montalegre, Berwick withdrew Popoli, d'Avaray and d'Asfeld in good order to Chinchilla del Monte Aragón. He estimated Galway's strength at rather less than his own. He knew Galway was short of stores. He guessed that his opponent would 'hazard a battle' in the belief that he would be hitting Berwick before his reinforcements came. He pushed his hungry infantry to Petrola and then Montalegre. Then he heard that Galway had raised the siege of Villena and was concentrating at Caudete and on 23rd April, Easter Eve, concentrated in turn at Almansa. Now, in Churchill's grim phrase; 'The wine was drawn and must be drunk'.

★   ★   ★

There are many better-known battle names. But few had quite the same emotional impact, viewed close to, the same sense of inevitability as Almansa. The few, tough English soldiers who came through it felt deeply scarred by that day and they and their comrades three years later would go into battle at Almenara and Saragossa shouting at their opponents, 'Remember Almansa, ye dogs!' Galway was presented with the need to fight a battle; Berwick with the means to win a victory.

Battles did not last so long then. From the firing of the powder-barrel until the issue was decided was a matter of sixteen hours and of these seven were taken up manoeuvring into position. The fighting itself began at about 3 p.m. and took place in five phases of which the first four overlapped in part, while the final one took place in the small hours of next day. These were: Galway's attack on the Bourbon right wing, its repulse and renewal; the almost victorious Anglo-Dutch thrust on the centre, its eventual wearing down and isolation; the Portuguese failure on the Allied right wing, after holding Bourbon attacks; the consequent effect of this failure on the Allied centre and left and the orderly withdrawal of 13 Anglo-Dutch battalions to the hills well clear of the battlefield; and their subsequent surprising surrender just after midnight.

Although Galway, das Minas and most of the other generals had left the field at about 5.30 leading what remained of their cavalry, and to this extent the victory was already Berwick's, it had been a very close fight and he did not know how much of the Allied army was intact. It was only when, after midnight, he received in astonishment an almost inexplicable offer of surrender from the still-intact thirteen battalions, that the victory became firmly his.

Piecing the various accounts together one can arrive at a reasonable picture of the battle. Berwick's dispositions seem to have been largely defensive. Apart from anything else he was as ever conscious of the fact that he had the only army which stood between Philip and the loss of the Crown of Spain and must not risk it. Then he was supposed to await the Duc d'Orléans who was some days behind the troops he was meant to be accompanying. Berwick's intelligence sources were however reliable, for the people of the province of Murcia were fiercely hostile to the Allies. But, to be quite sure, he sent out vedettes and these reported that the Allies were advancing on him. He realised he could not avoid a battle and he therefore recalled Pinto's force, which was no longer needed at Villena. Some of his generals wished him to stand behind Almansa, putting only a screen of second-line troops in the town, but he preferred for sound tactical reasons to be able to watch his enemy and react as needed. He therefore drew up his seventy-six squadrons and fifty-six battalions in front of Almansa 'in two lines according to the usual manner'. Estimates of his total numbers vary. He could have had as many as 30,000 but experts such as Wilson think he had at most 26,000 since many units were certainly not at full strength. He placed his Spanish cavalry on his right on rising ground towards Montalegre, his French cavalry on the left. Before him to the south lay the plain of Almansa which has been likened to the glacis of a fort and capable therefore of being swept by artillery. He placed his guns so as to do this, spread from right to left, under the command of de Rigollot.

Berwick explained his battle plan to his generals in groups and then addressed the Spanish soldiery in their own language, demanding that they show the Spanish qualities of fidelity and courage, and finally he told his French troops of his dependence on their discipline and firmness. As the human voice without amplification could carry only a short distance it may be supposed that this took at least three hours as he rode up and down the ranks while they formed.

'News being brought that the enemy was near the town of Almansa a great council of war was held, in which it was unanimously agreed to go next day 25th April to give them battle ... Accordingly, about three in the morning we began to march in four columns till we had passed the hilly country which was computed at six long miles and then, coming into better ground, the army formed and marched the other three miles in order of battle ...'

So much for the official report from Galway's *Narrative*. It looked a little different to that member of the Awkward Squad, Captain Hawley, to his immediate boss, General the Lord Erle, and to others during that thirsty march to an appointment with Fate. 'At break of day', says Hawley,

'the army formed into three columns with the baggage in the rear and left the Pass of Torres de Henrique. [This is about 12 miles east of Almansa.] At ten of the clock we saw the enemy's camp ... General Erle ordered the *corps de bataille* to form and sent me to Lord Galloway [sic] to say the ground was very ugly, full of rocks and bushes and some hollow ways or ravines, and the men all blown and tired.'

When Hawley found Lord Galway, about two miles off, the commander-in-chief, remembering the decisions of the council of war but tired no doubt after an early start, replied, 'You see the enemy are marching away and we must make what haste we can to engage them or they will be gone.' Nevertheless, properly concerned to rest his weary men, Galway ordered a halt. This was felt by Hawley (himself mounted and therefore not tired) to be a mistake. 'If he chose to surprise the marshal why then halt for an hour?' asks the captain rhetorically in his personal note. Returning to Erle, Hawley found

'the foot formed and marching up in two lines of battle. They halted at the top of a large, long mountain full of rocks and broken ground. It was indeed time, for in the foot both officers and soldiers were quite spent. The enemy were drawn up in good order and seemed to muster very thick.'

On being told what Galway had said, Erle 'made no other answer than this: "We are beat already".' As to numbers, Galway probably had a total of about 16,000, of which 8,000 were Portuguese levies largely of indifferent quality, 4,800 English, 1,500 Dutch, 1,100 Huguenots and 250 Germans. Of the English regiments six – Brudenell's, Toby Caulfield's, Mohun's, Allen's, Hamilton's and Farringdon's – had dwindled to virtually nothing owing to sickness, and the same applied to Blesset's Huguenots. The Royal Dragoons had spent an exhausting winter on outpost duty and had been sent to rest. Hawley's own troop of 4th Hussars had had to be 'incorporated' with others after its appalling journey from England. Hawley confirms the approximate total for he was himself ordered after leaving Caudete to stay at the end of the Pass of Torres de Henrique in order to count the numbers as the men defiled on to the Almansa plain. He records 13,400, but since in those days officers, N.C.Os and drummers were not included in the count and together numbered from one-sixth to one-eighth of the total, they and the rank and file together amounted to just about 16,000.

10.30. a.m. Berwick noted that the Allies were intermingling their horse and foot on the wings. This tactic, used by Marlborough at Blenheim and afterwards criticised by Macaulay, was forced on Galway because of shortages of cavalry. But it is true that Tyrawley's dispositions were criticised at the time by the insufferable Hawley: 'He [Tyrawley] scratched out [the Order of Battle] upon paper as for encamping, therefore it must not be changed according to ground or circumstances. Was this not ignorance in a general?' Erle was next senior to Galway among the English generals but was plainly in a bad humour that day.

12.00 noon. According to Hawley Berwick's second line, under d'Asfeld, was to be seen close under the walls of Almansa town, his Spanish troops being clearly poised to take on the Portuguese horse on the Allied right wing. There was no Allied reserve and the main battle of twenty-two Portuguese, nine Dutch and thirteen English battalions of foot were in the centre. On the Allied left there were nine English battalions of foot, and six Dutch, nine English and two Portuguese squadrons intermingled.

Hawley blames Galway for allowing das Minas to take the post of honour on the right. But the old Huguenot had no choice, under the military terms of the Methuen Treaty. He was certainly not feeling well, was probably aware of the attitude not only of Erle but of other English officers and had been worn down by the months of argument with das Minas. That sprightly old thing on the other hand was accompanied on this day by a young woman, his mistress, who according to varied accounts was either 'in a gay riding-habit' or 'dressed as a man'. Cantering to and fro she was eventually laid low by a musket ball during the battle.

Galway's wings were of one line only, two files per squadron, whereas Berwick's were two lines of three squadrons each, and unlike Galway he had a reserve. So, even though the Allied cavalry wings were supported by interspersed foot, Berwick's forces outflanked his opponent's. Galway appears later to have thought mistaken the decision to have his cavalry on high ground, for at 2.00 p.m. he is recorded by Hawley as coming from the extreme left to the centre to speak to Erle and Macartney, saying, 'He thought we were drawn up just wrong, for the foot was in the plain and the horse upon the hills where the foot should have been.'

2.15 p.m. To this, says Hawley, Erle replied: 'Did you not see this before? You should have thought of that five hours ago. 'Tis too late now. You must make the best of it. Have you any orders for me?' Galway appears not to have replied to this piece of nervous insubordination, for Hawley merely says, 'General Galloway went to the left to begin'.

3.00 p.m. The 'beginning' was, according to Hawley, signalled at three by 'blowing up [another] powder barrel, after which their batteries began to play'. Galway ordered Colonel Charles Dormer with a party of Essex's dragoons and probably also of Carpenter's 'to go and attack the battery over-against our left,

ALMANSA · phase I · 3.00 p.m.

N

Hill

Almansa Town

Bulkeley ☆

d'Asfeld ☆

Signal fired 3.00 p.m.

Wade

Southwell

V. Dohna · Shrimpton

L'Islemarais

☆ Erle

Guns

French Cavalry

☆ d'Avaray

Berwick ☆

Hill

Portuguese Infantry

Portuguese Cavalry (Stationary)

English Cavalry

des Mines and d'Ataleya ☆

☆ Pepoli

Dolmer (K) Fabrèque and Dragoons

☆☆ Galway Tyrawley

Carpenter

Guns

English Cavalry ☆ (Carpenter)

ALMANSA · phase II · 4.00 p.m.

Almansa Town

Bulkeley ☆

d'Asfeld ☆

☆ Erle

Spanish Infantry together

Berwick ☆

French Cavalry

☆ d'Avaray

Roper (K) and English Cavalry

Port. Infantry

Port. Cavalry (stationary)

des Mines ☆

Portuguese Cavalry (Stationary)

☆ d'Ataleya

Spanish Cavalry ☆

☆ Pepoli

English Dutch Cavalry

Galway ☆ Wounded 3.45 p.m.

Tyrawley ☆

English Cavalry ☆ (Carpenter)

Not to Scale

ALMANSA · phase III · 4.30p.m. – 5.00p.m.

N

French Cavalry

☆ d'Avary

Portuguese Infantry form Square

☆ das Minas and d'Atalaya

Hill

Portuguese Cavalry flee

☆ Almansa Town

French Infantry

☆ Bulkeley

Popoli

Spanish Cavalry

Carpenter + Dutch and English Cavalry

Hill

☆ Galway and Tyrawley

☆ d'Asfeld

Berwick ☆

Southwell

Wade

V. Dohna

Shrimpton

English and Dutch Infantry

not to Scale

ALMANSA · phase IV · 5:30 p.m.

Almansa Town

French and Spanish Infantry

French Cavalry

Popoli

Spanish Cavalry

French Infantry
Bulkeley

Erle

Galway
Carpenter
Tyrawley
+ 3,000 Cavalry

Hill

Hill

d'Aspeld

Berwick

Portuguese Guns

Portuguese Infantry Overwhelmed

To Onteniente

das Minas and d'Atalaya

13 English & Dutch form Square
Shrimpton
V. Dohna

To Caudete

ALMANSA · phase V · Midnight April 25-26th.

Almansa Town

Berwick Receives offer of Surrender

Caudete

Shrimpton and V. Dohna
+ 13
Surrender Early
26th April

N

which did much gall our horse. This was instantly executed but with ill success'. The guns, after firing for at most a quarter of an hour played little part in the battle. The main shock was between cavalry and cavalry or cavalry and infantry. And each time it was severe.

3.15 p.m. On the Allied left, Dormer's small force was now fallen on by 'eight to ten squadrons of their [Spanish] best horse with incredible fury', and was 'cut all to pieces'. The original couple of squadrons seemed to think that on their own they maintained a very obstinate and bloody fight near to two hours, but were at last overpowered by their far superior numbers and so cut off that not above four or five officers and ten or twelve private men were left in each squadron'.

But even in a small area it is possible for those intimately and bloodily involved in hand-to-hand combat to be unaware of what is going on a hundred yards away, and Galway had in fact ordered the English horse on the left to charge, while the Portuguese newly arrived to the right of him were to take up fighting once the English and Dutch were fully engaged. So three regiments of Carpenter's made for Popoli's main force and were followed in echelon of brigades from the left, and soon the whole Allied first line on the left was in contact, and, says Hawley, 'there was one continual fire for half-an-hour'.

Carpenter's cavalry were now within a hundred yards of Popoli's, while far away to the Allied left Dormer's men fought on, their colonel himself dead. Berwick now ordered Popoli to attack and being heavier and more numerous, this force pushed Carpenter's back fifty yards. Now however, the interspersing of infantry with cavalry showed some value. While the two battalions of allied infantry in the centre failed at first to break the first French line, the Allied second line, though 'too far off', came up and beat the French infantry of the centre 'shamefully'.

At the same time, while the English cavalry fell back, Southwell's and Wade's infantry, interlined with them, wheeled in and hit Popoli's cavalry on the flank, sending them back in their turn. Brigadier Killigrew seems to have been particularly active at this confused moment. Popoli tried re-forming and striking again but was once more repulsed. 'The enemy [cavalry], says Berwick, 'were overthrown but the fire of their battalions obliged our cavalry once more to retreat'.

This withdrawal took Popoli right back to Berwick's second line which was commanded by d'Asfeld. There seems little doubt that the marshal had placed this tough and experienced general just there *en cas de malheur*, and it was now that he made full use of him and his reserve of nine French battalions.

As Popoli retired d'Asfeld opened ranks to allow the cavalry to pass through in reasonable order and re-form behind him, while he in his turn faced Southwell's, Blood's, Wade's and Mountjoy's regiments who were by now themselves out of breath, over-excited, and pursuing Popoli 'with shouts and hollerings', as though he were a fox.

Bulkeley's men were fresh and fell on the Allied squadrons and battalions 'defeating them entirely', says Berwick. 'Our cavalry at the same time setting the enemy's left entirely in disorder' – while d'Asfeld saw off Wade's infantry.

4.00 p.m. It was at this time, when the stress was falling most heavily on the Allied centre and on its left wing that the Allied commander-in-chief was literally blinded for a while by a cut over his eyes. While Galway was having urgent first-aid, Erle grumpy and gouty as he was, kept up momentum, leading his English, Dutch and Huguenot infantry against Vincentilla's Spaniards and Labadie's French. Backed by Shrimpton with Breton's English, van Dohna's Dutch and l'Islemarais' Huguenots he drove his opponents right up to the walls of Almansa. Here they paused, and Amezaga, with a small force of cavalry, including the *Ordenes Viejo* regiment, held them off.

It was the crisis of the battle, when the Allied right wing, under das Minas and Atalaya should have tipped the scales by a charge, for the English and Dutch in the centre had 'carried all before them'. The Portuguese cavalry on the right, however, instead of attacking the French cavalry under the Walloon d'Avaray, sat tight. Perhaps had Galway been physically and mentally present he would have ordered this and the outcome of Almansa would have been different. But he was far away on the left wing and incapacitated.

4.30 p.m. Erle had no orders but realized that his infantry were exposed on their left and receiving little or no support on their right. He therefore sent his A.D.C., Hawley, to Count van Dohna, second-in-command of the Dutch and English foot in the centre, with orders to withdraw. Thanks to Hawley's notes we can catch a feel of the battle at this point. Van Dohna's Dutch, says Hawley, 'took the greens out of their hats'. Since in those days uniforms were easily confused and often worn out, men usually marked the side they were on by carrying some modest and easily adopted sign, a white cloth on the left arm, or a twig in the hat – as in this case. And in this instance too the Dutch 'beat the French march on their drums in order to deceive'. They and the English formed a hollow square.

On his way back from van Dohna Hawley records seeing 'seventy horsemen on rising ground with yellow liveries' and thinking they were Pearce's Dragoons. 'I was', he says, 'accidentally clothed that day in grey, faced with red and laced with gold. By accident I got near the people on the hill. Then

I saw they were carrying white papers.' They were Berwick's staff. 'At 100 yards I saw the marshal's star – he was on a little English bay nag.' The captain made his escape and though he was chased and his horse hit in the neck he managed to rejoin his own side.

Erle was now under intense pressure, and was trying to persuade two squadrons of Dutch horse to move to aid his infantry. But they refused. As the Dutch cavalry would not charge, Erle obtained from Lord Tyrawley Harvey's Horse under a Colonel Roper to 'chastize' some French battalions which had got too far ahead. Erle is reported as saying, 'As you have had no share of this day's work let us see what you can do to save those brave men there.' Roper wheeled his men in, followed by Erle himself. Roper was killed outright and Harvey's men were then the verbal targets of Irishmen in Berwick's ranks who 'called every officer . . . by their names as well as many of the men, asking them if they were mad and crying out they would give them good quarter. But, finding no notice taken of their offers they began their fire which made the squadrons peel away to the left, carrying off the four platoons on their right with them.' At this point Hawley was himself wounded in the thigh by a bayonet and his personally observed account finishes. But he still comments on the disaster of the last phase of the afternoon on the Allied right wing.

4.45 p.m. Here das Minas was still in command but apart from his age he may have been suffering from the shock of seeing his mistress killed – which had occurred by now. Hawley had little time for him – 'a sort of old woman who never did anything without consulting St António of Padua'. His second-in-command (and nephew), Atalaya, was a less dogged creature and a considerable number of his troops 'stayed where they were and asked for quarter'. Although a few squadrons immediately around das Minas stood firm and tried to help the Allied centre, the majority fled causing a panic in the second line among eight Portuguese infantry battalions and the Portuguese artillery under Mascarenhas. Of the eleven first line Portuguese battalions some formed square and were killed where they stood (a fact which San Felipe notes with admiration), but most fled when d'Avaray sent Colonel Saint Gilles after them with his cavalry.

By five o'clock, the battle was virtually over on the left and right Allied wings. Galway had been bandaged and, while General Carpenter led a charge by a Huguenot dragoon regiment, managed to get away with some 3,000 men from the Allied left and Generals das Minas, Tyrawley, Erle, Frisheim and Wade. They did not stop until they reached Onteniente, twenty miles away to the east on the road to Denia.

In the centre it was quite another matter. Here the English and Dutch infantry had earlier as we have seen driven the enemy before them with great success, pushing their first line on to their second and crowding the latter back into Almansa town. Had the Portuguese on the right charged, or even stood their ground Almansa would have been a different battle. As it was, 'they galloped away'. Indeed, in an anonymous account enclosed by Philip in a letter to his grandfather, there is a more critical comment.

> 'The Portuguese did no good at all. Their infantry laid down their arms crying "*Viva Philippe Quinto*." The English who were with them drew their swords on them and killed them, asking, "Why did you not advance instead of leading us into this?"'

The French cavalry could now fall on the Allied centre and did so. Many senior Allied officers had already been killed and some of the English and Huguenot infantry began to waver. Retreat for some was physically impracticable and some hundreds of men were ridden over by cavalry. Six battalions were crushed into a crowd that could do nothing but lay down their arms. The regiments involved were the Guards, the Marines, Mordaunt's, Bowles', Nassau's Germans and Welderen's Dutch. Casualties were extremely heavy and included eighty-eight officers killed. In Hill's regiment alone five officers were killed, five wounded and fourteen made prisoner. A particularly ferocious fight developed between Jean Cavalier's Huguenots from the Cevennes and a French Catholic battalion from the same province. These fell on each other with bayonet and sword, and out of 1,200 altogether fewer than 300 were unhurt at the end. Cavalier, himself wounded, was given a horse by an English officer and escaped. Voltaire says of this harsh fight that Berwick himself could never speak of it without emotion. Cavalier lost his second-in-command, five captains, six lieutenants, five ensigns and about 300 men.

Shrimpton and van Dohna managed to hold together thirteen battalions, five English, five Dutch and three Portuguese. Of the five Dutch these were in fact Huguenot. They formed a hollow square, 'which so well answered the design that the enemy could gain no advantage of them and by that means they retired from the field of battle with little or no loss, though still pursued till night parted them'. They ended up in some hills near Caudete seven or eight miles off, where they lay on their arms for the night.

After an emergency council of war the Allied generals sent a message to Berwick offering to parley. 'After a long consultation in which there were very warm debates, they came to the resolution of surrendering themselves as the French infantry had done at Blenheim.' Everybody not directly involved was mystified by this, including Berwick.

'How these brave men, after having fought so gallantly for so many hours and made so glorious a retreat could at last come to a resolution of surrendering to an enemy that was some miles from them and reckoned them quite out of his reach is not so easy to be accounted for, unless their excuse be admitted which was that the soldiers, after marching for nine hours and fighting about six could march no further; they had spent all their ammunition and had not so much as bread and water to refresh themselves with; they were strangers to the country and did not know of any place to retire to; besides all this, they thought themselves in danger of being pursued and attacked the next morning by the enemy's whole army, against which they could not pretend to defend themselves, being abandoned by all the horse.'

Berwick according to his own account was astonished

'and could hardly believe the officers who brought him this welcome message which did complete his victory. For till then it might have been called a drawn battle, the numbers of the slain being reckoned equal, our baggage safe and only a Portuguese train of twenty-two pieces lost.'

Not surprisingly, Berwick rapidly agreed to their proposals.

Galway says it was van Dohna who sent a note to Berwick. Hawley and others blamed Shrimpton. Both van Dohna and Shrimpton were involved, according to a verbatim account dictated soon afterwards in Madrid by *Maréchal de Camp de Guerre* de Cilly, one of two officers sent by Berwick to report to Philip V and thence to Louis XIV

'Das Minas had gone. Lord Galway was wounded ... About 1 hour after midnight at the moment of their departure Count Danna [sic] Lieut-General of the Dutch troops and Major-General Scylton [sic] of the English sent officers to the Duke of Berwick to ask him to make them prisoners of war.'

The phrase 'We have beaten them hollow' [*à plâte couture*] recurs again and again in accounts on the Bourbon side – first used by Berwick in a battlefield despatch and repeated by Amelot, de Bourk, and others. And there is no doubt that this was justified. What is more difficult is to establish the actual losses on each side. Dead and wounded among the Allies were estimated at 4,000 at least. All the artillery was reported taken (but this, numbering twenty-two pieces, was probably just the Portuguese, and Michael Richards with his few English cannon certainly escaped). There were 120 standards captured, bearing the arms of the polyglot regiments fighting for the Allies. And so abundant was the booty that for many days a horse could be bought for one *écu*, a coat for a few *sous*, muskets couldn't find a buyer and mules could be had for the trouble of catching. Berwick's own figures for Allied casualties were, according to his *Memoirs*, 5,000 killed and 10,000 prisoners. But this must be an exaggeration, since the total Allied force was only about 16,000 and some 3,000 at least had got away that night. Churchill estimates some 4,000 dead and wounded and 3,000 prisoners, but the latter figure may be low, for certainly the problem of housing and feeding the prisoners is a major preoccupation in the Bourbon correspondence for weeks afterwards.

Berwick's figure of losses by his own side has been questioned. In his *Memoirs* he admits to only 2,000 and some writers, such as Churchill, think this is only half the true number. His loss of senior officers was small. He names colonels Pollastron and de Sillery as dead and brigadiers d'Avila and the Duque del Sarno wounded, but that is all. And on 24th May he sent a table of losses of cavalry to Chamillart. The total is 1,604 killed and wounded of which the French number 1,187 officers and men and the Spaniards 417. He does not give the infantry figure so one would not be far wrong in doubting the 2,000. As usual he asks Louis for recognition of those who have done well such as d'Asfeld and Nanette's brother, M. de Bulkeley – whom he had sent to Versailles, where he received a senior command. The infantry figures for the French only are given in a letter from General Labadie to Chamillart of May 4th, regiment by regiment and summarised. Altogether 663 men were killed and 1,105 wounded. So, with the cavalry losses, the total must have been between 3,500 and 4,000. Many wounded inevitably died.

Berwick's prudent strategy had been crowned by a staggering victory. In Frederick the Great's view, it was the most scientific battle of the century. So clearly was Almansa his prize that Orléans, though chagrined at missing the battle, was generous in his praise of the marshal, writing on 27th April to King Louis

> 'I cannot refrain from telling Your Majesty that if M. de Berwick's glory is great, his modesty is no less, nor his politeness to me. He even wished to apologize because the enemy attacked him, and for having obtained so complete and signal a victory as this without me.'

★   ★   ★

In May 1707 euphoria on the side of the Two Crowns was accompanied by relative inactivity.[2] So unexpected had been the 'fortunate event' at Almansa that the French and Spanish Courts had failed to foresee it and had therefore no preparations and few means for following it up. The booty taken, though considerable, would not supply all that was needed. It was all very well for Philip to lay up those captured standards in the Church of Our Lady of Atocha, but places like Lérida and Tortosa would need artillery for siege work. And Orléans' proposed attack on Portugal would need more men. Berwick's pursuit of the Allies was 'very civil' by their own account, and his follow-up sedate. A large detachment received the submission of the city Valencia on 9th May. The walls were razed, the inhabitants fined and a new citadel built to cowe them. But many other strongholds of the kingdom – Denia, Játiva, Gandia, Alcira, Alcoy, Morella, Alicante – remained in Allied hands.

Meanwhile, Galway's strategy was mapped out in a letter from Paul Methuen, who had succeeded his father in Lisbon. 'I heartily wish,' he wrote to Sunderland on 19th May, 'that my Lord Galway may with the battered remnants of his army ... make head against them from the other side of the Ebro and preserve Catalonia during the whole campaign.'

The aftermath of Almansa went on a long time for Galway. He, Stanhope and Tyrawley had adopted for good reason an offensive policy. Peterborough, out of contrariness had before sailing opposed it. So had Noyelles for reasons of personal ambition. Erle had been crusty and difficult. Now Charles and his court threw the blame, however politely on the Huguenot, who was too proud to argue. Fortunately Tyrawley seems to have shown stout loyal qualities. He had the reputation for bravery and had shown this at Guadalajara and Iniesta on the retreat from Madrid. He was an Irishman and knew how to amuse and charm the archduke. And, as an English Lieutenant-General he had attended the council meetings at which the policy leading to Almansa had been discussed and could remind Charles and others of the reasons for it. Tyrawley did not claim to be anything more than a fighter. When, nearly four years later – it was still being discussed – Galway and he were under rigorous questioning in a House of Lords inquiry, he was to say engagingly that he had fought with the sword and not with the pen; he had not carried ink about with him nor kept a register; so he could swear to the main facts but could not recollect details after such a lapse of time. Indeed nothing was found written by him in the official records except his signature to the statement recommending an offensive policy. Now, as Galway recuperated his battered old body and waited for the situation to clear itself, Tyrawley seems to have been a tower of strength to his chief, and together their effort was rewarded.

Berwick collected flour at Valencia and moved with thirty battalions and forty squadrons north-eastwards towards the Ebro at Tortosa, behind the Allies, hoping to sweep them from the left bank of the river and, 'having baked sufficient biscuit', meet up with Orléans. By 23rd May his advanced guard was opposite Tortosa, driving the Allies out of the suburbs south of the river. Tortosa city being too much of an obstacle to tackle without d'Asfeld, who was attempting to subdue the remaining strongholds around Valencia, Berwick left the Chevalier da la Croix to watch it and toiled on up towards Saragossa. He knew that his royal colleague (four years younger than himself) was short of experience and with his customary carefulness wished to make sure that nothing was left undone. But it was a terrible journey. Catalan bandits and partisans 'were in defiles in the most difficult places but were put to flight by our grenadiers. Once through the passes it was easier.'

Berwick reached Caspé some eighty miles upstream from Tortosa on the south bank of the Ebro on 4th June and arranged for supplies of wheat, and also for boats to enable him to cross the river. On 6th June, using relays of horses, he met Orléans at Saragossa, returning two days later to Caspé. He still had to await cannon before he could attack Tortosa or Lérida. He records bitterly, 'Although I had written during the last winter to Chamillart nothing had been done and the artillery was not yet even at Pamplona.' Orléans gave him every discretion but there was nothing to be done but blocade Lérida.

Galway, having destroyed the bridge of boats at Tortosa and put in a strong garrison there and in Gerona, left the rest of his small infantry force at Tarragona and marched up the river Ebro. For the next three months 'we continued in marches and counter-marches observing one another's motions, our great care,' says an English account, to prevent the enemy passing the Cinca, 'which would have been of very bad consequence to us. For the country about Tarragona must have fallen into their hands unless we were able to make a vigorous stand, which we were not.'

As June passed into July and the heats became 'excessive'; there were crossings of the river; the Allies retired towards Lérida and then beyond, to avoid 'being shut up' there. Berwick obtained 'prodigious quantities of corn' in the region about Urgell. Garrisons were left at Alcañiz, Fraga and Monzón, so as to maintain communications with Aragon, but, 'since there was no hope of receiving the artillery and munitions needed for siege work', Berwick and Orléans recrossed the River Segre 'in order to be quieter during the great heats'. 'In their rear, though d'Asfeld and O'Mahony took Játiva and Gandia 'sword in hand', most of the coastal strongholds held out with the help of the Royal Navy. At his time of greatest frustration, on 18th August, Berwick received new orders from

Versailles. He was to leave Spain and transfer to a newly critical theatre of the war in Provence, where Toulon was under siege. He was as Louis explained in a personal letter, not even to serve as commander-in-chief under Burgundy, for Tessé was senior to him and, said Louis, 'I am satisfied with his services.' But it is noticeable that from late June onwards Louis was writing to Tessé at great length and frequency, as though taking control personally, commenting on enemy moves – ten days after they were made – and hoping that 'we shall be filled with glory and honour. I have every hope that you will be fortunate enough to render the enemy's projects futile.' Tessé is sent, moreover, blank commissions to fill in with names of men put in positions of command.

★   ★   ★

Berwick's arrival at Béziers in Provence on August 25th coincided with that of Philip's and María Luisa's first-born son in Madrid. This took place at ten o'clock in the morning in the Palace of Buen Retiro. As that date was the festival of St Louis and in honour of the child's great-grandfather, he was named Luis, Prince of Asturias.

Te Deums were sung and bells rung in cities, towns and villages throughout the realm. Prisoners were freed and exiles amnestied. Among these were the Conde de Lemos and the Duque de Infantado; the Condes de Palma, Puñon-rostro and Monterrey. These had had dealings with the Archduke Charles when he came to Madrid, and Monterrey had gone even further, seeking personal pledges from das Minas. Some, although freed from exile, were still not permitted to appear at court. In Paris of course the birth was celebrated with great joy. And even Victor Amadeus of Savoy, although in the Alliance against France, prided himself that through his two daughters in the enemy camp he was now the grandfather of 'the two legitimate heirs to the greatest thrones in the world'.

For the people of Castile – and indeed for most of Spain – the birth was a matter of profound importance. From now on Philip V, *El Animoso*, was *their* king, his son *their* prince. Never again would he be treated without respect, as had happened a couple of years earlier to the shocked amazement of Intendant Dupont at Pamplona, reporting in cypher on 'the lack of *empressement* with which the people greeted the king, the mayor appearing on his balcony in his dressing gown!' And although the Allies hurried to find a bride, a Princess of Brunswick, for their candidate, they were now too late. María Luisa had once more done a great service to her husband and to his throne.

On arrival at Béziers, Berwick heard that the siege of Toulon had been raised, and that the imperial army was in retreat, its rearguard, under Victor Amadeus, watched by the cautious Tessé. His journey had been for nothing. After two days' rest, he turned back towards Saragossa. Fifteen days later, he was with Orléans. Only the season had changed. The Bourbon camp was still weak in artillery, but the rivers were low, the ground hard and the heat diminishing. A new offensive was possible.

★   ★   ★

Berwick reached Saragossa on 12th September and made straight for Orléans' camp outside Lérida, where he found *Son Altesse Royale* in a changeable mood. He had marched his 22,000 men, of whom still two-thirds were French and one-third Spanish, including 6,600 cavalry, via Balaguer, taking his time over it and allowing himself unwisely to be tempted by Galway's movements to try and offer battle at Cervera. Galway was not to be drawn, however, so Orléans camped near Lérida, 'the right of his circumvallation on the Convent of San Francisco and the left on the Segre'. He built a special bridge over the river so as to speed his communications. It was made of wood and could be dismantled for transporting. He was impatient and wanted to begin the siege of Lérida before even the siege material had arrived; that or seek a battle. He did not even want to await the return of the 7,000 men who had accompanied Berwick to Provence. Indeed he proposed to Berwick that he should start breaking ground for the siege two days after the latter's arrival.

The marshal would not agree.

> 'Besides the town there was an admirably situated citadel – a very indigestible morsel. We had only fifteen battering pieces, little ammunition and not enough entrenching tools. It was quite possible therefore that we might miss Lérida and with a maltreated army be in peril on the disturbed borders of Aragon and Valencia.'

As far as the battle was concerned,

> 'One is never sure of winning a battle. If we were beaten, Spain was undone. If we won our bloodshed would only give us Lérida, so crippled were we with our poor commissariat and lack of ammunition. As soon as

we had the place we should move completely to the right bank of the Segre where we could defend ourselves in an excellent camp or if the opportunity offered attack the enemy.'

Orléans eventually agreed, no doubt persuaded not only by Berwick's superior age and experience but by the marshal's newly acquired honours. For his work at Almansa Philip, in mid-September, made him a grandee of the first class, and appointed him *Duque de Liria y Gérica* – titles which were formerly included in that of the sons of the Kings of Aragon, and which brought in an income of 40,000 *livres*. He was permitted to transfer the grandeeship and the dukedom to whichever of his sons he selected. Louis for his part made the marshal Governor of Limousin, worth 50,000 *livres* a year, with no duties to perform.

Heavy rain impeded preparations for the siege, washing away the bridge over the Segre, interrupting supply and preventing trenchworks. By 30th September, however, Berwick was satisfied and authorised de Légal's engineers to begin their approach to the walls. The assault trenches were opened on the night of 2nd October. The batteries were set up and ready to open fire on the 8th. The roster for the trenches, recorded in detail in Monchant's handwriting to ensure that those worthy of it would get recognition at home, has an inexorable air. These men were facing death or disfigurement.

The city had been fought over often before. Caesar had once extricated himself from being trapped between the two rivers and forced his opponents to surrender. Almost within living memory it had repelled Condé. Now it sat with its high citadel 300 yards square on a rocky escarpment, awaiting another onslaught. Though fairly well off for guns, its garrison was small, suffering from sickness and short of supplies. It was the usual Allied mixed bag of about 1,800 regulars and 800 *Miquelets*. But Prince Henry was a firebrand, and put up a fierce defence.

When the batteries opened fire Prince Henry replied with counter-battery and musketry from the citadel, whose guns could not be silenced by Orléans. He reported 'a frightful firing'. At length, however, a breach was made on the 10th at an angle where the town wall met the river and another in the curtain nearby, although Prince Henry sortied, destroying fascines and filling in trenches. The garrison fought off an assault by d'Avaray and fiercely resisted the grenadiers of the Auvergne who, under Captains Bêche and Polignac, made a lodgement on the evening of the 12th. Both men were recommended for the Cross of St. Louis. Although there was 'a perfect intelligence between the gunners and the engineers' and, according to Orléans, Berwick was 'doing marvels', the marshal preferred to wait until daybreak on the 13th before sending in his main assault.

The town was quite untenable as that day dawned and from the citadel Prince Henry begged for mercy for its inhabitants. It was not granted. Orléans and Berwick agreed that as their men's pay was, as usual, heavily in arrears, they must be allowed to loot. In any case the sooner the defenders' stocks of food were consumed, the sooner they would surrender, and it was late in the season. So the inhabitants were sent to join the soldiers in the citadel or risk being killed, and Orléans allowed systematic pillage for eight hours, two men from each squad carrying out 'the fatigue' of spoiling on behalf of their comrades.

Now it was a matter of attacking that 'indigestible morsel', the citadel. On the 15th Berwick admitted that they had no idea how to, and a week later they were still puzzled, while the guns of their enemies, high up and untouchable caused casualties. De Bourk was hit in the elbow while with Labadie and after weeks of pain felt himself lucky not to be crippled. Sapping and mining seemed to be the only way. 'If it is possible to take the citadel we shall do it,' said Berwick. But mining is a slow business and although deserters reported that the defenders were now small in number and weak in condition, there was no sign of yielding by 5th November. Moreover the rains had set in.

Galway tried to come to Darmstadt's relief and made to cross the river at Las Borjas. He was not strong enough to force an opposed crossing though he was in sight of the citadel on 5th November. Here a scout brought him a message from Prince Henry that he was down to bread and water. Galway had to reply with regret that he could do nothing except watch ineffectively. He was in any case being harassed by Zereceda, who attacked his advanced guard, killed fifty and took another fifty prisoners. 'The disproportion [of men]', wrote Stanhope to London, 'is so very great and our expectation of any reinforcement so very uncertain that I fear we must quietly see this place lost.' And so it turned out, for the rains helped make all movement difficult as well.

By 10th November the French mines were ready to be exploded. Perhaps luckily, in the prevailing rain this was not put to the test. In those days explosives were primitive. There were no such things as detonators or primers. Fuses were rough and unreliable. Portfires, if blown or rained out, had to be lit again with flint and tinder for there were no matches. However, the garrison's provisions ran out at this moment and Prince Henry beat the chamade. After lengthy parleys terms were agreed and on 14th November Henry and General Wills and the 800 who remained of the garrison marched out. As they passed Orléans he himself saluted them and walking up to Prince Henry, complimented him on the defence he had made. He even allowed him to keep three pieces of artillery. Orléans was at his best in this operation. He had personally supervised every-thing and the sight of him in the siege lines day and night earned him the respect of his troops and raised their morale. Even his eagerness in the face of Berwick's professional caution may have been of value. The total cost of Lérida to the Two Crowns was 800 killed and wounded.

It was recognized that it was now too late to besiege Tortosa before winter set in, though d'Asfeld was poised at San Mateo with some artillery. Orléans asked Philip for more cannon and supplies for the siege to be begun in February 1708. Galway, now joined by Prince Henry went into winter quarters at Tarragona, adding some men to the garrison at Tortosa. Seven months after that crushing blow at Almansa he was still in the field with an army. It meant keeping the Portuguese troops with him but this – although he could not know it – had the effect of preventing Cadaval's peace party in Lisbon from negotiating a settlement with Madrid.

Orléans left Berwick in charge of the main body and sent d'Arênnes to Morella, sixty miles inland from Tortosa with seven infantry regiments (Dillon's, Marly, Bourg, Maine, Charleroi, Orléans' and Berwick's) plus the Grenadiers of Miromesnil and 200 Spanish horse. Morella, an ancient walled town, is built in tiers on a hill, some 3,000 feet up. It was at this time garrisoned by the usual mixture under command of one Lucás de la Puerta who put up a spirited defence. There is a lengthy account of the siege by a Colonel Joblon, which tells that by 4th December there was no sign of surrender and that Berwick himself felt it necessary to come up, inspect the trenches and supervise. After much bombardment an assault was made 'at break of day' on the 11th. At 1.00 p.m. the chamade was beaten and a parley begun. This lasted eight hours and d'Arênnes could not report himself master of the place until midnight. He held eighty deserters whom he kept. The garrison of 730 marched out at mid-day on the 12th. D'Arênnes also picked up some cyphered enemy letters but could not read them, not that it really mattered. He was relieved that the siege was over. '*J'ay esté trop heureux d'y réussir dans une saison aussie rude.*'

Berwick was hoping to be able to return briefly for leave in Paris. (No doubt Nanette was pursuing 'Brochet' with letters.) But he could not. Orléans had himself gone to Madrid on December 8th to attend the baptism of the Prince of Asturias and was now on his way to bask in King Louis' approval. Amelot wrote that in view of this Berwick must stay for if he were to go, all the senior officers would follow his example and as the troops were already very undisciplined there would be 'terrible disorders'. Philip himself put pressure on to keep the marshal in Spain, though Chamillart wrote privately to Berwick saying that King Louis intended to employ him elsewhere in the Spring. At least the promised move may have been some comfort to Berwick's duchess who, according to Antony Hamilton, 'did not know which foot to dance on at the ball at Marly or the masquerade at St Germain, she was so desperate because you [Berwick] hadn't the courage to come here, using the pretext of the king's order. If you stay away much longer I don't know what will become of the poor thing, she's getting so fat.'

The expected recall was in fact deferred until April, 1708. In the meantime, Berwick did his duty, visiting cantonments and frontier posts. This at least gave him a good excuse to avoid the *longueurs* of court life in Madrid and in any case some of the positions were under constant watch and occasional attack. Against his express orders the Regiment of Louvigny, for example, had been sent to the remote region of Ribagorza where it had been surprised and cut to pieces by *Miquelets*. 'A sad affair,' said Berwick, 'for it had good officers and men.' On he went, to Saragossa to see Labadie, to de Légal's Aragon headquarters, to Lérida where the Marquis de Louvigny, separated from his regiment, was governor, and where new fortifications had to be built. It was now that the cathedral was converted into an ammunition store. And on the way he visited his newly awarded but dilapidated ducal castle at Gérica, and the lines being constructed to prevent any attack on Valencia from the direction of Tortosa. To the north his enemy still held Barcelona, Tarragona, Tortosa and much of Catalonia.

D'Asfeld, busily moving between San Mateo and Valencia, might worry about 'the thorny point' of Tortosa, but preparations were in hand for its capture. Of course worry made d'Asfeld seem harsher. In the Kingdom of Valencia, where the enemy now held only Alicante, Alcoy and Denia, he spent a lot of time on punitive measures. San Felipe goes so far as to say that there were scarcely enough trees left in the province on which to hang those who were considered rebels. It was Peterborough who, in a macabre moment once described a general as a 'hangman-in-chief'.

In the west, de Bay, the inn-keeper's son from Franche-Comté, had carried out a highly successful operation at Ciudad Rodrigo. A journal of the affair describes how the Allies had tried on 25th September to send their cavalry to safety at Almeida but had been prevented. The few English and rather more numerous Portuguese in the place were clearly not at their best. De Bay got into the suburbs on 3rd October and brought up siege guns. There was a brisk exchange of fire, the Allied batteries doing some damage, and musket fire was also heavy. But a determined escalade forced the Allies to capitulate on the 4th. De Bay was awarded the Golden Fleece by Philip for this exploit. No doubt it made him more opinionated than ever. Further south, Ossuna had taken Serpa and Moura, coming in from Andalucia. Berwick, riding briskly through the ever chillier and shorter Spanish days to carry out his last tour of inspection, could reflect with some satisfaction on the outcome of the year's campaigns.

CHAPTER SEVEN

Stanhope's War, 1708–09

Let Spain recall and England praise
The dreaded loss that froze the sun
And hid its face and dulled its rays
When the mount gaped to make a tomb.
> – Lines by a Jesuit priest on the immolation of
Colonel John Richards during the siege of Alicante, 4th March, 1709,
from Richards' Letter-Book in the British Library.

THAT winter was a time of intrigue, of rumours, of planning and of changes in command on both sides of the struggle.[1] Das Minas and Galway (now blind in one eye and permanently deaf) were recalled from Catalonia and sailed from Barcelona early in February with 1,800 Portuguese levies returning home. Galway had been gazetted commander-in-chief and ambassador to Lisbon in December 1707. Das Minas, now very definitely aged although anxious to serve even two years later, is little heard of henceforward. Berwick, as usual well informed, actually reported the two old generals' departure to Chamillart on 4th February, five days before it took place. With them sailed Erle whom Marlborough intended to put in command of 6,000 men based on the Isle of Wight for an amphibious blow in the summer against Abbeville across the Channel. This was never to take place but is one more example of Marlborough's forward contingency thinking – and later of his readiness to abandon a ploy which was not working out. It also represented a diminution of effort in Spain.

It was about now that the duke apparently decided that Stanhope should be tested in the Peninsula as commander-in-chief of the Anglo-Dutch units there. Local knowledge, a good understanding with Charles (on which Stanhope prided himself), energy, drive and the ability to view the enemy's situation as well as his own, all these Stanhope may have seemed to have. The last, a simultaneous combination of detachment and involvement Marlborough had in the highest degree. In Stanhope's case, though present, it was not entirely reliable. Another quality demanded of a general was once described by Lord Wavell, who compared it to that of a mountain gun. This weapon, after being carried on mule back through difficult terrain in foul weather and dropped fifty feet on to snow-covered rocks must still be capable of assembly and immediate function. This quality too Marlborough had, again to a greater degree than his protegé.

The captain-general now in his late fifties was perhaps looking on this man, young enough to be his son, as a potential successor. He took him to Holland, keeping him at his side, to expose him personally to Prince Eugene whom he had met 10 years earlier in Italy. But he did not give him firm orders until 8th April, and these were, in Stanhope's words 'to get out of Catalonia and enlarge our bounds'. This was the day before they sailed to Flanders, where Eugene duly gave the young general tips of the trade and a personal insight into a new figure about to descend on Spain from Vienna. Unwilling to go himself to Spain, the prince nevertheless insisted that German reinforcements must be commanded by an imperial general. It should have been de Noyelles, but just at the end of 1707 this self-centred, sly creature died suddenly – thus answering providentially Stanhope's often expressed wishes for his removal from the scene. The cause of death is obscure but San Felipe says that 'it was not without suspicion of poison since Charles had come to believe that the count had been corrupted by French gold'. That his departure was generally welcomed is confirmed by a later comment of Marlborough's. 'Between ourselves, I fear if Count Noyelles were living, matters would not go so easy.'

Since Eugene and de Noyelles were unavailable a respectable alternative had to be found and the lot fell on Marshal Graf Guido von Starhemberg. This officer, now fifty-nine, had been knocking around for years, chiefly in wars between the Empire and the Turks, and had the reputation of being cool, gallant, modest and upright. Significantly, dubbed 'the best general for the defence', he was also considered slow, cautious, phlegmatic and – understandably at his age – more of a desk soldier than an active one. According to Eugene's advice to Stanhope, the new commander knew as much as he himself did about war and should not be bothered with frequent councils but allowed to get on with the job.

Starhemberg arrived in Barcelona on 30th April, bringing with him one Imperial regiment (Reventlau's) one Italian, and seven Palatine regiments. The numbers were fewer than had been promised, thanks to inevitable problems about their pay, transport and maintenance. When in July they were joined by a further 3,000 horse and 3,000 foot from Italy, logistic arrangements were still poor and many of them took to looting. Starhemberg, although regarded by the likes of the Portuguese de Atalaya as a very poor substitute for Eugene, did some good work in bringing order out of chaos, and was insistent on being on good terms with the other generals.

It was not in Stanhope's make-up to follow anybody he thought too slow, as we can see from his behaviour on the way to Catalonia for the campaign. Travelling poste-haste with his new secretary, James Craggs, son of the secretary to the Ordnance Board and recently appointed English Resident at Barcelona, his trip took him via Düsseldorf, Innsbruck, Milan and Genoa. Stirring up the Imperialists, beating down the interest rate demanded by the Genoese moneylenders, hastening the embarcation of troops, he chartered two clean frigates and set out for Barcelona with 20,000 *pistoles*.

On arrival there he found morale low among the 2,000 or so English troops. Their habit of plundering had as we have seen made them unpopular but then their pay was always late and when it came was insufficient to buy supplies even from army stores. Officers neglected their duties and even uniform clothing was lacking. Stanhope bent the rules, allowing each company commander to keep fourteen vacant places in his unit, draw the pay for these and put it in a fund to help the private soldier. At 16s. 4d a day these vacancies were worth enough to bridge the gap for a company between the 14d. a day allowance to cavalrymen for example and the 17d. which food and forage actually cost. Stanhope insisted on proper clothing and arms including breastplates for cavalry, cracked down on absenteeism among officers and ruthlessly suppressed looting. It was not long before those under his command – including Brigadier-General Carpenter as cavalry commander – appreciated his attention to their needs and his way of bestowing praise where it was due. Captain John Cope – later to become well known as a general, though for the wrong reasons, butt of the rhyme 'Hey, Johnnie Cope are ye wauking noo?' in 1745 – wrote to Lord Raby in Berlin that the cavalry was 'in better order than had ever been known in this country' and that he was happy to serve under a general like Stanhope.

★   ★   ★

A *tour d'horizon* shows the state of Bourbon dispositions at Berwick's departure that spring. In Andalucia *le petit Renaud* and de Fiennes at Cadiz were still obsessed with possible threats from the Royal Navy at 'this little corner'. They even expected an attack on Seville. In Extremadura, de Bay was in charge but, as his English opponents noted, 'it was a particular happiness the Spaniards were so weak as not to be able to take advantage of the naked and unguarded state in which the Portuguese were at that time'. Only two not very good Scottish regiments had been sent as reinforcements and most of the Portuguese troops were still in Catalonia. De Bay had 12,000 foot and 6,000 horse but felt able to send out only a series of raids which had the sole effect of tiring out the troops engaged in destroying villages and driving off cattle. De Bay himself was sick at Badajoz part of the time and had to depend on de Aguilar. The Portuguese responded with similar futile activities until the heat drove all the armies into summer quarters in mid-July. When in the autumn of the year the second campaign followed, it was to be a similar exchange of useless barbarities inflicted by each side on the other at Elvas, Olivenza, Barbacena, Moura and Serpa. 'Fire, violence, rape and robbery were the only heroic exploits of either side,' says San Felipe sharply. Orléans had wished to send seven battalions to that frontier but had been persuaded to keep them for use in the north-east. Up in the north-west in Galicia and Navarre it was much the same story. Gramont 'had not a *sou* to pay the garrison of Bayonne,' let alone for anything else. In Valencia d'Asfeld was endeavouring to collect sufficient forces to take Denia and Alicante.

★   ★   ★

The chief mainland battleground was to be around Tortosa. Orléans reached Saragossa on 19th May, short of guns, money and provisions. Amelot was forming a company 'supported by fourteen of the richest individuals in Madrid' and hoped by this means to put the supply of victuals on a sounder footing. But up in Aragon the floods had removed bridges over the rivers Cinca and Segre so that the army had to cross at Fraga and take control of the river passage at Perello in order to deny the Allies their communications between Catalonia and Tortosa. D'Asfeld had collected fifteen cannon, 15,000 rounds of shot and 140,000 pounds of powder. And these, together with 50,000 rations of bread per day for two months and 200,000 rations of barley, he had sent forward to Orléans. But the latter noted grimly, 'The rivers are so full of debris that our guns cannot be moved by water.' Moreover, 'there is not a soldier in our 10,000 [sic] who has not been through hospital ... We badly need hospitals not only for the wounded but for the sick ... The roads are appalling.' On 12th June he began to surround Tortosa, making two bridges, one above and one below the town.

Tortosa, an ancient Roman town, guarding from its heights the only permanent bridge over the Ebro, was at this time some two miles nearer the sea than it is now, for each year alluvial deposits from the Pyrenees and elsewhere build up in the river delta. In 1708, as in 1938 when the Republicans controlled Catalonia and Franco's Nationalists Valencia, it was a key point. In 1938 the Republicans were beaten off with heavy losses. But in the earlier siege Orléans was more fortunate. A contemporary sketch in the Vincennes archives shows the plan of attack he concocted. He found the situation of the town difficult and the terrain equally so. Colonel Petit of the Engineers had done much to strengthen the Allied fortifications and the garrison was, as noted, composed largely of regular troops. Stanhope reckoned it at nine battalions, 4,000 men, 'and seven of the battalions very good old troops; they want neither provisions nor ammunition.' However, Braconelli, Orléans' chief engineer, was as skilled as Petit, and d'Asfeld had come to add his dour forcefulness to the besiegers. The Bourbons disposed of 14,000 men altogether and a battery of mortars and thirty cannon.

Although trenches were opened on 21st June there was little sign of progress by the 27th when the defenders emerged in some strength after counter-battery and 800 men in two columns filled in the attackers' trenches before withdrawing. It took five more days for Braconelli to construct breaching works from which to destroy the walls by gunfire and then the defenders in turn set his batteries on fire. However, sixteen days from the start the scarp had been pierced and miners had dug and sapped underground to within a few yards of the counterscarp. The attack on the covered way was offset by Colonel Petit, who sprang a mine killing a large number of the attackers. In his account written to King Louis on 11th July Orléans remarked on the 'heavy losses in the saps because of the terrain and the enemy's fire'. He resolved to attack the covered way once more, this time by night on 9th July, sending in

'ten companies of grenadiers, four on the left, two by the glacis on the right, with four in reserve. A lodgment was made but enemy fire was very heavy ... Eventually we got such a good lodgment in the covered way that the enemy decided to beat the chamade yesterday [10th]. I demanded that they give up the forts, the citadel and Harrés Castle but have not insisted on other articles of the capitulation.'

The garrison was almost out of food and Esseren was anxious to avoid slaughter of the citizens. Stanhope reported,

'We flattered ourselves it might have held out longer but it seems the works which had stood still most part of the winter for want of money had not been finished to my design. The garrison likewise did not answer expectation, especially the Palatines, above two thirds of which deserted either during the siege or on marching out.'

Orléans had already lost 260 killed and 630 wounded and expected more. The capitulation was therefore welcome to both sides. Of the 3,200 (Stanhope says 3,600) originally in the garrison a mere 1,200 marched out on 15th July, depleted by death, wounds, sickness and also by desertion. 'Many English, Germans and Dutch threw themselves', according to Orléans, 'into our ranks to desert.' Stanhope, however, indignantly rebutted the claim: 'The enemies, upon the marching out of the garrison, did most impudently break their faith, and partly by money but more by force took about 1,000 men out of the ranks.'

Starhemberg made no attempt to succour Tortosa. All that is recorded in the minutes of Charles's council on 20th July is that it was necessary to publish the capitulation 'to prevent pernicious rumours'.

★   ★   ★

Minorca was, perhaps, the weakest point in Bourbon Spain, just about under control thanks to the efforts of Diego Leonardo Dávila. He had been sent there as governor in January the year before. As a result of a visit at that time by Marshal Villars, Dávila had received some reinforcements. The fortress of San Felipe had been given a larger garrison. The inhabitants generally had then been rebellious and the Bourbon soldiers could not move a hundred yards without being shot at. Villars had landed four more battalions, bombarded Port Mahon's citadel and chased the rebels out of the town to Cape Mayorquin. Dávila had been firm, 'issuing punishment according to the rebels' deserts' and had got the inhabitants generally back to their jobs by promising that they should keep their privileges. In October he held a three-day fiesta in Ciudadella to celebrate the birth of the Prince of Asturias ('whom God preserve') with special masses, a theatre show, bull fights, lots to eat and drink, and the officers in full dress parading (more or less willingly) in torchlight between houses decorated with escutcheons. At the same time, writing about twice a week to Grimaldo in Madrid, he was naming disaffected nobles in other islands. But, although the defences were now fairly sound, like the Viceroy of Sardinia he felt that there would be little chance of standing up to the enemy if they came in force by sea.

Tindal attributes the decision to capture the island entirely to Stanhope, but while the general supplied the necessary drive and vigour he was in fact only obeying orders.[2] Certainly he had a strong interest in the place, which he never lost, but the Cabinet in London had long wanted it. Charles and Peterborough too had hankered after it a couple of years earlier and Marlborough wrote formally on 15th July 1708, 'I am so entirely convinced that nothing can be done effectually without the fleet that I conjure you, if possible, to take Port Mahon.' A similar letter came from Godolphin, instructing Stanhope 'to dispose of himself without loss of time to be master of Port Mahon.'

He received these orders while in camp with Starhemberg at Cervera and at once set out for Barcelona, finding there Brigadier-General Wade, just returned from London. In order that 'no time be lost in attempting a thing of such consequence and upon which our ministry lays such stress', he began at once to order men to be marched to Barcelona. Charles added his pleas for action but the Allied army in Catalonia could spare in the end only some 1,800 men – about 600 Neapolitans and Spaniards, Southwell's regiment of English (550) and about 550 Portuguese. 'I have likewise got handy', wrote Stanhope, 'ten battering guns, some mortars, a good number of bombs, 15,000 cannon shot and 1,000 barrels of powder.' He had Borgard in charge of this train and Lewis Petit came along as chief engineer. His A.D.C. was Captain Johnnie Cope. His force would, he thought, 'fall short of what will be wanting' but he intended to be off Majorca 'this day se'nnight'. He would hope to have sufficient force 'to take post and to make batteries against your [Leake's] arrival, when I hope you will spare us your marines, guns, powder etc. and crown all your services in these parts by the reduction of this important fortress'.

He was sure he could rely on Leake but he had to do everything in such secrecy that one of his staff wrote that he was 'going to imbarque on some expedition whither as yet is not publicly known', And Leake had had no time to send orders to the captains of H.M. ships at Barcelona, whose standing instructions were to protect the coast and who were within their rights in refusing to carry Stanhope's force to a destination which he was unwilling to specify exactly. Four English and two Dutch captains were so obdurate that Stanhope later wrote, 'I have in all this affair met with ten times more difficulty in dealing with the sea [Navy] than with the enemy.' But fortunately his brother Philip was Captain of H.M.S. *Milford* on station there, and he and a Captain Trevanyan (H.M.S. *York*) insisted on escorting the transports. After five days of preparation the force sailed with just these two as escorts, on 3rd September; they reached Majorca on the 6th, and took on 300 marines, sundry others and some more guns, bringing the total strength up to 2,000 of which 1,200 were English.

Stanhope had no idea of the size of Minorca's garrison but guessed, 'half are natives whom we expect great assistance from. If a sudden peace does not disintricate us from our difficulties I look upon the fate of Catalonia to depend on this expedition which I will push on the best I can.'

Leake was helpful as ever. He was in fact off Minorca on 5th September before the young general arrived. Without Stanhope's men he could do little but he detached H.M.S. *Defiance* to meet Stanhope and hurry him to Minorca and sent Captain Butler in H.M.S. *Dunkirk* to probe the forts guarding the harbour. Somewhat awed by the sight of this distant but considerable squadron the gunnery of the forts seems to have been inaccurate. The *Dunkirk* was the target of thirty-seven shots which'flew half a mile over her'.

There now arose the perennial problem of the return of the fleet to England in time to avoid the equinoctial gales. Abel Boyer gives an account of the affair in which he says Leake was 'backward to engage' and two generations later Leake's biographer goes out of the way to rebut this. Yet already Wassenaer had sailed most of his ships for Holland and Leake was aware, of course, of the grim example of Shovel's loss a year before. He could not risk losing important naval units by lingering too long over Minorca. It was not even as though he could obtain sufficient repairs and stores there when and if the island were taken. He must, he said, sail home with fifteen ships almost at once.

However, when Stanhope objected in writing, the admiral held a council of war on 14th September. It was agreed that all ships returning to England should leave the marines 'above their highest compliment', which would produce 500 for Stanhope. Rear-Admiral Whitaker was appointed to command a winter squadron of seventeen ships which was to return to base in Lisbon only when no longer required, and to provide the expedition with bread and all the cannon-shot not needed for the squadron's own defence.

Landing well away from the forts Stanhope marched first on Port Mahon which he captured on 14th September, just before Leake left. The population rose to a man in jubilation and even enlisted as militia. A detachment of 400 men sent on to Ciudadella obtained its capitulation on the 22nd. It now remained to capture the forts which guarded the approach to Port Mahon, without which the port would be no use. Of the three only Fort San Felipe presented a real problem. A strong, square structure with regular bastions and walls, it stood on an isthmus across which had been built a dry-stone wall, nine feet high with four towers at intervals, each armed with four guns. The garrison was estimated at 1,000 but in the event was nearer 1,600, of whom about 600 were French marines. The fort had 100 guns. The commander was Colonel de la Jonquière, described as 'an old officer who was sent there by way of punishment for not behaving so well as was expected from him against the Cevennois'. Poor man, he was to be punished again for Minorca. Dávila, the governor, seems like all the others to have been mistaken as to the size of the army element in the invading force.

Although thus indifferently led and expecting, from the size of the Allied squadron a landing by 10,000 or 12,000 men, the garrison rebuffed an attempt to land near the fort and a second attempt had to be made out of range of gunshot. This meant a very long and difficult approach.'We found great difficulties,' Stanhope reported, 'in landing and transporting our heavy artillery and stores through a country very rocky and where there are very few beasts of burden.' The 2,000 or so infantry were disposed on the skyline so as to make the garrison think them more numerous. This must have helped to fool Dávila.

Before leaving Leake had added to the train which now consisted of forty-two guns and fifteen mortars. 'With continued labour', said Stanhope, 'we did in twelve days get up all our artillery.' Much of the labour was provided by sailors, glad no doubt to spend time ashore. Stanhope personally supervised Borgard as he set up gun emplacements, staying until midnight and beyond. By 28th September he and Petit had got the first of two batteries of three and six guns firing on the towers of the drystone wall and silencing two of these. Borgard later added another battery.

Stanhope does not mention it himself, but wishing to avoid bloodshed and to get possession as soon as possible he adopted the device of ordering

> 'a great many papers to be writ in Spanish and French in which he promised very honourable terms to the besieged if they did not put him to the trouble of raising batteries; but if they refused he threatened that all the Spaniards would be sent to the mines and the French worse used.'

These papers were tied to arrows and fired 'into the suburbs and the vacancy between the fort and the stone wall where small parties were placed to observe us'.

It was one of these parties which fired a shot which killed Stanhope's brother, Philip, captain of H.M.S. *Milford*, 'a young gentleman of great hopes', who had been 'very active in engaging the seamen in this operation'. He had got two of his men to lift him so that he could see over the wall when a ball 'fixed to his forehead'. Since he died 'in doing service to Her Majesty and his country', wrote his brother stoically, 'I shall think his life well bestowed as I would my own.'

Stanhope intended, as there had been no response to his arrow-borne messages, to assault next day after further bombardment, but was bounced into doing so earlier by Wade's grenadiers on the right who, without orders 'found a way to get into it. To support them Brigadier Wade marched with what men he could find to sustain them, and got in.' Some little way off Stanhope heard the firing, collected the 'ordinary guard' from the battery and advanced on horseback, sword in hand. The enemy abandoned the wall and the two as yet undamaged forts and retreated into the citadel. The Allies lost only about forty men in this, the only action involved.

According to Cope, a small boy of twelve from the garrison was found that evening apparently spying on the camp. The general, instead of punishing him,

> 'loaded him with a great quantity of papers … that all those who would desert should have 2 *pistoles* each; half he writ in Spanish and ye rest in French and sewed them all round this said boy, tyed his hands behind him, and send him back to ye castle.'

Whether it was this, or the threat of the mines (of which the Spaniards were terrified) or the fact that there were a number of wives and children in the fort, consternation began to reign there. Wade's advance that evening 'even within reach of the enemy's fire' was so intrepid that 'it struck the garrison' (as one of the officers told our author [Cope]) 'with admiration and terror'. A council of war voted by a small majority to surrender.

'Next morning' reported Stanhope, 'they beat parley and at five o'clock in the afternoon the capitulation was signed, which 'I have not time to get trans-lated but is as they would have it.' Cope, youthful and contemptuous, wrote scornfully:

> 'Ye garrison seemed in very good condition and ye place prodigiously strong, so that everybody may judge ye governor was a Spaniard and an intolerable fellow to deliver up such a place without one cannon shott against it.'

This unkind view was to be shared by the French ambassador in Madrid – and indeed by Dávila, the Spanish governor himself, who acknowledged his fault and flung himself to his death from a prison balcony a few months after. In fact one round *had* been fired, and when Wade entered the castle to arrange the capitulation he found 'the large ball on the table which most of the officers had been wondering at'. The actual terms of the capitulation were that the garrison was to march out next day, 1st October, and be shipped immediately, the Spaniards to a port in Murcia and the French to Marseilles or Toulon. The magazines were to be handed over, the outer gate surrendered and arms piled in the court. The capture of the island with its 100 cannon, 3,000 barrels of powder, and most useful port was viewed with some admiration in Europe. Stanhope said severely, 'All things necessary to make a good defence [were there] except resolution in the garrison.'

A Spanish civilian governor was to be appointed but at Stanhope's insistence the garrison was always to be English. Later from Barcelona he urged over again that it must be made impregnable, even offering to stay on for three or four years to make sure. Eventually Sunderland agreed though insisting that the presence of English troops 'must be kept very secret' to avoid treading on Dutch sensibilities which had been aroused by special conditions Stanhope had negotiated with Charles for English trade with the West Indies. Stanhope argued that it would suit Charles very well to cede the island to England as a modest return for what she had done for him. But Charles was by now resentful of his dependence on England. He said it was impossible for him to cede the place without breaking his royal oath. In the end, the issue was shelved. But *de facto* Minorca remained in British hands.

The capture of Minorca was part of a Mediterranean strategy which embraced Sardinia (captured almost bloodlessly in mid-August). It gave the Allies invaluable bargaining counters and Britain a maritime stranglehold. From now on, fleets could winter in the Mediterranean. Stanhope's views of the importance of Minorca were such that when he was eventually ennobled in 1717 he chose Mahon as one of his titles. The views of the London government were the same. A medal was struck at the Tower (then the Royal Mint), showing the queen on one side and on the reverse Victory standing on a sea conch. A palm was in her right hand and in her left the Union Standard, the two islands appearing at a distance with this epigraph: SARDINIA ET BALEARIS MINOR CAPTAE MDCCVIII (1708).

★   ★   ★

After Tortosa d'Asfeld returned to take charge of affairs in the Kingdom of Valencia. It is no exaggeration to say that he did so rather like some avenging Scandinavian fury (he was of Swedish descent). His failure so far to capture Denia had embittered him for it had dimmed his prestige and exposed him to criticism.[3] He was determined to wipe out this affront by taking that place and Alicante. Stern, humourless, unforgiving, he only occasionally shows signs of humanity in the correspondence which he carried on in excellent French and a neat, clear hand.

Del Valle, appointed *corregidor* of Valencia city had wisely begun 'on a light rein' and then tightened up, but his stewardship was still appreciated, as witness a letter from the *alcaldes* thanking him for representing their problems to King Philip. D'Asfeld would tolerate no indiscipline in his troops and issued 'instructions to be observed in the Kingdom of Valencia to establish good relations between the military, the administration and others'; for example: 'the army shall protect churches, private houses and estates against insults and other hostile acts by the enemy.' Such instructions were rigorously carried out, and some clemency was even show to Alcira, 'where shortages of everything' caused him to excuse the town from paying for a kings' lieutenant.

On his arrival at the end of July he had fourteen Spanish and eleven French battalions and twenty-one Spanish and six French squadrons available in the kingdom, and he set about at once collecting more. By 10th September eight battalions and four squadrons were already on the march to Denia. D'Asfeld insisted that Orléans send him more troops and on 4th October His Royal Highness despatched all he could spare under Colonel Francisco Caetano, putting the rest in winter quarters. By the time d'Asfeld appeared at Denia he had about 12,000 men and a good train of artillery.

Stanhope had intended going straight for Denia once Port Mahon had been secured. As early as June Charles's council had realized that it was a possible target and attempts had been made to strengthen the garrison. Major Perceval, who had fought d'Asfeld off last time, was in command of a garrison of 227 officers and infantrymen and 200 marines, fifteen gunners under a lieutenant and a number of local Spanish volunteers. The governor of Alicante, John Richards, did his best to help. Having organised 1,200 of the inhabitants of Alicante into a militia, he managed to send 200 Spanish regulars and 150 *Miquelets* together with some grain in a convoy of small craft which arrived just before d'Asfeld and Ronquillo cut Denia off from the sea. Richards' private view was that the little town could scarcely hold out for more than nine days

Even if Stanhope had been able to get there he would probably have been too late to land. As it was, Admiral Whitaker had taken his squadron to Italy to escort Palatine German reinforcements for Catalonia (in the end they did not appear) and Stanhope had therefore to stay on in Barcelona. He had no warships and the French navy had sent four men-of-war to cruise unopposed off the Catalan coast.

D'Asfeld kept up a regular string of reports. In his view it was high time to concentrate on Valencia. The taking of Lérida and Tortosa covered Aragon and his enemies were at present closed in and feeding their troops with difficulty. Yet 'although Valencia had been reduced by force there were still a lot of *mauvais sujets* about'. By late September he was ready to tackle Denia, except that Orléans' reinforcements were taking their time. Guns and mortars, had however, arrived. The weather was bad and he wasted little time in opening trenches and planting batteries. On the evening of 12th November he sent in a general assault on the outer fortifications and the garrison retired to the citadel, this was totally cut off from any help from the sea, since Major-General Ronquillo at d'Asfeld's orders, had some days earlier occupied a Franciscan convent between the citadel and the port. D'Asfeld was determined to hurry and in reconnoitring the breaches between he was wounded. He did not let this interfere with his drive, for speed was all the more necessary because the weather was bitterly cold. Already there were indications that the whole of Europe was in for one of the worst winters ever recorded.

That same evening of November 12th he wrote to Chamillart:

'We have carried the lower town of Denia sword in hand although the breaches were not very practicable. I did not wish to give the enemy time to perfect their defences and they only resisted for an hour and a half while our grenadiers forced their way in and chased the enemy up to the heights. I do not yet know the losses.'

He appears to have given no quarter to any civilians he found, and next day began to bombard the citadel. His batteries working '*en chaleur*', he hoped soon to make a breach. In the citadel Perceval and Valera held on grimly but supplies were running out, and at last on 18th November after seventeen days of fighting (twice as long as Richards had forecast) they surrendered. D'Asfeld had captured fifty cannon and 80,000 pounds of powder.

Leaving a minimum of men to resore the fortifications d'Asfeld moved swiftly on Alicante, the last fortress in Allied hands in the kingdom for which he was responsible. The weather had temporarily improved but still no time could be wasted. He sent Ronquillo ahead, to reach the outskirts of Alicante by 3rd December. Recovering from his wound he himself left a few days later, arriving on 7th December and setting to at once to reduce the place.

*   *   *

By the end of 1708 John Richards, an English Catholic exile, had been governor in Alicante for well over a year and to judge from his letters he had found the job depressing.[4] It was now the last Allied stronghold in Valencia and must not be given up without a struggle, but its maintenance had hitherto been the responsibility of the impecunious Charles, it was in poor condition, and little help was forthcoming from British sources. Richards, however, did his best to improve the fortifications of the town and the citadel, known as the Castillo de Santa Bárbara, which stands high on a rock to the north-east of the town. Here he had during the latter part of 1708 built strong casemates and a hospital and hollowed out a large cistern, and he reckoned that at a push he could, with water from this and adequate food, guns and ammunition, hold out for a considerable time. After all, too, he may as a gunner have reflected, St Barbara the patron saint of artillerymen would be on his side. 'Our garrison,' he reported, 'is not a thousand men. Of these 400 are sick, we want physick and, I fear very much, provisions.' Sometimes, when Stanhope – himself short of everything – could do so he sent supplies but he had no men to spare, though Richards kept on with his requests. When the last grain transport came in early in November he did not hesitate to send 'succours' to Denia. His last letter about supplies is dated 20th November – a letter to Paul Methuen in Lisbon asking for some sea-coal. It arrived in December, too late.

Altogether the besiegers had 10–12,000 men and were determined to reduce the place before the next campaign, for the presence of even a small garrison there together with its possibility of sea supplies would mean leaving a larger force to watch it, and France was running out of men. Ronquillo's first care was to open trenches in such a way as to cut off the sea approaches. These trenches, which contained batteries facing the town in one direction and the sea in the other were very strong and well sited.

Having been unable to do as much as he had hoped to the town's defences, Richards decided to let it go. The nobility and the principal citizens were allowed to embark for Majorca. The remainder were allowed to capitulate and the Spanish cavalry were also permitted to go – but without their horses. During a brief truce of four days Richards withdrew to the Castillo with his English, Dutch and Huguenots. His mind had long since been made up. Writing on 25th October he had said, 'Here is neither troops, money, stores of war or provisions, our ffleets is gone [sic] two months ago,' but 'if the enemy do's come – and I juge they will I hope/trust [sic] in God to give a good account.'

D'Asfeld had decided what to do about the Castillo of Santa Bárbara:

'We are working without stopping at Alicante on *The Mine*. The Captain of the Mines [de Lorme] lets me hope that by the 15th of next month (February) at latest it will be ready. It will be a great thing if we can get that thorn out of our foot before the spring. Otherwise we would have to leave quite a large corps of troops there to blockade the citadel.'

From now on until March not only he but King Philip, Amelot and many others would be tensely waiting at varying distances while a chamber was hollowed out in the rock below the citadel, into which it was intended to place a huge charge of gunpowder. For Richards, too, the next few weeks, his last on earth, would be clouded by the menace of whatever it was – he did not know at first, though he could guess – that was going on under his feet.

For an account of the progress of this monster, which had been begun well before Christmas, we have the evidence of letters from a Colonel de la Cour (a gunner) and, thanks to him at secondhand, the reports he and d'Asfeld were getting from Captain de Lorme, the chief engineer. On 7th January de la Cour sent a letter to Paris with a plan of Alicante:

'There is difficulty in mounting cannon in the face of plunging fire from the citadel, which has already killed 15 or 16 peasants working on this and wounded 20. We have a battery of six guns on the mole, six more [along the shore] and 17 pieces in the great bastion of the Faubourg of St. Francis. Ronquillo wanted me to use mortars but I would not since the enemy are better placed to return fire with heavier pieces.'

It was impossible to assault the citadel since attackers could not approach the wall without being seen or find footholds. It was for this reason that d'Asfeld had decided on The Mine, though this operation too was fraught with difficulty since the rock was like marble and very hard to work.

After a month of continuous excavation de la Cour reported that they were only fifty-two feet in.

'M. de Lorme deserves great credit . . . I hope The Mine will be finished by 15th or 20th February but the rock is getting harder, and we have to use 6 lb. petards of gunpowder [to blast]. This shakes the citadel buildings though they are 20 fathoms above.'

So, in addition to the sounds of pick and shovel transmitted through the rock as a faint, sinsiter tinkle particularly at night, the besieged were frequently shaken by random explosions far below.

The project now began to catch the imagination of the Madrid court.

King Philip himself became rivetted by what was going on. By February 6th de Lorme was certain that The Mine would be ready for charging by the end of the month, when, wrote d'Asfeld, 'We can summon the governor to surrender, offering an honourable capitulation.' It is as though d'Asfeld, tough as he was, was beginning to have qualms about his 'infernal machine', that enormous explosive charge. It was going to use up a very large quantity of powder which might be needed for other purposes. And there were technical problems he had not foreseen. He wrote from Valencia on 13th February and again on the 20th, reporting that:

> 'I am going to Alicante to push on with charging The Mine at the end of February. It will be a problem transporting 1,200 barrels of powder from the town up to the rock, where the entrance is, without having an accident or being interfered with by 'artifices' [small bombs] thrown by the enemy from the citadel. I have ordered 800 goatskins to be prepared for carrying the powder .... I am going to see what remedy I can find to the obstacles placed by the enemy against our transport of powder. For seven or eight days they have occupied a rocky point from which they can observe the path to The Mine and our cannon have not yet been able to chase them away.'

King Philip was still in touch and had the cold shivers:

> 'The Captain of Mines says it will be ready by the end of the month and d'Asfeld will then go and summon the governor to accept an honourable capitulation. I do hope they do not oblige us to set it off for the 100 *milliers* of powder would have a terrible effect.'

On 25th and 26th February Richards got two letters out. To Stanhope he expressed his disappointment at having had no response to his recent requests for aid and goes on;

> 'Wee juge the enemy to be verry neare if not under our great cysterne where they are making a chamber which they pretend to charge with 1,200 barrils of powder, the consequences of which no mortal can juge, it being

the first myn of this kinde that ever was heard of ... You may be assured that we will stand it, tho' there may be some who are not altogether of this mind and indeed it is verry uncomfortably [sic] to heare our enemy working Night and Day under our ffeete.'

To his brother, 'Dear Mickey' he gives the same news.

'The enemy have brought their *Madriers* [wooden panels for closing the mine] to the mouth of the Mine so that I juge they will begin to charge to-night or to-morrow. The Almighty assisting us you may depend upon it that for my part I shall stand it, and in this case any man can only answer for himself ... Pray God send us a merry meeting.'

Now, 200 feet below the sounds of pick and petard ceased and the roar of gunfire on Richards' observation post drove his men away while d'Asfeld began to rush the goatskins full of gunpowder into the mine chamber. Further below in the town and suburbs civilians were being evacuated and thousands of Spanish troops stood guard against any attempt at break out.

Just about at this time there was an eerie exchange at midnight between Richards and his senior officers on the ramparts and an English ship's captain, who was later picked up with his ship and interrogated. A note in French at Vincennes records it briefly. A packet boat had left Cartagena on 23rd February

'at nine o'clock with a W.S.W. wind. This changed to north-east and blew us till midnight when we saw the flag of the Citadel of Alicante. After an exchange of signals we called them by voice. The Citadel asked who we were and I replied: Captain James Bolton of a Queen's ship carrying orders for him and letters from Lisbon to Barcelona. He replied that the Citadel was mined everywhere and that time was about to end one way or another. Water was low and he could expect no supplies from England or Lisbon. I asked: What will you do? He replied: I cannot give you my feelings for the town would hear. But we will take our measures, having heard what you have said. Tell the King [Charles] that they have nearly completed the mine.'

That unearthly yet matter-of-fact exchange between the ramparts and Captain Bolton was Richards' last personal contact with the English-speaking world outside the citadel. Within, there were still discussions, for not surprisingly although Richards himself was prepared 'to stand it', there were officers in the garrison who, as he put it, 'were not altogether of the mind'. Their discussions are carefully recorded in a document drawn up in Richards' hand in two columns. Coolly and dispassionately the arguments for surrender and against are marshalled in a most unusual and moving document. To keep up morale, Richards had ordered 'that it be publicly reported that he had discovered that the barrels were only filled with bran, for he was desirous that the soldiers should not be discouraged at the approaching day'. But he himself knew the truth.

The paper he wrote is worth reproducing in full:–

For the Surrender

1. That we have a terrible mine under us, the effects of which cannot be certainly known but it is possible it may blow into pieces the upper part of the Rock, at least it will open it, and destroy our water and it may be the Hospital where we have the much greater part of the garrison, which, should it do notwithstanding the mine should not open such a breach as to let in the enemy, where shall we have men to defend us?

Against

1. That we have a terrible mine beneath us is certain but the effects of it is [sic] not. It is therefore unjustifiable in the highest degree for men of our profession to do a certain evil out of fear of an uncertain one, for all that we shall probably lose by the mine is our great cistern; for it is not likely that we shall lose that *fausse braye* where we have, without rain, water for ten months, but should this unexpected evil happen us it will sufficiently justify our surrender. The enemy mine will either blow the Parade and dungeon [Keep] into atoms, or, what is more probable, only open it in divers clefts. If this be the only thing that will happen to us then may the enemy be as far from entering that way as they are at present, for we do actually experience that a very few men before the outside of the Rock can hinder them from coming up. But should they entirely blow away all that is above the chamber [?] of their mine, they will leave such a

stump as may easily be defended and give us time to consume our provisions with honour.

2. If we must be obliged to surrender after the blast of the mine when we have lost the greatest part of our men, suredly it will be better to do it before, and move them for an occasion when they may be more serviceable.

2. It being not probable that the Parade and dungeon should be blow'd into pieces, it is as certain that the hospital will subsist, and all that is in it, for unless the whole mass of the rock upon which it is found did be blowed to pieces, it may be shaken but it will not fall. But if we suppose this evil to happen, it is in no way to be reduced but by retiring the men into the lower parts of the castle leaving above only the necessary sentries that the enemy may not surprise us. As to the rest of this point I answer that we must not surrender before we be actually put out of a condition to defend ourselves, and this [not] out of apprehension of what is as uncertain as the effect of a mine. For at this rate no town is to be defended, it being certain that it cannot be done without the loss of men, and consequently it would be better to surrender the first day than the last, for as to the probability of being succour'd, I will be bold to say that none of them had as much reason to expect it as we.

3. It is the practice of war that when a garrison is reduc'd to the last shift that they should save themselves by a timely capitulation, and if we stay until the enemy has sprung the mine it may be we shall have none.

3. I grant that it is the practice of war to surrender when the town is reduc'd to an extremity, that the outworks are taken, that a breach is made in the body of the place, and the garrison juges themselves so

weak as not to be in a condition to defend it. But the case is quite otherwise with us, for the enemy has not taken nor indeed attempted the taking of an inch of ground from us. They have made no breach and our magazines are full of provisions of war and mouth, so that to surrender out of apprehensions only of what may or may not happen is in no way justifiable. I therefore conclude that we are to stand the effects of this mine, and if it is not possible for me to hinder them from carrying in their powder, that then we retire our guards from dungeon, sea battery and rock, leaving only the necessary sentries to the number of three or four and those of our best men in proper places that we be not surprised by any stratagem of the enemy's — leaving only thirty men up on the Hospital and the same number behind the traverse of the smith's forge, in order to stop the enemy in case they should attempt to come up any of the rocks, in confidence of our guards being retir'd, the which two guards will be sufficient to stop the enemy until the rest of our people can come in to their support. And for greater security I juge it necessary that there is a guard at Gorge's battery.

All accounts agree that d'Asfeld himself hesitated before going ahead, showing a humanity which he had not displayed before or would again. His own words tell the story:

'I summoned the Governor to surrender, offering a good capitulation but he answered very honestly saying he was resolved to defend himself. This made me charge the mine on the 28th [February] although the enemy could observe the road I was using from three sentry posts. We kept up such a cannon fire that we were able in the day to put in eighty *milliers* of powder without their seeing. On March 1st we continued to carry in powder with the same success so that the rest of the 120 *milliers* was in by 10.00 a.m. By 3.00 p.m. the wooden *madriers* [to tamp in the powder] were also in place. I thought it against humanity to set off the mine without summoning the Governor a second time which I did at 2.00 a.m. I told him the mine was charged and that to show I was not deceiving him he could send to look at it. He did so, but as part of the mine was masked by the wooden shields the two officers who came to reconnoitre [Thorneycroft and Pagez] thought I was imposing on them, not believing it was possible to put in 110 [sic] *milliers* in so short a time . . . I offered if they capitulated to blow the thing up in front of them afterwards. After hearing what the two officers said, the enemy refused to capitulate, which made me work diligently to put the mine into readiness.'

The mine gallery had been driven with great difficulty by de Lorme from the western face of the rock on which the citadel stood, facing towards the town. The barracks, casemates and hospital were on the eastern side. Richards instructed that those not on duty were to be withdrawn as far as possible. Probably on the morning of March 4th though it may have been at dinner on the 3rd, Richards, according to Archdeacon Coxe 'as a bravado, sat down to table with many of his officers over the very chamber of the mine.' At 8.00 a.m. sentries on the walls reported that people below the citadel were fleeing in crowds, and a corporal of the nearest guard shouted that 'a slight smoke' was climbing the rock face. This meant that the 'hose', technical term for a fuse, a canvas tube filled with gun-powder and leading into the chamber of The Mine, had been lit.

It is easy to imagine the unendurable tension at this moment.

Richards at this signal had ordered the guard to retire, and himself 'repared to the spot considered as most exposed'. With him, perhaps drawn by his personality in emulation, or perhaps afraid to show fear, went Thorneycroft, Sybourg, Vignoles and four other un-named officers. Within seconds The Mine blew up and 'with little or no noise made an opening in the rock on the very parade, of some yards in length and about three feet wide'.

The absence of noise is normal, for such a huge explosion nearby is felt rather than heard. A hideous uprush of hot gases, dust and debris drags the breath from the lungs, bursts the eardrums by drawing air from internal cavities in the head, blackening the vision, and shakes the whole body like a rag doll. Further away it would sound like a great clap of thunder. D'Asfeld reported 'a great tremor felt at more than half a league from the town'.

Into the opening in the parade ground fell Governor Richards and those who had stood with him, 'and the opening instantly closing upon them they all perished, though their bodies were not entirely sunk in'. Some of them must also have been blown into the air, for d'Asfeld later wrote of 'finding quantities of corpses, including several officers. In addition to those who were named as being with Richards those killed included the four nameless captains, three lieutenants and forty-two N.C.O.s and private soldiers of the guard.

D'Asfeld was optimistic. The Mine took

'part of the lodgings on the curtain wall, ruining the rest including a complete bastion. All that part of the Chateau facing over the town is entirely fallen and there is a breach in the second curtain. Their great cistern is ruined. Without a *vaine* [*cleft*] in the rock the effect would have been more considerable. To judge from the stones that have fallen every-where The Mine must have caused great disorder in the Chateau. Nothing confirms [this] more for us than all the cries heard since 8.00 a.m. I hope that [the fact that]their cistern will have suffered will facilitate our access to the Chateau, but as it is 400 feet up The Mine has made it inaccessible ... I hope that the disorder done by it will soon make the enemy surrender. It had little effect on the town, only 12 or 15 houses suffering.'

He was to be disappointed in his hopes. 'Even during the blast a cry of 'Long Live the Queen!' had been raised and rung amidst the ruins. The damage had been considerable – including that to the cistern, but only a couple of guns had been dismounted. Richards had been right in his estimate of the potential damage. As d'Asfeld noted, the rock face had in fact been made more inaccess-ible to an assault. The surviving commander, Lieutenant-Colonel d'Albon of Sybourg's Regiment, resolved to hold out as long as he had any provisions.

D'Asfeld waited for the end with increasing exasperation. He wrote on 3rd April to Chamillart:

'Thanks to the small amount of water in the Citadel at Alicante ... we can hope to be masters [of it] before the end of the month ... I beg you to believe that I will forget nothing in order to conclude matters for the Two

Crowns. As I have been forced to take many difficult measures during the last three years in order to overcome all the materials I lack, I shall continue to do my best.'

On that same day the Engineer de la Cour was writing:

'We know little of what has happened ... The enemy do not fire as much as they did ... D'Asfeld has ordered us to shoot deserters leaving the Citadel so as to ensure that the numbers are there to eat victuals and drink the water more quickly ... A deserter sent to the Mine chamber has found a way out. He says the garrison is divided. The English want to surrender but the *religionnaires* [*Huguenots*] who are mostly French, want to hold on to the end ... There are only two hands' [depth] of water in the cistern. The [acting] governor probably will not wait till the last drop ... We hope the citadel will surrender about 16th April.'

The effect of the siege on the Franco-Spanish troops had obviously been considerable.

'Our troops will not be ready for the campaign in May. They have had 300 killed and wounded since the siege began ... Crops are likely to be bad because of a prodigious host of locusts, a kind of grasshopper which attacked last year's crop. The peasants in Murcia, La Mancha and Valencia have been ordered to kill them but have been quite ineffectual. Now people will die of hunger. Bread costs three French *sous* for a pound of 12 ounces, more than double what it was last year ... After Alicante citadel has yielded of course fewer troops will be needed but the people [here] are so ill intentioned and blind to their own interests that they can only be held down by force. This is an accursed nation on which we cannot count unless we are masters.'

The garrison was beyond relief but at least it could be rescued. Stanhope and Byng made the attempt from Port Mahon on 1st April, but storms drove them into Denia, where they stayed until the 15th in order to avoid being dispersed. When at length they got to Alicante, Byng 'went in with men of war to batter the enemy's works and trenches.' Stanhope had wanted to land his troops that day but Byng insisted that the weather made it impossible. So with general agreement he decided to sign a capitulation, give up the citadel and take off the Allied survivors. At last on the 20th the garrison sallied forth 'free and with every military honour, glorious though defeated,' says an opponent. 'What

King Philip had lost in one day cost years to recover. This advantage was the archduke's to whom it had cost little and who held it, thanks to the pertinacity with which those who took and defended it grimly to the end did their duty.'

★   ★   ★

The Duke of Orléans had not been in Spain since October, 1708. Recalled to Versailles for consultations, he had given every appearance of intending to return. Louis XIV, however, had no intention of allowing him to resume command. His private designs upon the Spanish throne, which he considered his cousin unworthy to occupy; his intrigues; his trade in insults with the queen and Mme des Ursins; and his personal interest in a prospect of peace, which would at least enrich him with Allied brides and perhaps bring him a crown from the wreck of the Spanish monarchy: all were incompatible with his soldierly duties.[5]

Orléans' absence from Spain was much discussed in Madrid. Those who approved of him said he had gone of his own accord, while there were those nourished on little drops of poison dispensed by Madame des Ursins who was determinedly weaving a spell to trap him; and they said that he had been dismissed by King Philip for unspecified reasons. His going certainly had one effect, chiefly noticeable in the Bourbon armies of the north-east, a recurrence of bitter ill feeling between the French and Spanish troops.

Here de Besons was moving up to Saragossa and then Lérida to take over command with d'Estaing as his second. The Spaniards were commanded by de Aguilar, a capable and soldierly figure. Jacques, Comte de Besons, was now in his mid-fifties, and had recently been made a Marshal of France but despite this and his vigorous and neatly written correspondence he seems to have been a military second-rater. He and de Aguilar did not hit it off and San Felipe records in shocked tones:

> 'Never was seen an army in such discord from the commanders down to the lowest ranks – to such a degree as to encourage the enemy. Whatever the French undertook the Spaniards did their best to undo while in return the French did their best to foil the Spaniards, and all this, not out of emulation but from hatred. The Spaniards wanted the French to quit so that they alone could defend their country.'

San Felipe would have been less surprised if he had been present in Tessé's and Villadarías' camps before Gibraltar four years earlier, but he had then been in Sardinia. Now he was hearing about it at first hand. It is not surprising that things went wrong. As early as January d'Estaing wrote from Barbastro in the lowlands of the Pyrenees saying that for lack of cash to pay them he was having difficulty in keeping the troops happy. He notes particularly that the two Berwick Regiments were the most troublesome.

Still, there was nothing better for the men than a little action so he marched 3,000 of them seventy miles north into the Pyrenees and on 12th April attacked the little town of Benasque which stands nearly 4,000 feet up and fifteen miles inside the Spanish border. Situated on the River Noguera among the Aragonese Pyrenees it is not easily approachable and seems scarcely worth the trouble. The French took the town but were unable to capture the citadel. Short of food and ammunition, with few cannon and those only field pieces, and under frequent attacks from the garrison under General de la Puebla, d'Estaing started to mine the citadel but then found he had insufficient gunpowder. This all took weeks and produced no results, while he barely subsisted in the rough, barren countryside, surrounded by marauding *Miquelets* and rapidly losing men. By mid-June he had out of the 3,000 he began with only about 1,300 fit, having lost 450 killed and wounded and with many sick. It seems an extraordinary undertaking.

By now de Besons had reached Lérida via Saragossa – where he had as usual found everything lacking, had ordered tents and boots to be sent at once and d'Asfeld to send him five regiments of French infantry. From Lérida he ordered d'Estaing to withdraw from Benasque, a most risky manoeuvre, given that the *Miquelets* held all the passes along the winding, rugged 100 miles. The unfortunate d'Estaing and the residue of his force eventually reached base in July, to find de Besons having futile rows with the Spaniards, so short of food and stores as to be unable to order any action, though he spends ten pages at a time describing his proposals, and watching Starhemberg, his opponent, whom he describes as being 'inactive' although he was believed to have 23,000 troops. On both sides word had come through that the negotiations were going on. It would be foolish to be too zealous and waste lives if there were to be a peace. And Starhemberg, although his infantry were good, could only get Sardinian mounts which were unsuitable. His cavalry were therefore of poor quality. So he too did little.

On his return from Alicante Stanhope had tried with the marshal to prepare for a new campaign, but the countryside was bare and exhausted, supplies must come from England, the enemy were believed to be much more numerous and there was no sign of any reinforcements coming. Moreover Charles's court was much as it had been four years earlier, eliciting from Stanhope words which echo those of Peterborough:

> 'The ministers think of nothing but confiscations; entire new-modelling of Spain; suppressing the order of the grandees; changing their habits, which is already begun at court, where the Spanish ladies are ordered to dress after the German fashion; and I believe they would even abolish the Spanish language if it could be agreed between them whether High Dutch or Neapolitan should be spoken instead of it . . . The marshal does all he can and all that can be done; but has not the good fortune to please this Court better than his predecessors.'

Despite the difficulties of dealing with such a court, and the problems of supply – 'the greatest enemy we have is famine' – Stanhope suggested a project to clear French troops out of Spain using the Allies' central situation to attack de Noailles' force in Roussillon, separated as it was from the rest, drive it back into the Cevennes, and thus force de Besons to quit Spain to its rescue. This would open Aragon to the Allies. Starhemberg preferred to wait and see what happened about the peace negotiations; he would later regret having done so. Now he took up a position across the Segre from de Besons and the two armies listlessly watched each other for weeks during the high summer heats.

★   ★   ★

There is no point in our wasting time watching them, for over on the Spanish–Portuguese frontier, near Elvas, things were livening up. The two previous campaigns in this sector had been of excruciating dullness and lack of distinction – a few marches here and there, a few villages sacked, a general dodging of anything approaching action. Now there was a flare-up.

De Bay had been encamped since 19th April near Evora while his opponents were at Elvas. De Bay's force of 5,000 horse and 10,000 foot was entirely Spanish, apart from himself, de Fiennes and a few other officers. This had involved him in an argument. Madrid had ordered him to detach troops to Valencia and Catalonia but he had refused point-blank as he was, with his customary aggressiveness, determined to force an action. His opponents were a mixed force of Portuguese and British. Their commander, the Marqués da Fronteira, as was customary under the Methuen Treaties, shared his duties with old Galway, in his usual equivocal position as 'adviser', but the Huguenot nevertheless was also in charge of some 3,000 'English' infantry. These troops, described by San Felipe as 'highly selected', were in fact a *fricassée*, rehashed from the leftovers of the previous couple of campaigns, and included Pearce's dragoons, mounted theatrically by Peterborough in 1705 but now back on foot. Also present was Colonel Carles, who had been involved in the reconnaissance before Cadiz in 1702. Captured at Ciudad Rodrigo and later exchanged, he was now a major-general in the Portuguese army. Directly responsible to Fronteira was General the Conde de São João, in command of the Portuguese cavalry. They were all encamped on the right bank of the River Caya near Campo Maior, their nearest base being at Arronches.

On 3rd May de Bay decided to provoke his opponents into activity, so he moved his cavalry into a position directly opposite Fronteira and sent foragers right under the noses of the enemy into the surrounding area. This involved leaving his infantry well back but he appears to have felt it worthwhile, for he was trying to tempt Fronteira to cross the river, and he succeeded. Galway did his best to dissuade Fronteira but, whereas he had sometimes been able to sway old das Minas in the direction of good sense, he could not budge Fronteira. The Marqués left his Portuguese infantry such as they were at Arronches and on 7th May crossed over on to the plain of La Gudiña with all his cavalry, five guns, and one brigade of English infantry under Montandré.

The infantry he placed in the centre with Portuguese cavalry on either wing, and at about mid-day fired off his five guns. De Bay's right was commanded by Aytona and Caylus, his left by de Fiennes and Moscoso, all well tried men, and he immediately sent in Aytona against the Portuguese, who promptly wheeled and rode off, leaving the cannon to be taken. They were terrified of Spanish cavalry. So swift was their retreat that they caused disorder in the second line which São João tried to control. Galway sent up Sankey with some foot to support Montandré but as all the Portuguese horse now fled the English were left isolated and surrounded. São João, and about 900 men were made prisoner, but Montandré coolly formed square and withdrew in good order, losing only 150. Galway, as usual in the thick of it, had his horse shot under him and only just got away with his secretary, Major Bladen, to Arronches a few miles away. Next day the Allies camped at Elvas.

Although the Spanish infantry was far off when the Allied line was broken, the Portuguese left all their equipment and were only saved 'by the speed of their flight'. De Bay was criticised for keeping his infantry so far back and for not destroying the bridges over the Caya so as to catch the Allies on the wrong side. But Aytona and de Fiennes were unable to control their men who, after dashingly breaking their opponents, rode off in a muddled search for personal plunder. The Allied losses were about 1,700 altogether and de Bay's about 500. He had had a remarkable victory at La Caya but was able to gain little advantage from it.

Having recovered his breath Galway took up advantageous posts on the River Guadiana and put supplies into Olivenza. Under his advice on 9th May the chastened Fronteira took up a strong defensive position. De Bay did not feel capable of tackling this and soon withdrew into summer quarters.

Galway by now had had enough and recommended that never again should the British take the field with the Portuguese. He at least would not! As far as London was concerned this struck an answering chord. Long experience had by now shown the difficulties of acting in concert not only with the Portuguese court but in the field, or even at sea. There was always much talk, much selfish manoeuvring for position, and a minimum of effective action. So now it was decided to let them recover themselves and, if they could, get into a condition to do something on their own for a change. Meantime, perhaps a diversion into Andalucia would be useful.

★   ★   ★

Accordingly London decided that a landing-party be sent out in transports escorted by a naval squadron under Admiral Baker. Stanhope was sent instructions to raise troops in Catalonia, join those coming with Baker at Gibraltar and, taking command, make one more attempt on Cadiz. This half-baked scheme was frowned on by Marlborough who had written to Godolphin on June 14th 1708: 'There can be no doubt that Cadiz would be of great use. But I beg you to consider how impossible it will be to have any success unless it be done by surprise.' There could be no surprise.

Of course they none of them knew how busy *le petit Renaud* had been these past few years, improving the fortifications of the place. But London should have remembered the landing and withdrawal carried out by Rooke and Ormonde in 1702 and the appalling effect on the city – and on all Andalucia – of the behaviour then of the English soldiers. Stanhope certainly did, and realizing that with only at most 5,000 regular troops he would need the good will of the inhabitants, was convinced before he even set out, as he wrote to Starhemberg that 'the affair is impracticable.' He was half-hoping for peace, half-fearing an expected invasion from Roussillon. It was not until 20th August that he was able to sail, by which time the threat from Roussillon could be gauged: twenty-two battalions and twenty-five squadrons, all French, but under de Noailles, not Berwick, and in any case limited to foraging for corn, which was short in France, though they did surprise and capture a badly commanded battalion of Germans. Leaving the two armies wearily plodding up and down on opposite sides of the Segre, Stanhope in H.M.S. *Chichester* arrived at length at Gibraltar on 31st August. With him were Colonel Harrison's regiment from Minorca, 500 dismounted Spanish dragoons and Michael Richards with quite a good train of artillery. But there was no sign of Baker. He and his force were to be delayed for weeks by the weather. Galway and Wade sent reports on Cadiz and these and subsequent intelligence made it clear that to attack the place would need three or four times the numbers available to Stanhope. All the measures taken by de Fiennes and Renaud over the years had been justified. Cadiz was too strong, and the idea of a popular rising was a myth.

There was nothing to do, however, but await Baker. So Stanhope diligently examined how best to improve Gibraltar which he was

'sorry to find so much exposed to be insulted ... I must not conceal from Your Lordship the disorder and confusion I found the stores in, which is owing as much to the want of an inspector over them as the neglect and ignorance of the officer who is left here to look after them.'

He sent two experts, Paget and Phillips, to give Galway particulars of what Gibraltar needed by way of new work. Byng arrived on 27th September on his way home, with six ships which were meant to carry Stanhope back to Barcelona with his men. He brought alarming news of the Bourbon forces now outnumbering Starhemberg by two to one, and Stanhope was impatient to get back there, but could not leave until 27th October when Baker at length arrived. However the very fact of his being at the Rock had also prevented some Spanish forces from being sent to Catalonia.

'Uneasy' as he described himself while stuck at Gibraltar, Stanhope had heard on 12th October one great piece of news. On 11th September at Malplaquet, fifteen miles south of Mons, in Marlborough's words,

'We have had this day a very bloody battle; the first part of the day we beat their foot and afterwards their horse ... God Almighty be praised, it is now in our powers to have what peace we please, and I may be pretty well assured of never being in another battle.'

Even before Malplaquet, Louis XIV had resigned himself to the need to recall most of his troops from Spain to the north. Now the withdrawal was hastened. By the end of the year it was virtually complete. When Stanhope got back to Barcelona in December, he found both sides quiescent in winter quarters. The war in Spain was in a state of suspended animation. With no duties before him, save at home in Parliament, Stanhope packed his bags. It was to be a brief interlude. He would return in the spring, on the wings of war renewed.

CHAPTER EIGHT

The Swing of the Pendulum

Inconstancy and the Fortunes of War, or to speak more Christianlike the Instability of Humane Prosperity, appear'd in the most surprising manner; both parties being conquerors and conquer'd by turns.

> – Boyer and Tindal on the campaigns of 1710

LATE in March 1710 Lieutenant-General James Stanhope called in at The Hague to see Marlborough and Eugene. He hated what he called shilly-shally and was typically rushing to take up his appointment as commander-in-chief of the Anglo-Dutch contingent in Spain, this time even the more impatiently because his position was recognized by London as of key importance. Both the great captains, who had long known and valued him, realized the need for a reliable mainspring of activity in a sector which would otherwise have been in the hands of the inexperienced Archduke Charles and of the slow-moving Starhemberg; while Galway, hundreds of miles away in Portugal, ever-increasingly beset by age, illness and disillusionment, was awaiting his replacement

Stanhope was returning to a part of the world to some of which he had been introduced half his lifetime before, when at eighteen he had spent a year in Spain with his father, Alexander, then English minister to the court of Madrid. His Spanish and French were excellent. He had been tried in battle. He had energy. He had spent little of his life in England – except for schooldays at Eton and a couple of years at Trinity College, Oxford. He had had no time to acquire a wife and other hostages to fortune. Spain had already claimed the lives of two of his brothers; Alexander, the eldest, had died of a fever at Alicante in 1695 and Philip had been killed at the taking of Port Mahon in 1708. Later, in the patent for the peerage James Stanhope would be awarded in 1717 there would be a touching reference to this. And another brother, Edward, would be killed at the siege of Cardona a year later in 1711. A descendant, Charles, serving a century later at Corunna under Sir John Moore in the 59th Regiment, would be the fourth

Stanhope to leave his bones in Spanish earth. For James Stanhope fate awaited too but it would be defeat, not death, in battle.

His instructions, largely drawn up by himself, it would seem, were to take advantage of the withdrawal of French troops from the Peninsula and press for an energetic offensive. Charles was to be urged to offer amnesty to all Spaniards who defected from Philip. As Stanhope probably foresaw, the amnesty, delayed by inertia at Charles's court, was only ready in draft form six months later. All his considerable drive was to be required to build up a military offensive. He had had a promise from Emperor Joseph of 4,000 troops and carried bills of exchange on Genoa for money to pay them and the men who were already in Catalonia.

Accompanied by young James Craggs, his secretary and commissary, he travelled at a spanking pace, too hot for the younger man who wrote from Frankfurt: 'Mr. Stanhope and I arrived the 19th inst. [April]; he went away the same day by way of Swisserland [sic]; I was obliged to stay for my chaise which I had left to be mended six posts of. I hope to meet my master in Venice.' There was, as might have been expected, no hastening the German reinforcements and only 1,000 were ready by the time Stanhope reached Genoa. So he embarked these and on 10th May sailed with them and £80,000 in cash in order to be in time for the opening of the campaign.[1]

For that campaign Philip had as yet no commander-in-chief of standing. He had asked for Vendôme and would do so again – next time with success. His cousin Orléans was ruled out. In any case, Louis XIV engaged in devious and difficult peace manoeuvres, would not contemplate supplying a French generalissimo, since he was also overtly detaching French troops from that theatre. So King Philip had recourse to the veteran Villadarías who had been in embittered retirement in Andalucia since the failure to retake Gibraltar five years earlier. This worthy but elderly and now limited man took up his post in Aragon with Tzerclaes in command of the Walloon troops from Flanders and the Royal Guard, and Antonio de Amezaga commanding the Spanish cavalry.

Opposing them as spring came in was Starhemberg at Agramont, fifteen miles east of Balaguer, awaiting reinforcements. Stanhope joined him on 26th May with the English troops whose services had not been required at Cadiz in late 1709. They were not numerous but Stanhope was delilghted with their condition, for they were fully acclimatized:

'Though we have, at some time during this war, had more troops in Spain yet we never had so good an army. This I attribute to their having been landed in proper season and having had a winter in quarters to accustom them to the climate; whereas we have found by the experience of all this war that the men who have been landed in the spring or summer and have immediately been put upon service have mouldered away to nothing by sickness. If this war were to last I would have it laid down as a general rule never to have any Englishman sent into Spain at any other season than the beginning of winter.'

Independently of what his opponents were about, Stanhope was convinced that Charles must appear personally in the field, and on his way through Barcelona persuaded the archduke to do so. Then he and Starhemberg 'both did write to him and His Majesty did the next day set out from Barcelona with a very light equipage, and very suitable to his present circumstances and joined the army on the 7th of June.'

The two candidate-monarchs were actually facing each other across the battlefields.

At first Charles' situation bore 'a dismal aspect' because of the non-arrival of most of the German reinforcements. The Allies estimated that Philip's army in June numbered about 22,000 men in all, 'marching along the plain in our full view, to attack us' between Balaguer and Lérida. Philip was reported at Charles' headquarters to have announced 'that he was resolved to put all to a decisive battle'.[2]

Balaguer, captured by Starhemberg the previous year, was a useful strong-point. Indeed, as recognized at a council meeting of Charles' on 16th March in Barcelona, it was the only protection to the plains between Tortosa and Benasque. At a grand council of war in April it was resolved to take the field on 1st May. The army seems to have consisted by then of about 18,000 men.

As Villadarías considered himself superior in numbers he decided to try and surprise the Allies in their quarters and beat them before any major reinforcements could arrive. He led King Philip and the troops, some 20,000 foot and 6,000 horse, across the River Segre to offer battle. He was unlucky. North-eastern Spain was unlike Andalucia and snows melting in the mountains caused the river to overflow its banks and carry away bridges. He was cut off from his supplies and communications on the right bank. Yet Starhemberg, instead of attacking him, merely dug in. There was some mutual bombardment, but the Allied troops, being in trenches, suffered less. Philip had detached Amezaga to take a small citadel at Estadilla which he did, capturing 340 prisoners and leaving six companies as garrison. The whole business was inconclusive and Villadarías had to march, frustrated, back to his former quarters at Lérida.

On 11th June he tried once more to tempt his opponents but they stayed in a strong defensive position on rising ground overlooking the plain. On the 13th Villadarías came up to 'within less than half a cannon shot' (about 300 yards) of the Allied left wing. His army was briskly plied with gunfire which dissuaded them. On this occasion Stanhope, with eight squadrons of horse and eight battalions pursued them. He had two horses shot under him but the enemy lost some hundreds of their rearguard. In expectation of a battle Villadarías had left unguarded the passage across the Noguera, the river which divides Catalonia from Aragon so, pushed by Stanhope, Starhemberg took his army into Aragon. They hoped the Aragonese would rise and that this together with the Allied incursion would draw their enemy after them. It was at this time reckoned that Charles' force in the field consisted of thirty battalions and forty-three squadrons, compared with Philip's of forty battalions and sixty squadrons. When the Allies entered Aragon, camping at Portella on the far bank of the Noguera, they found that there was no rising of Aragonese, and Stanhope formed the considered view that 'the Castillians in general, and this army more particularly, are so riveted in the Duke of Anjou's interests that nóthing but force can dispossess him'. There had been few deserters, and of those few hardly any were Spaniards.

So far from following Starhemberg, moreover, Villadarías had invaded Catalonia, pushing parties towards Calaf and Cervera, two fortified towns at the eastern end of the plain lying outside the spur of hills which protects Barcelona. They tried to take the citadel of Calaf but met a hot reception which drove them off. They intercepted convoys occasionally and caused some alarm, but it was a futile exercise since within a matter of three weeks they ran out of supplies. All Villadarías had done in effect was to cause Stanhope and Starhemberg to call off their equally ineffective foray into Aragon and retire to Balaguer, there to await the ten battalions of infantry and ten squadrons of reinforcements – mainly German – that they had been promised and which arrived eventually on 26th July.

After thus fatuously each invading the other's territory the two elderly generals, one German and one Spanish, sat immobile for a month, glaring ineffectively at each other while the weather for a spring campaign waxed. Each had destroyed his own provisions in order to deny them to his enemy and both now paid the price.'Incapable', in San Felipe's words, 'of a large operation, both were eaten up by a slow war. The troops of King Charles could not leave their trenches and those of King Philip could not force them.'

This did not at all suit Stanhope, who now spent his time remonstrating with Charles and Starhemberg for their timid policy of sitting tight when with newly arriving reinforcements they were at least equal in number to their enemy. There was desultory talk of sending Norris with his squadron and some troops to Valencia but this was changed in favour of a minor amphibious raid on the Riviera coast with the object of linking up with the *Camisards* and opening an internal wound in the south of France. This proposal seems to have been used by Charles and Starhemberg as a satisfactory excuse for inaction. The raiders spent only four nights ashore from 24th to 29th July. Their efforts, however, as Boyer and others pointed out, were of considerable strategic value for they hindered de Noailles from joining Philip near Gerona with forces that might have tipped the balance, and permitted Charles to receive his reinforcements, 'which made way for two victories thereafter'.[3]

★   ★   ★

On the afternoon of 27th July there may have occurred the last example in European history, as far as is known, of a feat of arms which the Romans described as *Spolia Opima*, the personal killing by a general in single combat of his opposing commander. To this day the name of the general killed is not known with certainty. He was a Spanish cavalry commander whom some identify as Octavio de Medicis, Duque de Sarno, and some as Don Antonio de Amezaga. Although it is well attested that the slayer was General Stanhope he does not mention it himself either in his dispatch or his letters.

He had for weeks been arguing, hectoring and pushing Charles and Starhemberg into activity and, notably on this July evening, he forced and shamed them by personal example into doing battle. The site of the battle was Almenara, now spelled Almenar, then a small village some twenty miles west of the Allied headquarters between Balaguer on the Segre and Agramont, and about five miles south of Alfaraz where there was a bridge over the River Noguera.[4] King Philip's force was based at Lérida about fifteen miles from Almenara to the south-east. Philip's army could have got either to Alfaraz or to Almenara more quickly since its route would have been along the chord of a part circle, while the Allies had to move along the circumference. The capture of the bridge at Alfaraz was the key, and the presence of Stanhope on that day was of pivotal importance, since he supplied the drive which was otherwise lacking on both the Allied and the Bourbon sides. It was this that enabled the Allies to win the race for Alfaraz.

By noon on the 26th Stanhope's cavalry had a deep bridgehead across the River Noguera, when the enemy cavalry came up. Stanhope wanted to attack before the Bourbon infantry, which was a long way behind, arrived in force. But

Charles and Starhemberg 'seeming still determined not to hazard anything', prevented this. Stanhope fretted and fumed while the enemy cavalry formed up. He pressed the marshal several times more to permit an attack on the 4,200 horseman now drawn up by de Sarno in double line on the high ground facing him but as yet unsuported by infantry. His swift advance had given him a great advantage, and timing matters in battle. But still Charles and Starhemberg demurred. Boyer quotes a letter from the Savoyard envoy (who was there) dated 30th July: 'Mr Stanhope propos'd to push them. But Marshal Starhemberg did not presently come to it, judging that measures ought to be taken to sustain well the work begun.'

Stanhope's field of manoeuvre was narrow – as he later reported – and with the 14 squadrons which Starhemberg shortly sent to join him the cavalry wings had to be bent back at their outer ends. In the first line were Carpenter on the left with six squadrons of Harvey's, Rochford's and Nassau's; in the centre Belcastel with four Dutch; on the right Frankenburg and Pepper with ten squadrons. The second line was composed of 10 German and Dutch squadrons, so that altogether 2,600 Allied horsemen faced over 4,200. Behind the Allied cavalry were the infantry.

It was by now six in the evening, when in Stanhope's words:

'The enemies having gott up all their horse marched several squadrons down a little hill which was between us, upon which we all cried out 'Shame!' and I did earnestly press the King that we might have leave to dislodge them.'

One can picture him, his swarthy, eager face going crimson with anger and frustration as he shouted and argued with Charles and Starhemberg. His chaplain, Lenoir, says that he said loudly that if they let slip this opportunity he and his Dutch colleagues had orders to withdraw their troops – orders which he would instantly obey and leave the country. The delays and indecision, coupled with the men's burning wish for revenge for Almansa, raised feelings to a fever pitch.

It was seven o'clock, nearly sunset, 'when the army were still at a shilly-shally' (Stanhope's words) before Charles belatedly

'took a resolve to attack the enemy immediately because it was seven and he supposed they would take advantage of the night to remove to a stronger camp and retire and because he saw they were discouraged by reason of their ill situation.'

According to Tindal Count Atalaya gallopped to Stanhope from the king, 'to inform him that he complied with his desire and advice, but wanted to know, Who was to command?' 'Who but myself,' answered the general. With the sun 'not above half an hour high', Stanhope put himself at the head of the first squadron of Harvey's horse.

His 'very short speech' was noted: 'Keep close and do not break yourselves, the only danger. For I am sure you will be as firm as rocks and all the enemy squadrons will not be able to break you.' At his first approach, he found the enemy lines too strong. But 'The enemies', by his own account

'were so good as to give us the time we wanted; we brought up six squadrons and put our line in good order, which [now] consisted of sixteen in all . . . So soon as ever we were thus formed we attacked them and by the blessing of God broke their two lines.'

Villadarías took Philip on retreat to the shelter of Lérida, where they arrived at midnight. Stanhope did not claim *Spolia Opima*. His despatch commends everyone but himself. But there is the immediate report from the envoy of Savoy, written a day before even Stanhope's despatch:

'Mr Stanhope fought at the head of one of Harvey's squadrons and had a personal encounter with an officer of the enemy's and who by divers tokens is judg'd to have been Lieutenant-General Amenzaga [sic] reckon'd among the slain.'

The account in Mahon's history cannot be altogether dismissed, since Mahon went throughly through his ancestor's papers at Chevening. Here is what Mahon says:

'They [Spanish cavalry] were headed by General Amezaga and comprised the flower of the Spanish Army, more especially the royal guards. Finding their number so large, and the ground wider than that from which he had set out, the English general after ascending the hill, halted for a few minutes to bring up six squadrons from the seond line . . . As soon as these were formed the order to charge was given and most gallantly obeyed. In the onset, Stanhope's and Amezaga's horses closed and the two generals engaged in single conflict; an event not often seen in any age, but almost without parallel in modern times. Stanhope killed the Spaniard with a stroke of his sword; and the troops, animated by this example, fought with spirit as well as steadiness and soon retrieved by their united valour a first repulse of the German cavalry, pushed the first line of the enemy upon the second and at length completely routed them. Great bravery however was shown on both sides.'

The tradition of this case of *Spolia Opima* is very persistent, although Parnell, who for reasons of his own disapproved of Stanhope and could of course point to the confusion over the names of the slain, refused to believe it since the official reports – including that of Colonel Crofts who carried the dispatch home – made no reference to it. The London newspaper *Postman* of 22nd August, presumably using a verbal eye-witness report describes Stanhope and the Spanish commanders as having exchanged several cuts. Stanhope did not himself return to England until 1712. The medal presented to him in commemoration of the battle depicted a single combat on horseback. The medal was still preserved at Chevening when the last of the Stanhope line died in 1972. If the story of the encounter is true, its victim is perhaps more likely to have been de Sarno, the only cavalry general officially listed as killed.

The fall of darkness saved Philip and frustrated Stanhope. There was much recrimination on the Bourbon side. Although Villadarías had with Vallejo the rearguard commander, bravely fought off the pursuit and saved Philip from capture or worse – for he had been by no means the first to flee – it was generally considered that the old Spaniard and the Walloon Tzerclaes must bear the blame for the defeat. Villadarías was ordered to be dismissed, and sent back to Andalucia. De Bay was sent for from Extremadura to replace him. In letter after letter there are complaints about the Spanish generalship as a whole. De Bourk: 'Even the strongest partisan of Spanish generals says they are not fit to command and everybody, including the soldiers, say a *good* General is needed. Mahony: 'If King Philip is to succeed he *must* have a [good] general and minister, and these do not exist in Spain. The army is asking out loud for Vendôme or Berwick or somebody who can lead.'

★   ★   ★

On 12th August, when they had eaten all the grain they could obtain from the Lérida garrison and no further subsistence was available, Philip ordered his army to march to Saragossa, 100 miles to the west.[5] The next day, Stanhope 'saw the enemy plant their camp near Fraga on the other side of the river Cinca, which it was resolved we should pass that evening to attack them the next morning. But they marched all night towards Saragossa, so that instead of fighting we were put to a long, tedious march after them.'

The pursuit followed a thirsty road to the river Ebro. At Candasmos the Allies 'were in danger of perishing of thirst.' From Bujaralos,

'to incommode us the more the enemy had set fire to a very long heath we were to pass over. It is not to be conceived what we suffered upon such a march, smothered all that day with clouds of ashes, especially the foot.'

At Fraga, the two forces were within sound of each other's drums. Between there and Villafranca the Bourbon army, according to O'Mahony, 'had no bread or water.' Beside the Barranco de los Muertos – the Ravine of the Dead, tired and feverish, Philip hurriedly ordered his thirsty, exhausted army to camp as the merciless August afternoon sun crawled slowly through the sky above them.

Saragossa (more properly Zaragoza and named after Caesar Augustus) is a University city and a major religious centre devoted to the *Virgen del Pilar*. It was built of brown brick on the right (south) bank of the Ebro just above where two tributaries from the south (the Huerva) and the north (the Gallego) join it. The latter creeps through marshy ground on its way. The city is nowadays the centre of a huge and fertile basin. Even then it was militarily weak, being neither well-sited nor properly walled. Philip's chosen camp site on 19th August 1710 was such that if the Allies, coming up swiftly, reached the city he would have had no line of retreat. Starhemberg and Stanhope indeed had their camp about four miles off, with their left on the town of Pina. They were, however, on the other side of the river Ebro.

Mahoni considered the camp site dangerous.

'I told King Philip that for fear of losing time he would inevitably lose the army ... And his Sacred Person would be exposed to great peril ... This was so obvious that M. de Bay [who had joined Philip] at once gave orders and we marched at 11.00 at night, passed by the bridge and ford of the Gallijo [Gallego] and camped in the fork between the Ebro and that river. There was never a tougher march, to be true, or our men more tired. Both men and horses were being destroyed by the excessive heat and lack of victuals and forage.'

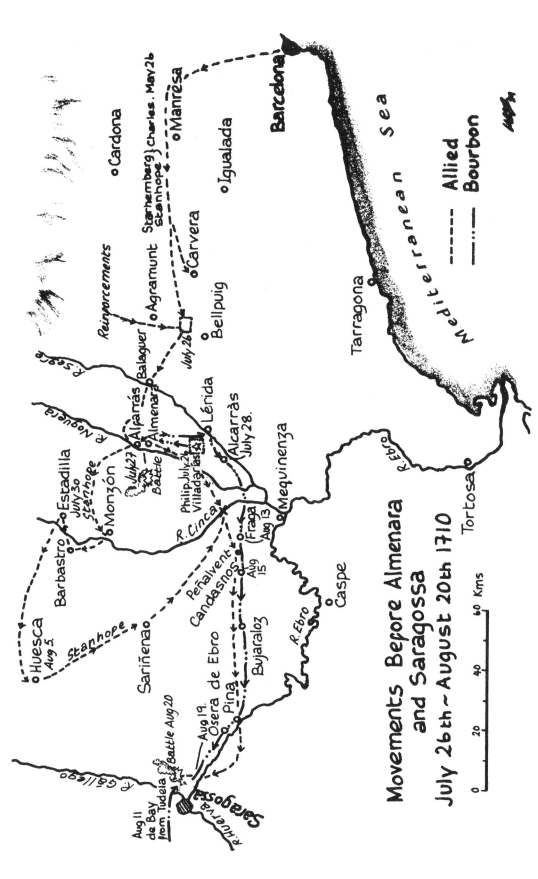

Movements Before Almenara
and Saragossa
July 26th ~ August 20th 1710

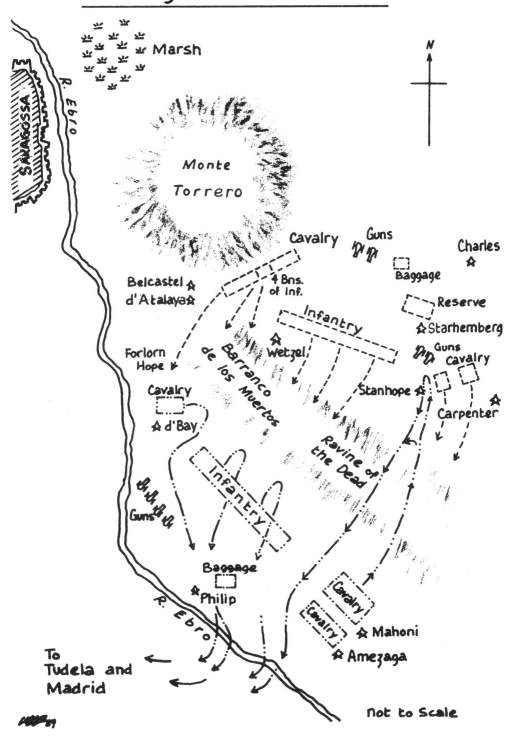

Battle of Saragossa
August 20th 1710

N

Marsh

SARAGOSSA

R. Ebro

Monte Torrero

Cavalry   Guns

Charles

Baggage

Belcastel
d'Atalaya

4 Bns.
of Inf.

Reserve

Starhemberg

Infantry

Forlorn
Hope

Barranco de los Muertos

Wetzel

Guns
Cavalry

Cavalry

Stanhope

Carpenter

d'Bay

Ravine of
the Dead

Guns

Infantry

Baggage

Philip

Cavalry

Cavalry

Mahoni

Amezaga

R. Ebro

To
Tudela and
Madrid

not to Scale

Both armies were exhausted, thirsty and hungry. Philip did not want a battle. Nor did Charles and Starhemberg, who considered that the fight would destroy the advantage gained at Almenara and that it was better to depend on the people of Saragossa or the chance of a favourable accident. But now once more Stanhope intervened, extracting permission from the elderly Palatine marshal to send Major-General Carpenter with 2,000 horse across a ford of the Ebro; he accompanied, 'as a volunteer', until so close to the enemy that Charles and Starhemberg would be forced to follow him. Carpenter later said that Stanhope's march had been contrary to orders. At all events the whole army was expected to follow, crossing by pontoon. So, at last the main body of the army reached the same side of the Ebro as their enemy.

> 'On August 19th at 6 p.m. His Catholic Majesty [Charles] drew up the army in order of battel within cannon shott of the enemy. Marshal Starhemberg and the rest of the generals went to see their [enemy's] dis-position. They rested with the Ebro on their left and the town in the rear, with their right wing of horse on the brow of a steep hill with a battery of eight pieces of cannon in their front.'

Both sides spent the night in order of battle. The two armies facing each other were not greatly different in size. After Almenara the Allies thought themselves smaller – with 13,600 Germans, 4,500 English, 3,300 Spanish, 1,300 Dutch and 1,300 Portuguese – about 23,000 in 37 battalions and 43 squadrons. Philip's was about 25,000, (thus slightly stronger in cavalry). It is more than probable that the Spanish army was as usual short of food. It is certain that the Allies, 'lying all that night at their horses' heads in readiness' among the olive groves and vineyards, went to battle fasting next morning, for the bread convoys failed to turn up. 'We lost many men this morning, who, prest by hunger and thirst, ventured to go and gather grapes in the vale between the two armies and were shot by the enemy's advanced guard.'

When the sun rose at six o'clock

> 'both armies play'd their cannon and General Stanhope who commanded our left wing found the enemy had march'd most of their horse from their left to their right wing. He obtained from the Marshal four battalions of foot which he placed at the left of our horse, and six squadrons of Portu-guese horse from our right beyond the four battalions, in order to stretch our left wing as far as possible towards the extent of their right. It is to be observed that the enemy lay in an oblique line from the Ebro up to the Hill.

So their troops on the Hill lay much nearer to us than those on the descent from it and on the plain.'

The beginning of the engagement was signified by 'the firing of two royal grenades', at 11 o'clock according to the *Paris Gazetteer* (whose reporter was not present) but 'at Noon', according to Stanhope's despatch.

'Our whole army, being drawn up in two lines, marched at once to attack the enemy in full front, except the four battalions interlined with the Horse, which were sent to advance and take post on the brow of the hill to give time for the wing of horse to form. Our left wing, from their situation coming first to the enemy began the battle which increased towards the centre and so towards the right till the whole was engaged. At first the enemy, with superiority of numbers and advantage of post, seemed to have the better of the day which they probably would have maintained if all our generals commanding on the left had not seasonably sent on fresh troops to support such as they saw push'd or disorder'd.'

Partly because of position, partly because of the temperaments of the commanders who were heavily engaged on either side – and of the degree of discipline they were able to impose on their men – the Allied right wing and centre were less harassed than its left and Starhemberg, Belcastel and Wetzel retained the advantage. It was far otherwise where Stanhope and Carpenter were involved on one side and O'Mahony and Don Joseph de Amezaga (not to be confused with Don Antonio, Stanhope's putative victim at Almenara) on the other. They were stronger than Stanhope, as the latter found when he came up against them. There is some disagreement as to who actually charged first. O'Mahony thinks it was he. Stanhope is equally convinced that it was himself, but this happens all too easily in moments of high tension such as this. At all events two of Stanhope's squadrons gave way under heavy fire and had to be re-formed, and the Portuguese horse on the Allied left was temporily driven back until Carpenter was squeezed on to his second line. While Carpenter fought it out with Amezaga, O'Mahony observed that 'two thirds of the Spanish cavalry of the right was pursuing the enemy left in a lively fashion'.

'I did my best to hold them in and would have succeeded if they had had more discipline and less ardour, but all my orders were useless. They pursued without hesitating the troops they had first broken and would not even stop at batteries of guns which I had taken. After killing the gunners they cut the hocks of the mules.'

Far too advanced, as he knew, he had lost contact with Amezaga while his men set about the baggage and reserves and approached close to a Carthusian convent in the rear where Charles had spent the night and was, perhaps, still closeted. Stanhope meantime, with fresh squadrons called up and those defeated earlier re-formed, was now trouncing Amezaga.

O'Mahony after a struggle with his impetuous men managed gradually at last to get them in hand and moving towards the main battle, where he was in time to see Philip's centre and right melting away. In the centre the Spanish infantry had mostly fought well. They had crossed the Barranco de los Muertos but here they were met with highly disciplined fire from Wetzel's Germans, and 'although they made a longer defence which lasted two hours', they were beaten 'with such slaughter of their men that the field of battle was covered with the dead'. The Allied infantry pushed through what remained of the Spanish centre and right up to the city walls.

Starhemberg, once committed, was giving of his professional best. Not only was he supervising his infantry but he displayed a cool grasp of the overall situation. When he was told that Stanhope had defeated the enemy's right but that O'Mahony's squadrons were in the rear and falling upon the batteries, 'That is no great matter', said the marshal, 'if General Stanhope has beat the right we are sure of a compleat victory'.

The official English dispatch to London is quietly triumphant.

'We took all the cannon, and most of the colours, so that out of forty battalions not above 4,000 escaped and of sixty squadrons the same proportions. His Majesty [Charles] entered Saragossa that night, being received with the acclamation of the people and all imaginable expressions of joy. The citadel capitulated and the garrison were made prisoners.'

Starhemberg, coming up to Charles said, 'We have won the battle and the Monarchy.' Stanhope's final summing-up, repeated to several correspondents later, probably represents the feelings of many of his compatriots, like those who had turned up under the walls of Almenara: 'It was a day to retrieve Almansa.'

Philip and de Bay did not stop until they reached Tudela, forty-five miles from Saragossa. The Allies considered that their enemy's losses had been 12,000. The Spaniards officially record 3,000 killed and wounded and 5–6,000 prisoners, including 400 officers. Their figures for material lost are 'seventy-two colours, twenty-two cannon and much baggage.' Only some 7,000 men appear to have reached Tudela with their leaders, but Starhemberg's comment to Charles on the evening after the battle was over-optimistic, for just as Galway after Almansa had managed to re-form his troops as they came in, so de Bay now began the same agonising but necessary process. The Allies were still far from winning, for while they basked in their success and permitted themselves in their over-confidence their normal futile disagreements, the very gravity of the situation would make Philip draw on hidden reserves of fortitude and enable him to obtain critical and effective help from his grandfather. In just over three months, the situation would be totally reversed.

★   ★   ★

On 24th August accompanied by a very modest-sized guard, Philip reached Madrid to find the court and population in appalling disarray. It was even being said that Madame des Ursins, with the approval of King Louis, had persuaded him to make peace, leave Spain, and accept some sort of kingdom in Italy. This may have been what she was herself putting about, but María Luisa would certainly have disagreed and the king himself does not appear to have entertained any such idea. On 24th and 25th August he gave orders for money and provisions to be found somehow and sent to Aragon for the troops there and for 5,000 reinforcements to be called up from Extremadura. He was certain that although Aragon lay open to the Allies and they were in Saragossa itself, those cities and towns he still held there, in Valencia and parts of Catalonia would remain loyal and that his governors in those places would hold out for him.

He had previously asked Louis for Berwick or Vendôme to come to Spain and undertake what he could not rely on his Spanish generals to do properly, but so far he had been refused. Now he wrote again, asking also that de Noailles should be given troops so as to carry out his longed-for wish to invade Catalonia from Roussillon and cause a diversion. Berwick's reputation still stood high and if Louis had ordered him he would have gone back to a place he disliked, to do what looked like the impossible. But as the marshal himself records, 'the king would not withdraw me from the command of the frontier of Italy.' So Berwick was not to go to Philip's aid, and it would appear that Philip had anticipated this, for

'A council [in Paris] resolved that the Duc de Vendôme, on whom King Philip had already bestowed the command of his forces should set out immediately for Navarre to be at the head of the troops who are to be reinforced with detachments from the several parts of France.'

This decision appears to have been taken on 19th August even before Saragossa. St Simon notes that Vendôme was laid up with gout on August 19th and that Torcy and Voisin visited him; that he went to Louis's court and had a long audience of the king in his private chambers, taking his leave after dinner and riding to Sceaux, whence he left for Spain. Even with the gout he could be swift when he wanted to be.

Philip meantime had other decisions to make, moving the queen and the seat of government out of danger, galvanising grandee support for the renewed liaison with France. He established his headquarters at Valladolid and packed the queen off to Vitoria.

Vendôme received news of the Battle of Saragossa while he was at Bayonne. Here he was joined by de Noailles, under orders to probe the precise situation in which Philip now stood. Was the grandees' adhesion to France sincere? Would Philip really be able to extract himself? The young king was always the subject of gossip in Paris, often malicious and designed to diminish him in the eyes of his cynical old grandparent. Indeed, just at this time St Simon reports the ready acceptance at court of Allied propaganda to the effect that whereas Charles had been directly involved with his army in Saragossa, Philip 'had distanced himself from the battle'. In his saddlebags de Noailles carried a memorandum, prepared by Torcy, proposing that Philip should abdicate. He met a point-blank refusal, returned to see Louis at Marly on 14th October and, after reporting on this tricky confrontation, was sent south-east once more to Dauphiné. It had been just one more heartless but understandable gambit on Louis' part, and it had failed. By the time de Noailles reached Valladolid for a second time, Philip was feeling himself to be in a stronger position. He had 12 to 13,000 men, now well paid and armed, and with de Noailles had come Vendôme to weld them into a fighting machine.[6]

Louis-Joseph, Duc de Vendôme was coarse, unattractive, but on his day undeniably able. Among other offensive habits, St Simon dilates upon his holding morning meetings of his staff while seated on his close-stool. Unliked because unlikeable, he nevertheless represented hope for Philip. Sometimes called a Titan because of his size, he was now fifty-six, slovenly in dress and generally repulsive. He had hastened to leave France, barely saying goodbye to his new Duchess, for he was in one of his active phases, anxious to restore his reputation by military prowess in Spain. As he halted at Bayonne he had bullied the local commander, the conceited, ineffectual Marshal Marquis de Montreuil into sending troops after him. On his way through Navarre he had ordered the French fortresses to be denuded of garrisons, and bursting with energy he had reached Valladolid on 17th September. Here he continued to throw his weight about. The French reinforcements were to be sent to Aranda del Duero. De Bay, who had been reported as ill – Blécourt said it was because he was upset at being placed under Vendôme – was to return to Extremadura to confront the Portuguese. Vendôme was now exhibiting a demonic vigour and although all these moves took time to mature there was a certainty about them which must have compensated for the company of the marshal's disagreeable personality. By comparison the Allies were as Stanhope would say, at the shilly-shally.

Elation at their victories was natural, particularly after the strain of the long march from Lérida, and no doubt the inhabitants of Saragossa were being obliging, however hypocritically. But the Allies havered endlessly about what to do next. By 27th August all they had decided (at a council of war presided over by Charles) was to send detachments to Tarazona and Tudela and march the rest of the army to Calatayud, an ancient fortified Moorish town built on an arid hillside about fifty miles west of Saragossa. Biscuit was sent for from Balaguer and more was to be baked in Saragossa. And as an afterthought the generals were instructed to avoid any disorders by their troops.[7]

Five days later, at Calatayud, there was still no decision. The various opinions of those present at what were by now typical councils of war, were recorded at length. It all boiled down to deciding between marching on Madrid or into Navarre or both. Aragon and Catalonia were too short of food to be worth going to. Castile was enemy territory, but advantage could be taken of the enemy's consternation by going to Madrid at once. Some of the council wanted to divert the German squadrons at present in Catalonia to blockade Tortosa, Mequinenza, Lérida and Monzón (now once more in Bourbon hands), and to mount an expedition into Valencia, but these were or should have been secondary.

While they argued, the only decision taken was to move in the general direction of Madrid. By 13th September their slow march had brought them only to Sigüenza, some eighty miles on the 180-mile way to the capital and they were still arguing as to whether it was better to continue the march to Madrid or turn towards Navarre. At least the idea of a move on Valencia was scrapped, if only because Admiral Norris could not now be expected to keep his fleet near the Spanish coast but must return to Port Mahon.

Stanhope, by now certainly restraining his impatience with difficulty, insisted that Madrid must be occupied at once. The negotiations at Gertruyden-berg had broken down and King Louis could withdraw his offer to disown his grandson. The London government needed a further success. It was too late in the season to fight through Navarre and in any case, there were so many routes by which the French could send reinforcements that the Allies could not possibly cover them all. So, keeping a line of possible retreat towards Saragossa (where 500 English convalescents could act as rearguard), the advance continued towards Madrid. At Alcalá de Henares, on September 20th, a bare twenty miles from Madrid, the futile discussion still continued.

Atalaya, the Portuguese general, appears to have inherited some commonsense from his uncle, old das Minas. Nobody, he said, could have believed

> 'that the glorious battle before Saragossa would have had so little effect on the spirit of the Castilians. It was clear that almost everybody known for his blood, his learning or his money was following the Duke of Anjou, since none had come to Alcalá to render obedience.'

It was therefore essential to send a detachment of a thousand horse to Madrid to oblige the city to obey Charles. 'Don Diego Stanhope', armed with letters from the archduke was to lead it. Charles had opposed such a course throughout the long march but, 'remembering what had frequently passed [before] would not contradict his generals and absolutely consented to go on to Madrid'.

★   ★   ★

Philip had agreed in advance to the temporary appointment of one Antó-nio de Sanguineto as *corregidor* of Madrid in place of the Conde de Jarosa who had gone with his king to Valladolid, and empowered him to do what was needed when the Allies arrived. So on 21st September 1710 it was he who was waiting. 'The municipal authorities in the capital,' says the Imperial Relation of 24th September, 'appointed four honourable gentlemen to ride forth and in the name of the city prostrate themselves at His Majesty's feet.'[8] It was common talk that Charles had been doubtful about going on to Madrid – indeed about the whole strategy to which Stanhope's pressure had committed him. Charles had written to his queen, 'They [the English] will take all the glory of it if it is a success, and I the blame if it goes wrong.' Now, however, Stanhope set up his own quarters in La Florida, while, according to the account of a supporter of King Philip

> 'For three nights in a row the candles burned before the Blessed Sacrament, the lights in the churches were turned low and the bells muffled, for the sacristans were mortally afeared of the English heretics and, their eyes glued on the chalices, they spent their days and nights convulsed with terror.'

How did it seem, viewed from Valladolid? It had of course been realized that those who had to stay in Madrid were in for a thin time of it, but it was justly supposed that their loyalty to Philip would remain undimmed. For many of them the last memory they would have of the royal family was of the queen, her hair *à la béguine* to hide the ravages of scrofula, showing herself on the balcony of the Palace, her little son in her arms, and calling out to them 'with courage, grace and strength'. In times when the spoken word was stronger than the written, this spectacle would have been described (and embellished) to those who had not seen it by those who had, with all the greater poignancy. Philip had directed that the *madrileños* were not to indulge in activities that would bring retribution, merely to avoid helping his enemy. So, to begin with, they were sullen but no more.

While María Luisa and her son were on their way to Vitoria, Vendôme, having taken time to raise troops and review the situation, had arrived at Valladolid. He was thinking of spending the rest of his days in Spain, where his rank could be accommodated at not too great a cost. On taking leave of Louis, the latter had offered him 50,000 crowns for expenses, but he had declined, saying, 'Sire, I have found means myself for this campaign and hope not to be even of any cost to Spain.' It was probably with a view to the future that his treatment of Philip was reasonably polite. It was indeed he who, it appears, induced the grandees to sign another letter of loyalty to Philip for transmission to Louis, and he even seems to have kept his temper under control when some of them added to their signatures the words, 'noble as the king'. He merely asked one of them, 'Dare you call in question the nobility of the House of Bourbon, the oldest in Europe?' To which the Spaniard replied, 'True, but remember that after all King Philip is a Frenchman and I am a Castilian.'

Though of royal descent himself, Vendôme's family tree was relatively modest and the royal blood had been acquired on the wrong side of the blanket. He therefore seems to have suppressed his indignation, accepting more readily such manifestations of Castilian pride because they were accompanied by an inhabitual zeal in the provision to Philip of men, money, arms and supplies. The marshal was the first to appreciate and make use of this. His strategic sense told him that the real danger was that of a junction between the Allied troops in Madrid and the Portuguese coming in from the west.

He joined the army at Aranda del Duero, moved on to Esteban de Gormaz, collecting there reinforcements from Castile, Galicia and Valencia, and thence via Tordesillas to the golden city of Salamanca where he laid in stores of corn and forage before marching to Plasencia. From here, so often the focal point for frontier operations in this war, he was able on 17th October to secure the bridge over the Tagus at Almaraz, forty miles to the south, just before the Portuguese could come up, if indeed they were to do so, and thus keep the two Allied armies separate.

Stanhope had been sent from Madrid to Toledo with orders to take a party and advance along the Tagus to effect a junction – as Vendôme envisaged – with the Portuguese but, to his no doubt vividly expressed rage, there was nobody there to meet him but the enemy and he withdrew. For, left to their own devices – Portmore, the replacement for Galway, had not yet arrived – the Portuguese were lumbering towards the junction with all the sluggishness of which they were capable.

Since the battle at the River Caya in May 1709, in fact, the Portuguese military effort had dwindled disastrously. There were reasons for this, political and diplomatic as well as financial. The latter were considerable. Attempts had been made in 1707 to reform the army but these were unsuccessful since the Portuguese were dependent on the Allies for wheat and clothes. There was no barley for horses and these too were short. The Portuguese government also depended for cash on the Dutch and the British. The Dutch had paid nothing, merely reducing the figure of Portuguese debts on their books. The British had adopted a policy of payment by results, and as the results had been meagre the payments had been likewise – and late. Considerable numbers of Portuguese troops were still up in Catalonia whither das Minas and Galway had led them and their absence was resented in Lisbon.

The essential imports of corn were put in the hands of an Englishman, Arthur Stert who had been Admiralty agent in Lisbon and was a merchant of some substance. Payment was to be by delivery of 4,000 barrels of gunpowder in England which had been charged to the British subsidy and were no longer needed, but the cumbrous bureaucracy of the day meant that Stert's agents in London, Clarke and Stevenson, did not receive the money, having instead to accept tallies on the tax on wine, which were discounted at 15%. The Portuguese embassy in London complained that no corn was arriving in Portugal. Galway on the other hand said that plenty was coming in but that local agents would not pay the going price. The Portuguese government complained that much of the grain was bad on arrival, but the quality was poor because of the delays and these were caused by attempts to corner the market, supplies for the army even being intercepted and sold at a high price to the public.

Galway by now had had enough and the Portuguese, too, were exasperated with him. He had never given up trying in Portugal, for it was not in his nature to throw in the towel. Nevertheless he was a martyr to gout, often unable to hold a pen, and it was a miracle that he was well enough to board ship for home. He had known for some time from the newspapers that he was to be replaced by Portmore, but his letters of recall were delayed and it was the beginning of October when at last, under Portuguese protocol, he could take leave of King João. Meantime he had done his best to build up new regiments, although he had no hopes of more than a defensive. Stanhope should perhaps have been put on his guard earlier by a most unequivocal letter from him.

> 'All I can expect or desire is that we may make show or noise enough to hinder your enemies from sending the troops they may have on the frontier against you. One could believe from their conduct that the Portuguese court had a secret treaty with the enemy, especially when Cadaval says publicly he is sure that the Spaniards will undertake nothing against them, but I believe these people have not the ability to do such a thing and I am almost positive there is nothing in it. But with a young king who does not love affairs or understand them and yet would make people believe that it is he that manages and that he is not governed, the person that has most credit with him is the inquisitor-general, who is very hearty in the public cause but without ability or understanding; and the Duke of Cadaval, hated by everybody and very much disaffected in this way, assumes the authority and has everything done as he pleases. You may judge by this short description in what an ill posture the affairs stand here. I hope you so much my friend as to pity me, to have to do with these people, working all the time without the least hope of success.'

'Your Majesty,' Vendôme told Philip, 'has gained more by the possession of the bridge at Almara than the archduke gained by the battle of Saragossa.' Yet the Portuguese seem unlikely to have kept their rendezvous in any case. Vendôme added a prediction that was to be more than fulfilled: 'Not even fifty thousand men will enable the Allies to maintain themselves at Madrid.'

*   *   *

Movements of Armies ~ September~December 1710

Scale 1:2.500.000

Allied
Bourbon

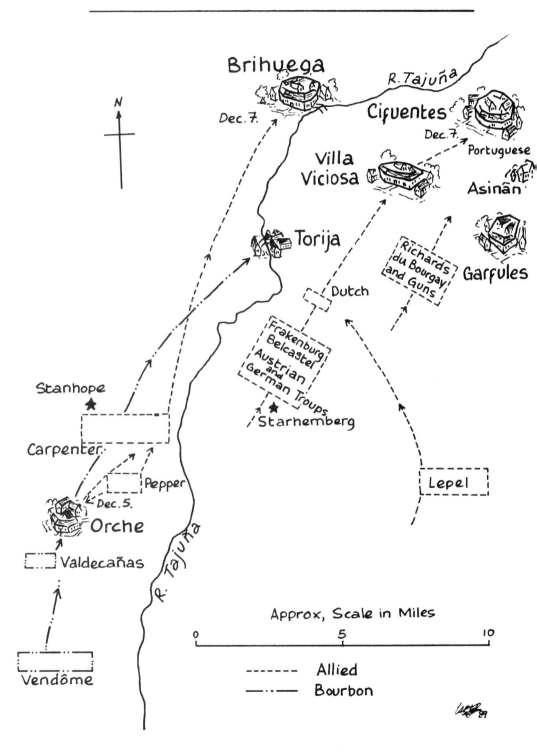

Approaches to Brihuega and Cifuentes
December 9-10th 1710

Brihuega

R. Tajuña

Cifuentes

Dec. 7.

Dec. 7.

Portuguese

N

Villa
Viciosa

Asinän

Torija

Richards
du Bourgay
and Guns

Garfules

Dutch

Frakenburg
Belcastel
Austrian
and
German Troups

Stanhope

Starhemberg

Carpenter

Pepper

Lepel

Dec. 5.

Orche

Valdecañas

R. Tajuña

Approx. Scale in Miles

0   5   10

Vendôme

- - - - - Allied
-·-·-·- Bourbon

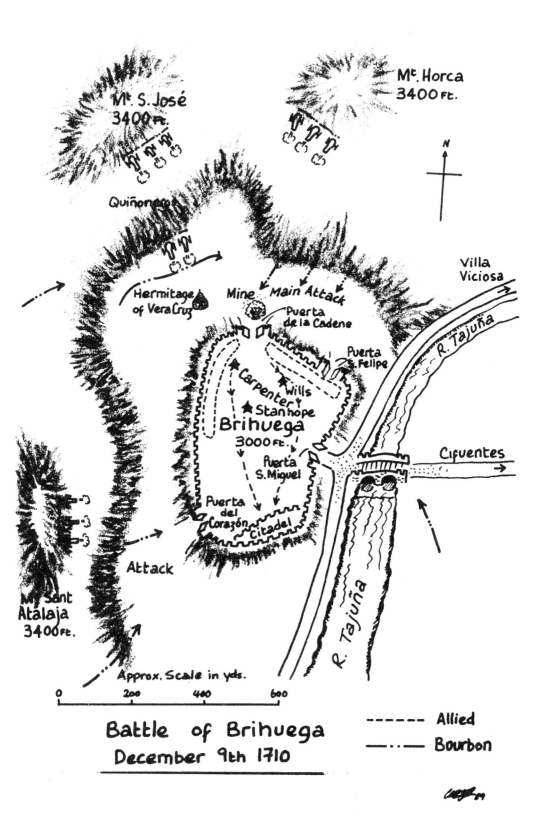

Mt. S. José
3400 ft.

Mt. Horca
3400 ft.

N

Quiñones

Hermitage
of VeraCruz

Mine   Main Attack

Puerta
de la Cadena

Villa
Viciosa

R. Tajuña

Puerta
S. Felipe

Carpenter

Wills

Stanhope

Brihuega
3000 ft.

Puerta
S. Miguel

Cifuentes

Puerta del
Corazón

Citadel

Attack

R. Tajuña

Mt Sant
Atalaja
3400 ft.

Approx. Scale in yds.

0   200   400   600

Battle of Brihuega
December 9th 1710

------ Allied
-..- Bourbon

Stanhope, the first to enter the city, had been struck by the general grief of the people on being occupied and their devotion to Philip. A few of the nobility, mostly of the lesser kind, came forward to accept Charles. These men were known to Starhemberg by the sardonic description of 'New Christians', a term formerly applied in Spain to converted Moors and Jews. Stanhope called them 'traitors', Lichtenstein 'outlaws', Perlas '*desperados*' and Charles himself 'the miserables'. Men appointed by Stanhope as magistrates in order to keep some form of order, were called traitors and said to be there only to supervise the theft from the houses of the loyal of goods handed over to the Allies. Although 40,000 crowns a month were demanded from the citizens for the upkeep of the army, it proved difficult to collect and money was as short as ever. Secretly, people who had pigs, chickens and other mobile stock removed them from the city. Bread, fish, wine and meat were scarce and vegetables not to be had at all. The wretched troops, hungry as they were, appropriated food and drink wherever it was found and scoffed it, often with ill consequences, particularly for the English. For, as the contemporary Lord Ailesbury records,

> 'Our soldiers are not good for to suffer heat and want of victuals, and besides being the most disorderly in the world, great devourers of fruit, and that could not abstain from wines when these came their way, which would fling them into fluxes and calentures [diarrhoea and fevers].'

The hospitals filled with sick whom, according to San Felipe, the local doctors took pleasure in killing off by secret means. Stabbed or knocked on the head in dark alleys, unwelcome in a far-off land, it is no wonder that the morale of the Allied troops, raised high by Almenara and Saragossa, rapidly crumbled.

There was now moreover no promise of help from Portugal. Stanhope sent express after express to Lisbon, but Portmore had still not arrived to replace Galway. Another battle would have been welcome, 'which would in all probability have been decisive' had the Portuguese come. 'If they do not,' Stanhope said grimly, 'we shall have some difficulty in making a retreat into Aragon.' The surrounding hostility, exacerbated by guerrilla attacks and the insecurity bred by sparse and false intelligence were undermining even his élan.

If Charles' advisers were unhappy about being in Madrid they do not seem to have known what to do about it. All through October Charles, Starhemberg and Lichtenstein refused to leave the capital, insisting stubbornly that it would look like a retreat, that they would risk harassment by Philip's cavalry, that resources were so short that hospitals could not be provided and the sick and wounded would have to be abandoned. Starhemberg is said to have told Charles, 'Let us leave what we cannot destroy,' and the army marched on 7th November to Cienpozuelos, then a village some twenty miles to the south; falling back on Toledo. According to San Felipe, the moment the last Allied soldiers had marched out, King Philip was acclaimed in absence by the population with such demonstrations of fervour that Charles could have heard them from his marching station in the midst of his army. A few days later, the archduke rode for Barcelona with an escort of 2,000 horses.

★   ★   ★

Starhemberg had endeavoured to make Vendôme think that he was proposing to winter in the Toledo region. When it became obvious that his deception was not succeeding, and in order to spread the demand for virtually non-existent forage and food as widely as possible, he ordered the army to advance in three columns by nationalities, and to make for three separate cantonments in the region of Cifuentes. They were under appalling pressure. 'The country people of Castile had taken up arms to fall upon our troops and plunder our baggage, which we prevented on all sides with the greatest care imaginable.'

Starhemberg himself led the centre column, consisting of Austrian and German troops together with the Dutch as a vanguard towards Cifuentes itself, some sixty miles from Guadalajara. The Austro-German and Dutch troops were under the immediate command respectively of Generals Frankenburg and Belcastel, and Atalaya with his few Portuguese was sent in the right-hand column towards Asiñan, to the east of Cifuentes. Control seems in particular to have been lax over Stanhope and his English column. It is probable that Starhemberg had by now decided that life would be easier if he let his dashing young English subordinate have his way. According to his later report, 'The English troops in this late season, believing that they would find provisions in Brihuega and subsist better there, took that road.' So Stanhope, the Lieutenant-Generals Carpenter and Wills, and Brigadiers Pepper and Gore and all the English troops, took the left-hand and rearguard position. Starhemberg had pointed out that this might well mean that they might be uncomfortably close to the enemy, but the Allies believed that Vendôme could not possibly close in so soon on them along the appalling Spanish roads from 160 miles away in Talavera and Casa Tejada where they had last been heard of. About 5,000 weary, disillusioned Englishmen, and at most a few hundred Portuguese, marched along the River Tajuña towards Brihuega, about twelve miles west of Cifuentes. Thanks to the roughness of the country this short separation was a good five hours' march in late 1710.

During skirmishes on 5th December, the English outposts under Pepper located Vendôme's army perilously close, its skirmishers already at Orche. An anonymous Royal Dragoon has left a lively account:

'The enemy Squadroones began to advance up to us, we being but four squadroones of Dragoons . . . ahead of the foot by reason of the speed of our advance. But Brigadier Pepper said: 'Gentlemen, I brought you on and I will carry you off', which we thought was more than hee could doe fur we *coulde see their whole army in motion* [my italics]. But our commander says to us: 'Gentlemen, to the right about and march as slow as your horses can goe. But our four squadroones we made eight and these did [each] engage one of the enemie. But our Captaine that commanded the squadroone turned taile. Peper [sic] seeing he was at the head of the squadroone that I was in, he clapt spurs to his [horse] and rode up to the Captaine and said unto him: 'D—n you, Sir, doe [ye] run?' Says he to Pepper: 'No, Sir, my men will not stand.' Pepper says to him: 'You are a lyer, Sir'. Then Pepper headed that Squadroone himself and beat the squadroone of the enemie and turned to us againe. So we kept on marching very slowly and every litel wile faceing abought to the enemie.

Slowly the four squadrons rejoined the main body now nearing Brihuega. According to Pepper's later self-defence, his warnings to Stanhope were brushed aside. It is a pleasant self-indulgence to imagine the conversation when they met up that evening:

Stanhope *(impatiently)*:   Yes, Mr. Pepper, what is it?
Pepper: I have just had a skirmishing with a large body of enemy horse at Orche.
Stanhope: Ah! Vallejo, no doubt, or Bracamonte. They have been snapping at our heels these past days.
Pepper: No General. 'Twas their whole army in motion.
Stanhope: That cannot be. Our intelligence two days since noted them at Talavera, forty-five long leagues away. No army, surely no *Spanish* army, could ever cover that distance in a se'nnight, let alone two days.

Pepper: But, Sir . . .

Stanhope: Mr. Pepper, be about your business as I must about mine. (*Turning to a commisary*): You there, Sir, we must find corn, and let us hope there is a decent bakery in yonder God-forsaken village.

Well, it could have happened. Brihuega was not much of a place, and to Stanhope arriving at eleven on a dark winter's night it must have seemed worse than it was, though there was a bakery at least. In 1710 it had about 1,000 houses (it has a few more now) and was surrounded by an old Moorish wall of limestone, mud and gravel. It is about 3,000 feet up on the Alcarria Plateau, which is riven by deep clefts through one of which runs the River Tajuña. Viewed from the south the town rises steeply from the river up an escarpment surmounted by a Moorish citadel, crumbling, like the wall, and although sheer above the river, of little defensive value. Of the wall itself, Stanhope said, '[It] is nowhere flanked and in very few places broad enough to put men on it'. Since it was late at night it is probable that he did not observe that Brihuega is closely overlooked by a number of hills some 400 to 500 feet high, the most prominent being the Horca and the Cerro de San José to the north. These, since the introduction of cannon to warfare, had made the town of little defensive value. There are four gates to it, the Puerta San Miguel on the south-east corner, the San Felipe and Cadena on the north side and the Corazon on the west. From the San Miguel gate a road leads down to a bridge and in those days a ford 'two gunshot' (about 500 yards) from the town, across the Tajuña in its narrow gorge.[9]

Sunday 7th December would have brought a depressing awakening had the Allies known what was to befall. But there were corn and other supplies in limited amounts at Brihuega and so Stanhope, believing that he was only menaced by irregulars, sent word to Starhemberg that he would spend the day there, baking bread, before joining the marshal. That morning he sent a detachment to secure the bridge and the ford, only to find it occupied by Spaniards. He still thought these were irregulars under Vallejo who could, when he marched, be driven off. The latter had after the skirmish reached Torija, nine miles from Brihuega the evening before, where a peasant told him of Stanhope's position, whereupon he marched to join up with Bracamonte and together they occupied the bridge. They also cut Stanhope's communications with Starhemberg when Vallejo captured the small cavalry force which formed the link.

Pepper claimed that he wished to place outposts around the town and perform a reconnaissance but was forbidden by Carpenter, acting on Stanhope's orders. Afterwards Stanhope was widely censured for not having taken these precautions. Yet in hostile country he could not risk outposts who would have been easily cut down or captured. And he had not sufficient numbers for a reconnaissance in force. His essential error was to miscalculate the speed of Vendôme's march.

On Sunday 7th December, in Stanhope's words,

'At about eleven of the clock before noon, there appeared some horse upon the hills near the town ... About three in the afternoon they began to show some foot, till which time nobody with me, nor I believe did the Mareschal, imagine that they had any foot within some days' march of us ... Such was the disposition of the country, so favourable to them, so averse to us, that during the eight days they marched [having left Talavera on the 1st], no advice came to us of it; in short by five o'clock [on Monday December 8th] we were surrounded by 6,000 horse and 3,000 foot.'

The rest of the Spanish army came up during the night bringing the total to 'thirty-two battalions, 8,000 cavalry and thirty-two pieces of cannon, some whereof were twenty-four pounds'.

This meant that Stanhope's opponents were about five times his number. He had no artillery and very little musket ammunition – so little that his men 'could not molest' the Spaniards. 'This made it impracticable for us to think of retiring, so we made the best dispositions we could to defend ourselves, and sent the Mareschal an account of what passed.'

Starhemberg did not get Stanhope's message till eleven that night, for his messenger had to sneak and dodge his way through enemy lines. The marshal's habitual slowness was exacerbated, in rumour, by envy, and, in reality, by the tardiness of his artillery. By the evening of Tuesday, the 9th, Stanhope still had no news of him. He was penned in the citadel of Brihuega, having contested every step in the narrow streets. Only about 700 rounds of ammunition were left; about 2,000 of the enemy were in the town, which was in flames. 'I thought myself obliged in conscience,' wrote Stanhope, 'to try to save so many brave men who had done good service to the queen and will, I hope, live to do so again. So about seven of the clock I beat the chamade.' He offered to surrender at discretion but Vendôme, having heard Starhemberg's signal guns, had no intention of letting such a band of tough fighters be anywhere in the area when Starhemberg came up. He therefore insisted on a stern though honourable capitulation. The garrison was to come out on 10th December; officers and men would bring out all their baggage without search; Vendôme would allow officers and men of each regiment to remain together; they could all march direct to places near the sea where exchange could be made and at a maximum of three leagues (nine miles) a day; they would be protected from insult and given bread. Wounded and sick, left at Brihuega, would be fed and cared for. Unfortunately few of these promises, hastily made, were kept.

Stanhope in his dispatch writes of 600 killed and wounded as compared with 1,500 lost by the enemy. San Felipe puts the Spanish figure at 2,000. By chance, the battle, thus begun on the Feast of the Immaculate Conception of the Virgin (December 8th) finished on that of Santa Leocadia. As she was the patron saint of Toledo the Spaniards, despite their losses regarded Brihuega as a fitting revenge. 'Providence,' said San Felipe, 'does not take chances and Divine Justice never forgets.' For Stanhope, it was the end of his military career and the start of a long period of calumny.

Starhemberg, however, was about to show how his stubborn, defensive qualities could foil even a capable opponent who outnumbered him by nearly two-to-one.[10] His report of the events of 10th December opens with a certain understandable undercurrent of nervousness:

'We arrived as night was coming on within a league of the town [Brihuega] and I instantly ordered some cannon to be fired ... We found the enemy drawn up in order of Battle ... I thought I ought not to abandon so considerable a body of men [the English in Brihuega, whose surrender was as yet unconfirmed] which was the reason that obliged me to hazard a battle though the enemy army was much superior to mine, especially in horse, besides that the ground was less advantageous for us than for the enemy, we being in a plain and under great difficulties to form ourselves in a place which was open on all sides...'

It was about three in the afternoon and there were only two hours of daylight left, when 'The enemy', Starhemberg continues,

'began their attack in good order and with great vigour and having flanked our right wing in some places which however we recovered immediately. But our left being entirely routed, the enemy attacked us in the rear... The horse of the [Allied] left wing went off quite on the first shock of the enemy together with seven battalions so that I found myself reduced to fight with twenty battalions and sixteen squadrons, which was one to three.'

Luckily for Starhemberg, the attraction of loot again proved too strong for the Spanish cavalry. Not only had they come upon his artillery train and most of his baggage (in the rear) but

'they met with another great booty. Many persons of quality and distinction (chiefly ladies and ecclesiastics), having left Madrid to follow Charles
to Saragossa or Barcelona, fell into their hand with a great number of
coaches and all the riches they could bring away. Unfortunately for them
they came into the field of battle, which was on the high road just before
the action began and could not proceed for fear of falling into the hands of
the partisan Vallejo. The enemy's right wing being thus employed [in
looting] the Marshal fought the left with great slaughter and success till
night when both horse and foot retired in disorder.'

O'Mahony confirms this: 'I returned to find our left not so happy, having retired two leagues.'

Despite the debâcles on the wings, the battle still raged in the centre. The Allied cavalry broke the first line of their opponents, a large number of whom turned tail and fled. De Aguilar coming up from Vendôme's left wing began to recover the situation but was held off by Starhemberg. He, like Villaroël, formed the men into a 'hedgehog' and thus kept control while night fell.

Up to now the Spaniards had lost about 4,000 killed and wounded (not 6,000 as Starhemberg said) and the Allies slightly fewer, though they had also lost what counted for much from the point of view of morale: colours and standards. Moreover they had now no mules and could drag away neither their own recaptured cannon nor what they had taken from their enemy, so they had to break up gun-carriages and burn the wheels and spike the weapons. Their baggage had also to be left. Vendôme in a well-reported *coup de théatre*, sent for the standards taken from the Allies, spread them on the ground, and said, 'Your Majesty shall have the most glorious bed that ever monarch slept in.' But it was Starhemberg who had marginally had the better of the fight and even the usually hostile San Felipe says of him,

'Never did a general of any army show more presence of mind in such a
bloody action . . . only the courage and skill of Starhemberg kept order and
carried out a fighting retreat.'

For retreat it must now be since he had no supplies and no transport. Indeed at a council of war that night of the 10th all his weary generals except Villaroël advised surrender. Starhemberg insisted on waiting for daylight for he was sure he had won time for an orderly retreat. At break of day he was able to confirm this and began to retire towards Aragon, albeit O'Mahony was marching parallel to him all day, still at gunshot range and gloating because the Allies 'could not even save a shirt'. 'The French', said María Luisa in a letter to Vendôme's duchess 'were so exalted that they were almost running mad with joy.'

CHAPTER NINE

'No High Flags, no Clamorous Haste'

I leave you, but my thoughts will be with you,
for I shall never forget your loyalty and love,
and believe me I shall always be at your service.
I leave my coaches for the use of your city.
– Parting words of the Empress Isabel Christina to the council of Barcelona
at her embarkation on 19th March, 1713.

ACCORDING to the Duque de Moles, young King João V was changing. In fact he was growing up and now began to breed legitimate offspring on his 75,000 *cruzado* bed. He eventually became a king to be remembered. Perhaps it did not matter that he never showed any aptitude for war or administration, for he developed an ability to take rapid decisions and to stick to them, and this may have been of service to his small country in dealing with the greater powers. Moreover he satisfied his people with display. Fond of music, with some appreciation of literature and the arts, and strongly religious, he spent the wealth of Brazil on adorning churches and organising religious ceremonies. But this was for the future. In November, 1710, when Galway's successor arrived, João was still under the thumb of Cadaval and his colleagues.

Sir David Colyear, Earl of Portmore, the new commander, was the elder son of a Scotsman, Alexander Robertson, who had settled in Holland where he had property and changed his name. The son had fought well for William of Orange and come to England with him in 1688, losing an eye but being awarded an earldom. Macky called him

'one of the best foot officers in the world; is very brave and bold; hath a great deal of wit; very much a man of honour and nice that way, *yet* married the Countess of Dorchester and had by her a good estate [she had £5,000 a year from the Irish Establishment]. Dresses clean. Towards 50 years old.'

The English forces in Portugal, according to a muster in October 1710, had had a total of 2,046 infantrymen which was about 1,300 short of full complement, and by February 1711 this had only improved to 2,738. Although, including Portuguese troops, the Allied force of 17,000 out-numbered that of de Bay, the Portuguese front was now entirely secondary and there was even less than the rudimentary co-ordination that had once existed with the Allied forces in Catalonia.[1] In February 1711 Admiral Jennings arrived at Barcelona from Portugal with five regiments. So delayed was he and so bad were communications that he was expecting (two months after Brihuega) to find orders from Stanhope for the men's destination. Although João objected, he had taken them on to Barcelona after waiting a month for further reinforcements meant to be coming from Ireland. When these at length came in May 1711 Portmore, by now doubtful of much action, felt that they might just as well go on to Barcelona too for all the use they were, for there was still an acute shortage of horses. Some had been actually traded for across the Spanish border; but this source was limited by natural Spanish objections; there were none in Portugal itself; and imports from Ireland were impossible as the London government was not interested in paying for them. There were, moreover, even difficulties about the new regiments Galway had so painstakingly been forming. One of these was a regiment made up in Charles' name of Spanish deserters. His special representative, Stampa, who was on bad terms with Charles' permanent ambassador, Cienfuegos, and feared that the regiment's costs would be charged against his master's subsidies, asked Portmore to disband it. Portmore refused.

The recapture that month of Miranda do Douro in Tras-os-Montes, the only Portuguese success in the spring campaign, was flawed. All the prisoners were released and there was no follow-up. A possible advance to the south of Badajoz, suggested by Portmore, was abandoned, since the release of the prisoners appeared to be connected with certain secret negotiations between Spain and Portugal. These were brought to light when a French merchant, Joseph Hallère, made available to Portmore some copies of alleged correspondence between de Bay and the Portuguese Secretary of State, Mendonza. Hallère's story was that he had for some time been regularly carrying letters between the two countries proposing a secret cease-fire north of the Tagus, with France sending thirty warships, to be paid for by Portugal, in order to safeguard her costs.

That there was something going on, although no official truce had been signed, is indeed quite certain. For, tucked away among the French documents of 1711 there is a cyphered note from de Noailles to Voisin dated 18th April, pressing to be made a captain-general and to be allowed to stay on in Spain. The note goes on, 'The Portuguese are waiting to negotiate a peace but King Philip is having difficulty in finding someone trustworthy to send to Lisbon.' And King Louis, writing to his grandson on 3rd May says of the emperor's death, 'I think this event will advance the negotiations you have begun with the Portuguese. Success there is important and you should not worry if it costs something to obtain.'

When taxed with the negotiations the Portuguese – who of course knew that if they signed a clandestine treaty all the Spanish troops on their border could have been sent to reinforce Vendôme in Catalonia – expressed resentment. They made the excuse that they were only acting 'in order to produce a general peace'. The better to palliate the matter, the young das Minas was extremely active and vigilant in forwarding the preparations for the campaign. Forty days' rations were sent to the forces at the front and a half-hearted sally was made across the Guadiana with twenty battalions, forty-six squadrons and a regiment of artillery. The territory was largely Portuguese but Spanish-occupied. Leaving garrisons at Albuquerque, Campo Maior, Elvas and Olivenza behind them, the Portuguese captured Safra (these border towns had long been used to this sort of thing) and exacted a 'contribution' of 13,000 dollars. There was even talk of besieging Badajoz and cutting Bourbon communications with that city. But de Bay, despite the peace feelers, was on the alert. He retreated at first, but took sundry small castles and towns, Vimiera, Puebla and the like, and then threatened Elvas. At this the Portuguese in turn retreated, and although their army stayed in the field for another three weeks before going into summer quarters, there was no more fighting.

When the autumn campaign began there was plenty of corn available but nothing had been done about setting up supply stores for the army, and there were still no fit horses. Portmore had been instructed to reduce the number of British troops in Portugal and some, including Barrymore's regiment, had been sent to garrison Gibraltar. Even the English generals were by now opposed to taking the field, for there was widespread talk of peace negotiations. This at one stage made the Portuguese decide that 'they must in future stand on their own bottom' and recruit troops. But at the same time a political storm blew up when some of King João's subsidy was held back to pay the Portuguese soldiers still in Catalonia. This was rubbing salt in the wounds, for the long absence of these men from their homes was resented. But the English paymaster in Lisbon refused on instructions from London, to pay the subsidy without making this deduction, and this did not encourage the Portuguese. After a brief period of futile marching to and fro in Tras-os-Montes there was no further action in 1711 in that sector.

★   ★   ★

On 11th January 1711, the Duke of Argyll had been officially appointed commander-in-chief of the English forces in Spain (as announced in the press months before), to replace Stanhope, at £20,000 a year. He had spent nearly ten weeks in London trying to ensure political support. Although he had shown wisdom and statesmanship over the Act of Union of 1709, he now seems to have evinced great naiveté. He certainly did not hoist in the fact that since the military situation in the Peninsula was virtually deadlocked the new Government could seize on this to break away from the policy of No Peace Without Spain, and that he himself was expendable.

Travelling overland through the Netherlands (where he impolitely failed to call on Marlborough for he was still in the middle of a personal tiff with him, only later resolved), the Palatinate and Italy he had only reached Genoa on 8th May, having left England at the end of March. Here he began to realize the mess into which he had been precipitated. From English agents and Italian bankers he discovered that the army's finances were in ruins – only £40,000 had been sent to Barcelona for the troops since Saragossa seven months before. The administration was in complete disorder, since the generals were all prisoners, and the Bourbon command had been carrying on a winter campaign of which nothing had been reported to him. While Starhemberg struggled northwards from the field of Villa Viciosa, de Noailles had launched his invasion from France, aiming for Gerona, advancing through the Pyrenean passes with 18,600 men and a considerable siege train.[2] Starhemberg had to face the fact that he could not reinforce the city. His forces were far away, weak and exhausted, and roads were difficult in winter. For his failure to do anything he received a pettish rebuke from Charles but it is difficult to see what steps he could have taken at that time.

Even de Noailles, whose men were fresh, found the affair a considerable strain because of 'the worst enemy of the French – the weather'. The artillery was supposed to be in a good state, de Bruelh reporting (from Bellegarde) that firing was 'extremely lively', but de Noailles and Barillon, writing to Voisin on 8th January, 1711, when the siege had been going for fourteen days, thought otherwise. Guns were not numerous enough. Powder and lead were short. Food was difficult and the 1¼ million *écus* needed for pay was being delayed in Roussillon. After three weeks of entrenchment and fighting the French camp was flooded by heavy rainfall. They were short of mules and there was no meat. They had already lost 89 killed and 167 wounded, and the defenders under Tattenbach kept making successful sorties. But de Noailles was determined to finish the job before succour could arrive for the garrison. So, into the trenches went in succession, day after day, Generals Baylus, Balaincourt, d'Arpajon, Tournon, de Guerchy and Périgord. Some of these, despite considerable battle experience, were so discouraged by the conditions that they recommended raising the siege. But the lines of circumvallation were now complete, so that no relief could reach the place and de Noailles persisted. On the morning of 23rd January mines destroyed the Virgin Rampart and the wall at Santa Lucia and the assault was ordered. Twice the defenders drove off the French. The third assault was led by de Noailles himself with great dash and courage and the defence was driven into the upper town, many prisoners being taken. There was a two-day pause during which bombardment continued; then, just as a fourth assault was ordered the governor beat the chamade and offered to hand over the city provided the outer fortifications were left standing. This was refused but Tattenbach later promised to capitulate in six days if no relief came in. The fortifications named after the Constable, Queen Anne (erected by Stanhope), the Cavalry and the Capuchins, would be handed over and the garrison would march out with full honours of war. Knowing that relief was impossible, de Noailles agreed, writing to Philip on 26th January, 'Sire, Gerona is in the power of Your Majesty.' French losses numbered 348 killed and 512 wounded, altogether the equivalent of nearly half the total numbers of the garrison. Among the considerable assets which fell into the victor's hands was a large pharmaceutical store containing 5,711 different drugs, essences, syrups and pills. More significant were the strategic consequences. Apart from garrisons in Gibraltar and the islands, the Allied presence in Spain was now confined to a beleaguered fragment of Catalonia, surrounded by land, tenable only by virtue of succour by sea. If the will to war in London weakened, the lifeline of Habsburg Spain might be cut off. In the reduced compass and straitened circumstances of early 1711, continued resistance by Charles would be impossible.

*   *   *

The course of the war in Spain had frequently been influenced by events beyond the Peninsula. Intrigues at Versailles, Marlburian victories in Flanders and Germany, hopes of a wider peace settlement in divers capitals, had all, at times, a greater effect on the Spanish theatre than the indecisive oscillations of the early years of the war or the slowly grinding Bourbon successes since Saragossa.

Now circumstances were to be transformed again by an outside event more adventitious than any of these. In April, 1711, the Emperor Joseph was struck by smallpox at home in Vienna. So rapid was the effect of the disease that Charles in Barcelona only heard that his brother was ill on the day he actually died, 17th April. When the news reached Philip's court in the second week of May, de Bourk wrote to Voisin, 'not everyone believes it but some are consternated'. Ironically, for Charles, too, this sudden opportunity to claim a great empire caused almost as much 'consternation' as comfort. He automatically succeeded his brother as King of Hungary and Bohemia, but the Imperial crown was elective. He might not be able to count on his allies to support him in simultaneous attempts on two almost indecently corpulent inheritances. To leave for Vienna would imperil his tenuous foothold in Spain. To stake all on Spain might jeopardise his election as emperor. Yet the struggle in Spain was a cause to which he was committed and about which he was convinced. So, although he should have gone at once to Vienna, he was determined to stay in Barcelona. Wratislaw and Prince Eugene wrote begging him to come home, but he considered that he had won so much Spanish and even more Catalan trust that he could not let down his loyal subjects, particularly the Catalans. The Imperial throne should be looked on as a fulcrum upon which to lever up a hold on Spain. He was to stay on in Barcelona for five more months, his *Despacho Universal* and *Junta de Guerra* recording dozens of items no doubt important to the individuals concerned but of minor consequence to the war as a whole. Royal decisions are as usual noted in the margins on such subjects as: the formation of a regiment by the Conde de Cifuentes; accusations against Sola, the Governor of Cardona; service records of Spanish, Portuguese and other officers in Naples; the economic situation in Benasque; requests for junior appointments and some promotions; punishment for deserters; the release of four galley-slaves in Genoa; orders for stores; trade between Milan and Naples; the fortification of Ibiza. All the minutiae of wartime management but no major policy-making.

Of much greater potential significance was a direct approach to him attempted by his rival at this time. Philip knew a good deal about the strength of Charles' forces and of the lack of money in Barcelona. He knew that Charles had had to send out a letter, signed on his behalf by Perlas, speaking of his 'paternal love' for his people and withdrawing an earlier order for the collection of funds. This had nearly caused a rebellion, the collectors had to flee from the infuriated populace. So, after consultation with Vendôme, de Noailles and his other advisers, Philip wrote on 19th May a careful letter to be sent across the lines to Charles. De Noailles sent a cyphered copy of the draft to Voisin and King Louis was kept well in the picture. The letter, although its transparent earnestness is swathed in the pomposity natural to royal missives, deserves quotation. 'Sire, my brother,' it began.

'It is time to leave ordinary laws in the hands of Providence and to adopt the road we ought to take. The death of a brother whom God has just removed from Your Majesty, leaving you the Crown Imperial, provides certain solid reasons for us to come together, and for a peace to be equally established for all Europe. My Religion has decided me to take the initiative, when the Turkish and Hungarian revolts are failing, [and] although German Protestants have joined the ranks of the Electors of Bavaria and Cologne. It is this which encourages me to forget and stifle motives of [self-] interest or private resentment, for the Church and Religion are in danger.

It is this that drives me to offer everything in my power to [assist in] placing on your head a crown which for so long has been the inheritance of your House. Seven years of war in this continent have given you little in the way of return and we [really] must come to an accomodation. The justice of my cause and all my own confidence persuade me that God, who has put [this] crown on my head will keep it there. So [please] do not think of this offer as coming from anything but a heart penetrated by God and [earnest for] the preservation of the Catholic faith. I know Your Majesty counts on [your] allies but these have their own private interests; and it is bad policy to try and profit from trouble by causing some new event [to take place]. It is for this reason that I [now] approach you.

I am convinced that it is quite as fine and glorious [as fighting] for us to try and end this war, despite the justice of my cause ... I do not mean to waste a moment in letting all Europe know that it will not be my fault if peace does not replace war at the first oppportunity which God has provided for the good of [all] our nations.

I recognize you as King of Bohemia and assure you that you will find my sentiments all that you could desire. If you wish to enter into broader discussions you can speak to me in confidence ...'

It was a sound and it would seem an honest attempt, but the letter was returned unanswered. It had been addressed to 'The King of Bohemia'. Even 'The King of Hungary' might have been better but neither was sufficient. How could Charles accept either when he considered himself King of Spain? It might be that King of Hungary was the senior title, but in replying how could Charles address Philip? He could not call him king, and to call him the Duc d'Anjou would only have caused offence and they would have got nowhere.

It was not Philip's approaches, but the importunings of his friends and the impecuriosity of his treasury, that gradually affected Charles's resolve. A music-lover, he had even introduced Italian opera to Barcelona for his wife's benefit, but had had to discontinue performances when asked by the authorities of the city to do so as an economy. Subsidies from England had failed to arrive, thanks to the change of government there. Though £1.5 million had been voted for furthering the war in the Peninsula, only about £200,000 had so far come through. Money sources in London were wary of the new ministry despite a disinterested offer from the dismissed Godolphin to use all his influence to help raise funds. So short had Charles been all along that when a few months earlier a jewelled sword had been presented to Starhemberg, the archduke had had to get Stanhope, as one of his last acts before the previous campaign, to advance the £1,342. 10s. it had cost. Now in mid-1711 the archduke could not even leave Barcelona unless carried by the Royal Navy. Impassively, as he now had the habit of displaying himself, he insisted on taking his own time, making his own decisions. He *would* be King of Spain, he affirmed, for that had been his mission in life. He even considered, as a last resort, an approach to France to negotiate a peace, though this was allowed to lapse. His correspondence with Wratislaw shows his determination in the face of events beyond his control, amidst deteriorating relationships with the authorities in Barcelona over money, and under the nagging, insoluble difficulties of supporting a military force to resist the Bourbon winter campaign and to provide for the forthcoming spring one.

But in the end he realized that stubbornness was futile, that he must move himself upstairs to be emperor. He wrote of waiting in Barcelona until the result of the Imperial election had been announced but Wratislaw forcefully pointed out that if he did so he might be cut off from Italy by the winter – he could not go overland – and arrive too late to accept the election. So, at last he caved in and wrote that he would return to Vienna, leaving his queen as regent in Catalonia. This was a political necessity. When he announced this to his Junta at Camp Pobla d'Aguiló on 1st September, the generals were unanimous that the queen must stay, 'so as not to leave the subjects feeling abandoned'.

On 27th September 1711 Charles sailed away for ever from Barcelona. He was leaving the Peninsula with far less state than he had entered. Seven years earlier half a Royal Navy first-rate's main deck had been stripped and converted into special quarters for him. Now, although he was escorted, according to the *Milan Gazette* of 21st October, by forty-three English and Dutch ships, the most that Admiral Jennings could do was to have his flagship, H.M.S. *Blenheim*, scrubbed, and to lay in a store of charcoal for braziers.

★   ★   ★

When in June 1712 Vendôme lay dying by painful and unpleasant degrees in the little coast town of Viñaroz, his thoughts may well in his distress have turned fitfully to his frustrations. In September, 1711, when campaigning resumed after a summer of inconclusive negotiations, he had once more been in one of his dynamic moods, determined to finish the war in the Peninsula by capturing Barcelona and Tarragona, thus eliminating Charles' precarious foothold in Catalonia for ever. It would have set the seal on his own occasionally chancy but successful efforts to save the crown of Spain for Philip. It might have restored to him the full approval of King Louis. Yet now, two seasons later, the war was still twitching on in a grim analogy to his own throes.

There was in fact no question of either side obtaining victory or surrender in 1711. The forces of the Two Crowns on one side and those of the Allies on the other were like two all-in wrestlers locked in a grapple late in a bout. While still able to inflict hurt they were almost too tired to feel injuries when inflicted. But Vendôme had tried hard.[3]

The armies of the Two Crowns were drawn up roughly on a circular line from Gerona in the north-east round to Tortosa in the south. The northern sector was de Noailles' and the southern Vendôme's, but the latter was the senior and it was to him that Philip rightly considered that he owed the recovery of 'some of his losses' and to whom he therefore deferred. As a result of Brihuega,

'obedience had been offered by many towns and castles which had served as retreats for ill-intentioned *Miquelets* . . . The establishment of His Catholic Majesty on the throne seemed to be announced by Brihuega and the capture of Gerona.'

Balaguer, Cervera, Solsona and numerous other towns, abandoned by the Allies, were occupied. De Noailles ordered de Fiennes to march towards Ostalrich, take it, and set up magazines there, but the latter did not dare attack the place for lack of equipment and supplies and because the Allies had been reported as receiving reinforcements. Several camps were set up on the way from Gerona but these in the end served only as strong points from which to levy contributions and later in the year as winter quarters. De Noailles was less enthusiastic than Vendôme. He had evinced joy when he heard in June 1711 of the opening of peace negotiations. De Fiennes was openly discontented and bloody-minded. It would not be long before, in response to orders from Vendôme and de Noailles (from Saragossa and Corella respectively), he would write saying it was impossible to carry on.

'Regiments lost to Dauphiné and enemy troops established near Ostalrich in greater numbers than mine make the job impossible. The six battalions I've been sent are so weak that they are barely enough to man the communications posts. I cannot from this region draw a body of troops sufficient for such an enterprise.'

It all in the end thus devolved on Vendôme, and even his robust energy and drive were frustrated. At a council of war discussions centred first round a siege of Cardona, which was proposed by d'Aguilar and supported by Valdecañas, followed by the placing of troops between that city and the enemy army. De Aguilar put his case forcibly, Valdecañas with more tact. Neither had any effect on Vendôme who was intent on moving on Tarragona and Barcelona, sometimes favouring one as a priority, sometimes the other. but as *hors d'oeuvres* he was determined to have Prats del Rey, a small, badly fortified little place 'of no importance' on the way near Igualada and occupied by the Allies, and simultaneously to send de Rozel to capture Benasque, and d'Arpajon to take Arents while de Muret made for Urgell. De Rozel, whose force was largely militia, was held up by the snow but d'Arpajon, after taking Arents in July with the help of de Guerchy and a couple of regular regiments (Auvergne and Chazel) and some artillery, went to help de Rozel. Eventually they surrounded Benasque with entrenchments by 11th September and three days later the governor, Jorge de la Bastida, surrendered. (He and his garrison were in for a most uncomfortable time as prisoners-of-war.) The Conde de Cazalèdes was put in as governor. On 16th October Castelleón fell without a bombardment.

So far so good for Vendôme, who had moved up via Calaf and Cervera towards Prats del Rey. Valdecañas had taken the former and de Muret and Clairfontaine the latter. The cavalry were now mustered at Agramont and the infantry at Balaguer. Against the advice of his generals, Vendôme pressed on. De Aguilar's pique at not having his views accepted was sharp and gossips fanned the disagreements, in particular Julio Alberoni, Vendôme's confessor, the Parmesan priest of humble origin, who was already beginning to be a figure in the world.

Starhemberg and Argyll had meantime taken steps to counter Vendôme's moves and protect Barcelona. The various roads and passes were occupied with picked cavalry and Starhemberg withdrew his main force from beyond Prats del Rey, leaving sufficient strength there to tempt his opponent. The country was very dry and Vendôme had to sink wells to get water. Some Allied troops were left within the walls, some outside on the same bank of the river and the rest behind the place on rough ground leading to a little hill. Even the flatter terrain was a mass of mounds and ditches and unsuitable for cavalry, of which Starhemberg was short. He kept one of the town's gates open and protected and through this, as Vendôme approached on the 25th and began his bombardment, the inhabitants left with all their goods. So, when next day Vendôme attacked and was unsuccessful, he was wasting his strength on a mere heap of dust and ashes. Nor did he fare better when he came up against Starhemberg's troops on the river bank.

Lieutenant Doyle recounts how Starhemberg on the 27th was in a mill 'not a mile off' with 1,700 German grenadiers and ten English companies with Argyll at hand. The summer heats were over and it was a pleasant day. A bombardment killed seven of Molesworth's men but, before the French infantry could attack, so far from withdrawing Argyll pushed Molesworth forward, supported by Edward Stanhope's and Mark Kerr's regiments and six companies of grenadiers in the rear.

Molesworth exhorted his men who 'gave a shout which made the French brigade tremble' and led them down to the waterside where

'they received fire without shooting back and then gave them such a charge, firing by platoons that in ten minutes he sent back two battalions with his single one, at which time six companies of grenadiers that was to sustain him came up and behaved like angels. The enemy brigade was indeed entirely broke to our battalion only and the six companies.'

French reports later spoke of the British having four battalions engaged there and said that these were forced back. But Doyle insists firmly:

'We had pursued them within forty paces of their whole line at which orders were sent from my Lord of Argyll to desire Colonel Molesworth to face his regiment to the right and return to his ground in the line of battle, which he did with the loss of two Lieutenants and fourteen men.'

For this brisk little engagement, described in the *Evening Post* of 29th October as 'a mere cannonade', Molesworth's men were warmly praised by Argyll and Starhemberg, the former sending them an 'an ox and ten sheep' with which to celebrate.

Vendôme had suffered something of a check to his plans. He seems nevertheless to have been insistent on continuing towards Barcelona and attacking Starhemberg on the way, leaving Cardona until later. And on this the argument with de Aguilar and Valdecañas persisted hotly. De Aguilar became so incensed that he wrote to Philip asking leave to quit the field. When no answer came he sent in his resignation from all his offices – captaincy of a royal guard, senior generalship of infantry, chancellorship of the council of Ordenes, and so on. The king accepted this and on returning to court de Aguilar was allowed to pay his respects but was later advised to leave Madrid when the court returned there in November. 'Thus at the end of the war the services of one of the ablest and most experienced generals was unused.'

In the end, however unwillingly, Vendôme decided that his projects were now impractical since the year was so far advanced. He therefore withdrew to Cervera and from here on 15th November sent de Muret to attack Cardona. He himself was still full of confidence but his subordinates, Neuville and de Fiennes, according to their letters, were fearful of 'some coup by Starhemberg such as an amphibious descent on Tortosa.' Observers further away, such as Bruelh at Bellegarde across the frontier, believed that Starhemberg, piqued by the 'affront' he had received at Villa Viciosa, was planning 'a great revenge. We are on the eve of a great action in that country'. This was of course far from reality, but there was something in it, for Starhemberg *did* attempt to take Tortosa.

But he too had his setbacks. He sent General Wetzel with a modest land force to recapture Tortosa on 25th October, and although de Bourgay's regiment had earlier won a small engagement and succeeded in preventing their opponents from occupying and fortifying a ferry point on the Lower Ebro, near the town, Wetzel's attempt failed. There was a lack of security and spies warned the Tortosa garrison, and at the same time the Allied force at Tarragona failed to co-operate.

Wetzel attacked during darkness and attempted to take a tower near the San Juan rampart. The sentries were alerted by the noise and the garrison turned out and took up arms, the governor, the Conde de Glimes, rushing to fight only half-dressed. The Allies' scaling ladders were destroyed but the assault party took over a demilune near the rampart, which had been left without a guard. All the action so far had been outside the city. Now Wetzel's men tried to take the fortifications between it and the River Ebro, but they came under small-arms fire from the rampart. As dawn broke they tried to destroy the gates of San Juan and Templense with battering-rams. Fierce musket fire prevented this but their own made it difficult for the garrison to man the ramparts. Glimes himself showed considerable courage and appears to have been well supported by a chief sapper called Tanuil and the colonel of the regiment of Pamplona.

Wetzel tried to turn the shoulder of the San Juan rampart, which was close to the city. He was foiled by Colonel Francisco Bustamente, chief gunner of the garrison, who, with support from three infantry regiments, Seville, Murcia and

Palencia, drove the Allies off. Thus, says San Felipe sententiously, 'was punished the arrogance of a difficult enterprise undertaken in the belief that the Spaniards were careless'. Wetzel, in his precipitate retreat, left about 400 men in the demilune and the San Juan redoubt and these were made prisoner.

The result of this little fiasco was to strengthen Starhemberg in his determination to hold on to what he had, and this produced a modest but bloody act of resistance to Vendôme in the siege of Cardona, where General Eck was governor. Cardona was a small town some fifty miles north-west of Barcelona, set high on a hill; its citadel was easy to defend and dominated the surrounding area. Eck's garrison totalled 1,200, two German and one Spanish battalion, when de Muret and d'Arpajon arrived with 3,000 men on 15th November and began to attack the town with cannon. Eck put up a tough defence but after only two day's bombardment the town itself was 'being ruined by the cannon' which enabled de Muret to take it 'sword in hand'. The assault was however costly to Vendôme's force. Melun was on the left, d'Arpajon in the centre and the Conde de Suders on the right. And although the town was taken the citadel put up a ferocious resistance and an assault on 30th November was called off. De Muret then ordered the citadel to be mined but the weather made this impossible. All he could do was continue the siege, erecting contravallations against persistent heavy attacks by Raphel Nebot's *Miquelets*. But his siege works were not enough to prevent Starhemberg sending reinforcements to Eck.

According to an account sent to London by Lord Forbes (who was still serving with the Army), the Palatine Lieutenant-General Pathee was detached from Igualada with a force of about 4,000 men and considerable supplies. These consisted of about 3,000 Palatine troops, some *Miquelets*, and 500 to 550 English – chiefly from Edward Stanhope's own regiment (formerly Inchquin's) and under his command. Their orders were 'to lay hold upon any occasion' to relieve the citadel. Pathee fought a skilled action. His cavalry, hussars and the volunteers of Casanova, were placed in the plains to keep off enemy cavalry and the rest of the force marched in this order: Stanhope and his foot in the lead; 200 grenadiers under Count Guel; 400 *Miquelets* under Colonel Geschwindt; the provision wagons for the citadel; 800 foot under Colonel Schonberg with 500 dismounted Imperial dragoons. Raphel Nebot joined them on the 19th.

At 5.00 in the morning of the 21st December, Pathee's force attacked de Muret's from a number of directions. Guel went in on one height and Stanhope on another. De Muret's troops – twelve companies of grenadiers and four battalions of foot – fought 'with such resolution that they put them [the Allies] in great disorder.' Stanhope stood his ground until the rest of the Allies were rallied and drove off their opponents 'at push of bayonet' down the hill he had taken. It was a highly confused affair, and the Allies' first two assaults had failed. Although the Germans had been beaten in one or two places, Stanhope in the end appears to have carried the day, capturing the French General de Melun, who died of wounds a little later.

De Muret had lost about 2,000 men and had been unable to prevent supplies and reinforcements being passed through to Cardona's garrison. Accordingly, on Christmas Day at two in the morning, taking the advantage of thick fog, he withdrew to join Vendôme at his main headquarters, having had to abandon twenty-two pieces of artillery, all his baggage, and his sick and wounded. The Allied casualties had been relatively light, about 300, but they included Edward Stanhope. Like his brother Philip at Port Mahon, he had been in the forefront of the fighting when he received a shot in the body. He died at Manresa on the 23rd. 'The town to which he was carried before he expired, out of respect for his name, suffered his body to be interred in the hospital burying-ground, a favour allowed to no other Protestant officer.'

The news of Cardona had spread fast, for the siege had been anxiously watched. Yet, while de Fiennes, Neuville and the rest were nettled by the Allied rejoicings in Barcelona ('salvoes and fireworks'), it is possible to detect a certain relief behind their publicly and officially expressed 'profound chagrin'. It had been a dreadful few weeks. Would the war *never* come to an end? Even this mini-campaign had meant that some two-and-a-half thousand men, mostly in their early manhood, had met death, disablement or disfigurement.

Even Vendôme's demonic urge to win a military solution faltered in the winter of the new year. His subordinate generals wished only to mark time for a negotiated peace. The king's coffers were empty. The marshal's calls for further sacrifice went unechoed, even unheeded. De Noailles refused to serve; de Muret considered his chief 'intolerable'; Bergeyck, who was in charge of finance, despaired of satisfying Vendôme. When the marshal was incapacitated by gout in late February, 1712, even the king was relieved. Philip had already decided to replace him, first with Valdecañas, then with Tzerclaes.

In the circumstances it might be thought that Starhemberg could have made hay of his opponents, but in fact the Allies were little better off. Long before winter had set in Argyll, furious at lack of support from London and disillusioned with the Catalonia campaign, had returned to Barcelona from the field stating that he was ill. Thence he sailed with some of the English troops to Minorca, despite understandable protests from the Catalans that they were being abandoned. He was by now so deeply convinced that Spain did not suit him and could do without him that he returned to England for some months leaving Lord Barrymore in command. His Lordship complained continually of lack of money and bread. Starhemberg received reinforcements of German troops via Italy which more than replaced Argyll's English but he was only sent 10,000 *pistoles* in money and was thus very short. Nor was Argyll likely to help or even to be able to. The momentum of the peace negotiations, sluggish though they were, were overtaking the torpid progress of the war.

★   ★   ★

Within six weeks of the opening of the Peace Congress at the Town House of Utrecht in January, 1712, France suffered a series of extraordinary dynastic catastrophes. Louis had taken the loss of his fifty-year-old son a year earlier relatively philosophically, for he had after all an apparently ample number of legitimate successors. Now smallpox intervened once more, first with the Duchesse de Bourgogne (María Luisa's sister). Though much beloved and never prepared to believe ill of anyone, she was not good-looking. Her teeth were poor and she suffered from goitre, but her skin was clear and her eyes 'adorable'. In mid-January she had tooth trouble and a fever and was wearing, like her sister, a *béguine*. She was in great pain, and opium and bleeding in the foot were tried, but without result. On 11th February she was mortally ill, confessed and took the Sacrament, dying next day.

Her husband, the second dauphin, had never had the disease but watched over her for the last three nights of her life. Now he in turn caught it and, no doubt at a low ebb after the loss of a wife he adored, he immediately prepared himself for death, having an altar brought to his bedroom. Emetics and bleeding were, not surprisingly, ineffectual and on 18th February he too died, at the age of thirty. After a somewhat wild youth he had been taken in hand by Fénélon and had become affable, patient and almost too pious. Small, dark-complexioned and slightly hunch-backed, he had nevertheless been looked on as a suitable successor to his grandfather. Now he was gone.

The couple had two sons, the Duc de Bretagne, aged five, who now became the third dauphin in less than a year, and his extremely delicate two-year-old brother. The five-year-old asked not to be called dauphin because 'it was too sad'. Both little boys went down with smallpox caught from their parents, and the third dauphin died at midnight within a few days. The younger, now the fourth dauphin, survived through a fortunate lack of medical attention. While the nine doctors present concentrated on his brother, opening a vein (which killed him), the nurses locked themselves away with the younger boy and when, on 9th March the doctors wished to open one of his veins, his governess refused to allow it and merely kept him warm.

This series of deaths destroyed all the assumptions on which the peace process had been based. The negotiators had hitherto relied on the fact that there were three lives between Philip and possible inheritance of the Crown of France. Now, suddenly, two of these had been snuffed out and the third seemed unlikely to survive. Louis was receptive to a solution devised in London. This was that Philip should renounce the throne of Spain on acceding to that of France; Spain and the Indies should go to the Duke of Savoy and his heirs; and France should receive in recompense Piedmont and Savoy. Savoy, the Empire and the Dutch agreed to this new proposal, although they had no guarantees. Louis had privately advised the English that he would extort his grandson's renunciation of one or other alternative by force if necessary, although he was sure that Philip *could* not renounce France and probably would not renounce Spain. At least it was for him a ploy that bought time.

So, in late May, the messengers were on the way to Madrid from Versailles; England's Tory ministers were full of hope that they had found the answer. If Philip agreed to renounce Spain and the Indies to Victor Amadeus, it would separate those possessions from the House of Bourbon and the Whigs would be unable to raise the cry of 'No Peace Without Spain', for Victor Amadeus was an ally. On 28th May the government felt confident enough to tell the House of Lords that a peace based on Bourbon renunciation of Spain was on the way. But they were counting their chickens prematurely.

For Philip, now twenty-nine, had survived over a decade of kingship, of disappointments and hardships, and had recently tasted victory; and he reached quite independently a decision which showed that he had taken to heart advice his grandfather gave him when he ascended the throne of Spain. He would be a good Spaniard. His adopted country had in turn adopted him, called him *El Animoso*, and shown faith in him. He would be true to it. He would *not* renounce Spain, and he firmly said so. In a solemn declaration before the *Cortes* on 5th November 1712, he announced that he would keep Spain and renounce the throne of France.

★   ★   ★

The immediate effect of Philip's decision was to infuse new life into the war in Spain. For on the Portuguese front, the Spaniards were anxious to secure their frontier before a peace settlement should supervene and renewed operations before their king's decision was formally promulgated; while in Catalonia, Charles and his supporters, who faced ruin if Philip's cause prevailed, were resolved on a last throw.

De Bay, short of matériel and apprehensive of the coming rainy season, was extremely reluctant to begin operations. But the key frontier town of Campo Maior, near Elvas, was an irresistible prize. The marqués accepted the order to take it, swearing in his truculent way that he would take Estremós as well. Why should he not say so, at least? For his force was far stronger and he had a low opinion of the Portuguese.

The Portuguese, however, managed to send in some 800 grenadiers as reinforcements, led by an Irishman called Hogan, a French Protestant engineer called Maffey and the Portuguese Conde de Ribeira. A lucky shot blew up the main Spanish magazine and Campo Maior managed to hold out, for it was the turn of de Bay's men to show that they were sick of fighting. Guns were surreptitiously spiked and officers killed by malcontents. When, on 17th October de Bay assaulted, he was repulsed and the garrison sallied out against him. It was a stalemate. A week later the rains began, putting an end to movement, and an official letter arrived at Lisbon from Dartmouth announcing the suspension of arms between Britain, France and Spain. Despite political pressure from Madrid, the military command seemed resolved not to try too hard against Portugal. On 8th November they raised the siege of Campo Maior. On 5th December, the Portuguese proclaimed the general armistice signed at Utrecht. As 1,200 or so English troops from Portugal were marched to Gibraltar, they were fêted everywhere by Spaniards delighted that the long war was at last apparently over. The hated heretics had become symbols of peace.

In Catalonia, however, while the British evacuation was effected smoothly the Imperial army was not included in the truce; nor was Catalan ardour diminished. Gerona had been under blockade almost since its capture by de Noailles. Charles insisted that it must be taken; Louis XIV was aware that, if his grandson was ever to rule in Catalonia, the blockade must be broken. De Fiennes had tried three times to break the siege. Tzerclaes was temporising. Louis decided to send Berwick. On 10th December, 1712, the Marshal was back in Spain.

By 26th December thirty-four battalions, forty-one squadrons and thirty guns had been assembled from Germany, Dauphiné and Provence and were at Toulon. Since the country was hostile and difficult and it was winter, Berwick arranged for 'a sort of fleet to sail abreast of us so as to provide necessary supplies – though one is never certain of anything when one depends on the wind'. By the 29th they were at Figueras and only waiting for bread from Rosas. Starhemberg, knowing of Berwick's approach, had at first thickened the blockade using thirty-six battalions and thirty-seven squadrons collected from all over Catalonia and on 15th December had proposed a capitulation, the walls of the town to be razed. When Governor de Brancas refused, the Austrians attacked three times without success, even when they sent 700 Germans in at the Capuchin fort. Meantime, Berwick's march continued, the weather improving so as to assist him. On 1st January he was at the crossing of the River Ter, only ten miles or so from Starhemberg, firing three rounds of artillery to let Brancas know that he was there. But the approach to Gerona was no easy matter. Berwick's order of battle still exists, with Generals de Fiennes and Caylus; d'Arênnes and de Bourk; d'Asfeld and Carafa; Dillon, Cilly and Broglie. By this time Spanish squadrons seem also to have joined him, giving him a total of sixty-three.

A strongpoint, the Costa Roja, blocked the high road, accessible on the left bank of the Ter but too strong to be tackled. On the other side of the river the country was mountainous and easy to lose oneself in. So, while he feinted at the Costa Roja and sent 600 dragoons to drive off *Miquelet* patrols on the right bank of the river, he determined to cross and make his way round through Torella. The threat of crossing was enough to convince Starhemberg – ever cautious – that his communications might be endangered and on the night of 3rd January he decamped – as the French put it, 'he did not consider it useful to wait' – and marched to Ostalrich, leaving some artillery, provisions and ammunition. He was fully justified, for his force numbered only 10,000 regulars against Berwick's 22,000. It was the feast day of St Geneviève, patron saint of Paris, but Berwick had a heavy cold and was cheered only by the news from four deserters that Starhemberg had gone. Though as usual complaining of shortage of wagons to bring supplies from Figueras and Rosas, he put two infantry brigades and all his dragoons to occupy high ground and made contact with Brancas, sending supplies into the beleaguered town. In a report to Philip, the governor underlined the hardships. The last three months (out of eight) were the hardest and poorest when they were reduced to eating cats, dogs and rats.

When, on 8th January Berwick entered the town (still with a heavy cold) he was greeted 'with the highest acclamation and a salute from all the artillery'. The bishop was ill and could not conduct the *Te Deum* in the cathedral. Berwick wrote to Versailles on 9th January that although bad weather and enemy interference were delaying the unloading of his supply tartans, 'most of our job is done'. In fact Bâville, the intendant of Languedoc, had been most effective in getting provisions as far as Rosas, and by 21st January Gerona was revictualled for eighteen months. The marshal's letter was taken to Versailles by his brother-in-law, Henry Bulkeley, to whom Louis gave 12,000 francs for travel expenses, promoting him to Brigadier with a pension of 4,000 écus a year. Philip wrote graciously to Berwick and awarded the Golden Fleece to Brancas.

It is a sign of deterioration in Franco-Spanish relations, however, that Voisin told Berwick to raze Gerona's walls – it was a strong place too near the frontier from Voisin's point of view. Berwick would only do so if Louis gave approval and the old king did not like to, since it would have upset Philip. So Berwick turned for home, leaving twenty battalions and twenty squadrons in the Lampurdán and returning the rest to their original stations.

The emperor took the setback very ill, telling Starhemberg he could not understand the withdrawal by such an experienced soldier. At Ostalrich, Starhemberg was openly accused of cowardice. De Fiennes reported hearing that the Austrian could not leave his quarters since some Catalans had 'adorned the front (of the house) with chicken feathers and nailed three chicken claws to the front door'. Although Rialp wrote to console him, Starhemberg was naturally furious, and indeed these last few weeks of his military career were enough to try a saint. He had neither firm knowledge of the situation nor instructions, and he was the one on the spot on whom everything depended. Tzerclaes was moving slowly towards Tortosa and Ceva–Grimaldi was closing in on Cervera. The whole front was crumbling.

Charles should have paid earlier heed to Prince Eugene, who told him that Catalonia was untenable. But he and his wife were both gripped by a genuine emotional commitment which made it impossible to renounce the country unreservedly. When Isabel Christina left to join her husband on 19th March, 1713, she declared it 'the saddest day of my life'. When Charles finally authorised complete evacuation, it was out of military necessity, not political realism. He did not explicitly release the Catalans from their allegiance; he avowed a continuing interest in their welfare. His equivocation encouraged them in a tragic resistance which prolonged the war in Spain beyond its term in the rest of Europe.

CHAPTER TEN

The Agony of Barcelona

Charles and Isabel have left us flat.
The English have ratted.
The Portuguese have signed.
The Dutch will sign.
And we shall be hanged.

— Street-rhyme sung in Barcelona in May, 1713

And what good came of it at last?
That I could not well make out
But 'twas a famous victory.

— Robert Southey, *After Blenheim.*

STARHEMBERG had been told to keep his evacuation orders secret, probably because Charles dimly realized the dangerous consequences, to those Catalans and Spaniards who had supported him, of his abandoning them. Starhemberg, in his quandary, therefore hedged, telling the Commons that 'far from preparing to leave, he had no new orders'. Although he thus deceived them, he protested vehemently on 23rd March to Charles in Vienna and Zinzendorf, the Imperial negotiator in Utrecht, that

'it is impossible to leave the Catalans, without their privileges and with little security, in the power of their enemies — and the same for a large number of Castilian, Aragonese, Valencian and other families who are refugees in Barcelona and for whom it is impossible to find transport.'

The marshal concluded by saying that he declined to take any responsibility 'before God or the world' for the evils that would result.

In mid-May, Admiral Jennings arrived with his squadron. Now, at last, Starhemberg advised the *Diputació de Catalunya* (representing the whole Principality) and the city's Council of 100 that he hd received the emperor's orders to evacuate. Naturally there was immediate uproar and Starhemberg himself was the recipient of personal abuse. He withdrew his troops from the ramparts and moved them into camp outside, he himself remaining alone in the city under a guard provided by the *Coronela* (the militia of which we shall hear more).

Formal arrangements for the handing over of Barcelona, Tarragona, Cardona and other garrison points had to be detailed, and a joint commission was called, to meet at Cervera. Ceva-Grimaldi attended for the Bourbons. Jennings, who had been well received by the people of Barcelona, appears not to have been apprised of exactly what was happening, but sent two English representatives, Swanston and Westcombe, and the Allied team was led by Starhemberg's deputy, Königseck.

Meeting at 8.00 a.m. on 13th June at Ceva-Grimaldi's quarters, Königseck, as he reported next day to his chief, first raised the question of the Catalan traditional liberties or *fueros*, only to be told that this was a matter to be decided in Utrecht under the general peace. When Königseck pressed further, Ceva-Grimaldi replied, 'That can be left to us.' He later explained privately to Königseck that, though he had been ordered by Popoli to deal 'suavely' with the Catalans, he could not enter into a capitulation with them and that if the Allies persisted 'it would be the worse for them [the Catalans]'.

So the Convention of Cervera failed to discuss, still more to take care of the Catalan position, and when this became known there was deep disquiet in Barcelona, for 'all the friends-so-called of Catalonia had agreed that the *fueros* were finished'. Meetings of the various councils and juntas were held and over the next few days feelings rose, particularly among the artisan classes. A number of nobles, who met on 16th June and decided 'to elect representatives with ample powers to make submission', were visited that night by 'masked men who told them and their families that they were traitors to their country, and if they did not change their views they would experience the utmost rigour'. There is thus little doubt that it was the artisans and their employees who were about to be the backbone of the resistance, using the powerful weapon of their *Grémios* or guilds – a kind of cross between a worshipful company and a trade union – to force the hands of the more pacific nobility, ecclesiastics and *Diputació*. As de Fiennes reported, 'Many of the nobility wish to accept King Philip's clemency, but the *canaille* have the upper hand and threaten them day and night.'

For Starhemberg – and by now for Jennings – tension increased daily. On the 21st they secretly met Ceva-Grimaldi again. On the 22nd Starhemberg admitted to the council that there had been another meeting which, like that at Cervera, had failed as far as concerned the Catalan *fueros*, and agreed that the matter should next be discussed by the *Cortes* or parliament of the three *Braços*:

Militar (nobility), Ecclesiastic, and *Real* (the Commons). He was thanked for this though in fact he was only buying time for himself. He did not tell the authorities that at a further secret discussion with Ceva-Grimaldi at Hospitalet, Swanston and Westcombe had actually signed a Convention, to include a cease-fire from July 1st and Barcelona to be handed over fifteen days later, Tarragona being retained by the Allies as temporary quarters for troops awaiting evacuation.

This was not at all what the Council of 100 had been led to expect, and although it only became known in full later, with the publication of an anonymous broadsheet, *The Crucible of Fidelity*, deep suspicion and consternation once more seized the city. Again the councils and juntas met. This time, the ecclesiastics also assembled, and intervention by the saints was invoked in the packed churches.

When weeks later Isabel Christina heard of all this, she burst out in a fury that Starhemberg's conduct was 'something which I could never in my life believe could come to pass'. She would have been fairer in blaming her husband.

Popoli, the Bourbon commander, on the other hand, wrote to Philip that he had no reason to doubt Starhemberg's good faith, and that in order to have his forces ready to take over when the Germans left on 15th July he must move at once, on 26th June. He, Tzerclaes and Patiño had already formed their plans and he had instructed Caetano, Captain-General of Valencia, to send troops to Tortosa, to be available to surround and take over Tarragona. The French contingents, now at Cervera under de Guerchy, were to march to Igualada and Martorell, ready to concentrate on Barcelona, while he himself moved to Montblanch. Franco-Spanish detachments were being sent to take Cardona and Berga, and Seu and other places in the mountains.

Faced with an arbitrary demand from Jennings that embarkation be brought forward, Starhemberg's nerve cracked. He dared not inform the council, who expected him to protect the meeting of the *Cortes*, planned for 9th July. On 29th June he left his quarters by a garden gate, as though going for a stroll, while his *Coronela* guard continued their watch on his front door. He made for the Portal Nou entirely alone and entered his coach (presumably there by pre-arrangement), making directly for the camp by the River Besós where his troops were awaiting embarkation. He did not return to the city but the *coronela* continued honourably to guard his front door until after he sailed. The embarkation began on 2nd July and continued for three days. Among those travelling was the archbishop, of whom it was unkindly but perhaps justly said that he had only come to the city to raise money and by occupying his See to make sure of his right to his cardinal's hat.

The first batch of evacuees reached Vado on 8th July, about 2,000 having been left under General Graf Wallis as a rearguard, to be evacuated a few weeks later. Catalonia was now officially on her own, abandoned by her last ally. According to San Felipe, there were some thousands of German troops who had been in the place long enough to form local attachments and had deserted Starhemberg to serve as volunteers in the defence; he probably exaggerates and they seem unlikely to have been very numerous, since the marshal was strict in imposing the death penalty for desertion. So, as this stage there were probably at most in the city some 5,000 regular troops of one sort or another and a host of militia and volunteers. Perhaps it is not surprising that Philip and Popoli should expect immediate surrender or at worst a collapse after a few rounds of bombardment, but something totally different took place. For although Louis XIV advised his grandson to play for time and use diplomacy, Philip was resolved on revenge and this in turn provoked a stiff reaction in Barcelona.[1]

★   ★   ★

What was to be the last parliament of Catalonia met in a series of sessions from 30th June to 6th July. Each of the three *Braços* met separately. The *Militar* and the Ecclesiastic were all along disposed to consider treating with Philip's government, though the former was subjected to passionate oratory by Francisco Ferrer de Ciges in favour of resistance, and the initial votes of forty-one nobles for submission were gradually whittled down. It was, however, the *Braç Real* (the Commons) which was most obdurate. After days and nights of argument, at 6.00 a.m. on 6th July a Proclamation of War was brought out 'to the sound of eight trumpets and eight drums'. It was cried by the Town Crier throughout the city on the 9th. A printed copy of this document exists, signed by Joseph Vilar. Defiant, dignified, desperate and somehow pathetic, it ends, 'God keep you many years.'[2]

In an outburst of religious fervour on the part of the citizens the patron saints, particularly Santa Eulália, were invoked again for miracles and the sacred relics mobilized. On 17th July the image of the *Virgen de la Merced* was carried in procession to the cathedral. The organisation of the fighting forces proceeded apace. The *Coronela* was a militia corps based on the *Grémios* and consisting of forty-eight companies in six battalions, at this stage numbering all-told about 5,000. The battalions' names were Most Holy Trinity, Santa Eulália, Santa Madrona, Our Lady of Grace, and so on, and the colonel-in-chief was the

Marqués de Vilana. Each company was formed by a trade or group of trades, such as confectioners, shoe-makers, dyers, linen-makers, and each maintained a hospital in the Convent of Santa Clara, manned by six surgeons. The *Coronela* was rather more than a Home Guard, if only because it had long been in existence; but it could only be used in static defence.

Three regular Cavalry Regiments, the San Jorge (Colonel Berenguer y Novell), San Miguel (Colonel Vinyalls) and The Faith (Sebastián Dalmau) were formed and some Hussars equipped. Seven infantry regiments were mustered, one mainly German and one, known as the Forsaken, Valencian. Fusilier regiments were recruited for service outside the city and companies of gunners, miners and engineers for within. The total strength was between 12,000 and 16,000. Barcelona also boasted 123 bronze and sixty-four iron cannon, twenty-three mortars and ten bronze and twenty-eight iron mortars capable only of throwing stone balls – and therefore somewhat ancient.

The Council of 100 also decided in principle to raise a squadron of armed ships to guard communications with other places on the coast and with the Balearics, from whence food would have to be brought. They tried to find seven ships but only succeeded in obtaining five, one of which already belonged to the city, the other four being English merchant ships, which were commandeered and armed. To these the Dalmau family, rich merchants in the vanguard of the resistance, added three of theirs, armed with twelve to sixteen guns. The Dalmaus also provided 210,000 *livres* towards improving the city's defences.

As the blockade and later the siege progressed, the Council of 100 acted through the *Novena*, a small committee consisting of the *Conceller en Cap* (Chief Councillor), initially Manoel Flix, and eight others. This helped to streamline matters but even in the desperate last days there were always disagreements and the enthusiastic amateurs were often at loggerheads with the professional soldiers, particularly with Villaroël.

Antonio de Villaroël, born in 1656 in Barcelona, was nevertheless a Castilian, his family stemming from near Toledo. He had served in the Spanish army from youth. In the early part of the war, he served in the Bourbon army under Orléans in 1707 and under Berwick at Almansa. Disillusioned by 1709, he had resigned his commission, been arrested and then released, and joined Charles' forces, fighting in 1710 at Villa Viciosa, where he distinguished himself. From this distance in time he seems to have been, like John Richards, a good man for whom things did not go right. In 1712 he should, with his experience and ability have been employed by Starhemberg in some senior posting. Perhaps he was too pessimistic – certainly he was a military realist – and somebody in Charles' entourage, probably Vilana y Perlas (Conde Rialp), was against him. So it was not until March 1713, when Sormani went sick, that he was appointed Inspector of Infantry. Though by then a loyal subject of Charles, he found Starhemberg's activities most unsatisfactory and resigned, joining with other generals 'in the just cause of King Charles III and to keep the liberties and privileges of Catalonia' – for the *fueros* were the one sure rallying point. When, after Starhemberg's departure he was nominated *Chefe Maior* by the *Junta de Guerra*, he only accepted it as being 'by nomination of his prince'. Charles now officially recognized him as an imperial general. He was, however, to find it increasingly difficult to get his orders carried out and his views listened to, and near the end he would resign the post of *Chefe Maior* in desperation at the irrational decisions forced on him. Yet when the final crunch came in the siege he continued to serve bravely and effectively, taking many difficult decisions, suffering a severe wound and afterwards a lengthy period of harsh imprisonment. A gaunt, determined-looking, melancholy man, he might have modelled a century or so earlier for Cervantes' 'Knight of the Rueful Countenance'. During the siege he was noted as 'showing energy, wisdom and knowledge of war above the common level', but it was in a hopeless cause. A popular song of 1715 would picture the City describing him as 'My noble son Villaroël, whose fame still echoes.'

Although determined on the policy of '*Fueros* or death', and prepared to do all in their power, the Council of 100 still hoped for help from England and Vienna, and wrote to ask for it. But at this time the emperor had no ships in which to send men and supplies – and in any event he had signed the Convention of Evacuation, which prohibited this. And Queen Anne, though sympathetic to Catalonia, led a country now committed to peace. 7th July 1713, indeed, was appointed in London as a day of public thanksgiving for the 'safe and honourable peace lately concluded'.

Poal and Nebot were sent out from the city to try, with other partisan leaders, to prevent strongpoints being taken by the Bourbons and to interrupt their supply lines. The first major attempt, at Tarragona, failed. Here Starhemberg had turned a blind eye and Wallis had himself left the place to go to Ostalrich, so that Nebot might take it if he could. But the garrison commander, an Italian called Toldo, considered himself still under orders to hand over to the Bourbons and march to Mataró for evacuation. Hurriedly sent from Barcelona, Nebot was delayed by lack of money to pay his men, and could not move until Amadou Dalmau came again to the rescue and sent him 400 doubloons.

By the time Nebot reached Tarragona on 11th July the Flemish General, Marquis de Lede, had arrived a few hours earlier with a small detachment and when Nebot appealed to the municipal council to join him there was confusion. In the end, as more Bourbon troops arrived, the council declared Tarragona an

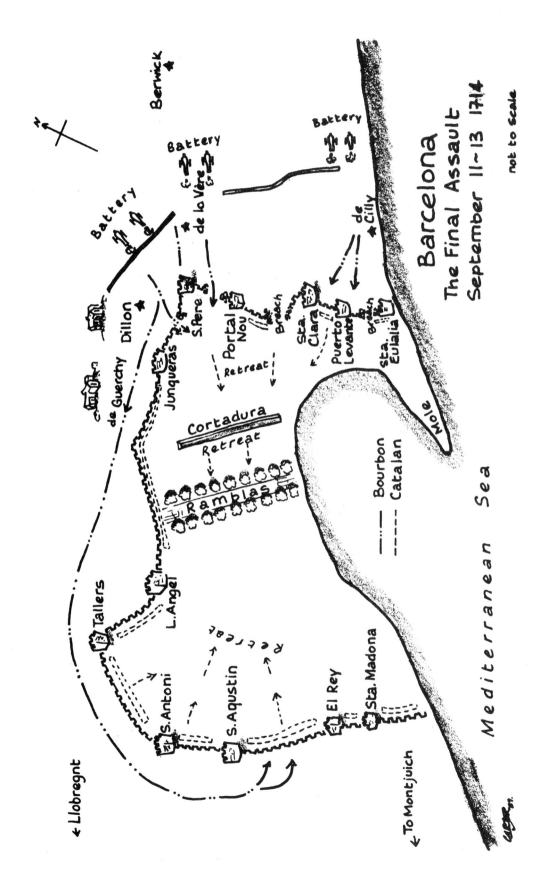

Barcelona
The Final Assault
September 11–13 1714

not to scale

Berwick

Battery

Battery

Battery

Battery

de la Vere

de Cilly

Dillon

de Guerchy

Junqueras

S. Pere

Portal Nou

Breach

Sta. Clara

Puerto Levante

Breach

Sta. Eulalia

Retreat

Mole

Cortadura

Retreat

Ramblas

Bourbon
Catalan

Mediterranean Sea

Tallers

L. Angel

S. Antoni

S. Agustin

Retreat

El Rey

Sta. Madona

To Montjuich

Llobregnt

open city and accepted Lede as governor. Elsewhere the small numbers of Catalan regulars and the occasional resentment aroused in the ordinary citizen by *Miquelet* excesses resulted in similar surrenders. Only the little town of Reus, fifteen miles or so from Tarragona, declared against Philip and stood out for Charles and the *fueros*.

By the time Popoli arrived at Igualada he may have thought all was going well. He was certainly being insufferable. When the former Imperial garrison from Tarragona reached Martorell he sent them on to Mataró in humiliating circumstances. He approved when de Fiennes, suspecting treachery at Riu de Arenas, threatened to hang local councillors. When Lede asked what he should do with captured volunteers, Don Restaino Cantelmo Stuart, Duque de Popoli, to give him part of his resounding title, instructed, on 20th July, that they and their officers should be hanged, together with one in ten of the *Miquelets* and the rest sent to the galleys.

On 29th July he sent a trumpet to the Sant Antoni gate of the city with a note couched in threatening terms: 'If you do not open your gates this day and submit to my obedience and the indult [pardon] which His Catholic Majesty has been pleased to grant ... You will be treated as obstinate rebels.' This *billet doux* should have been acknowledged by Flix, the *Conceller en Cap* but he lacked resolve and, after talking to Villaroël, called together the *Junta* of political affairs. This in turn set up a small committee which included Villaroël and formally 'received' Philip's message. After brief deliberation they replied, using the same trumpet, 'We are resolved vigorously to oppose all the enterprises of the enemy as we have done in the past.' A similar demand sent by Popoli to Majorca was turned down by Rubi, the viceroy.

Ordered by Popoli to demand Wallis' immediate removal from the scene, Ceva-Grimaldi wrote to the Graf referring to the stipulations of the Treaty of Utrecht and the Convention of Hospitalet. Wallis stolidly fudged his answer. He had considered that in turning down Popoli's terms and refusing to hand the city over, the Catalans were disobeying the orders of their king and emperor, but he had a certain sympathy with them. While at Ostalrich he even offered to sell them 600 horses for use by the *Diputació Militar* in order that that body, the only trained Catalan cavalry, which had been shipped to Arenys del Mar so as to be available for field operations, should have mounts. The sale, however, fell through for lack of money and of harness and eventually some 258 of the horses were left behind at Vich. Soon afterwards Wallis and his 2,000 men moved to Mataró when on 3rd September they were evacuated by a Royal Naval squadron.

By now Popoli's forces surrounded Barcelona in the plains. His right was on Hospitalet and his cavalry kept communications with the sea, where a small squadron under General Rios was anchored by the tower at the mouth of the River Llobregat. The vessels had been abandoned there by Barcelona. His centre was in the Convent of Grace and his left on the Clot and San Martí, this sector being manned by French troops under de Guerchy. It is true that in general the force lacked quality but it was far more numerous than those it was intended to assail. However, the latter were behind strong walls which ran between the gates. The people's spirits were high, they were expecting miracles, they were digging trenches and loopholing the walls of houses. They were set for battle. And, as Neuville put it, writing to Paris from Gerona: 'Majorca can furnish men, Sardinia corn and horses. The rich merchant, Dalmau ... bears it all at his own expense.' Even the students formed a regiment and took their turn on the ramparts. But although Villaroël had given orders for strengthening the defences, the work took much longer than in his view it should, for the different *Juntas* and other committees argued interminably and instead of getting on with it, bombarded him with letters. There were numerous small sorties leading to skirmishes and Popoli attempted to take the Santa Madrona Gate, only to be driven out with a loss of forty-five men killed and wounded. His people also had to put up with some plunging fire from the heights of Montjuich to the west.

At a council of war on 19th September at which were present Popoli, Ceva-Grimaldi, Patiño, Verboom and several Spanish generals, but not de Guerchy (perhaps Franco-Spanish friction was at work), there was a warm discussion about the next stage. Should the Bourbon army stay where it was, fairly close to the city walls or should it withdraw and prepare winter quarters on the more distant line from the Llobregat north through Mount Tibidabo? Verboom, the hired Dutch engineer, and others pressed that it should stay put, partly because a withdrawal would be bad for morale, partly because it would make it easier for the defenders to sally out and to obtain supplies. It was decided to stay, but Popoli's forces had lost what momentum they had had. Pay was slow in coming, winter was not far off – as we have observed, it was far more severe then, at the end of the Latin ice age than it is now – and food was difficult. De Fiennes, noting that a flotilla of nine ships was at Cartagena, loading ammunition for them, wondered when it would arrive. He had just replaced Brancas, his junior, of whom he was jealous, as governor of Gerona, the latter having been sent to Madrid as ambassador. De Fiennes ended a letter, 'The court of Madrid have only two choices over Barcelona. Either the king comes himself to be at the head of his troops and besiege it, or it must [continue to] be blockaded.'

At the end of the year Popoli, after more weeks of indecision, sent his men into winter quarters in barracks. There had been much desertion and among those left many were exhausted, particularly the French, by the *chevauchés* after Poal's, Nebot's and Amill's irregulars.

On the other hand the defenders of Barcelona had reason to feel encouraged. First, they had had supplies from Majorca and the convoy that brought these in had been formed into a squadron under Miguel Vaquer. This was active in seizing any vessels it came across, notably a French boat which was (probably exaggeratedly) said to be carrying 100,000 *livres*. Vaquer also took a couple of English vessels, to the annoyance of the Rear-Admiral, Cammock. Philip sent a squadron under Pintado to prevent such depredations, but this timidly based itself well out of reach of Barcelona. It was only when the French Admiral Jean-Baptiste Ducasse (or du Casse) – who had been Benbow's opponent in the Caribbean in 1702 – arrived with French ships-of-the-line in March 1714 that the blockade by sea began to be effective. Du Casse, the son of a pork butcher in Bayonne was an attractive man who had risen by sheer merit. Tall, thin, humane, witty, gentle and courteous, he was as fiery in battle as a corsair, and even St Simon, snob that he was, had praise for this self-made man. He was not to be there long, however, dying of apoplexy in June 1714.

Secondly, Popoli's army had had to waste time and energy chasing the guerillas which, even after being dispersed, still constituted a threat to his lines of communication. Although he himself had had some artillery and ammunition supplies these were so far limited. He had, for example, only six mortars in early 1714.

Thirdly, his shortage of money had forced him to place further levies on the local population and this had aroused such feelings that he felt he could not demand anymore contributions from them. On 2nd January 1714 he had therefore asked for help from Madrid and this had brought Orry to his side. Orry always took a hard line and the result was only a heightening of local resentment by the addition of 'unheard-of taxes', and a resumption of irregular warfare.

Barcelona, realizing this, sent orders to the partisan Poal to organize a general rising. At Cardona Poal found feelings strong enough to begin doing so, and together with Amill, who had rejoined him with 400 fusiliers, coming by sea via Arenys del Mar, and Brickfeuss, he fought a number of successful skirmishes. Early in February he was further reinforced by Antoni Puig y Sorribes, brother of the victim of Berga, and by Joan Vila y Ferrer, who broke out of Barcelona through the Levante Gate with 200 volunteers of the Horse of Sant Jaume. Though this operation was an encouragement to Barcelona it was never really strong enough to do much damage. 25,000 men would have caused real havoc, but there were at this time only about 5,000 insurgents and the most they could do was to prevent Cardona being attacked. This they did by forcing

Popoli to disperse his force into flying columns of up to 2,000 men under Bracamonte, Vallejo, de Thouy, de Fiennes and Mortemart, under whose pressure the guerilla effort eventually waned once more. A small sortie by the *Coronela* at the end of January and a minor naval engagement on 24th February were without much effect.

The 'war of sword, knife and punishment' was bringing Popoli no nearer to the capture of Barcelona, and he was making repeated requests for the means to undertake a proper siege. Such requests – and this was a further reason for Barcelona's unbreakable confidence – had to be sent to France via the court of Madrid, which was known to be riddled with intrigue and rotten with incompetence, and also believed to be on bad terms with the court of Versailles. That belief, although the people of Barcelona could not be fully aware of it, was well founded, and it provides the ultimate explanation of the long delay between Popoli's summons to surrender in July 1713 and the storming of the city in September 1714. It shows the effects of a kitchen cabinet on the conduct of high politics and war.

★   ★   ★

Under pressure from the formidable Madame des Ursins, Philip was holding up the signature of a peace with Holland, demanding on her behalf the Sovereign Principality of Limburg in the Spanish Netherlands, worth 30,000 *livres* a year. England and Holland had agreed, but the Emperor Charles, to whom the Spanish Netherlands had by now been ceded, would have none of it. The Dutch were perfectly prepared to hand Limburg over to her but could give no guarantee that she would continue to own it, while at the same time they demanded that Philip should sign the other articles of the treaty which had already been agreed. He refused to do so and the peace treaty was thus held up on this single point.

Philip's obstinacy can be explained by his character and circumstances. It was probably all the greater than usual because of the loss that he suffered at this time, which left him even more than ever at the mercy of Madame des Ursins. On 23rd September 1713 María-Luisa had been delivered of her third son, Fernando, the second to survive. There were rejoicings – Popoli at Igualada, had ordered salvoes and a *Te Deum* – but these were generally muted, for the queen herself was in the last stages of tubercular disease. It was surprising that the baby was born at all, let alone that he was stout and healthy, for soon a postmortem would show that most of his mother's insides had been consumed away and that there were stones in bladder and kidneys. The labour had been relatively easy but thereafter she had been in a continual fever, grown rapidly weaker, and had died on 14th February 1714 at the age of twenty-five. Philip was shattered. He had depended on her. Now she had gone but her powerful friend – and Philip's – was still there in a key position, as mistress of his household, governess of the Prince of Asturias and the other royal infant, and confidential adviser of twelve years' standing. Respect for his wife's memory imposed two demands on a king whose rational faculties seemed numbed by shock. First, he must treat the Catalans as 'rebellious scoundrels', with the severity which, as we know from the British ambassador's despatches, she demanded before her death. Secondly, he must honour his promises to Madame des Ursins, even at the cost of postponing peace with the Dutch and so, by a chain of consequences, alienating France and denying himself the help he would need for the reduction of Barcelona. In particular, Louix XIV made the despatch of reinforcements and the loan of the Duke of Berwick, contingent on the conclusion of the general peace. Philip was, in short, for sentimental reasons, to place himself in a position where he could neither conciliate the Catalans nor easily defeat them.

★   ★   ★

Within Barcelona work on the fortifications continued a little spasmodically and recruits were drilled or trained. At the end of March they made a considerable sortie with the intention of destroying Popoli's powder magazines. Bâville, writing of it from some way away in Marseilles, says that 5,000 took part (clearly an exaggeration) and were repulsed by French troops 'with much vigour and without loss. Some rebels were killed and 60 made prisoner'.

The mission entrusted to Poal and other leaders had begun with some dash and not a little brutality. De Fiennes reported that Poal had taken some 860 Walloon and Spanish prisoners and had cut their throats 'ten by ten', sparing only 100 officers who were taken to Cardona. Many villages had risen and at one stage de Muret's communications with Roussillon were completely cut, while d'Arpajon had to send his mail, like Popoli, by sea. But the gradual build-up of flying columns, whose job was to 'exterminate wholly this insolent rabble', squeezed the *Miquelets* too severely for them to be as effective as was hoped and by March 1714 they had largely shot their bolt. Nevertheless Cardona, under the staunch leadership of Desvalls, its governor and Poal's brother, remained firmly in support of its sister city.

Majorca, to which Charles had in late 1713 sent Verneda, father-in-law of his *Despacho* secretary, Rialp, was still, under its viceroy, Rubi, a source of supply, which the Spanish navy, even when reinforced by the arrival of du Casse and four French warships, was unable to intefere with. Du Casse brought in supplies for the besiegers. But apart from Philip, even the most optimistic Bourbons could not believe that an expedition could be mounted to take Majorca until after Barcelona had been captured. And from time to time, indeed, so far from Barcelona's supplies being threatened, the occasional Bourbon convoy from Roussillon was intercepted at sea by Dalmau's little squadron.

★   ★   ★

At the end of March, Popoli received from Philip a letter which though couched in gentle terms, carried the implication of severe dissatisfaction – at least in Versailles:

> 'Brancas has shown me a letter from the King, my grandfather . . . by which you will see [copy enclosed] that he wishes the Duke of Berwick to undertake the siege of Barcelona, and that only on that condition will he let me have the troops which you have been asking me to obtain from him. I am too much your friend not to see the mortification this will cause you, and you can count on me to do all that is necessary, and to keep you informed of the measures I am taking about it.'

Popoli was not such a fool as not to see the implications. He therefore decided to take some pre-emptive action, so as to strengthen Philip in his resistance to Berwick's appointment, for he wished neither to be dismissed nor to serve as a subordinate in an army of which he was at present commander-in-chief 'after working like the best of dogs', as he put it. He set up a battery of six mortars in the village of the Clot, about a mile from the Portal Nou. Like most of his projects this was ineffective. Firing about 150 rounds a day produced little result for the mortars' range of 2,500 yards did not enable them to reach any important targets in the city. Indeed, it was counter-productive, for Villaroël ordered a redoubt to be strengthened in the convent of San Francisco, mounted six guns there and began counter-battery. To make things more awkward still, he sent out some cavalry and three companies of *Coronela* as infantry to attack the mortar crews and this made Popoli cancel his bombardment. D'Arpajon, writing to Voisin, noted that the morale of the citizens had been unaffected: 'We've been throwing in bombs for three days. The rebels don't seem much frightened. They are the most fearful *canaille*.'

In the meantime, on 6th March, the Emperor Charles had, to Philip's annoyance, finally signed the general treaty of peace. The King of Spain was now the only non-signatory. The letters in which Charles conveyed the news to Barcelona were characteristically ambiguous in sense and were interpreted in the city as good news. They seemed to imply that French troops would now be withdrawn, for after all Barcelona's king, the Emperor Charles, was now apparently at peace with King Louis. This should surely mean that 'the Duc d'Anjou' would have to do what he could with his own resources, which were clearly quite inadequate. There was much rejoicing. D'Arpajon, from Martorell, wrote:

> 'Barcelona ... having heard that peace had been signed, fired off all their artillery. Next day they sent out a *pour parler*, saying that they were no longer at war with France and saw themselves as loyal subjects of the Emperor. They will not accept King Philip as their legitimate monarch, calling him the Duc d'Anjou ... Something must soon burst.'

A *Te Deum* sung in Barcelona's cathedral as part of the celebration, was, alas, not only premature, but totally mistaken, for Louis was now determined 'to remove this thorn from our foot', and was still only waiting for Philip to cave in and sign the Dutch Treaty before sending in Berwick with reinforcements to finish off the rebellion. He had no intention of leaving an active hornet's nest of rebels just across his frontier, and the treaty contained no exemption for Barcelona. He was, moreover, no less determined that whatever was done should be done properly – by Berwick.

In a last attempt to stave off his grandfather's conditions Philip now sent Orry who 'governs Spain under Madame des Ursins' – to Barcelona to assess the chances of success without French help. While casting a beady, experienced eye over Popoli's preparations (which he was in the event to find wanting), the minister also brought with him 125,000 *pistoles* and full powers to negotiate a settlement if possible, by a mixture of threat and bribery. He was even permitted to hint to the Catalans that they might be allowed to keep some of their privileges, though at the same time he was to insist that if the citizens resisted they must take the consequences.

By another of those coincidences which, together with outbreaks of religious and patriotic fervour coupled with ferocity, so characterise the fall of Barcelona, Orry's arrival took place just as the *pour parler* mentioned by d'Arpajon, indicated a misplaced peace initiative – on their own terms – from the citizens. It is as though the gods were determined to prevent a peaceful solution, let alone a happy ending. For while Villaroël was certainly hoping for a reasonable, acceptable peace, and one which he could sell to the more intransigent of his colleagues, Orry was to demand an unreasonable one. He was under pressure to produce a quick answer, though he had not been given the means – and was not temperamentally suited – to obtain one.

Villaroël's anxiety for a peace was no doubt in part prompted by the continual problems he had with the so-called government of the city. In February an enthusiastic captain in the *Coronela* had endeavoured to set up a 'Lower Chamber', manned by lieutenants and ensigns of the *Coronela*, to usurp authority. He had failed and been dismissed, but was otherwise left unpunished. In March the *Diputació Català* had dissolved itself and the affairs of the city were in the hands largely of the Conde de Casanova, a strong advocate of resistance who had replaced Flix as *Conceller en Cap*. Despite the urgency of the situation the tangles of municipal disorganisation were such that practical measures were neglected. Villaroël had been having to bombard his civilian colleagues with letters, trying to get them to provide the necessary labour to work on the fortifications. Having himself served under Berwick at Almansa, he was aware, as they were not, of the marshal's ruthless drive and ability. If Berwick were coming – and so lax were security measures in the Bourbon camp that Villaroël had almost certainly heard of the probability – Barcelona was in for a bad time of it. All the more necessary to continue with the fortifications, while at the same time trying to discover for certain what was going on.

So, on 24th April, the *pour parler* was begun. Sebastián Dalmau was sent out at 4.00 p.m. under a trumpet, to advise the nearest French general, de Guerchy, of the signing of the general treaty and ask what were to be the next moves by the French. De Guerchy sent a Colonel Monteil, who received Dalmau courteously, confirmed that there was a truce between France and the Empire (official news of the treaty had not yet arrived), but added that the French troops before Barcelona would stay put. He advised Dalmau that he and his colleagues should not look on the French as their friends. And he added that the Two Crowns intended to besiege Barcelona in due course, as the Catalans 'were in rebellion against their lawful monarch'. When Dalmau returned to Barcelona the citizens were even more confused, for they now began to realize that they might have been mistaken in their interpretation of Charles' letters. They debated again whether they should continue to resist and decided that they must, for Charles was still their king, not Philip, and the *fueros* were all-important.

Meantime, as the city authorities argued and deliberated, Orry had at last reached Popoli's headquarters, with his son, on Friday 28th April, after a brush on the way with a *Miquelet* ambush, which did not increase his equanimity. When Dalmau returned to the Bourbon camp to resume negotiations Orry began politely enough but the mood changed when Dalmau said he was not empowered to treat about delivering the city. Orry then began to bluster, threatening to send over 50,000 shells unless the city yielded, to which Dalmau replied that this was hardly the way to reach an understanding, that Villaroël had a considerable number of troops, and that the citizens would fight as well.

'Why should they', asked Orry, 'when they did not do so in 1705?'

'That was because Velasco did not then consult them.'

D'Arpajon backed Dalmau up: 'It is true that Velasco lost Barcelona.'

Orry then cooled down a little and offered an amnesty to all, without exception, to which Dalmau replied stiffly that the Catalans did not need pardon, for they had 'followed the prince who had gained Barcelona and other places in Catalonia'. He agreed, nevertheless, to take Orry's message back, and was given until 7th May to return with a reply.

Orry had already lost hope of agreement well before the deadline date. On 4th May he wrote to Philip what can only be regarded as the letter which finally determined that Barcelona would be besieged:

> 'It is not a matter of bombarding Barcelona, for that will produce no results. Barcelona must fall to a formal siege, and this is impossible unless we have the reinforcements from France, whose march has been halted because Your Majesty has not signed the Dutch Treaty ... If Your Majesty persists in making the peace with Holland dependent on the concession of the sovereignty [of Limburg] to Madame des Ursins, France, the archduke [sic] and Holland will support the rebels and make war.'

Coming from 'the creature of Madame des Ursins' this was indeed straight talking. On 20th June, the treaty with Holland was signed at last, and Madame's ambition sacrificed.

★   ★   ★

The reason for the lack of any definite reply from Barcelona after 4th May was only known later. Villaroël himself had publicly recommended reaching a settlement, probably with the overt or tacit support of a number of responsible soldiers and citizens. But the *Junta General*, under the unanimous pressure of the Commons, approached the Vicar-General of the See, who, after a meeting of the Ecclesiastics on 9th May, proclaimed that to defend the city was a 'just' action in the service of God. This stopped any movement towards settlement.

At Olesa, in the countryside, Poal's partisans held a council of war, where it was agreed that they were not strong enough to come to Barcelona's aid and could only continue the guerilla war. On 19th May sixteen of Poal's men came into the city by night to bring the citizens the news that from now on they could expect no help from the province.

They could, however, expect a new effort from Popoli. He was determined to attempt some great coup before losing his command – as it now seemed he must – to Berwick.

On 9th May he ordered ten companies of grenadiers, 1,500 fusiliers, 300 horse and 600 pioneers to take the enemy battery which was firing on them from the Capuchins. Preparations, however, were sluggish and it took till the 11th for the attack to be mounted, in two columns. Trenches were opened half-way between the Bourbon lines and the city. The Convent of the Capuchins was an essential strongpoint for the defence, so Villaroë had it fortified by an engineer, Verarde, and threw in four companies of foot and a company of volunteers under Major Armengol, to assist the fusiliers who were already there. The attack began at last, at 4.00 a.m. on the 16th, but this did not succeed until the night of the 17th/18th, the defenders losing six officers and sixty-five men, including one of the best *Miquelet* commanders, Colonel Rau, while the attackers lost seventeen officers killed and wounded, including the high-born Fleming, Torcy, and 468 men.

Alongside the Capuchins was another strongpoint, the Convent of Jesus, connected to it by an earthwork, and it was here that the defenders retreated when they had been cut off in the gardens at the rear of the Capuchins. Watched by Villaroël from the Angel Bastion, Bellver, who was in command at the Convent of Jesus, held on until the 20th, then retreated after blowing the place up together with the *Casa de Mercader* alongside it.

Despite a very fiery defence, the city thus lost two of its most important strongpoints, an event which might have caused a major drop in morale. Yet on this very day the Council of 100 met to approve again the decision 'to go on fighting to the last drop of blood'. There had been a meeting of the War *Junta* on the 16th (just as Popoli's assault began), attended by all the soldiers, Sebastián

Dalmau, Eximeno, Blas, Ferrer, and the Portuguese Gregório Saavedra; only Bellver had been absent, unwell. The Council of 100 considered the decision of the War *Junta*, and despite the loss of the Convent of Jesus, ratified the decision to fight on. This was typical of the mood of the majority. The worse the news, the more determined they were.

By 22nd May batteries had been erected, at Popoli's direction, in the gardens of the Capuchins and at 10.00 p.m. that night a ferocious bombardment of the city began, only interrupted by heavy rainstorms. No attempt seems to have been made, curiously enough, by the defenders to place cannon on the ramparts at the Tallers Gate, the Gates of the Angel, Junqueras, San Pedro or the Portal Nou, from any of which counter-battery would have been effective. The reason for this is not known.

Popoli ordered a hail of terror. Thirty mortars and six cannon were to fire on the centre of the city, to include the Ramblas and the Convent of San Francisco. There was much damage and a considerable number of casualties and some panic set in. People left their houses half-dressed in the glare of fires and to the thud of explosions. But by next day steps had been taken to move the women and children and the old to temporary quarters out of range, on the slopes of Montjuich and, as is the way with cities under bombardment, the inhabitants grew accustomed to the noise and nuisance, and a paradoxical calm returned.

Next Popoli, hearing of the movement of the population out of his range, tried to persuade Admiral du Casse to bring his ships round to face Montjuich and fire on those who were settled in encampments there 'in order to spread the terror'. But the old admiral was a chivalrous creature and he disapproved of the idea. Never, he said, in his life had he heard of such a thing, and, calling his officers to a council of war, decided that, unless directly ordered to do so by King Louis, 'they would not fire on the defenceless'.

Popoli's problems multiplied. Martorell and Mataró were isolated by a new effort on the part of Poal's irregulars and Bracamonte needed reinforcements. Eventually communications were re-opened but it had taken many men away from before the city. His total forces were down to some 12,000 foot and 4,000 horse and nothing like enough engineers. The weather was exceptionally unfavourable; he had not been able to open trenches properly and rain kept halting his batteries.

And now, at last, Berwick had had his final instructions from Louis. Fifteen French battalions had resumed their march, together with a cortège of officers including Dupuy-Vauban and his engineers. At the beginning of July 1714 there is a change in the whole tone of the correspondence in the French archives, a new sense of drive and purpose, easily detectable even after nearly three centuries. There is a feeling that matters are at last in expert hands. Optimism returns, though it is a little premature, for much would happen – and a great deal of it unpleasant – between 1st July, when Berwick crossed the border into Catalonia and 11th September when the true horror took place.

Within the city there was optimism of a kind too. This had no proper basis, but what counts at such times is what people believe, and the citizens of Barcelona were now for the most part living an existence in which hard facts meant nothing; sharing a euphoria which in no way reflected the hopelessness of their situation. Leonidas would have understood it.

★   ★   ★

July 7th 1714 saw Berwick arrive in the lines before Barcelona, accompanied by his eldest son, Lord Tynemouth and his stepson, Sarsfield, the Earl of Lucan. He also brought with him a fever which he was unable to shake off throughout the next four months, though this does not seem to have affected his commonsense, his energy or his military professionalism.

Before leaving Narbonne on 22nd June he had received his first set of instructions from Philip. Summed up, these were: if Barcelona surrendered before siege works were begun he might promise to intercede on behalf of the citizens; if not they could take the consequences. Himself bearing no particular rancour towards them and being usually considerate, he would wish to spare women, children and churches and to prevent pillage. But he always carried out orders, and these seemed to him so 'un-Christian' and so likely to be counter-productive that he wrote at once over Philip's head, to King Louis, asking for permission to use his own discretion.

In his *Memoirs* he is contemptuous:

> 'I was not surprised at such sentiments from the Spanish court; ever since the accession of Philip its behaviour has been arrogant, and from the discontent this has aroused it has often found itself on the brink of a precipice. Ministers talked of their sovereign's greatness, the justice of his cause and the wickedness of those who opposed him. Yet, while those opposed to him were his 'enemies', he treated those who supported him as merely doing their duty.'

Louis warned his grandson, 'You must treat them [the Catalans] like a father and not set them against you. Believe me, I speak from experience. Give Berwick more freedom, because there will be loyal people in Barcelona and they could be hurt just as much.' Philip relaxed, but only a little. On 29th July he wrote a second set of orders allowing Berwick to intercede on the Catalans' behalf, after as well as before the siege had begun.

Berwick spent a few days on a careful personal reconnaissance, occasionally drawing musket fire, before finally deciding on his assault plan, about which he wrote a long letter to Louis on 13th July. It was the plan proposed by Verboom:

'Having looked at the whole of the city I have decided to attack from the Besós side [i.e. north-east]. An attack via Montjuich would have been most difficult because the cannon the rebels have there would enfilade our trenches. The Capuchin front has five bastions and re-entrants and would have been difficult under heavy fire. Where we shall attack has only three bastions and although these and the curtain walls are very high the ditch is only six feet wide. And the approach will be easier for there are also a number of little mounds near the place where we can place five or six battalions [under cover] so that they are alongside the artillery park. It is true that our parallels will be in low ground and if it rains there will be a lot of mud, but this is the dry season. Acuña, Vincentilla and Courten will open the trench with four battalions of Spanish grenadiers, three of the Normandy Regiment, two of Artois, the Royal Artillery of France, three hundred horse, ten companies of grenadiers and 2,500 pioneers in reserve.'

To Berwick and his officers, the siege looked to be an easier assignment than it finally proved. This is because of the incalculable effect, when things became desperate, of most citizens taking up arms. Women, children, old men and monks all did so. Some 500 of the latter, apart from hearing confessions and acting as stretcher-bearers, also took up the arms of dead and wounded men. A French soldier gave the professional view:

'It may be said of the Barcelonese that there are few examples of so stubborn a resistance as theirs. If it had been the deed of regular troops they would have earned immortal glory. But people who rise up against their sovereign do not deserve the name of brave men.'

The defenders' reaction to the opening of the trenches took Berwick by surprise. The first parallel was about 500 yards from the city walls and ran from the seashore, across, facing the Santa Eulália Bastion, up past those of the Levante and Santa Clara and then, using a dried-out water-course, parallel to the Bastion of Portal Nou. With 2,500 pioneers at work a good deal of progress was made by dawn on the 13th, for some reason without any interruption by fire from Barcelona until daylight. But the summer night was so short that the work was not completed. There was a gap at the end near the sea and the trench had no support in the way of a redoubt. 'This meant', explained Berwick to Louis on 13th July,

> 'that at one o'clock in the afternoon the rebels carried out a sortie of 300 cavalry and 3 to 4,000 foot [in his *Memoirs* he says 6,000] along the seashore. They got right behind our trenches and killed ten or twelve Swiss pioneers. They were chased out by our grenadiers and by pickets from our positions. Our cavalry beat theirs, killing about sixty and taking a lieutenant-colonel prisoner. We lost only eight horse. [Since then] cannon fire from the town has been heavy and thirty or forty of our infantry have been killed and a Swiss captain wounded. At the same time as our left was under attack the rebels assaulted our parallel from the front with all they had, but our battalions being behind the curtains they [the rebels] were forced to return to the covered way. A great many must have been killed by our heavy fire. This evening we shall continue our parallel to the sea and close it with a big redoubt in its middle. After completing these works we shall go ahead to establish batteries. I think they will be able to fire in ten days. Vauban and Verboom have done good work on the trenches and the general officers in the trenches did very well against the sortie.'

It was unorthodox to attempt a major sortie so early in the siege. Castellví says it was initiated by Villaroël in the hopes of putting Berwick off his stroke – as to some extent it did. It may also have been tried for the sake of morale, as 'the ordinary people did not like to see the enemy working so tirelessly.' Villaroël, in this account, returned surreptitiously to the city and spoke again to Casanova who, with the other senior councillors agreed, but to the general's annoyance, insisted on including men from the *Coronela*, of whose usefulness he had doubts. Altogether his total force was about 1,000 infantry, some dismounted dragoons and 450 horse. Bellver was in command of the left. About 200 were killed, though Castellví, like Berwick, gives a higher figure.

What is strange about the affair is that an experienced soldier, aware as he was of Berwick's ability, should have thought it sensible to undertake a major sortie on the very first day against so powerful a besieging army. It seems more likely that the amateurs, including Casanova, the *Conseller en Cap*, known to be 'intransigent for resistance', insisted on the sally and pressed Villaroël against his judgement; and that, as his position as commander depended on an antique and somewhat half-baked consensus, action was taken to show the amateurs the limitations of the capabilities of the forces disposable. At all events such a large venture into the open was never again repeated, although the defenders did sortie on many occasions on a more modest scale.

The siegework continued, the first parallels being completed by 15th July, and a new parallel opened between the entrance to the Bastion of Santa Clara on the left and the angle flanked by the Portal Nou; and next night the batteries were installed and a communication trench 'sustained by two redoubts', excavated towards the Capuchin monastery. For the time being both sides contented themselves with cannon fire, on the defenders' side using, as well as ordinary cannon, their ancient stone-throwing guns. An informant in Berwick's camp sent word to the city that there was a 'spy' at high level in Barcelona who was passing information to the enemy. Villaroël spoke of this to Martí, who was in his special confidence and had commanded the right wing in the sortie. It was Martí himself who turned out to be the 'spy', for at 10.00 o'clock that very night he crept out of the city on a pretence of having orders to do so, accompanied by his brother, by Brigadier Muragall and others, mainly friends and relations. Many of them had been involved in the original rising in 1705 and Martí himself had fought well only a couple of days before. But he had for some time been in touch with Popoli 'through a couple of ladies of ill fame'. Now he went over to the other side, telling Berwick that the populace at large wanted to arrest Villaroël, suspecting him of a desire to capitulate; as soon as a breach was opened, he and the regular troops would surrender and beg for Philip's mercy, but the ordinary people were as obstinate as ever. It could be that Martí was aware of Villaroël's doubts but not of his soldierly loyalty. Berwick, although prepared to make use of such people in the past did not do so now. Martí and his friends were sent to prison at Peñiscola.

On 22nd July Berwick went at night to the trenches again, and ordered additional cannon and mortars to be sent up. These 'marched in with two pairs of kettledrums, four trumpets and a company of hautboys marching at their head and answering each other alternatively'. Straw had been laid in addition to help the band drown the noise of movement. By now sufficient progress had been made, in normal siege conditions, for the marshal to announce that St James's Day, July 25th, his own patronal feast would be a special day. On that day the siege proper was to begin. But by then the citizens had also been active. A proclamation had ordered that everybody except monks and priests should work on the 'great intrenchment' – the *cortadura* parallel to those ramparts which were being demolished by the fire of Berwick's cannon. Houses were being pulled down and a huge ditch dug to act as a second line of defence and it was rapidly being completed. A wooden bridge which might have offered an easy entry was burned down on purpose.

All this was probably seen by an English naval officer, Captain Gordon of H.M.S. *Launceston* who had anchored at the port with orders from Admiral Wishart to deliver a note to the city council demanding reparations for English ships and cargoes which had been commandeered. Wishart, like the French General de Guerchy, was at least polite enough to write in Catalan, which is more than can be said for Philip's own officers. Gordon was courteously received and given a proud and touching reply to the letter he brought: 'Being altogether without resources, abandoned by everybody, we throw ourselves at the feet of the Queen of Great Britain, imploring her support.'

They could not know it, but the poor woman was dying and the question of who was to succeed her was of far greater importance in England than the destiny of a former ally. Gordon, a sympathetic enough character, agreed willingly to take this reply and was thanked by being given 'an ostentatious and copious refreshment followed by a musical concert.' Next day, before sailing, he was invited by Sebastián Dalmau to 'a splendid lunchon and a gift of sweet and dry wines – at a distance of only 500 yards from the trenches opened by Marshal Berwick'. The defenders were showing pathetically misplaced good manners, for their ex-ally had indeed abandoned them for ever.

Their plight was indeed dire. From the ramparts the menace of the Bourbon batteries could easily be seen, twelve of eight or ten cannon each, plus a mortar battery concentrating on part of the city wall towards which the creeping siegeworks were nibbling away. At night on the 24th the guns ceased fire, though apprently scarcely affected by the counter-battery of the defenders.

Then, on St James's Day at 4.00 a.m., Berwick went into the trenches and joined General de Robeck and his Number Two, d'Havré (or d'Avaray), cousin of the man killed at Saragossa in 1710. Mass was said and the chaplain was asked to bless the guns. Then these opened fire again and continued till nightfall, 'playing on the walls, and the Bastions of Santa Eulália, the Levante, the Santa Clara and Portal Nou – and on the new *cortadura* behind them.' It was exactly a year to the day since Popoli had arrived before the city and unsuccessfully demanded its submission.

From deserters Berwick learned that powder and water supplies in the city were running low – it was the dry season. And when on 26th July he received a letter, sent under trumpet by Villaroël, he returned it unopened, saying that the city must open its gates and surrender at discretion. Later he regretted this, when he learned that all the letter contained was the militarily correct notice that his own quarters would not be subjected to bombardment.

While the bombardment continued for the next five nights and days, Villaroël did his best to cover all the defensive points. He even placed the *Coronela* in the crucial Levante and San Pedro Bastions, for he was extremely short of men. All that could be done was to hang on grimly. On the night of 30th July Berwick again went to the trenches to observe the assault. Arthur Dillon was lieutenant-general of the day and was in command of the extremely fierce attack which now took place in two columns, led by eight grenadier companies, from the parallel only thirty yards from the salient angles of the Bastions and therefore too close for traversing fire. The covered way had to be abandoned by the defenders for sheer lack of numbers and the besiegers made a firm lodgment in the counterscarp which they proceeded to fortify in their turn. A vigorous counter-attack next day failed to dislodge them, though some 400 were killed and wounded, including Brigadier Courten, who had led one of the two columns. From the third parallel Verboom began to mine beneath the walls while four batteries were erected in the covered way itself. Verboom's mines were attacked with particular fury and on one occasion, on 3rd August, twenty-four men under an Aragonese Ensign, Adrián, and a sergeant completely destroyed one near the Santa Clara Bastion.

Far too late there now arrived, carried by an Imperial colonel, Juan Francisco Ferrer, an offer from Emperor Charles to deliver Barcelona and Majorca to Philip, provided the Catalan *fueros* were preserved. Ferrer's arrival at Barcelona coincided with that of Philip's second set of instructions to Berwick, dated 29th July, with its bitterly obstinate terms. So out of touch were these instructions with reality that Berwick, sending them on to the Duc de Maine, now minister for war, remarked, 'In Madrid they make projects based on a total lack of knowledge when it would seem only natural for them to consult those on the spot whose job it is.'

Bombardment yielded scant results. Berwick waited till he thought the fire from the city was slackening. Then, on 12th August, a full month after the first assault, orders were given for a fresh attempt. Arthur Dillon was again general of the day – he seems almost always to have been picked for this task when there was an assault. The sap leading to the covered way was complete in front of the Portal Nou and Santa Clara Bastions, the galleries for blowing in the moat walls were ready and the breaches 'practicable', to be made increasingly so by a mine under the flank of the Portal Nou. Dillon, with Camp Marshal Castillo and Brigadiers Torrecusa and Ordoño, commanded ten battalions of mixed French and Spanish infantry, six grenadier companies, 300 horse and 2,000 pioneers. At break of day the mine was set off as a signal and the besiegers forged forwards. Initially they were fortunate in establishing a foothold, but this was no ordinary siege and an hour later they were driven out by a determined sally. Losses were heavy on both sides, the attackers admitting to thirty-seven dead and ninety-seven wounded and claiming 300 among the defenders; but the latter were still in possession. Berwick felt that this was because the breach had not been wide enough. A renewed assault on the 13th at night gave the assailants a hold on the Santa Clara Bastion though at further heavy loss, including Brigadier Pollastron, badly wounded, and Brigadier Sauneboeuf, killed. After some eight to ten hours of hand-to-hand fighting, in which even Capuchin friars and Jesuit priests were reported to be active, the situation was at stalemate.

Next day, 14th August, the defenders threw in all they had and recovered the positions they had lost, the besiegers thus having nothing to show for this murderous and bloody attack on the Portal Nou and Santa Clara Bastions. During the three days of this action the besiegers probably lost two-thirds of those engaged and the defenders a third – because they were more sheltered. There were many deeds of great gallantry on both sides but Berwick was not satisfied with the behaviour of his men: 'Our troops were shaken by the confidence of the enemy attack and did not return [it] with sufficient vigour.' Indeed Ceva-Grimaldi was reprimanded for not trying hard enough.

Exhaustion in the city was now even more extreme, the *Coronela* in particular being described as very tired. Pickets could not be placed out of sight for fear of desertion. A boat brought a message from Rubi, Viceroy of Majorca, that Admiral Wishart was offering to mediate; it appears that he had now received orders to help rather than hinder the defenders. But his attitude was suspect; Berwick would not listen; and Barcelona was determined to fight on.

In his *Memoirs*, Berwick says:

'The enemy's stubborn resistance caused me to cease similar attacks, yet it was hard to see how otherwise the place could be taken. Our engineers, who were only conversant with the routine of their job, could advise nothing better than a general assault of the breach in the curtain wall between Puerta Nueva [Portal Nou] and Santa Clara. Surely anyone making such a proposal must have been off his head. The flanks were intact, the breach was mined, a strong entrenchment lay beyond [the ramparts], *coupures* had been made in the ramparts on either side of the breach. At length, after having taken a long walk and thought deeply I decided so to open the front of the attack as to enable us to go in in full battle order. And so, without exposing myself to further checks I went to work steadily, pushing forward batteries, and bore patiently the murmurs of the officers who were getting tired of the long drawn-out operation.'

His own health was now very poor, and the fever persistent.

The detachments he had sent into the country were not at this time very successful in suppressing the rising there; so that was a further preoccupation. Bracamonte, after revictualling Berga, fell on and routed Poal and 3,000 *Miquelets* in a ravine and twice more broke up other insurgent bodies. But Poal persisted and soon had actually collected a force estimated at 10–12,000 armed peasants whom he led to within eighteen miles of Berwick's headquarters. They were eventually defeated and driven off by de Thouy, González and Bracamonte and began to disperse; only to gather again and force the garrison of Mauresa to retire to the citadel. Little quarter was given in this savage form of warfare, and prisoners from Poal's force were hanged as a deterrent. Yet it all took time and troops. Berwick had to send d'Arpajon with four French battalions and some cavalry to help de Thouy and Mortemart. It was not until 31st August that he could write; 'Mortemart has beaten [Poal] hollow at the foot of the mountains.' The guerrillas sent word into the city that they could do no more.

By then, Berwick was hoping to quicken the pace of surrender by turning the screw of hunger. Deserters in scores provided a general picture of the situation in the city, a grim mixture of fervour and starvation. Priests daily preached penitence to packed, hungry congregations. Troops, while prepared in principle to face gunfire, were becoming mutinous for lack of bread. They were not alone. At nightfall women would break the law by stealing out through the breaches to beg for food at their enemies' trenches. The arrival of three store-boats from Majorca on 29th August caused a near-riot as people fought their way to find food. An attempt by the authorities to introduce rationing was too late, for those who had been astute enough to hoard would not give up what they had hidden away.

A council of war on 1st September considered a muster of available troops. Only about 1,800 regular horse and foot remained, augmented by about 4,500 *Coronela* who were now too tired to do much, and a further 6,295 elderly men and boys under fourteen. After a lengthy discussion Villaroël postponed a decision until the 2nd, probably because he knew that the predominant *Braç Real*, militarily ignorant, would not see sense and needed a firm hand. Next day he and other professionals, 'as officers of the Emperor Charles', gave their views individually in writing, the vast majority in favour of capitulation. The place was in ruins and stank like a charnel house. There were no drains, smoke from burning buildings mingled with other stenches. There was no food. And the bombardment was continuing and growing in intensity. Moreover on that day there was a heavy rainstorm from early morning until 10.00 a.m., adding to the sordid scene. Admittedly it destroyed the attackers' trenches but it also flooded the mines of attacker and defender alike.

Accounts vary as to what took place at this time in Berwick's camp. He certainly held a council of war at which all his generals were present. They appear to have been in favour of calling on the city to surrender without another attack. He says himself that he yielded to their view, that he knew of the state of the city's defences and that he wished to save bloodshed. He may well have known from indirect contacts that Villaroël was in favour of capitulation, but he could not be sure of the attitude of the populace and may have feared that their resistance would harden if they were to hear of intervention elsewhere on their behalf, however ineffective. Above all, at the back of his mind, Queen Anne's death and Louis' feeble health may have raised thoughts of what he might, once this affair was over, be able to do perhaps for his family if his half-brother were to be King of England; or of what might happen to them all if Orléans became Regent of France. And his fever persisted. It was an anxious time for him.

At any rate he decided to beat the chamade. Some accounts say this was on the 4th but it is certain that he did so on the 3rd after his council of war. In his *Memoirs* he says that 'on the 3rd I yielded to the requests of my general officers in sending an intimation to this place'. This also fits in with the names of the officers of the day, General de la Croix, Camp Marshal d'Esterre and Brigadier d'Avaray. De la Croix sent a Major Montesquieu to call out from the trenches that Berwick 'washed his hands of the bloodshed and horror that would take place in the assault he would have to order if the rebels did not surrender at discretion', and to ask that this message should be sent to Villaroël.

It was heard by the Portuguese Colonel Saavedra who sent an immediate note to Villaroël, which was at once transmitted to the council. Montesquieu waited for two hours before being told to return next day, and the *Novena de Guerra*, the inner committee, met in the city. Whatever was decided by the *Novena* had still to be approved by the *Braç Real* who seemed as unlikely as ever to be agreeable to capitulate. At their meeting on the 4th Feliú de la Penya indulged in some lively oratory, opposing any accommodation. Casanova has gone down in history for wishing to capitulate but in fact he was probably still in favour of continued resistance. Very early in the morning of the 5th the *Braç* sent a long, slightly incoherent message to the *Novena*. At first they would send no reply to Berwick. Then they would send a refusal. All hope might have gone but they were still hoping for a miracle. Villaroël refused at first to pass on a negative reply. Then he agreed to let it go but insisted on resigning as commander-in-chief. They accepted his resignation but it was kept secret, and eventually he stayed on to fight on a personal basis.

It was then that the Commons took three decisions, carried by twenty-eight votes to four. They would first nominate Our Lady of Grace, patroness of the *Coronela*, as commander-in-chief (and henceforth the statue was present at all meetings). Secondly, they issued a decree raising more money for the defence, and in particular to pay the *Coronela*. Thirdly, they would ask for God's help.

It was, in Canrobert's epigram on an incident a century and a half later, 'magnificent, but not war'. And it was ineffectual. Berwick had decided to wait no longer. It had taken three days before the reply was actually read out across trenches to be heard by d'Asfeld, now general officer of the day: 'The Three Estates of Barcelona have resolved unanimously neither to make nor to receive any proposition for surrender.' The reader of the message added, 'Does Your Excellency wish for anything more?' D'Asfeld made no reply. Berwick commented coldly, 'There's a bold answer! We have reason to hope that in a little while they will regret it.'

By 10th September the breaches were capable of accepting a broad frontal attack. One indeed would take a battalion in line abreast. The rains continued, with heavy squalls of wind. Once more the damp put out the defenders' mines, making their job more difficult. The assault was to be made on the 11th. Arthur Dillon was in command of the right and centre with largely Spanish but some French troops, and de Cilly of the left, with mainly French soldiers. Altogether thirty-one battalions of foot and thirty-eight companies of grenadiers were formed up at nightfall at the openings in the covered way, and with them were 1,100 pioneers, forty-nine miners and forty gunners, 500 dragoons and 200 horse. Berwick himself commanded a reserve of eleven battalions, eight companies of grenadiers, 350 pioneers, fifteen miners and ten gunners, with de Guerchy and de la Vère to assist him. The right was to attack the Portal Nou, the centre the curtain wall between this and the Santa Clara Bastion and the left the curtain next to the Levante Gate. As the inevitably tedious job of marshalling these large numbers in confined spaces went on, the tension was acute in the Bourbon ranks.

Then at dawn on the 11th the signal to attack was given by a triple discharge of ten heavy cannons and twenty mortars. The assault began. Somewhat to the surprise of the besiegers the city's batteries were slow to open fire and the defenders equally slow to form up. De Cilly was initially held up by the

Barcelona
The Siege Builds up
July~August 1714

not to scale

- Main Attack
- Secondary Attack

Powder Magazine

Tallers
L'Angel
S. Antoni
S. Agustin
El Rey
Sta. Madona

To Montjuich

Ramblas

Cortadura

Juniqueras
Convent of Jesus
Capuchin Convent

Communication Trench

Guns
water

S. Pere
Coronela
Portal Nou
Breach Aug 6

Breach Aug 6
mines
Covered Way

Sta. Clara
Puerto Levante
Sta Eulalia

July 15
2nd Parallel July 15
1st Parallel

Sortie July 14
Guns
Retreat July 15

Mole

Mediterranean Sea

Bourbon
Catalan

Levante Gate, but a party of grenadiers came at the defenders from the flank and shoulder. After some brisk fighting the defenders were thrown out of all three Bastions, the Castilian flag raised and the throats of anyone remaining on the spot cut. Even the *Cortadura* was abandoned and the attackers poured into houses and churches.

After taking the *Cortadura* the Visconde del Castillo (Villadarías' son) told his Brigadier, the Visconde del Puerto to advise de Guerchy and Dillon by a shout that 'the great trench' was not mined, and then moved to the right. However, the French General de la Vère now came up from the reserve (presumably with leave from Berwick, one does not know) intent on commanding the sector, 'so as not leave all the glory to the Spaniards'. After a fierce argument it was agreed that Brigadier del Puerto should command, apparently under the joint orders of de la Vère and Castillo. The movement was thus delayed and this delay coincided with a staunch effort of defence in the Bastion of San Pere, which stood on the way to the Tallers Gate. Reportedly 'as calm as if he were pondering tactics in his dressing-gown', Berwick ordered that the attack on San Pere should be discontinued and entrenchments dug to protect the troops and enable them to penetrate towards the Ramblas (which is now the fashionable promenade running north and south towards the harbour). He also sent in a further ten battalions from the reserve to support Dillon in this move and the Irishman resumed the advance, reaching the Arboleda.

It was now 8.00 a.m. and the defenders still held the San Pere Bastion, but the attackers' blood was up after their appalling repulse and another assault was made, only called off by Berwick himself going to the spot and commanding immediate obedience to his orders. He later commented bitterly that this piece of hot-blooded insubordination had caused him some hundreds of totally unnecessary casualties.

When the attack began at dawn Villaroël had been in his house 'awake and sitting in a chair, waiting to go on board ship'. He had been offered a frigate, after his resignation as commander-in-chief, to take him to Majorca. Hearing the alarm bell he at once decided as a professional soldier to do what he could to help the defence. Finding a horse he rode to the Plá del Borne, where he met two senior councillors, Pinós and Placencia. He sent them to the city hall to say that a major effort was required and that now was the time to bring out the sacred Banner of Santa Eulália. He then set about placing detachments in positions to tackle the assailants from whichever direction they should come, including San Augustín and Sant Antoni. Cannon were mounted in the doorways of shops and other buildings on the Ramblas and orders were sent to Colonel Vila to send powder from Montjuich – for in the usual confusion a ship bringing supplies had not been unloaded. Those manning the various positions were given ammunition, victuals and brandy 'to refresh them'.

Casanova, the *Conceller en Cap*, insisted on carrying the banner when it was brought from the cathedral, while the two others, Pinós and Placencia held the cords which spread it, and together they paraded it round the defences, followed by men of the Third and Sixth *Coronela*. Villaroël even detached thirty horse to accompany the procession. Such was the shortage of men that this parade seems to have been, for all its morale-building intentions, a touching but futile effort. From about 8.00 a.m. until 10.00 the banner was carried round while the hand-to-hand fighting went on; then Casanova was badly wounded and the aged Placencia insisted on carrying it. When it reached the breach between the Portal Nou and San Pere it was recognized by Verboom from the enemy lines, though others described it as 'a black flag carrying a skull and crossbones'.

By now the situation at the Levante front was dangerous for the defenders. The first wave of the assault, under Brigadier Chateaufort, a Provençal who had left religious training to serve in the Spanish Army, had been held up by Colonel Vilana but now the assailants, reinforced, were driving towards the Mediodia Gate, until Villaroël contrived to find enough men to halt them. He held a brief meeting with Pinós and Placencia and tried to mount a counter-attack at either end of the defence lines. He is reported to have given the troops a rousing exhortation but it is doubtful if many heard it, for the noise must have been appalling. He then positioned himself at a point between the Plá d'en Llull and the Plá del Borne but was severely wounded and had to hand tactical command of the post to Captain Bordas and overall command to General Sans, while he was taken into a dressing-post to have the musket ball removed.

Another incident now took place, a mixture of bravado, pathos and farce, when two members of the *Diputació* of Catalonia brought to the *Novena* the Banner of San Jordi, the flag of the Principality, and wished to parade it as well. General Sans, who had much to worry him, said it would be more of an embarrassment than a help, that it would need a huge guard and that men were in short supply. What was needed most was food. He was right, but 'this painful and humiliating withdrawal of the symbol of the Catalan nation meant that the city was beaten. All felt at that moment that they were defeated.'

It was by now 11.00 a.m. and there was a temporary lull in the firing. A meeting of the *Junta* had begun at 8.00 at the house of one Gorgot near the Plá de Junqueras. Villaroël was still under treatment, and those present included Feliú de la Penya, Sayol – Lieutenant-Governor of Catalonia – Sebastián Dalmau, and others, plus an important figure, Francisco Ferrer, who had been sent to Barcelona by Rubi from Majorca to try and obtain mediation. It was a lively meeting full of polemics and cries of betrayal. Ferrer pressed to be allowed to intervene but received no clear agreement. By the time it was over it was near mid-day and he went to see Villaroël, who instructed him, on his own authority, to beat the chamade but first to return to see the representatives of the Three Estates and obtain their agreement. Ferrer, however, had clearly had enough of polemics and went first to canvas other professional officers. All considered that the city's forces were incapable of any further action. Castellví was sent on horseback to consult officers who were with the Banner of Santa Eulália, now at the San Pere Bastion, with the same result. When Ferrer and Castellví returned to the Commons, these were still arguing among themselves. So, in the end it was back to Villaroël who, wounded and exhausted, took the final decision to capitulate, encouraged no doubt by the sensible Ferrer. It was by no means the least courageous of many brave acts on the part of Villaroël at this time.

The first contact with the besiegers was in fact made by Thoar, who, announcing himself as a brigadier asked to see de la Vère, the sector commander. There was some affable talk but Thoar took a rather haughty line in demanding a parley. De la Vère passed the request back to Berwick as Thoar returned to his lines. It was now four o'clock, and after the heavy rains the area outside was like a swamp. Thanks to Villaroël, the Commons tardily agreed to join the initiative and a mission of three deputies was sent via the breach at the San Augustín Gate. It represented the military, ecclesiastic and civil authorities and consisted of Ferrer himself, Jacinto Oliver and Mariano Durán. Conducted to Berwick's quarters, they adopted, like Thoar, a haughty tone, demanding a parley, but Berwick would have none of this.

> 'I answered that it was now too late [for that]. We were already masters of the city and had it in our power to put everyone to the sword, and I would not listen to any proposals on their part except of submission at discretion to His Catholic Majesty and imploring his mercy.'

They continued to argue but he refused to listen and they withdrew. At 8.00 p.m. he sent his son, Tynemouth, to tell the city authorities that if they did not surrender by daybreak he would sack the place. It was not until after midnight that the three-man commission reached the Commons and few of them were about, so unofficial discussions probably continued all night until 8.00 in the morning of the 12th, when a full meeting took place in the council room of the hundred, at the end of which it was decided to submit. The three men were sent back once more to see the marshal.

There does not seem to have been a formal capitulation. A document prepared by Berwick had been printed but it was not signed:

'Although the City of Barcelona has been exceedingly tardy in approaching His Majesty and beseeching him to show clemency towards it, Marshal the Duke of Berwick is of his very disposition so kindly that he is loath to have recourse to all the rigours permitted him by the Articles of War, and has been graciously pleased to spare the lives of all the people and inhabitants of Barcelona and of all those who do at present abide there. He has commanded moreover that the City shall not be put to the sack, and that all the citizenry shall be permitted to continue to reside in their own homes, and that no proceedings shall be instituted against those who have in the past shown disloyalty to the King. All those regular soldiers at present in the City shall remain there at His Majesty's pleasure as is laid down in the Articles of War. Their lives shall be spared.'

The fact that this was not signed may have been because it was contrary to Philip's instructions. But Berwick gave his word that the citizens' lives would be safe and that there would be no plunder in order, he explained later, 'to preserve for the King of Spain a rich and flourishing city from which he could by this means hereafter obtain considerable revenues.' To avoid his own troops going on the rampage he would not allow them into the place on the 12th,

'lest, night coming on before I could have settled everything, confusion and plunder would have ensued. I therefore thought it proper to conceal from everyone all I had been concluding with the deputies, and pretended to prepare all things for a general assault next day. I sent word to the rebels to keep a good guard on their barracks and entrenchments in the evening. However, I took possession of Montjuich. On the morning of the 13th the rebels retired from their posts, and our troops, having beaten the *générale*, marched through the streets in such [good] order that not a single soldier broke ranks.'

The Spanish royal guards were put on the churches, convents and the Royal Palace. The right of the army entered by the Calle San Pedro, the Portal Nou and the Portal del Angel, the left via the Palace to the Portales de Mediodia and Pescatória and the centre by the Santa Clara and Plá d'en Llull. A total of sixteen battalions, 400 dragoons and 400 horse formed the garrison. Berwick concludes:

'The inhabitants were in their houses, in their shops, and in the streets, looking on our troops passing by as if in time of peace; a circumstance perhaps incredible that such profound quiet should in an instant have succeeded to so much confusion; and, what is still more wonderful, that a town taken by assault should not be plundered; this can only be ascribed to God, for all the power of man could not have contained the soldiers.'

He was perhaps a little too modest, for he certainly had his men well in hand after a murderous sixty-one days of hard battle, and few other generals could have done as much. Within the city were vast quantities of shot of all kinds ('enough for another siege') and much other war matériel, but very little gunpowder and, above all, even less food. It was observed that the inhabitants 'were recognizable by their pallor'.

Estimates of losses on the two sides vary. The affair at San Pere Bastion alone had cost Berwick about 2,000 men – one regiment, the Orléans, losing all but five of its officers – whereas the defenders' loss there was less than 600. The marshal put his losses at 10,000 killed or wounded; his son at 8,000 of whom 5,500 were French and the rest Spanish. Tynemouth estimated the total defenders' loss at 6,000 but clearly this was pure guesswork. Sanpère y Miquel, after a close reckoning, says that the besieging army lost 2,000 more than the besieged. Probably the best estimate is that of Verboom, given in his letter to Grimaldo:

'For the two months of this siege Berwick's losses were 2,000 dead and 6,000 wounded; those of the defenders 3,500 dead and 5,000 wounded. But the latter figure does not include the unknown number of deaths from starvation and other causes, and as many of the participants were volunteers it is even more uncertain. On top of this, the material destruction had been appalling. One-third of the city's houses had been completely demolished, another third were in bad condition, and few of the rest were without some damage.'

Perhaps some of the 'profound quiet' on which Berwick remarked was explicable as apocatharsis, the aftermath of a huge, orgiastic blood-letting, the kind of thing that followed the less appetizing Roman games, a public execution for treason in 17th-century England, or in modern times in Spain a *corrida de toros*. It was not, of course, a total quiet. Firearms were for the most part handed over, though no doubt a few were hidden in cellars or buried in gardens. Gentlemen were permitted to retain their swords but there were cases of soldiers stripping the owners of these by force. So many of the city's men had been killed or were for the present under guard that it was largely the women who opened the stalls (*tiendas*) to sell what little was available the day after the surrender. Here again there were cases of bad behaviour. 'Some officers, under a pretext of buying, took without paying, using foul words to the men and women selling.'

This did not however last long. Berwick had expressly avoided imposing any indiscriminate hanging or other violence on the inhabitants. He himself entered the city on 18th September and had a good look at the situation, setting up at once a new *Junta* or local committee of administration under the presidency of Patiño, with a membership culled entirely from Catalans known not to have been involved in the 'rebellion'. As this could hardly have done much about disputes between the soldiery and the citizens, he appointed de Guerchy as military governor and Maulevrier-Langeron as king's lieutenant. De Guerchy, hearing of the forced seizure of swords, had them returned to their owners; and, when informed of the fact that 'Spanish soldiers had been outrageous, taking without paying', gave orders for them to be found and shot.

Berwick would have preferred to leave the city in the hands of a Frenchman like de Guerchy, who spoke good Catalan, but the French troops were due to return to France – many had indeed marched away within a matter of weeks and most were to leave by the end of the year. Philip therefore insisted on appointing his own nominee as governor and selected, of all people, Tzerclaes. But by then the marshal, himself on his way home, did not bother to protest.

Twenty leading rebels, including Sebastián Dalmau and Villaroël were shipped to imprisonment at Alicante. In 1715 they were transferred to Corunna on the north-west coast. Here the Emperor Charles wrote to Villaroël, sending money to help him escape, but the attempt to do so by sea was discovered and he was shifted once more, this time to Segovia. It was not until 1725, after the Treaty of Vienna, that he would be released, to die, aged eighty-six in 1742.

On 18th September, the same day that Berwick entered Barcelona and heard a *Te Deum* sung in the cathedral, the city of Cardona surrendered to Mortemart. Poal and other *Miquelet* leaders had gone there to await a capitulation. It was a strong place, winter was not far off, and after the shattering siege of Barcelona Berwick did not want a prolonged investment. The garrison, under Poal's brother, Desvalls, was therefore offered advantageous terms and took them, though Philip characteristically protested.

There remained Majorca. From Palma, the capital, on 13th October the Viceroy, Rubi, wrote to Berwick asking for the island to be included 'in the accommodation with Barcelona', and Berwick sent General d'Adoncourt with a small squadron of six vessels to arrange this. The British government were suspected, however, with some justice, of wanting to keep the island for themselves and Wishart had warned Rubi to do nothing in a hurry. Orry wrote at some length to Versailles about this. 'England is showing ill will and must not be allowed to profit from her offer to take over Majorca.' He had even gone so far as to ask Berwick to go there himself, but the marshal had had enough. His troops were on their way to France or going into winter quarters. He, Berwick, 'was so exhausted by fatigue that I hadn't the strength to do anything'.

He left Barcelona via Sarriá and travelled slowly, visiting his estates at Liria in the province of Valencia with his son, Tynemouth, whom he intended to be heir to them. On 28th October he was welcomed enthusiastically by the populace as he rode into Madrid. Philip was affable despite the marshal's disobedience to his orders. Tynemouth was awarded the Golden Fleece and the wounded Lucan given a company in the Royal Guard. The duchies of Liria and Gérica were constituted a *mayorazgo* or entailed estate and Tynemouth was formally recognized as heir. Berwick received a pension of 100,000 *livres* and a diamond-hilted sword which had once belonged to Philip's older brother, the late Charles, Duc de Bourgogne. In bestowing it Philip made a graceful enough speech: 'My brother was very fond of you. He had a high opinion of you, so I think you will enjoy receiving something that comes from him.'

★   ★   ★

Majorca and Ibiza witnessed the last convulsion of the war. Rubi remained in undisturbed control and in February 1715 Charles ordered the Graf Daun in Naples to send 2,000 men, of whom 200 were Germans, from Sardinia to reinforce him. Then, within a month he ordered the viceroy to evacuate the place, apparently realizing that the population was not particularly martial and was quite prepared to accept Philip as king. Wishart was still at Port Mahon as commander-in-chief of the Royal Navy's Mediterranean squadrons and he and Lord Forbes, now Governor of Minorca, actually helped the passage of these troops. Philip, as usual obstinate and impatient, sent d'Asfeld with an expeditionary force, which occupied most of the island, though Rubi hung on in Palma, hoping to exact guarantees of traditional liberties. On 22nd June, however, a conference of the citizens and ecclesiastics of Palma made it clear to Rubi that they were not formed of the same resistant stuff as the people of Barcelona. At this point Lord Forbes came to Palma and by his mediation arranged for evacuation by Rubi and occupation by Philip's forces.

★   ★   ★

Catalonia lost her *fueros* formally when in June 1715 the New Plan for Spain was published and the Catalan institutions were integrated with those of the rest of Spain. Bolingbroke, perhaps in self-justification, had proclaimed that the Castilian privileges would be more use as they would give the Catalans the entrée to the American trade. No such thing occurred, though the political and administrative effects were otherwise lasting; and this hurt, for it was for such independence that the people had sacrificed so much.

On the other hand some of the traditions continued, such as that of the *Grémios*, and the sturdy Catalans turned to and made the most of the resources available to them. It is probably, however, an over-statement to say, as does Voltes Bou, that 'their old zeal for the *fueros* was sublimated into an inimitable enthusiasm for prosperity'. The citizens of present-day Barcelona would surely accept the judgement of Enric Prat de la Riba in 1889 that 'the sacrifice should not be a model, since it was inopportune and inconvenient to the interests of the region'. A rational approach to Catalan autonomy had been resumed since the restoration of democracy in Spain. 1714 was not 'the end of the Catalan nation'. That nation did not take kindly to the construction by Philip in 1716 of the *Ciutadella*, a fortress, just to the east of the city, or to the pulling-down of houses and straightening of streets so that the citizens might be prevented from causing trouble by a whiff of grapeshot – either from the *Ciutadella* in the east or from Montjuich to the west. The *Ciutadella* was demolished in the 1860s, to make way for a public garden, just when Napoleon III, with the aid of Baron Haussmann, was adopting precautions similar to those of Philip in order to control the people of Paris.

For Spain as a whole the War of Succession had a unifying, centralizing and modernizing effect. More coin was circulating than ever before. There had been no plague, and the fighting had not affected most of the ancient cities and towns. The New Plan, initiated by Orry and Bergeyck provided a mainspring for improved efficiency of government, and the removal of the burden of administering possessions in northern Europe and Italy made the job of running the home country easier. Philip resented the loss of these possessions and fought a series of wars, 1717–20, 1727, 1732–35 and from 1739 until his death in 1746 in an attempt to rebuild piece-by-piece the empire of his predecessors and provide principalities for his large family. Apart from such relatively minor struggles, the history of Spain in the XVIIIth century did not greatly tempt historians until nearly 100 years later. By then steam was running out of the Bourbon dynasty, and yet, when Napoleon tried to impose extraneous control on her, Spain rose as a whole to the tocsin of 'Death to the French' and fought another Peninsula War. As Plato said, 'Only the dead have seen the end of war.'

Bibliography and Notes

Abbreviations

Add.MSS.	Additional Manuscripts, British Library
Adm.	Admiralty Papers, Public Record Office
AGI	Archivo General de Indias, Seville
AGS	Archivo General de Simancas
AHN	Archivo Histórico Nacional, Madrid, Sección de Estado (except where *libro* is specified)
Atkinson (1931)	C. T. Atkinson 'Brihuega', *JSAHR*, xxxi (1931)
Atkinson (1938)	C. T. Atkinson, ed., *War of the Spanish Succession* (Camden Society Special Publications, v, 1938)
Atkinson (1944)	C. T. Atkinson, 'The Second Front in the Spanish Succession War', *JSAHR*, xxvi (1944)
Ayala	I. López de Ayala, *Historia de Gibraltar* (1782)
Baudrillart	A. Baudrillart, *Philippe V et la Cour de France* (1890)
B. De C.	Biblioteca de Catalunya, Barcelona
Berwick	James, Duke of Berwick, *Memoirs* (1779)
BIHR	*Bulletin of the Institute of Historical Research*
B.L.	British Library
Bolingbroke	Henry, Viscount Bolingbroke, *The Study and Use of History* (1728)
Boyer	A. Boyer, *The History of the Reign of Queen Anne, Digested into Annals* (1703–13)
Bruguera	*Història del Memorabel Sitio y bloque de Barcelona* (1872)
Burchett	J. Burchett, *Naval Transactions* (1720)
Burnet	G. Burnet, *History of His Own Times* (1833)
Burton	J. H. Burton, *History of the Reign of Queen Anne* (1880)
Byng Papers	W. C. B., Tunstall, ed., *Byng Papers* (Naval Records Society, lxvii and lxviii, 1930)
Campbell	J. Campbell, *Lives of the British Admirals* (1779)
Carleton	G. Carleton, *Military Memoirs*, ed. C. H. Hartmann (1929)
Carreras	J. R. Carreras y Bulbena, *Carlos de Austria y Elizabeth de Brunswick-Wolfenbüttel* (1902)
Carr-Laughton	L. G. Carr-Laughton, *The Battle of Velez-Málaga, JRUSI*, lxviii (1921)
Churchill	W. S. Churchill, *Marlborough: His Life and Times* (1936–40)
Clowes	W. L. Clowes et al., *The Royal Navy* (1898)
Corbett	J. Corbett, *England in the Mediterranean* (1904)
Coxe, *Marlborough*	W. C. Coxe, *Memoirs of John, Duke of Marlborough* (1818–19)
CSP Dom.	*Calendar of State Papers, Domestic Series*
Dangeau	Marquis de Dangeau, *Journal*, x (1860)
Deplorable History	*The Deplorable History of the Catalans from the Time of their First Engaging in this War to the Time of their Reduction* (London, J. Baker, 1714)

Dickinson (1967)	H. T. Dickinson, 'The Recall of Lord Peterborough', *JSAHR*, xiv (1967)
Dickinson (1969)	H. T. Dickinson, 'The Earl of Peterborough's Campaign in Valencia', *JSAHR*, xlvii (1969)
Dickinson (1970)	'Correspondence of Henry Bolingbroke and Thomas Erle', *JSAHR*, xlviii (1970)
DNB	*Dictionary of National Biography*
Dungay-Tronin	*Mémoires*, ed. St Malo (1929)
Duro	C. Fernández, *La Armada Español* (1934)
Feliú de la Penya	*Anales de Catalanya*, iii (1709)
Fol. Bons.	Colecció Bonsom, Biblioteca de Catalunya, Barcelona
Fortescue	J. Fortescue, *History of the British Army* (1889)
Francis	A. D. Francis, *The First Peninsular War* (1974)
Francis (1966)	A. D. Francis, *The Methuens and Portugal* (1966)
Freind	J. Freind, *The Earl of Peterborough's Conduct in 1705–06* (1707)
Full History	*A Full and Impartial History of the Expedition to Spain in the year 1702, Extracted from the Journals and Memoirs of the Generals* (1712)
Hargreaves-Maudsley	W. N. Hargreaves-Maudesley, *Spain under the Bourbons* (1977)
Hills	G. Hills, *Rock of Contention* (1974)
HMC	*Historical Manuscripts Commission*
JSAHR	*Journal of the Society for Army Historical Research*
JRUSI	*Journal of the Royal United Services Institute*
Kamen	H. Kamen, *The War of Succession in Spain* (1969)
Landau	M. Landau, *Geschichte Karl VI als König von Spanien* (1889)
Leake	G. A. R. Callender, ed., *Life of Admiral Sir John Leake* (Naval Records Society, li and lii, 1920)
leg.	*legajo*
Llave	J. de la Llave y García, *El Sitio de Barcelona 1713–14* (1903)
Luttrell	N. Luttrell, *Brief Historical Narrative, 1678–1714* (1857)
Macaulay	T. B. Macaulay, *History of England* (1858)
Mahon	Philip Stanhope, Lord Mahon, *War of the Succession in Spain* (1831)
Marlborough	Dispatches
Mommerqué	R. Mommerqué, *Mémoires du Marquuis de la Villette* (1844)
Monti	R. Monti, *História de Gibraltar* (1805)
Noailles	Adrien, Duc de Noailles, *Mémoirs* (1865)
Owen	J. H. Owen, *The War at Sea under Queen Anne* (1938)
Parnell	A. Parnell, *The War of the Succession in Spain* (1888)
Petrie	C. Petrie, *The Marshal Duke of Berwick, Picture of an Age* (1953)
Portà	A. Portà i Bergadá, *La Victòria Catalana de 1705* (1984)
Prestage	E. Prestage, *Portugal and the War of the Spanish Succession* (1938)
PRO	Public Record Office
Quincy	Marquis de Quincy, *Histoire militaire de la Règne de Louis le Grand* (1725)
Roncière	C. de la Roncière, *Histoire de la Marine Française* (1932)
Rooke	*Journal of Sir G. Rooke*, ed. O. Browning (Naval Records Society, ix, 1897)
Russell	F. S. Russell, *The Great Earl of Peterborough* (1887)
St Simon	Duc de St Simon, *Mémoires*, ed. B. de Bois Lille, ix–xxiv (1879–1911)
San Felipe	V. Bacallar y Sanna, Marqués de San Felipe, *Comentarios de la Guerra de España y Historia de su Rey Felipe V El Animoso* (1957)
Sanpère	S. Sanpère y Miquel, *Fin de la Nación Catalana* (1905)
Soares da Silva	*Gaceta em forma de carta* (1931)
Stebbing	W. Stebbing, *Peterborough* (1890)
Tessé	*Mémoires et lettres* (1806)

Tindal	N. Tindal, *Translation and Continuation of the History of England by M. Paul de Rapin-Thoyras* (1757–63)
Torrington and Pococke	*Torrington Memoirs and the Journal of the Rev. Thomas Pococke* (Camden Series, xlvi)
Trevelyan	G. M. Trevelyan, *England under Queen Anne*, 3 vols (1930–34)
Trevelyan (1931)	G. M. Trevelyan, 'Peterborough and Barcelona', *Cambridge Historical Journal*, iii (1931)
Vincennes	Dépôt de Guerre, Vincennes
Voltes Bou (1953)	P. Voltes Bou, *El Archiduque Carlos de Austria, Rey de los Catalanes* (1953)
Voltes Bou (1973)	P. Voltes Bou, *Barcelona durante el sestierno de Carlos III* (1973)
Warburton	E. A. G. Warburton, *A Memoir of Charles Mordaunt, Earl of Peterborough* (1853)
Williams	B. Williams, *Stanhope* (1932)
Wilson	C. T. Wilson, *The Duke of Berwick, Marshal of France* (1883)

Chapter One

1. Accounts of this episode appear in Parnell and Campbell as well as in the *London Gazette* 3835, and in the N.R.S. (Rooke). The *Full History* is a useful source. Boyer and Tindal touch on the affair and PRO Adm. 1/5262–4 contains accounts of Munden's court-martial and those of Benbow's captains.

2. The best English account of the silver fleet is in Kamen, but Francis, Churchill and Trevelyan also provide some well digested material. For Benbow's operations see Clowes (ii, 367), Campbell and Tindal and the *DNB*. Adm. 1/5262–4 covers the courts-martial.

   Details about individual ships and personalities are to be found in *AGI* leg. 2631, 2632, 2633, 2634, 2710, 2714, 2716, 2717, 2720, 2721, 2745, 2755 & 2756.

3. This affair was a muddle and reports on it are contradictory. Churchill (i, 647), Francis (p. 31 ff.), Kamen (p. 177 ff.) and Trevelyan (i, 270–82) are to be trusted. Clowes (ii, 377) gives a brief account. Tindal and Boyer provide some information and the earliest printed account is the *Full History*. Burnet and Burchett supply brief accounts, as does Luttrell.

   Francis has also published two pieces which are of assistance: 'Prince George of Hesse-Darmstadt and the Plans for the Expedition to Spain of 1702', *BIHR*, xlvii (1949), 58 ff and *The Methuens and Portugal* (Cambridge, 1966), pp. 18–23. There are references in Wilson and in Berwick (i, 185). Mahon makes good use of his ancestor's letters but follows San Felipe's emotional account, including the tale about the Governor of Rota (p. 48 above). Macaulay seizes on this too as the excuse for an orotund paragraph. The *DNB* provides useful summaries on Ormonde, Rooke, Hopsonn, Fairborne and Graydon, and there is an amusing reference to the last-named in Ollard (p. 254).

   Parnell, basing his account on the dispatches, makes no mention of the Governor of Rota. Nor does the only account I could find in AHN leg. 542. This is a little strange since Villadarías, who was in local command and would have been responsible for hanging any governor, was a compulsive letter-writer, as will later appear.

   The English documents used are: Rooke, pp. 61–76 (though Rooke's Journal is not always to be relied upon); PRO Adm. 1/4317 (Log of H.M.S. *Royal Catherine*); B.L. Add.MSS. 3125 (Raby papers). 28, 946, f. 281 (Southwell, Cadiz correspondence, orders dated 3.10.'02); 28, 056–58 (Methuen Letters); 28,925 (Vigo correspondence); 29, 126 (Log of H.M.S. *Britannia*); 38, 159, ff. 20–21 (Ormonde's Journal); B.L. Harleian MS. 7025 (Account of Vigo); *HMC* Ormonde iv, 319 ff. and viii, 44–51.

4. The attack on Vigo is covered by the same secondary sources as in n.3 above, especially Clowes, ii, 381. In particular, Boyer, Tindal and Mahon are vivid and Churchill and Trevelyan are always lucid. San Felipe is relatively brief (pp. 49–50); he accuses the English of using 'inhuman artifices', which seems to mean some kind of Greek fire. There is no other reference to this.

   In addition to the Rooke, *Leake* is useful, as are: PRO Adm.52/266 (Master's log of H.M.S. *Ranelagh*); H.C.A. 32/48 (Prize Papers); and *Inquiry*.

   Kamen in 'The Destruction of the Spanish Fleet at Vigo', *BIHR* 1966, p. 165, refers to the wealth of military detail in AGI and much of this chapter is based on leg. 2631, 2632, 2633, 2714 and 2716. It is now, too, that I begin to draw on Vincennes 1695, 1696, 1697, 1791.

5. The best description of the diplomacy of this phase is in Francis (p. 59 ff.). This author has also published 'Some Reflections on the Methuen Treaties', *Report on the 5th International Colloquium on Portuguese/ Brazilian Studies* (Coimbra, 1963, pp. 315–352). Trevelyan (i, 265, 307) and Churchill, Parnell, Tindal and Boyer devote varying amounts of attention to the negotiations. Wilson has a brief note on Savoy and Mahon makes use of the Stanhope letters. There is a strange difference between the apparently poor level of victualling in Shovell's fleet as recorded in Rooke and his own statement in *Inquiry*. I draw on B.L. Add.MSS 29, 590, ff. 130–395, and 28,056 (Godolphin's Papers and Methuen Dispatches) and PRO Adm. 52/11 (Log of H.M.S. *Adventure*).

   Views from the other side are provided by San Felipe who has very little on the treaties but records Shovell's rows, while St Simon writes of differences between Chamillart and Torcy. Vincennes files 1695, 1696 and 1697 contain Orry's correspondence with Versailles.

Chapter Two

1. Two of his biographies in English are useful, Wilson and Petrie (1953). His own laconic, but – like their author – honest *Memoirs* are of immense importance. These have been used by most historians of the period but few if any seem to have examined his contemporary letters and despatches and those he received in reply. The first of these now appear in Vincennes files 1786–89 and 1791. The *Avertisement* in no. 1786 and many of the letters are useful as a guide to the thinking at the time of King Louis and his ministers. They also illustrate the daunting difficulties facing the French civil servant Orry, who had been sent to help Philip and his *Despacho Universal* or council to provide finance for the War.

   San Felipe as usual offers continuity but not always accuracy. Villars' remark on Berwick (p. 66) is quoted from G. Mallison, *Prince Eugene of Savoy* (1888), p. 257.
2. Parnell (pp. 69–70) and Mahon give some account of the archduke's journey from Vienna via Holland and England to Lisbon, the latter quoting letters from James Stanhope and his father. San Felipe has relatively little to say, but the best accounts are in Francis and Portà. On the Bourbon side, Berwick (i, 215 ff.), St Simon and above all Vincennes files 1780, 1787, 1791 and 1793 are full of interest.
3. Francis, Petrie, Wilson, Mahon and Berwick (pp. 228 ff.) are the chief printed sources. On Galway, Agnew is excellent and Macky worth quoting. The *DNB* provides useful summaries on the Richards family, Galway, Schomberg and Borgard. The Stanhope correspondence has often been quoted and much of it is printed in Mahon. Original English documents are: B.L. Stowe MSS. 467, 4–7, 34, 48, 60–67; B.L. Add.MSS. 28056, ff. 8, ff. 115; B.L. Add.MSS. 31, 141; B.L. Add.MSS. 22231 (letters of de St Pierre) PRO SP 89/18 and 103, 138, 142 and SP 105/73 for the build-up of Allied troops. On the Bourbon side, Vincennes files 1786, 1787, 1789, 1791 and 1793 as before, and AHN, leg. 259–60, 262, 264, 542 and 552.
4. On the campaign, more sources are printed by Tindal and Boyer. As usual the Stanhope correspondence is most useful. In Vincennes 1791, I use particularly the correspondence between King Louis and Berwick about the latter's recall from Spain.
5. On the 'kitchen cabinet' in Madrid, authors have hitherto relied on the Memoires of Noailles (ii. 41), Tessé and St Simon. Baudrillart (185, 227) provides an account. Francis and Parnell say relatively little and San Felipe is somewhat dull. Trevelyan refers to 'two modern books by Taillardier and Miss Maud Crutwell', but I have not read these. Vincennes files 1786–87, 1789, 1791, 1793, 1883–5 have an extraordinary immediacy, as they contain the day-to-day correspondence on the subject from Orry, Berwick, Tessé, Gramont, Chamillart and King Louis himself.
6. Printed sources on the naval operations in 1704, including the fiasco in the Gulf of Lions, are in Rooke and *Leake* (pp. 158–184), which give reprints of the original Journals and Narratives. Parnell (p. 47 ff.) and Owen are based largely on these. Burnet (v, 388) is biased against Rooke. Clowes (ii, 392–397) is brief but reliable. Francis provides a full account. Original documents are: PRO Adm. 51/4317, 4277 and 4357 (logs of H.M.S. *Royal Catherine*, *Nottingham* and *Suffolk*) and full official reports appear in *HMC House of Lords MS.* (n.s.), vi, 152, and in PRO SP 42/67, f. 56.

   On the Bourbon side there is relatively little. San Felipe, p. 72, describes Darmstadt's landing, and there is a brief account in Roncière, vi, 345; Baudrillart gives an account.

   AHN leg. 572 has some Velasco correspondence early in 1704 about the fortifications of Barcelona. Feliú de la Penya has observations at first-hand on Velasco. Portà i Bergadá (pp. 217–32) is most informative, providing a great deal of data, including the names of Catalans who joined Darmstadt and were present at the taking of Gibraltar.

Chapter Three

1. Macaulay's typical piece of heavy inaccuracy provides the opening. As if to make up for this, his kinsman Trevelyan (i, 420–430) is quite as vivid, much more exhaustive, and his references are invaluable. He quotes in particular: Corbett (i, 503–6), Burchett (pp. 666–76) and Lediard (ii, 789). *London Gazette* No. 4045 carried Rooke's first report. Francis (p. 111 ff.) and Parnell (p. 47 ff.) are brief but excellent for references. Burnet (v, 388) is as usual biased against Rooke.

Tindal and Boyer (iii, Ap. XXIV) provide contemporary views and J. H. Owen (p. 90 *et seq.*) is clear. Churchill's account is brief but as usual lively. Portà i Bergadá (p. 238 *et seq.*) gives a brief account based to some extent on Hill's *Rock of Contention* (pp. 169–75). F. Sayer, *History of Gibraltar* (1862), p. 113, has been used. London's attitude about Gibraltar at the time is given in: J. Addison, *Present State of the War* (1736), iii, 245. *HMC* Coke, p. 42; *HMC* Dartmouth, p. 197. The Imperial *Diario*, or Lisbon Account is printed in Hargreaves-Maudsley, pp. 21–5. On the Bourbon side there is relatively little contemporary material, presumably because the capture of the Rock came as such a surprise. See Berwick, i, 162 ff. San Felipe, pp. 73–4, is brief but introduces the tale of a quarrel over which flag the Allies flew. López de Ayala's account, written in 1783, is unreliable; Duro, vi, 63 is little better and Monti is much the same. Ayala does, however, quote the San Roque archives (as does Trevelyan) and the dispatches by Salinas to Villadarías of 2nd August, 1704.

2. Parnell (p. 50), Trevelyan (i, 420) – only two pages, Churchill (surprisingly very little) and Francis (pp. 116 and 126) all give accounts of the Battle of Velez Málaga. Trevelyan refers to Corbett (ii, 524–535) and Burchett (pp. 678–80) as well as to Troude (i, 219–55), and Mommerqué to St Simon and other observers. Francis adds material from Darmstadt and from Vienna. Boyer (iii, 107–112 and Ap. XXV, 65) and Tindal (xiv, 656) are lively and the former includes some French material. Owen's summary (pp. 90–98) is as usual excellent but Mahon is somewhat cavalier in his treatment of the event. Mahon is blisteringly critical in his analysis. The article by Carr-Laughton (*JRUSI*, 1923, pp. 367–90) is good. Rooke's despatch of 27th August was published in *London Gazette* of 29th September 1704. Rooke, *Leake*, Byng and Torrington and Pococke (pp. 157–614 and 197–8) are important. *CSP Dom.* Naval, p. 7, is the source of the quotations from Darmstadt's letters to Galway and Charles. On the Bourbon side, in addition to the sources cited by Trevelyan, Roncière (vi, 354) is dispassionate, though brief. San Felipe (pp. 74–6) contributes some purple passages but is surprisingly unbiased in his conclusions. St Simon provides only what was public knowledge at Versailles.

   The Vincennes files (1786) and AHN leg. 525, 552, 559 and 597 contain some original papers, though not a great deal and largely second-hand. In the Biblioteca de Catalunya (Barcelona) the Foletto Bonsom Collection includes the following: F.Bons.9550 (a poem about the battle), F.Bons.9425 (a brief inaccurate news item), F.Bons.9549 (A Spanish translation of Toulouse's dispatch. An English translation is to be found in *HMC* Portland, viii, 143.)

3. On the subsequent events of the summer, Parnell, Mahon, Wilson and Petrie use Berwick (i, 169 *et seq.*). Wilson's account is good (pp. 17–87). Mahon is brief and so is Luttrell (v, 440). Francis (pp. 98–103) bases his brief account on Berwick and Tessé, but also uses the Dutch *Rijksarchief* as well as the original English documents given immediately below. Hills (p. 187 ff.) also refers to these. Tindal, xiv, 667, is more informative than Boyer. Original English documents chiefly used are: B.L. Add.MSS. 28, 056 ff. 38, 115, 168, 172, 178–9, 188, 220 and 226; B.L. Stowe MSS. 467, ff. 63–7; PRO SP 89/18, ff. 211, 217–8. Bourbon accounts, are in: San Felipe (pp. 81–83), Dangeau (x. 105), Tessé (ii, 137–8) and Noailles (ii, 332, 356). I follow all these but provide additional contemporary material from Vincennes, some of which does not seem to have been published before: Files 1786–7, 1789, 1791, 1793, 1880, 1885, 1887–8 and 1890. File 1793 contains an ill written but vivid report on the court-martial of three Irish soldiers in the 2nd Berwick regiment, and file 1890 the letters between King Louis and King Philip.

4. Churchill provides little on the siege but Trevelyan (ii, 33 ff) gives a most exciting account, drawing *inter alia* on Corbett (i, 536). Francis' account (128–149) is also based on Corbett but in addition cites the *Rijksarchief*, the *Kriegsarchiven*, Künzel and Dangeau. Hills (pp. 187 ff.) is an important recent account. Boyer (iii, 146) and Tindal contribute, as does Fortescue (i, 446–50). Portà i Bergadá (p. 212 ff.) emphasises the Catalan contribution. The original English documents are used by most English historians. On the other side of the hill there are Feliú de la Penya (iii, 52); Roncière (vi, 376) and Ayala.

   Although some authors have used Tessé (i, 187–350) and he was indeed closely involved, nobody in England seems to have consulted his original letters and dispatches, or those of Villadarías and others who were carrying out the siege. Yet these papers provide a compelling and previously unpublished insight into the Franco-Spanish problems and the appalling differences of view between the individual commanders of the besieging force. It was this that in the end tipped the scale towards the Allies – particularly as the latter were able to take advantage of a most capable English Naval Commander: Vincennes files 1786, 1789, 1883 and 1888. AHN 525, 542, 559, 565, 577 and 755 contain the Villadarías correspondence and much else.

Chapter Four

1. Parnell, Trevelyan (ii, 46 ff.) and Francis (p. 171 ff.) describe the gathering clouds, but all rather briefly. Boyer (iv, 156 ff.) and Tindal provide much that is helpful, e.g. King Pedro's speech impediment. The English documents quoted are: B.L. Add.MSS. 9, 115 (Coxe's correspondence); 28,056 (Godolphin's letters from Methuen); PRO SP 89/18 (despatches from Portugal) and B.L. Stowe MS 467 (Letters of John and Michael Richards). On the Bourbon side, M. Chamblay's forecast is in Vincennes file 1883. In general the Vincennes files become more informative than ever and are worth comparing with Tessé. Those used are: 1883–6, 1888 and 1890. File 1892 has much grim detail about the treatment of deserters and other offenders. The account given to Tessé by the Lisbon spy is in 1884, and his own outspoken and treacherous letters about King Philip in all these files have to be seen to be believed. AHN leg. 542 contains much material hitherto unpublished.

2. Early biographers of Peterborough such as Warburton, Russell and Stebbing tend to follow, quite uncritically, Carleton and Freind. (Sir Walter Scott and Dr. Johnson were both taken in by Carleton.) Ballard, writing half a century after, is more sceptical. Trevelyan is equally so. Mahon takes the Earl too readily at face value, but he was writing just after Sir Walter Scott. Burnet (i, 209–15) is unreliable. Churchill (ii. 58) is brief on the subject but later turns savagely on the Earl. Swift, a friend and possibly the recipient of eleemosynery aid from 'the ramblingest lying rogue on earth' is cynical about him, yet friendly. Francis (pp. 171ff; 197ff) is very useful but too much inclined to follow Mahon (pp. 159–65 and 203–8). Mahon gives most of Stanhope's correspondence and there is more in the Kent County Record Office. Some of Methuen's correspondence is at the Methuen family home, Corsham, Wilts. Tindal is as usual a good secondary source (xvi) and so is J. H. Burton. B.L. Add.MSS. 28,056–5 (Methuen's letters) and PRO S.P. 94/76 (Despatches from Spain) are valuable. Teonge (pp. 226–7) exhibits the Earl as what in the 1980s became known as a 'Hooray Henry'. Parnell (pp. 114–38 and 316–26) does a richly deserved demolition job on Peterborough, whom he loathes, but he goes perhaps too far. Tindal is as usual highly informative but Boyer has little until Barcelona is reached.

   Of the foreign accounts Portà i Bergadá is a mine of information on Dutch naval movements. San Felipe (p. 95 ff.), though well-informed about Allied preparations, does not mention Peterborough which would have infuriated the Earl!)

   The English documents used include Richards' papers and those of de St Pierre in James, B.L. Add.MS. 22, 231; 31, 134; 31, 138 and B.L. Stow MS 467; also B.L. Add.MSS. 28,056. (ff. 206, 243, 285, 293); and PRO SP 89/18 (ff. 247, 263, 273, 276); SP 105/74, ff. 307, SP 79/3 (ff. 502, 510–13, 527, 531 (Crowe's despatches); *HMC* House of Lords MSS (n.s.), vii, 361, 378, 410, 500–6 (Secret Instructions); PRO Adm. 52/266 (Master's Log of H.M.S. *Ranelagh*); 51/242. (Log of H.M.S. *Devonshire*).

3. Original material is from Vincennes files 1884, 1885, 1886 (from where the summary cited on p. 170 is drawn) and 1890, and AHN (eg. 264–5 and 272).

4. Portà i Bergadá (p. 293 ff.) is again a mine of information. Trevelyan (ii, 63 ff.) and Churchill (ii, 58–63) are reliable but Burnet (v, 209 ff.) is not. Mahon is only fairly good. J. H. Elliott, *The Revolt of the Catalans* (1963) pp. 71–7 is instructive. Francis (p. 171 ff.) again is excellent. Tindal and Boyer (iv, 146 ff.) provide good accounts, but Parnell (pp. 114–38) has to be watched as he is so biased against Peterborough; though he does supply many useful references. Carleton (pp. 122 ff.) and Freind have been much quoted but are almost totally unreliable. A document unearthed and printed in Atkinson (1938) and used here for the first time in this book, is the memoir of the anonymous Royal Dragoon. On the Bourbon side, Vincennes 1884–7 and 1890 provide the French viewpoints and information, and AHN leg. 265, 267, 272, 281 and 283 the Spanish.

5. Additional printed sources on Montjuich are *DNB* (for Norris); Full History; Portà i Bergadá (pp. 461–4); and Trevelyan (1931).

The controversy about the respective roles of Darmstadt and Peterborough has never been properly resolved. Carleton and Freind are deservedly discarded. Parnell's destructive essay does seem to destroy Peterborough's claims, but Trevelyan considers that Richards' evidence in favour of the Earl is totally compelling, and having read it, so do I. St Pierre, the stolid dragoon colonel, is further evidence for Peterborough which cannot readily be discarded. Parnell goes too far in trying to make Peterborough out to be a coward. For all his faults the Earl was *not* one. The evidence from Boyer cited on p. 195 above is in iv, 146 ff. French and Spanish accounts do not mention the Earl (San Felipe, Feliú de la Penya and Castellvi).

Portà i Bergadá and the Richards Journal (B.L.Stowe MS. 467, f. 38) and Narrative (B.L.Stowe MS. 471, f. 15) are of particular value. So is *Leake*, pp. 297–306. Darmstadt's funeral is described in 'a naval officer's' letter, cited in *A General History of Europe* (1705), p. 328.

6. For the fall of Barcelona see also Boyer (iv, 170), where the Capitulations are printed, Voltes Bou, and Sanpère y Miquel (p. 195) for reference to Popoli and his duchess. Fol.Bons.715 is a full copy of the *Deplorable History of the Catalans* to which reference is made in the final chapter. 5673, 5675 and 5677 are printed broadsheets showing Velasco's unpopularity. Vincennes files 1887–8 and 1890 supply the news as it first reached the French.

7. For the Portuguese front, Francis' description (pp. 152–170) is excellent. Fagel's apologia was printed in England in 1708 and is quoted in Boyer (iv, 156–70). Tindal and Mahon have little to add. On the Bourbon side Berwick (i, 280) describes his activities in the Cevennes, and so therefore do Wilson and Petrie. San Felipe (pp. 100–2) has little that is useful. But the Vincennes files 1887–8, 1890 and 1892 are excellent (1889 has been lost.) AHN Leg. 280 provides some information.

Chapter Five

1. Accounts written in English on Peterborough's campaign of 1706 are usually based on Carleton and Freind. Even Trevelyan (ii, 147 ff.), though he writes of Peterborough's 'light mind' and does not accept everything, treats the Earl too kindly, in the light of the documents available on the other side. Francis is more sceptical and Parnell is totally unbelieving. Where St Pierre is involved we have the evidence of a straightforward, meticulous man, by no means a blind admirer, though sometimes mesmerized by his volatile boss. The *Journal of the Siege of San Mateo* by Jones (1707) seems to be truthful, but I have only seen excerpts. Dickinson (1964) is slender, but his (1967) article is far better. It is interesting to note that as he writes he becomes more critical of Peterborough. Arent Furly's note on the council of war at Alcobacer is in B.L.Add.MS. 28,058, f. 393, the minutes (also printed by Freind) at ff. 9–10.

San Felipe (pp. 103–4) might be expected to say something but merely records gloomily the losses of towns in Valencia and Catalonia. But there *does* exist quite a lot of evidence from the other side, hitherto unpublished, which throws some light – and doubt – on previously published work.

Part of this is in AHN leg. 292, 296 and 2902, which contain the correspondence of the Spanish General de las Torres, the Irish officer Don Simon Connock (or Cornock), and letters from Daniel O'Mahony himself – the man whose reputation Peterborough claims to have blasted by dirty tricks. To judge from these, the Earl's attempts to undermine O'Mahony were totally unsuccessful.

The other part of the evidence is in Vincennes file1976. This contains ambassador Amelot's correspondence with Versailles in early 1706. Full as it is of fears and doubts, it seems to brighten when O'Mahony appears in Madrid 'sent by de las Torres to give an account in detail'. The Irish colonel was *not* in disgrace but had been sent from Valencia to give a reliable report to the Madrid court. De las Torres was driven from San Mateo *not* by Peterborough but by the weather, and de las Torres' chief concern was the threat that he was to be replaced by Arcos. There are numerous letters and dispatches about Peterborough and how 'enterprising' the enemy is being, so clearly the Earl's campaign was having an effect, but he and his friends are guilty of untruth and exaggeration.

2. The only really reliable English source on Peterborough's behaviour in Valencia is St Pierre, in his Journal and letters (see Chapter 4, n. 2 above). His activities are put in perspective by the accounts from the Bourbon side. AHN leg. 281, 282, 283, 297, 298 and 2902 are most informative, and these, together with Vincennes files 1976–7 and 1986 have been extensively used for these pages.

3. On the siege of Barcelona, despite Peterborough's claims, Churchill, Trevelyan (ii, 145 ff. and chapter notes), Francis (p. 219 ff.) and of course Parnell, set the record straight. But at the time the Earl's friends in London took care that the public should credit him with responsibility for the successful defence. Even Tindal (xvi, 276) and Boyer (v, 124 ff. and 297) make no attempt to correct this, though Boyer does print a *Journal of the Siege* by an officer present (v, 121). As Trevelyan points out, naval reports were often written up by civilians and Leake's own papers and journals (*Leake*, pp. 297–356) were not published till half a century later.

   Francis and Trevelyan both refer to the original English sources. Of the French and Spanish sources, San Felipe contributes, Berwicks (i, 223 ff.) has a bearing. Trevelyan cites Tessé's published letters. However, many remain unpublished, and these, as well as correspondence from other officers such as Legendre are to be found in Vincennes files 1976–81 and 1989. The *avertissements* or summaries which normally begin a file are often useful.

   AHN leg. 272, 281, 283, 297 and 298 contain much information. Feliú de la Penya has sources of eye-witness material and Voltes Bou is useful. St Simon occasionally provides some material but is second-hand. B. de C. MS 421 is Castellvi's record.

4. On Leake and the winter squadron, Parnell (p. 137 ff.) and Francis (p. 197 ff.), are informative, the latter as usual using Dutch as well as English sources. Mahon (pp. 159, 205, 208) also gives much of Stanhope's correspondence. Tindal is useful too and Boyer (vi, 114–30) prints a *Journal of the Siege*. B.L. Add.MS. 28,057, ff. 226 and 407 (Methuen correspondence), B.L. Stowe MS. 471 (Richards' papers); PRO SP 94/76 (despatches from Spain); and *Leake* have been useful. Castellvi provides an account from within Bercelona in B. de C. MS 421.

   On the other side San Felipe gives little, but Vincennes files: 1976 and 1977 have Amelot's and others' correspondence, a good deal about Berwick and the Portuguese frontier, the flight of Philip and María Luisa, and much of Tessé's corrspondence.

5. Additional sources for what follows are Tindal (xvi, 281 ff.) and Burton (ii, Ch. 10). Mahon prints Stanhope's letters. Methuen's are in Marlborough's *Dispatches*, ii. B.L. Add.MS. 31,134 has St Pierre's relevant letters and 28,057 Methuen's to Godolphin. *HMC* House of Lords MSS.(n.s.) vii, 404 covers Peterborough's money problems. San Felipe (p. 104 ff.) describes the eclipse of the sun as does Tindal.

6. As Berwick returns to the Peninsula his English biographers follow him. Mahon gives a very full account (pp. 190 ff., 203, 230, 248, 257, 276). Francis (p. 222 ff.) has much to offer and very useful references. Boyer (v, 275 ff. and vi) and Tindal provide contemporary comment. Owen (p. 65 ff.) describes the French raid on the Tagus. B.L. Add.MSS. 28,057, ff. 116, 119, 125, 127, 131 give particulars of John Methuen's efforts. On the Bourbon side Berwick (i, 223 ff. and 284 ff.) can be supplemented by Vincennes files 1976–7, 1986 and 1989, which are rich in letters from him, Madame des Ursins and Amelot. AHN leg. 280, 282 and 292 are also useful. San Felipe (p. 117 ff.) is informative. The *Memoirs* of Dungay-Tronin are cited by Francis on the Tagus raid.

7. Berwick gives a full account but should be supplemented from Vincennes files 1977 and 1986, for his letters are even livelier. These files shed light on the Madrid court, on Amelot's panic, Tesse's loss of nerve, the activities of Legendre, the attitude of the grandees, Orry's trip to Paris, as well as some captured Allied correspondence. AHN leg. 282 contains the correspondence in which Galway and das Minas try to suborn Richebourg. Wilson (p. 124 ff.) quotes the Memoirs of la Feuquière and correspondence between des Ursins and Maintenon.

8. My account is drawn from AHN Documentos del archiduque Carlos, Libros 9832 and 9852.

9. Published work on this subject is considerable: e.g. Mahon (p. 196 ff. and App. xi-xxxi); Wilson (p. 131 ff.); Francis (p. 230 ff.); Trevelyan (ii, 154 ff.); Leatham; Petri P. 191 ff.); Tindal (xvi, 281 ff.); Parnell (p. 191 ff.); Boyer (v, App. 82); Carleton (p. 272 ff.); Freind (p. 84) and Kamen (p. 291). Dickinson (1967) gives a good picture, but it is based entirely on English sources. I have also used the Vincennes files 1977, ff. 241, 243, 276, 301; and 1978 ff. 1–20, 32, 37, 40, 42, 49, 62 and 64.

10. Corbett (ii, 550), Williams, Parnell, Stebbing, Ballard, Francis, Wilson (p. 141), Tindal (xvi, 292), Trevelyan (ii, 158) and Owen (p. 67 ff.) all deal with naval affairs in this phase. *Leake* gives a full account. On the other side, Quincy (p. 252 ff.) and Roncières provide something, but Vincennes files 1977, ff. 6, 208, 241, 286, 289, 295 and 296, and 1978 f. 46 are more vivid. AHN leg. 323 is useful.
11. Berwick's biographers, Wilson and Petrie, Francis (p. 234 ff.), Tindal are used. Mahon (App. xxxiv-xl) is useful. Kamen (pp. 112, 146, 157, 164, 189, 191 and 198) provides a very full account. On the Bourbon side see Berwick (i, 327, 338) and Vincennes files 1978, f. 89, 1979 and 1981 on Berwick's operations in the remainder of the year.

Chapter Six

1. Almansa is recognised by most English historians as of great importance, though some over-estimate its effects.

    Printed sources used here are: Churchill (ii, 233 ff.); Tindal (xvi, 404 ff.); Trevelyan (i, 287 ff.); Francis (p. 242 ff.); Mahon (p. 230 ff.); Boyer (vi, 18 ff.); Kamen (p. 371 ff.); Coxe *Marlborough*; Hawley, *The Earl of Galway's Conduct in Spain and Portugal* (1711); *Full Inquiry*.

    Original documents are: B.L. Add.MSS. 31,134; 28,057; 9,092 (Coxe, Letters to Marlborough); 9,116 (Coxe, Correspondence with Spain) Stanhope MS. of 16th January 1707 (Deposition of three generals supporting Galway's decision) in Kent County Record Office. On the side of the Two Crowns see Berwick (i, 356 ff.). I have drawn on Vincennes files 2048 (*Avertissement* and ff. 207, 229, 258, 260, 268–9, 280, 284, 286); 2049 (ff. 10, 20, 108, 118); 2051 (ff. 31, 63); 2052 (ff. 4, 126, 141, 172); 2106 (passim); Noailles (ii, 403); San Felipe (p. 129 ff.).
2. Additional sources on the aftermath of Almansa are Torrington (p. 141), Tindal (xvi, 412), Hargreaves-Maudsley (pp. 25, 31, 37); Marlborough's *Dispatches* (iii); *Byng Papers*; Boyer (vi, 24 ff.); Mahon (Appendices); O'Connor (p. 330); *HMC* Egmont, ii, 223; *HMC* Mar and Kellie. Galway's narrative is in *HMC* House of Lords MSS (n. 5.), vii, 947. Vincennes file 2050 and AHN leg. 993 of 7/9/1707 supply material on the autumn campaign.

    The correspondence between Bolingbroke and Erle, – Dickinson (1970) is valuable. See also *HMC* Bates ii, 146 ff. and Bath i; On the Bourbon side, see Baudrillart (i, 275 ff.) and of course Berwick (i, 340 ff.). Vincennes files 2048 ff. 31, 40, 50, 52, 64, 67, 153; 1979, 1981 and 1980 have been used, as they have much that is fresh. In AHN *libros* 793d is useful for Charles' council meetings.

Chapter Seven

1. Changes on the Allied side are described by Parnell (p. 271), Mahon (pp. 243, 260 and App. LI), Francis (p. 258 ff.) and Churchill (ii, 301, 398). AHN 993d described Charles' councils of war. Marlborough's *Dispatches* (iii, and iv) supply material about Stanhope and Francis (1966) is full of information.

    Vincennes file 2104 provides excellent details of the picture as seen from Madrid, Paris and Berwick's Headquarters.
2. Parnell (p. 271), Francis (p. 268), Tindal (xvii, 72) and Boyer (vii) all give excellent accounts of the Minorca episode, as does Campbell. N.R.S. again is useful. Stanhope's despatches and letters (Mahon App. LXX ff.) are very vivid. B.L. Add.MSS. 22,231 has Cope's correspondence and Marlborough's *Dispatches* iii on Minorca and Mediterranean strategy. San Felipe (pp. 148–51) contributes; Vincennes Files 2105, 2107 and 2177 and AHN leg. 3468.
3. Francis merely refers to the fall of Denia but Mahon (p. 259 and App. LXXVIII and LXXXV) has been frequently used. Carleton was an eye-witness. *HMC* Egmont (Perceval correspondence) and San Felipe (p. 164 ff.) are useful but the best original material is in Vincennes file 2105. AHN leg. 346 and *libros* 993d, f. 363 add details.
4. It was Churchill's brief note on Alicante (ii, 522–3) which first made me think of writing this book. Parnell (p. 262) makes a brief reference.

    Tindal (xvii, 194), Boyer (vii, 97) and Coxe, *Marlborough* (iv, 373) make references. Mahon

(p. 277 and App. LXXXIX) gives Stanhope's point of view. I use B.L. MSS. Stowe, 458, 459, 466–81 especially 475 (Richards material); *HMC* Egmont, ii (280–2); *Byng Papers*; Torrington; AHN, *libros*, 997d, f. 476. Vincennes files 2177 and 2179 contain d'Asfeld's and others' reports and Philip's correspondence with King Louis. There is a good account by D.G. Chandler in *History Today*, xix (1969), 475, though it is based only on English sources.

5. Mahon (pp. 262–4 and App. LXIX), Tindal (xvii) and Marlborough's *Dispatches* iii are useful sources. Francis (p. 275) makes a brief mention. Landau (p. 477) shows that Charles was aware of what was going on.

   St Simon (xv. 307) is fairly reliable as he knew Orléans well, but the most rewarding source is Madrid *Legajo* 3468, which contains full notes on the interrogations of Flotte and Regnault.

Chapter Eight

1. Printed sources used are *DNB* and Macky; Churchill (ii, 301 and 981); Tindal (xvii, 217, 244, 286); Parnell (p. 373); Boyer (vii, 79 ff.); Mahon (p. 294 ff.); Francis (p. 279 ff.); Williams (p. 247).

   Original documents are: PRO S.P. 90/77; *HMC* Townshend 64,376.

2. On the Bourbon side see: St Simon (xix and xx), San Felipe (p. 197); AHN leg. 382 and *libros* 993d, f. 574 are used here.

3. Brief notes on this affair are to be found in Parnell, Mahon, Trevelyan and Boyer (x, 82 ff.). Vincennes file 2254 contains references.

4. Mahon (302 *et seq.*); Tindal (xvii, 286 ff.); Boyer (vii, 85 ff.); Trevelyan (iii) and Atkinson (1944) are the useful secondary works. Stanhope's dispatches and letter in Kent County Record Office; London *Postman*, 22nd August, 1710, San Felipe (p. 195) for the Bourbon side and Vincennes file 2253 for many excellent references are valuable primary sources.

5. There are secondary printed accounts from the Allied side in Francis (p. 309 ff.); Mahon (p. 307 ff. and App. CXV); Tindal (xvii, 289); Boyer (viii, 90 ff.); Parnell (p. 284); Williams (p. 99); and Atkinson (1938).

   See PRO SP. 94/97 has Captain Cosby's account (he was Stanhope's messenger). Mahon (Appendices) and the Stanhope MSS (Kent County Record Office) are obviously invaluable. San Felipe (p. 199 ff.) can be supplemented and corrected by Vincennes file 2253, to which the *avertissement* warns, 'As there were no French troops left in Spain the account is not exact and relies on the correspondence of Blécourt (Amelot's successor as ambassador), de Bourk and Mahony.' But Mahony in particular provides colourful touches to what is known not only of this battle which he calls 'our *choc* of 27th July' but of the later actions in the campaign in which he played his customarily vigorous part. An invaluable account is by an anonymous Royal Dragoon trooper, who is much more informative about the end of the campaign than the beginning. He was present at the Battle of Saragossa and later at Brihuega, where he was made prisoner. Half a century afterwards, when he was over 80, he wrote a relation of his time in Spain for his 'children and his children's children'. They probably read it, but afterwards it lay unknown until published in Atkinson (1938).

6. For the Bourbons see San Felipe (p. 202); Berwick (ii, 98); St Simon xviii, 126 and xx, 108–124; Moreno is a useful secondary work. Vincennes files 2253, 2255 and 2257 contain the correspondence quoted.

7. Secondary sources on the Allied moves are Francis (p. 31 ff.) – particularly good on correspondence from Charles's Court; Williams (p. 100 ff.); Boyer (vii, 104). AHN *libros* 993d, ff. 594, 602, 612, 620 and 623 refer to the discussions at Charles's council.

8. Printed accounts of the Allies' re-occupation of Madrid are in Mahon (p. 317 and App. for Lenoir and Stanhope Letters); Francis (p. 302); Tindal (xvii, 307); Boyer (x, 108); Moreno; Trevelyan (iii). I quote from AHN *libros* 993d, ff. 624–5. Hargreaves-Maudsley (pp. 37, 39, 40, 41) prints contemporary documents. San Felipe (p. 203), Noailles (iv, 159) and St Simon (xx, 117, 124 and 416) have been used. Vincennes file 2253 and AHN leg. 2898, 3469 and 3487 supply my new material.

9. There is a good deal of printed material on Brihuega, eg. Mahon (p. 330, and App. for letters CVII etc.); Williams (pp. 97, 105 ff. and two good maps of Brihuega); Tindal (xvii, 287 ff.);

Boyer (x, 64, 119, 125); Parnell (p. 288 ff.); Atkinson (1938); Burnet (iv, 17); Coxe, *Marlborough* (iii, 160); Cunningham (ii, 333); Trevelyan (iii); Swift, *Journal to Stella* (ii, 122); *HMC* Portland v, 219, Ormonde (N.C.) vi, 44 and viii, 316 and House of Lords MSS (n.s.) viii.

St Simon (xx, 130, 141, 422 and 445), San Felipe (p. 212 ff.) and Moreno (p. 27) are useful on the Bourbon side. I have used Vincennes file 2253 throughout, and AHN leg. 3469.

10. Printed accounts of Villa Viciosa. Tindal (xvii, 300), Boyer (x, 119); Parnell (p. 292); Francis (p. 319); Trevelyan (iii, 313) and Mahon (p. 342) -- can be supplemented from PRO SP 92/27, 92/28 and 92/29 (Peterborough and Chetwynd dispatches). On the other side, St Simon (xx, 419) and San Felipe (pp. 217 ff.) – can be compared with Vincennes file 2253.

Chapter Nine

1. Printed sources used here are Francis (pp. 323, 332, 342, 353); Churchill (ii, 804); Boyer (x, 91, 133); Tindal (xvii, 367, 383); Prestage, Soares da Silva; *HMC* Morrison, p. 47; Macky; AHN *libros* 994d, 995d, 996d and Vincennes files 2328, 2330, 2331 and 2333 have been used throughout.

2. Printed sources: Parnell (p. 300 ff.); Tindal (xvii, 384); Francis (p. 359 ff.); Kamen (p. 237 ff.); Boyer (x, 83, 87, 352 ff.); Mahon (p. 362); *HMC Various Collections* viii, Portland v, 17; San Felipe (p. 221 ff.). AHN Leg. 811, 2327; Vincennes files 2328, 2329, 2330, 2331, 2332, 2404 and 2405; and Fol. Bons. 5659–5777 are drawn on here.

3. Secondary sources: Churchill (ii, 910, 914, 940, 964 ff.); Tindal (xvii, 431, 453, 547 and xviii, 28, 29, 176, 194, 320); Francis (pp. 348 and 386 ff.); Mahon (p. 316, 364, 370); Boyer (xi, Introduction and 280); Wilson (p. 334 ff.); San Felipe (pp. 228, 234); St Simon (xxiii, 123 ff.); Dangeau (xiv, 376); Voltes Bou (Plates VI, XI, XIV, XV). Primary sources: B.L. Add.MSS: 22,206, f. 402 (Bolingbroke letter); PRO. SP. 94/79, 94/80 (dispatches from Spain); *HMC* Portland iv, 622; Hargreaves-Maudsley, p. 45; Torcy (ii, 180); Berwick (ii, 99); AHN leg. 427, 760, 2327; Vincennes files 2404–6; Fol. Bons. 7794.

Chapter Ten

1. Tindal, (xvii, 236; xviii, 108); Francis (pp. 367, 370); Wilson (p. 344); San Felipe (237); Voltes Bou (p. 299); Sanpère y Miquel (pp. 59–70, 79, 81,89, 93, 95, 119–121); Llave (pp. 53, 101, 103) are useful accounts of the background to the siege of Barcelona. I draw from Vincennes file 2466, ff. 1, 19, 30, 31, 43, 66; Fol. Bons. 715. and B. de C. MS 421, v, 23–30, 34–7.

2. Documents of the government of Barcelona during the siege can be studied in the original files of the Arxju de la Corona d'Aragó in the vice-regal palace in Barcelona. Many have disappeared but some, marked Gen: 121, 123 and 126 are still there. Number 121, which is in the best condition, consists merely of the acounts of the Regiment of the *Diputación*. The other two, though bound in calfskin with a toggle, are in a poor state. Number 126, in sixteen folders, contains 'The Papers Belonging to the Archives of the Ancient Generality of Catalonia', which are the minutes of the *Junta* of 36 from June 1713 onwards. This *Junta* met every two or three days. It was attended by varying numbers and dealt largely with pay, promotion and discipline. The *Junta* of Provisions' meetings are also recorded.

Other important primary sources on the siege are AHN leg. 427, 450; Fol. Bons. 654, 715, 3035, 3040; AGS Guerra leg. 3787, Estardo leg. 2864, f. 3; Vincennes files 2466–7 and, above all, 2488 (especially ff. 26, 40, 45–7, 53, 55, 60–156, 167–250); B. de C. MS 42, v, 129 ff; *Deplorable History*; Hargreaves-Maudsley pp. 52, 58; Berwick, ii, 263 ff.; Quincy, vii, 369 ff; St Simon, xxiv, 105, 112–13, 207 ff. on the 'intrigues'. The accounts in Sanpère, Voltes Bou, Carreras, San Felipe, Llave and Bruguera are generally important.

Index

W